Exam Ref 70-339: Managing Microsoft SharePoint Server 2016

Troy Lanphier

PUBLISHED BY
Microsoft Press
A division of Microsoft Corporation
One Microsoft Way
Redmond, Washington 98052-6399

Library of Congress Control Number: 2016934335
ISBN: 978-1-5093-0294-9

Printed and bound in the United States of America.

1 16

Microsoft Press books are available through booksellers and distributors worldwide. If you need support related to this book, email Microsoft Press Support at *mspinput@microsoft.com*. Please tell us what you think of this book at *http://aka.ms/tellpress*.

This book is provided "as-is" and expresses the author's views and opinions. The views, opinions and information expressed in this book, including URL and other Internet website references, may change without notice.

Some examples depicted herein are provided for illustration only and are fictitious. No real association or connection is intended or should be inferred.

Microsoft and the trademarks listed at *http://www.microsoft.com* on the "Trademarks" webpage are trademarks of the Microsoft group of companies. All other marks are property of their respective owners.

Acquisitions Editor: Karen Szall
Developmental Editor: Karen Szall
Editorial Production: Cohesion, Inc.
Technical Reviewer: Jeremy Taylor; Technical Review services provided by Content Master, a member of CM Group, Ltd.
Copyeditor: Teresa Horton
Indexer: Lucie Haskins
Cover: Twist Creative • Seattle

To my kids and my wife: Thanks for sharing my evenings with the occasional writing effort. I appreciate your love and support - KBO.

—Troy Lanphier

Contents at a glance

Contents

What do you think of this book? We want to hear from you!

Microsoft is interested in hearing your feedback so we can continually improve our books and learning resources for you. To participate in a brief online survey, please visit:

www.microsoft.com/learning/booksurvey/

Chapter 2   Authentication and security   77

Chapter 5 Manage search capabilities 279

Chapter 6   Plan and configure cloud services   339

Introduction

Although this book was written primarily to help you prepare for Exam 70-339: "Managing Microsoft SharePoint Server 2016," it is also intended to be a reference that you can refer to during your experiences with SharePoint Server 2016. In several cases, the steps to perform the more advanced tasks are shown in this book to help you feel comfortable with related questions on the exam, as well as provide a reference on how to perform the task in a real-life situation.

The 70-339 is an advanced solutions examination, although the level of detail in this book might exceed content required for the exam. This does not mean there won't be specific questions about steps required to perform a task or requirements needed to install a service application; what it does mean is that you should not focus on minutia such as being able to spell out a command correctly or knowing every possible parameter for the command. Instead, focus on the concepts, the overall steps involved with a task, and the required components needed for a solution.

If you focus on these concepts and go through the tasks in this book, you will be well on your way to passing the exam. It should be noted that this 2016 exam requires a broader spectrum of experience, as it combines concepts that were previously covered in two separate tests: 70-331 (Core Solutions of Microsoft SharePoint Server 2013) and 70-332 (Advanced Solutions of Microsoft SharePoint Server 2013) exams. If you didn't previously take these tests, don't worry; just expect that there are a lot of potential topics to be covered.

This book is generally intended for exam candidates who have four or more years working with SharePoint Server and related technologies such as SQL Server and Windows Server. Candidates should have hands-on experience with a multiserver SharePoint farm, specifically focusing on planning, implementing, and maintaining this farm. This experience includes (but is not limited to) the areas of high availability, disaster recovery, capacity planning, and exposure to Office 365 and hybrid implementations.

Despite having multiple years of experience with a multiserver SharePoint farm, it is doubtful that exam candidates will automatically have experience with each and every technology set covered by the exam; thus, they should focus on the areas in which they have the least experience or understanding. Also, any of the newer features recently added to SharePoint Server 2016 will likely receive additional coverage on the exam.

This book will help you prepare for the exam, but nothing can take the place of real-life experience. In an effort to make the exam content an accurate measure of product knowledge, the test might include a series of case studies along with the standard multiple-choice questions. Expect to see questions that present you with a business and technical problem, then require you to place steps in order and answer questions in which you have to choose the right set of items from a large list of possible answers. In these cases, previous practice with the actual implementation of the functionality covered in this book will help you far more than just trying to memorize facts and answers.

This book covers every exam objective, but it does not necessarily cover every exam question. Only the Microsoft exam team has access to the exam questions, and Microsoft regularly adds new questions to the exam, thus making it impossible to cover specific questions and answers. You should consider this book a supplement to your relevant real-world experience and other study materials.

If you encounter a topic in this book that you do not feel completely comfortable with, use the reference links provided in the text to find more information, then take the time to research and study topics in which you lack experience or understanding. A great deal of planning and implementation for SharePoint is available on MSDN, TechNet, and other blogs and forums.

Organization of this book

This book is organized by the "Skills measured" list published for the exam. The "Skills measured" list is available for each exam on the Microsoft Learning website: *http://aka.ms /examlist*. Each chapter in this book corresponds to a major topic area in the list, and the techniques in each topic area determine a chapter's organization. If an exam covers six major topic areas, for example, the book will contain six chapters.

Microsoft certifications

Microsoft certifications distinguish you by proving your command of a broad set of skills and experience with current Microsoft products and technologies. The exams and corresponding certifications are developed to validate your mastery of critical competencies as you design and develop, or implement and support, solutions with Microsoft products and technologies both on-premises and in the cloud. Certification brings a variety of benefits to the individual and to employers and organizations.

> **MORE INFO**   For information about Microsoft certifications including a full list of available certifications, go to *http://www.microsoft.com/learning*.

Acknowledgements

Several people are involved in the development of a book such as this; from an author standpoint, I'd like to thank Karen Szall as well as Lisa Flinchbaugh and Kim Spilker who helped to finish this project. Jeremy Taylor of Content Master was my technical reviewer, and provided top-notch feedback, particularly around the hybridization of SharePoint. Finally, thanks to Mary Stone and Chris Norton for helping close this effort out.

On the home front, I'd like to thank my family and friends for putting up with me being the occasional writing hermit. In particular, I want to thank Marlene Lanphier, who always seems to be available when I need someone to listen to a particular portion of this text.

Free ebooks from Microsoft Press

From technical overviews to in-depth information on special topics, the free ebooks from Microsoft Press cover a wide range of topics. These ebooks are available in PDF, EPUB, and Mobi for Kindle formats, ready for you to download at:

http://aka.ms/mspressfree

Check back often to see what is new!

Microsoft Virtual Academy

Build your knowledge of Microsoft technologies with free expert-led online training from Microsoft Virtual Academy (MVA). MVA offers a comprehensive library of videos, live events, and more to help you learn the latest technologies and prepare for certification exams. You'll find what you need at *http://www.microsoftvirtualacademy.com*.

Errata, updates, & book support

We've made every effort to ensure the accuracy of this book and its companion content. You can access updates to this book—in the form of a list of submitted errata and their related corrections—at:

http://aka.ms/ER399/errata

If you discover an error that is not already listed, please submit it to us through the same page.

If you need additional support, email Microsoft Press Book Support at *mspinput@microsoft.com*.

Please note that product support for Microsoft software and hardware is not offered through the previous addresses. For help with Microsoft software or hardware, go to *http://support.microsoft.com*.

We want to hear from you

At Microsoft Press, your satisfaction is our top priority, and your feedback our most valuable asset. Please tell us what you think of this book at:

http://aka.ms/tellpress

We know you're busy, so we've kept it short with just a few questions. Your answers go directly to the editors at Microsoft Press. (No personal information will be requested.) Thanks in advance for your input!

Stay in touch

Let's keep the conversation going! We're on Twitter: *http://twitter.com/MicrosoftPress.*

## CHAPTER 1

Design SharePoint Infrastructure

The previous version of Microsoft SharePoint has often been discussed as if it were two distinct products: SharePoint 2013 and SharePoint Online. SharePoint 2013 provides traditional IT organizations with the option of either federating with SharePoint Online or adopting an exclusively on-premises stance, in which all servers and development efforts are kept within the boundaries of the server room. If the federated SharePoint Online option is enabled, additional "cloud first" functionality is available to the organization's users.

As you prepare for the 70-339 exam, you'll be challenged to instead consider SharePoint 2016 and SharePoint Online as a single product. Although your organization might initially choose to implement SharePoint by using only on-premises functionality or only in the cloud, it's more likely that you will find yourself implementing fully hybrid environments of SharePoint before too long. Planning for the overall infrastructure in the near term will make the initial environment more scalable and robust.

Skills in this chapter:

- Skill: Design information architecture
- Skill: Plan installation
- Skill: Plan a hybrid cloud environment

Skill: Design information architecture

SharePoint implementations require both flexibility and scalability to be considered successful. A *flexible* SharePoint environment enables change to take place in the structure and layout of the implementation with minimal impact to the user base, and a *scalable* SharePoint environment accounts for the necessary growth required to meet changing business objectives.

This section reviews the taxonomical, navigational, and structural considerations that should be decided on prior to implementing your SharePoint environment.

Design information architecture

This section relates the concepts of information architecture to planned implementations of SharePoint, including how to capture metadata with a focus on optimizing reuse and searchability.

Design an intersite navigational taxonomy

The concepts of sites and site collections are core elements of basic SharePoint navigation. A *site* is the most granular element in this taxonomy and is formed from a combination of lists and libraries. When sites are functionally, navigationally, and administratively grouped together, this grouping is called a *site collection* (see Figure 1-1).

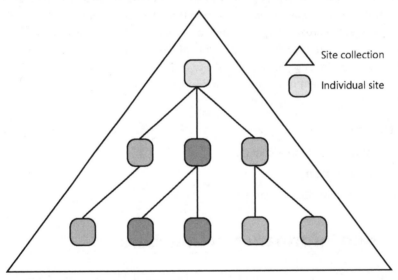

Site collection

Individual site

FIGURE 1-1 A site collection and its sites

The first site created within a site collection is known as a *top-level site*, and it often defines the navigational relationship with all its subsites and their subsites (children, grandchildren, and so on).

Creating sites within a single site allows for a fairly straightforward navigational structure that is easily configured. As you begin the process of adding subsites beneath the top-level site, the creation process offers the chance for you to add the newly created sites to the overall navigational structure and also to inherit the structure to the site you are creating. This so-called *structural navigation* allows the navigational component of SharePoint to be easily customized to a point as the organization changes and grows.

SCALABILITY ISSUES

The issue with placing all content within a single site collection is not initially apparent to users, as they are busy adopting and configuring the new environment. This increase in activity can cause the site collection (and the content database in which it is stored) to grow quickly; this growth subsequently poses an issue, as it's not possible to have a single site collection span multiple content databases. As subsites are added and duties are delegated, the site collection begins to become unwieldy, affecting components such as security groups and permissions inheritance.

CURRENT AND GLOBAL NAVIGATION

Current and global navigation refer to the two major navigation page areas present in traditional web design (also known as the inverted L), as shown in Figure 1-2. *Current navigation* generally contains links to content within the current site, whereas *global navigation* is often used to link multiple sites together.

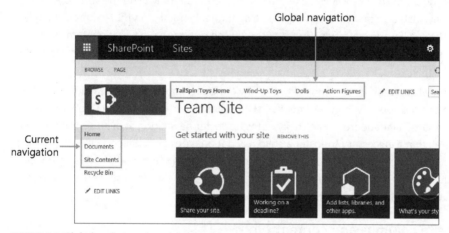

FIGURE 1-2 Global and current navigation

As this chapter focuses on intersite navigation taxonomy, this section concentrates on the global navigation section, although the current navigation section might be mentioned in a limited capacity.

> **NOTE** When site collections are created in SharePoint, the template chosen for the top-level site influences which functionality will be present by default for sites in the site collection. Some site templates, including the Team Site, do not have current and global navigation enabled by default. Instead, these controls are replaced by more basic tools that provide limited link customization functionality, known respectively as Quick Launch and the Top Link Bar.

ORGANIZATIONAL CHART NAVIGATION

One of the simplest site taxonomies to build echoes the layout of the organizational chart. Users visiting the site are immediately greeted by a navigational menu system with links to each major unit in the company (human resources, information technology, accounting, and so on).

As with any configuration, there are benefits and drawbacks. In this case, configuration requires little effort to set up on the front end and might be sufficient for a smaller organization, but is it suitable for a growing company? Basing navigation on the structure of the organization can end up being quite restrictive and inflexible.

Organizational navigation might be accurate when the site is first configured, but your organizational structure itself might change. Several factors can cause broken or incorrect links within a site, such as new or divested acquisitions that alter the SharePoint navigational structure. A sudden shift in this structure to accommodate organizational change can result in broken bookmarks or errant search results.

FUNCTIONAL NAVIGATION

The challenge is not to necessarily make the navigational hierarchy echo the structure of the company; instead, consider focusing the navigational hierarchy on the actions of people who visit the site. Functional navigation is based on the notion that navigation items should function as verbs, possessing both action and specific intent (for instance, "check my benefits" instead of "HR").

Deciding which items get promoted to the navigation requires some interaction with the respective business units. When you meet with these units, it is important to throw the rule book out: A large whiteboard, some sticky notes (to foster navigation activities), and an open forum are all that is necessary to foster a solid navigational design. Challenge the members of the group to act as normal business users visiting the site. Don't be afraid to make mistakes. These requirements form only an initial understanding of how the site is to be used; navigation can be refined by using site metrics as time progresses.

Design site columns and content types

There are two distinct types of columns within SharePoint: list columns and site columns. From a functional perspective, the two are identical, with one major difference: Only site columns are reusable.

LIST COLUMNS

As an example, consider a new list for a small company's building management that will be used to assign a desk to a worker. The company currently has two offices, one in Houston and one in San Antonio, with only one building in each city. The plan is for the organization to eventually expand into other states.

The requirement is to capture a simple series of metadata elements (such as user name, office location, and phone number), and for each office to maintain its own version of the list.

Within each office's list, you could build simple list columns to capture each of these distinct pieces of metadata (also known as *information types*).

So far, so good—maintaining two distinct lists for two separate offices isn't really that tough. Adding values to each list requires you to visit its site and office list to make changes. As the company begins to add sites (and more office sites and lists), maintenance of these list columns becomes more error prone and time consuming.

SITE COLUMNS

The next step on the path to reusable metadata is to build site columns instead of list columns and then associate the site columns to a list or library. The major benefit of moving from list columns to site columns is extensibility; metadata that was assigned to a single list column can now be associated to that same column, but in multiple lists.

Site columns are similar to list columns, but they are hierarchical in nature. When a site column is instantiated on a particular site, that site and all its child sites inherit the site column and its properties, allowing you to maintain the column from a single location within the structure.

Figure 1-3 shows the inheritance of three site columns within a site hierarchy. This example is oversimplified, but you can see the inheritance of site columns based on where they were initially created.

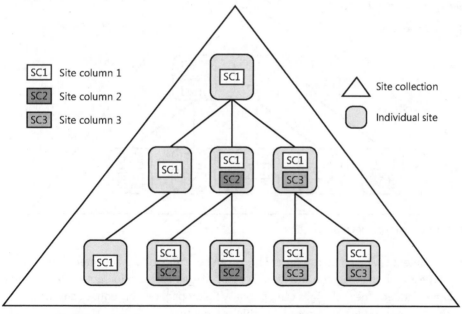

FIGURE 1-3 Site column inheritance

Site columns are hierarchical, inherited from parent to child. After a site column is created, a list can be assigned to that column (along with its information type and all metadata). If the metadata associated with the information type changes (for instance, adding a new color choice), this change can be propagated throughout any list that had previously been assigned to that site column.

Both list columns and site columns are defined by the type of content they possess (also referred to as the column's information type). Most of these information types are scoped to the particular list or site column, meaning that metadata contained within the column is available only to sites residing within that site collection.

CONTENT TYPES

A content type allows you to manage groupings of similar items in a list or library. These attributes not only provide descriptive information about the item (metadata and properties), but also provide activities that can be associated with each item (workflows, information management policies, document templates, and other features).

As is the case with site columns, content types behave in a hierarchical fashion and are inherited from each parent site to its child in the same site collection, as shown in Figure 1-4.

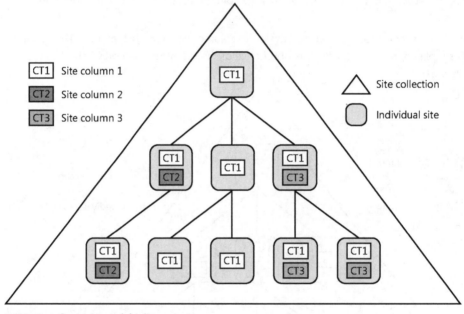

FIGURE 1-4 Content type inheritance

After a content type is created, a list or library can be assigned to that content type. If the content type is then changed at a later time (for instance, a new retention policy stage or new site column is added), these changes can optionally be propagated throughout any list or library that had previously been assigned to that content type.

CONTENT TYPE HIERARCHY

All content types are related and form an ecosystem of documents, items, pages, lists, and libraries. For example, when you provision a new document library, the default content type assigned to it is Document. If you wanted to build a hierarchy of legal documents and have Contract (a more specific document type) as one of the available content types, its content type hierarchy might look something like Figure 1-5.

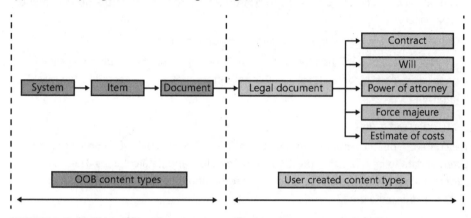

FIGURE 1-5 Content type hierarchy

In this case, you might assign a core set of site columns to the Legal Document content type and then assign workflows, retention policies, and more site columns to the individual child content types (Contract, Will, and so on).

Site collections are automatically populated with a series of content types that are themselves composed of out-of-the-box (OOB) site columns. The number and type of content types provisioned depend on two different factors:

- **Site template** The template you choose when provisioning a new site
- **Features** The features you select to add to an existing SharePoint site

So far, we have a series of site columns that can inherit managed metadata, but the content type is still limited in application scope to the site collection. If you build multiple site collections for your implementation (and you should), you'll need a mechanism to make metadata available beyond the site collection boundary without having to build the same information type over and over again in each new site collection. For that, we will use the Managed Metadata Service (MMS) and a concept known as the content type hub.

CONTENT TYPE HUB

Although content types can easily be defined within the boundaries of a site collection, we've not yet seen any provision for creating a content type that can be used in multiple site collections; this situation is quickly remedied by the use of a content type hub.

A *content type hub* is a site collection specifically configured to provide content types to other site collections. The individual content types are syndicated by the MMS; the process is fairly straightforward:

1. The MMS is configured to allow the content type hub to be the only source for centralized content type syndication.

2. The MMS connection is configured to consume content types from the hub's content type gallery.

3. Content types are placed in the content type hub for syndication.

4. Content types are published by the Content Type Subscriber timer job on a regular basis (every hour by default) to all web applications that are connected to the MMS application.

EXTERNAL CONTENT TYPES

External content types incorporate Business Connectivity Services (BCS) functionality to enable external data to be represented within SharePoint lists and data columns. These content types are metadata that represent connectivity information to data, data definitions, and behaviors applied to the data.

Information provided via the use of external content types is reusable, mimicking the behavior of normal content types within a site or site collection. Users who interact with an external content type do not have to be aware of the underlying data type, connection type, or security present. External content types also allow for the creation of lists and data columns within SharePoint that function identically to their native SharePoint counterparts.

The information represented by external content types is provided by BCS and surfaced in SharePoint by specific Web Parts:

- **Business Data Actions** Displays a list of actions associated with an entity defined in BCS (for example, an external list) and made available to a user, such as sending email or editing customer information

- **Business Data Connectivity Filter** Filters the contents of a connected Business Data Web Part by using values from an entity

- **Business Data Item** Displays the details of an entity instance (for example, an item) from a business application, such as a particular customer or order

- **Business Data Item Builder** Creates a Business Data Item based on URL query string parameters, then provides the output to other Business Data Web Parts

- **Business Data List** Displays a list of entity instances (for example, items) registered in BCS, such as displaying a list of customers or orders

- **Business Data Related List** Displays a list of related entity instances from a business application, such as showing all orders related to a particular customer

External content types and item pickers are also available for use within SharePoint along with profile pages, which can display details about a particular item. If more functionality is desired than what is presented by the OOB tools, development by using external content types is available via the SharePoint and client object models, or by using Representational State Transfer (REST) URLs.

> **NOTE** As it happens, the release of SharePoint 2016 does not correspond to an updated release of the SharePoint Designer tool; thus, business users of SharePoint 2016 continue to rely on the use of the 2013 release of SharePoint Designer for many tasks, including the creation and integration of external content types by using BCS.
>
> SharePoint administrators and developers can alternately continue to use Visual Studio for the creation of external content types.

Design keywords

Within a SharePoint 2016 site, descriptive *keyword metadata* (words or phrases) can be directly assigned to any list item or document and are often created by individual users on a site. Enterprise keywords are stored in a single term set within the MMS. This specialized term set is nonhierarchical and simply called the *keyword set*.

Adding keywords to a list item or document is fairly straightforward, but requires a bit of configuration prior to use. The basic configuration process requires the MMS connection to be configured as the default storage location for keywords. Once this is complete, the enterprise keywords site column can be added to content types.

CONFIGURING THE DEFAULT STORAGE LOCATION

Configuring the default storage location requires access permissions to Central Administration, specifically to the MMS application or connection.

To configure the default storage location:

1. Open Central Administration and select Application Management.
2. Under Service Applications, select Manage Service Applications.
3. Scroll down the list of service applications, and click the blank area next to Managed Metadata Service Connection.
4. On the ribbon, on the Service Applications tab, click the Properties icon.
5. On the Edit Managed Metadata Service Connection page, select the This Service Application Is The Default Storage Location For Keywords check box (see Figure 1-6).

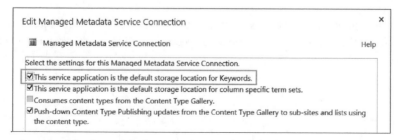

FIGURE 1-6 Selecting a default storage location for keywords

ADDING THE ENTERPRISE KEYWORDS COLUMN

Next, the Enterprise Keywords column must be added to a list or document library (see Figure 1-7); this column allows the user to enter multiple keyword values to describe an item.

FIGURE 1-7 Keywords added to a document in a library

Once keywords have been added by users in the enterprise, these values are reflected within the Managed Metadata term store. Note that keywords are located under the System, Keywords group; none of the specialized term sets within the System group enables you to build any sort of hierarchy.

Keywords that are regularly used by business users in the organization can be reviewed and moved into term sets; doing so enables the keyword to become centrally managed as a term and moved into appropriate term sets. In other words, the keyword effectively makes the transition from folksonomy to taxonomy.

To transform a keyword into a term, right-click it and select Move Keyword (see Figure 1-8).

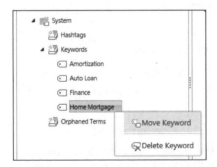

FIGURE 1-8 Moving a keyword to a term set

A series of destinations appear; at this point, you can select a term set (see Figure 1-9). You can also decide whether this word can continue to be used as a distinct keyword outside of this term set.

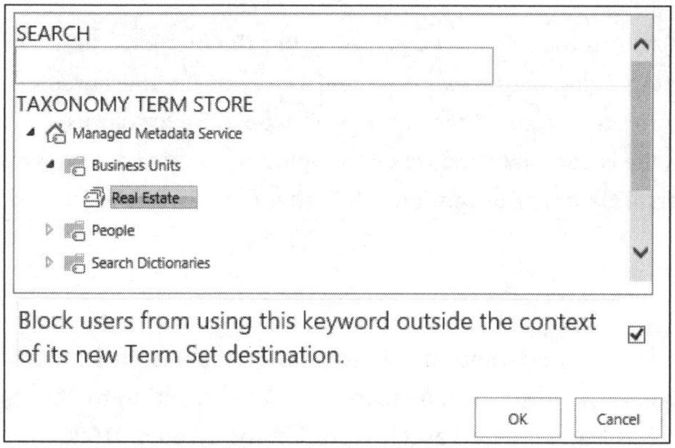

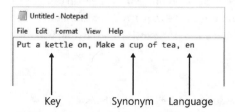

FIGURE 1-9 Choosing a destination term set

> **IMPORTANT**   This conversion is a one-way process; after a keyword has been changed to a term, it cannot be reverted to a keyword.

Design synonyms

The ability to define synonyms in SharePoint requires the use of a thesaurus, which is uploaded to SharePoint by using PowerShell cmdlets. The use of a thesaurus in SharePoint 2016 provides two benefits to search users:

- The ability to define multiple names for the same items; for example, searching for "put a kettle on" will return search results that include the phrase "make a cup of tea"

- The ability to use acronyms in search; searches for CEO will return results that include "chief executive officer"

CREATING THE THESAURUS FILE

Creating a thesaurus for use in SharePoint is a straightforward process; essentially, you first build a text file as a comma-separated value (.csv) file and then import it to SharePoint by using a PowerShell session.

The manner in which the thesaurus is created truly matters. Each entry in the thesaurus is comprised of a key, a synonym, and a language; each should also be contained in its own line. By using our previous examples and building entries in English, our entry would look something like Figure 1-10.

FIGURE 1-10 Key, synonym, language: one set per line in thesaurus

> **IMPORTANT** Uploading a new thesaurus file to SharePoint overwrites the previous thesaurus entry (they are not additive). Also, you might want to retain a copy of the thesaurus .csv file outside of SharePoint because there is no way to retrieve or export the thesaurus once uploaded. Once the thesaurus file is complete and ready for upload, save it as a .csv file with UTF-8 encoding to a Universal Naming Convention (UNC) share that is accessible by a SharePoint server in the farm.

IMPORTING THE THESAURUS FILE

Importing the thesaurus requires the person uploading the file to possess the Search Service Application Administrator permission and be able to run a PowerShell session within the farm. In this example, the Thesaurus.csv file has been created and is stored in the \\16SP2016RC \PowerShell share. To upload the thesaurus (PowerShell shown in Listing 1-1):

1. In Windows PowerShell, set a variable to the Search service application.

2. Import the thesaurus by using the Import-SPEnterpriseSearchThesaurus cmdlet.

```
$searchApp = Get-SPEnterpriseSearchServiceApplication
Import-SPEnterpriseSearchThesaurus -SearchApplication $searchApp -Filename
\\16sp2016rc\\powershell\thesaurus.csv
```

Once the thesaurus file has been successfully imported, the console will report the message, "Dictionary imported successfully," as shown in Figure 1-11.

FIGURE 1-11 Dictionary imported successfully

> **NOTE** The SharePoint Online component of Office 365 does not currently include the ability to upload a thesaurus; thus, the Import-SPEnterpriseSearchThesaurus cmdlet is only for use with on-premises versions of SharePoint 2016.

✔ Quick check

- You join a new company whose SharePoint administrator recently quit abruptly, and have no access to their files. The SharePoint environment has been in production for a while now, and some of your users have requested new thesaurus entries be added to the farm without losing any of the existing entries. Can you help them?

Quick check answer

- Unfortunately, without a copy of the thesaurus entries (.csv file) that were previously uploaded, you will be required to re-create the thesaurus file from scratch.

Design Promoted Results

Promoted Results are weighted or promoted to be preferred responses to a particular search query. For instance, if a corporate user were to type in a search query that happened to include a key phrase such as "Benefits" or "Onboarding," you might want to direct them to the Human Resources website.

Promoted Results do not use keywords as triggers, instead using the query rule functionality for this task. To be effective, SharePoint Farm Administrators, Site Collection Administrators, and Site Administrators all have a hand in optimizing search results. To this end, Promoted Results can be configured at the following levels:

- **Search application** Scoped within the boundaries of the particular Search application
- **Site collection** Scoped to a single site collection
- **Site** Scoped to a single site

BUILDING QUERY RULES

Promoted Results are configured by adding query rules at the appropriate level (Search application, site collection, or site). Query rules can be found in three places: (1) under Queries and Results, Query Rules in the Search service application, (2) under Query Rules in Site Collection Administration, or (3) under Query Rules in Site Settings.

Adding a query rule requires only three steps: Select an appropriate search context, specify one or more query conditions, and then specify the resulting action.

> **IMPORTANT** SharePoint 2016 does not allow you to alter any of the built-in query rules. If you wish to build a query based on an existing rule, you must first make a copy of it; then you can alter the copy to meet your requirements. The Edit menu of a *built-in* query rule is always unavailable.

 Quick check

- An experienced SharePoint user in the enterprise requests that you create a Best Bet for search in the farm. How would you go about doing this?

Quick check answer

- Best Bets were replaced in SharePoint 2013 by Promoted Results. From a user standpoint, the function is very similar. Use a query rule to offer Promoted Results for users in search.

Design managed properties

Items within a list or library have metadata stored in columns, such as author, title, and subject. The metadata captured from these populated columns (both built in and user assigned) is initially stored as crawled properties.

To make crawled properties useful within SharePoint search, managed properties must be created and mapped to the crawled properties. Although this process can be done manually, the majority of the time, SharePoint can do the conversions for you.

> **NOTE** It's easy to forget: Assigning a standard column to a SharePoint list or library will give you a crawled property, but will not automatically create and map this property to a managed property. If you wish this process to happen automatically, first build a site column, then assign it to the list or library.

Creating a managed property at the site collection level and adding it to search requires just a few steps. In this example, we will be adding a site column called Phase to the Documents library, then making sure that SharePoint search is picking up the contents of the column.

1. Create the Phase site column.

2. Assign the Phase site column to a document library.

3. Create or edit an item in the list, adding metadata in the column you just created, then start a search crawl to create and map a managed property to the crawled property.

4. Verify that the property was created and mapped.

The Search Schema page within Site Collection Administration shows all of the managed properties, but you need to view the mapping between crawled properties and managed properties. Select Crawled Properties.

In the Filters section of the page, enter **Phase** into the Crawled Properties text box, and then select the green arrow to filter the properties. You should now see the Property Name ows_q_TEXT_Phase (the crawled property) and the Mapped To Property of PhaseOWSTEXT (the managed property), as shown in Figure 1-12.

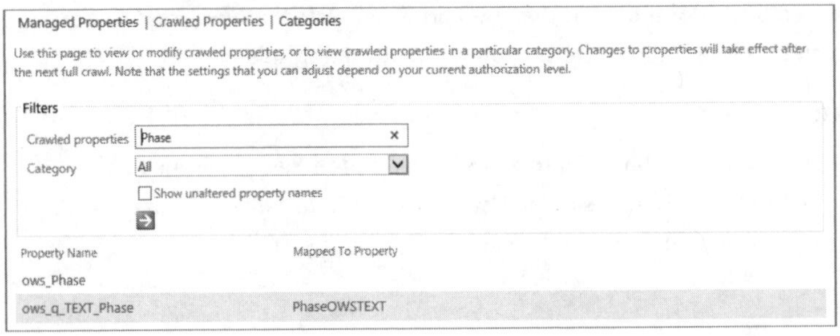

FIGURE 1-12 Crawled properties, showing the managed property mapping

If you need to have a managed property be sortable or refinable, you will create and map it from Central Administration in the Search service application.

 Quick check

- One of your experienced users complains that the values of their recently created SharePoint columns aren't searchable. These columns were initially created as site columns, but aren't showing up in Search Schema. There are column types, including values recorded as strings, booleans, and choices. How can you help?

Quick check answer

- It's likely that search crawls have occurred, but a full crawl hasn't yet occurred. Initiating a full crawl will cause the crawled properties to map to managed properties, except for the columns that are set up as choices. These columns will need to be created from Central Administration and then mapped manually to managed properties, as choices cannot automatically be mapped to a managed property.

Design durable links

Durable links is a way of assigning document links that remain functional when moving or renaming documents within a SharePoint 2016 site collection. In earlier versions of SharePoint, this was an issue because documents were exclusively assigned absolute URLs, which changed when a document was relocated or renamed.

This functionality is dependent on Office Online Server, the successor to the Office Web Apps server, and will not function without Office Online Server configured in the SharePoint farm. The resource ID of a document (docID) is stored within the content database and assigned to the document. When a user selects a durable link to a document, Office Online Server looks up the document by docID and then renders the document.

Design document library accessibility

There are several accessibility improvements in SharePoint 2016:

- Keyboard shortcuts allow you to do standard tasks without having to use the ribbon, by using shortcuts that seem familiar to Microsoft Office users (such as Alt+N to create a new document).

- Multiple documents can now be uploaded by using the Upload command (Alt+U) in a document library.

- File menus in SharePoint are now right-click enabled, allowing you to download, open, share, rename, delete, and more.

- Quick previews of videos and images are now available by hovering over or clicking them.

> **NEED MORE REVIEW?**   For a complete listing of accessibility improvements in SharePoint 2016, read the Document library features section of the article entitled "What's new in SharePoint Server 2016" at *https://support.office.com/article/What-s-new-in-SharePoint -Server-2016-089369b5-c3d4-4551-8bed-22b2548abd3b.*

Plan information management policies

In an increasingly litigious corporate world, the ability to regulate the life cycle of content is no longer an optional feature for an enterprise content management (ECM) system; it has become a core requirement.

SharePoint 2016 provides specific functionality designed to regulate the creation, interaction, and disposition of content. An information management policy is a set of rules that can be assigned to any given piece of content. These rules (also known as policy features) then define behaviors, such as the retention schedule, auditability, or markings (bar codes and labels) for a given piece of content.

> **NEED MORE REVIEW?**   For more details on the creation and use of information management policies, see the TechNet article entitled "Plan for information management policy in SharePoint Server 2016" at *https://technet.microsoft.com/library/cc262490(v=office.16) .aspx.*

There are four sets of policy features available in SharePoint Server 2016: retention, auditing, bar codes, and labels.

RETENTION POLICY FEATURES

Documents that have to comply with legal regulations often have a retention requirement. This requirement essentially regulates the amount of time that a document can (or should) be legally discoverable within any given ECM system.

After a retention policy feature has been enabled in SharePoint, a retention stage must be added to describe how the item will be managed according to the information management policy. This retention stage requires two elements to be valid: an event and an action. A third element, recurrence, is utilized only when certain actions are selected.

> **EXAM TIP**
>
> **Although one stage is the minimum requirement for a retention policy to be considered valid, it is possible to build multiple stages as required by your business stakeholders.**

AUDITING POLICY FEATURE

A vital element in any information management policy, auditing enables key personnel to monitor how a document is interacted with and by whom. When the auditing policy feature is enabled, any combination of the following events can be audited:

- Opening or downloading documents, viewing items in lists, or viewing item properties
- Editing items
- Checking out or checking in items
- Moving or copying items to another location in the site
- Deleting or restoring items

> **IMPORTANT** Increasingly, SharePoint Administrators are requested to provide auditing information for the environments they support. SharePoint 2016 provides the ability to generate Content Activity, Information Management Policy, Security and Site Settings, and Custom Reports. Events generated specifically by the auditing policy feature described in this section can be viewed in Site Settings, Site Collection Administration, Audit log reports.

BAR CODE POLICY FEATURE

Due to legal regulation and other concerns, documents are sometimes still rendered as paper documents. Printed versions of these documents must still be managed; thus SharePoint's information policies include the bar code policy feature.

When enabled, this feature creates a unique identifier value for a document and then inserts a bar code image of that value in the document. Although the default bar codes are compliant with the Code 39 standard (ANSI/AIM BC1-1995, Code 39), you can use the policies object model to add other bar code providers.

LABELING POLICY FEATURE (DEPRECATED IN SHAREPOINT 2013 AND 2016)

This policy feature is strictly provided in SharePoint 2016 for backward compatibility and should never be used in new information management policies. The purpose of this policy feature was to enable fixed text or document properties to be applied to the printed version of a document.

CREATING A NEW INFORMATION POLICY

To create a new site collection policy, follow these steps:

1. In Site Settings, Site Collection Administration, select Content Type Policy Templates.

2. On the Policies page, click Create to build a new information management policy.

3. Enter a name and description for the policy, then add a policy statement that will appear to users when interacting with items subject to this policy.

4. Choose and configure the pertinent policy features as applicable.

EXAM TIP

Site collection policies are scoped to a single site collection. For the sake of consistency, it is possible to export a policy from one site collection, then import it to another for reuse. Be familiar with the steps required in this process.

ASSIGNING AN INFORMATION MANAGEMENT POLICY

Information management policies can be assigned in three different ways:

- Policy features can be associated with a site collection policy template; that policy template can be associated with a content type, list, or library.

- Policy features can be associated directly with a content type; the content type can then be added to lists and libraries.

- Policy features can be associated directly with a list or library.

Note the hierarchy in the three different applications of information management; the more direct the application of policy features, the more difficult the administration of the features would be across multiple libraries, lists, or sites. After the policy has been applied at a high level (for instance, the top of the site collection), all subordinate levels using the same content type must inherit all information management policies present.

DISABLING A POLICY FEATURE

Any of the four policy features can be disabled from Central Administration. A good practice is to choose which of these features are in use within your organization, and prohibit the use of the rest (particularly the Labeling policy feature, which is deprecated). To disable any of the features in Central Administration, select the Security link. Within the Information Policy section, choose Configure Information Management Policy.

Plan search for sensitive and nonsensitive content

Data loss prevention (DLP) queries allow users responsible for managing sensitive content to locate content that might not belong in SharePoint sites, in accordance with corporate governance policies. These sensitive information types are templated, and they are identical for use between Exchange and SharePoint 2016.

> **NEED MORE REVIEW?** For more details on templates available for use with DLP as a whole, see the TechNet article entitled "Sensitive information types inventory in Exchange 2016" at *https://technet.microsoft.com/library/jj150541(v=office.16).aspx*. Note that not all of these templates are enabled within SharePoint Server 2016 by default.

Search enables DLP users to find sensitive information types based on patterns defined by a regular expression or a function, and also make use of keywords and checksums. Proximity ratings give the DLP user a confidence rating (85 percent, 75 percent, 65 percent, or 55 percent) in the type of information retrieved.

EXAM TIP

The configuration of DLP queries is the first step toward gaining an understanding of sensitive information deployed in SharePoint. Understand how to create a query and which actions can be added to it. For more information, refer to the Office article entitled "Create a DLP query in SharePoint Server 2016" at *https://support.office.com/article/Create-a-DLP-query-in-SharePoint-Server-2016-c0bed52d-d32b-4870-bcce-ed649c7371a3*.

Sensitive information types might include content such as bank routing numbers, credit card numbers, identification card numbers, and passport numbers; there are more than 80 template types available overall, although only a subset of these is available by default in SharePoint 2016. These types are specified by templates and are activated by DLP search queries put in place via an enterprise eDiscovery Center. When configuring the query of a search, the scope can be configured to search everything in SharePoint or to narrow the scope to one or more site collections.

Plan compliance features

DLP policies complement DLP queries, allowing an organization to identify, monitor, and automatically protect sensitive information across the SharePoint farm. DLP policies are created and stored in a Compliance Policy Center.

Each new DLP policy requires that you select a policy template, select the number of instances of sensitive information that triggers an event, and then send an incident report when new content is saved or edited. Optionally, the user can be notified via a policy tip when their content contains sensitive information, and this content can also be blocked (but potentially overridden by the user).

Although many sensitive information types are accounted for OOB in SharePoint 2016, it's possible to extend this functionality via Document Fingerprinting. Document Fingerprinting allows you to convert business documents (contracts, intellectual property, and other documents) into sensitive information types.

As we look to a hybrid installation of SharePoint 2016, we find that DLP is extensible in Office 365. If you have a predefined, text-based document template that you want to turn into a sensitive information type, Document Fingerprinting can be used to prevent the transmission of that document outbound, by using Information Rights Management (IRM).

IRM also permits users in the organization to configure item-level encryption via Information Rights Management Services, both on-premises and in the cloud. This level of content control maintains the governance requirements of the organization and prevents sensitive information from being made available to external users.

Plan managed site structures

Site structure design is a key concept in a SharePoint farm, affecting everything from capacity planning to navigational structure.

Earlier in this chapter, we defined the relationship between sites and site collections. A site is the most granular element in a given taxonomy and is formed from a combination of lists and libraries. Sites are functionally, navigationally, and administratively grouped together, into one or more site collections.

Within a site collection, moving a subsite around is fairly straightforward, requiring only that the Publishing Infrastructure feature be enabled:

1. Open Site Settings, Site Administration, Content And Structure.
2. Next to the site you want to move, click the drop-down arrow and then select Move, as shown in Figure 1-13.

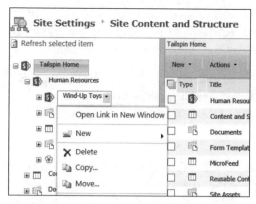

FIGURE 1-13 Moving a site within the Site Content And Structure menu

3. Choose a destination site and click OK.

Moving sites between site collections is another story. Sites within a site collection share administrative groups, content types, permissions, policies, and other items, which are provided only within that site collection. Although it's technically possible to copy a site to a different site collection by using the Export-SPWeb and Import-SPWeb PowerShell cmdlets, doing so does not make the newly copied site a full-fidelity copy of the original. Some permission and document settings are copied over, but other components (such as workflows) will not be transferred.

As their SharePoint implementations grow in size, most large organizations tend to focus on building multiple site collections rather than implementing fewer site collections with more sites and subsites. The problem then becomes one of navigation, which is addressed via a combination of two navigation types: path-based and metadata-based.

PATH-BASED NAVIGATION

When two site collections need to be included in the same navigational structure, path-based site collections can be used. These site collections are associated to one another by using managed paths. Two distinct types of managed paths are available for use: explicit and wildcard.

- Explicit managed paths enable two site collections to be put into the same URL path. For instance, if you had a site collection at *http://your.url.com/*, you could create an explicit managed path (for example, */yoursite*) to store another site collection at *http://your.url.com/yoursite*.
- Wildcard managed paths enable one site collection to be the "implied" parent of several site collections. Doing so requires two things:
  - All site collections are nested under a path that itself is not a site.
  - All site collections in the wildcard are at the same URL level.

If you had a site collection at *http://your.url.com/*, you could build a wildcard managed path (/projects) to contain all your projects, each in its own site collection. So the projects would be located at *http://your.url.com/projects/project1, /project2, /project3*, and so on. If a user decided, however, to navigate directly to *http://your.url.com/projects*, there would be a problem because there is no site at that level, only the wildcard managed path.

> **NEED MORE REVIEW?** For more details about creating and implementing managed paths, review the TechNet article entitled "Define managed paths in SharePoint Server 2016" at *https://technet.microsoft.com/library/cc261845(v=office.16).aspx.*

METADATA-BASED NAVIGATION

Although path-based navigation is useful, navigation can be further improved by way of managed navigation. Conversely, your navigational design might choose to hide path-based navigation, instead arranging logical site collection navigation by the use of metadata alone.

> **EXAM TIP**
>
> There really is no right answer here: Your organization will likely use both of these navigational elements. For the exam, be familiar with both of these navigational concepts and the mechanisms for setting them up.

Using the MMS, a navigational structure can be generated on a fairly dynamic basis, tying multiple sites and site collections together into an organized (and exceptionally flexible) structure. It should be noted that the navigational structure is generated on a per-site collection basis, with every site collection setting up a term set for its own use.

Managed navigation is dependent on one or more term sets, which are nothing more than a grouping of terms within the term store. Each term set defines a navigational structure, and multiple navigational structures can be utilized, even within a single site collection (if desired).

Within a site, global and current navigation can each use a term set for navigation. Note that global and current navigation *cannot* use two separate term sets—only a single term set can be specified on the navigation settings page of a site. The individual terms can be set to show in global navigation, current navigation, or both.

> **NEED MORE REVIEW?** For more details about creating and implementing managed navigation for site collections in SharePoint 2016, review the TechNet article entitled "Overview of managed navigation in SharePoint Server 2016" at *https://technet.microsoft.com/library /dn194311(v=office.16).aspx.*

Plan term sets

Term sets are part of the larger set of MMS functionality present in a SharePoint Server 2016 ECM solution. A term set is nothing more than an intelligent grouping of related terms; terms are nothing more than metadata that can be associated with items in a SharePoint list or library.

As discussed previously, MMS encompasses two distinct groupings of metadata: taxonomy and folksonomy.

- **Taxonomy** The more formalized of the two groupings, taxonomy is hierarchical and deliberate in nature and includes terms and term sets.
- **Folksonomy** The more casual of the two groupings, folksonomy imparts items with metadata by using tags or keywords, generated by individual users; no hierarchy can be implied or defined.

EXAM TIP

SharePoint administrators are often not the people who define term sets. Most term sets start as tags and keywords (folksonomy) and are then promoted to more formal status as part of a term set (taxonomy). Be familiar with how this transition takes place.

TERMS

One of the more interesting behaviors of terms is that they can be nested up to seven levels deep. Additionally, you can designate certain levels of terms as "unavailable for tagging," meaning that you will be using them only for navigational purposes (such as grouping topics by letter; for example, A–F, G–J, and so on).

TERM SETS

Term sets with SharePoint are stored within a term store, which is stored within an MMS application. A SharePoint implementation is not limited to a single metadata service application; multiple service applications might be present to service different legal or organizational functions.

Term sets can have a status of either open or closed. An open term set enables anyone to contribute a new term; a closed term set enables only contributors and owners to add a new term.

IMPORTANT All metadata elements in SharePoint share the same hierarchy: MMS applications, taxonomy term store (organized by language), term set group, term sets, terms.

DEFINING TERM SET FUNCTIONALITY

Colors (red, green, blue), sizes (small, medium, large), and fabrics (polyester, wool, cotton) are all examples of valid term sets; their values would be considered terms within a SharePoint environment. Additionally, these term sets could be grouped into a larger term set group, such as clothing.

LOCAL VERSUS GLOBAL TERM SETS

As term sets are being designed, it is important to consider the audience who will be consuming the metadata. During this design phase, questions such as these often arise:

- Does everyone in the enterprise need access to a particular term?
- Is the term specific in scope?

- Who should be managing the term set?
- What is the desired "footprint" of the term set?

A SharePoint MMS application is associated to a web application via the service application proxy. Terms provided via the proxy can be assigned to items within the desired SharePoint web application; the only consideration that must be made is one of scope.

Term sets are assigned by way of the Term Set Management Tool, which can be used at two distinct levels, local and global:

- Local term sets are scoped to a single site collection and are created via the Term Set Management Tool in Site Collection Administration.
- Global term sets are scoped to an MMS and are created via the Term Set Management Tool in Central Administration.

> **NOTE** You might notice that both types of term sets are intended to be administered by power users. Site collection administrators familiar with the administration of term sets are often those whom you will work with to formalize global term sets for use across multiple sites and site collections connected to the MMS. Either farm administrators or appropriately trained business stakeholders can be granted access to administer global term sets within the MMS instance management page in Central Administration.

CORE TERM SET PLANNING

Members of a particular business unit often volunteer to be early adopters of this information management strategy and are advocates for a successful ECM implementation. It is a common misconception that term set designers have to be technical to design an effective metadata taxonomy; truthfully, they do not.

Working with an enterprise librarian or design team, it is quite preferable to involve this group of term set designers in planning simply because they have firsthand knowledge of the products and processes that are pertinent to their segment of the business.

> **NOTE** Microsoft provides two distinct metadata planning worksheets in Microsoft Excel format. Both of these sheets can be found in the TechNet article entitled "Plan terms and term sets in SharePoint Server 2016" at *https://technet.microsoft.com/library/ee519604(v =office.16).aspx*. The Term Sets Planning worksheet provides a basic worksheet intended for manual term set implementations, whereas the Detailed Term Set Planning Worksheet can be used for more in-depth design and can be directly imported (.csv) into the Term Store Management Tool.

Successfully implementing a term set involves five core activities: identifying each term set, identifying a term set owner, designing term set groups, defining the term sets themselves, and creating the term sets.

IDENTIFYING TERM SETS

Identifying which items belong in a term set (and at what level) is often the hardest part of the entire metadata process. The amount of metadata present in a business can be overwhelming, but there is an easy way to overcome the initial shock: Look for the pain points. Specifically, you are looking for places where even a limited application of metadata could streamline processes and make information more readily searchable, such as the following:

- Custom columns, particularly those that enable the selection of one or more values (such as choice fields)

- Words or phrases that are being regularly used to tag an item (from folksonomy to taxonomy)

- Metadata that users often use to sort or filter items in a list or library

- Acronyms or abbreviations for a function or product

- Items that are, by definition, hierarchical in nature (for example, inventories)

Items that probably should not be included in a term set might include:

- Items that have column metadata fields that have already been provided with the SharePoint framework (built-in columns)

- Boolean (yes or no) values

- Items that might have different values in different segments of a business

- Items that have no well-defined values

IDENTIFYING TERM SET OWNERS

A term set owner is the person or group responsible for the maintenance of terms in a particular term set. As an example, if a business has locations that are added and removed on a regular basis, the term set owner is the person who performs the additions and deletions of terms from the term set.

In more formal term sets (global term sets, in particular), the term set owner is often not a single individual but a small team of people who are responsible for the overall correctness of the term set.

DETERMINING TERM SET GROUPS

Term set groups define security for a particular term set; they also provide for the logical grouping of term sets. Users can be designated as contributors for a term set, and these people can be enabled to manage a particular term set in the group. Additionally, individuals can be designated as term set group managers, enabling them to assign and remove permissions to a term set (or sets) as required.

DEFINING THE TERM SET

After owners are defined for a particular term set, they can choose to either define the term set on their own or designate contributors to a term set to more fully develop the term set. To define a term set, users must be able to answer three distinct questions:

- What terms belong in any given term set?
- How are terms organized with a term set?
- Who are the designated contributors for a given term set?

CREATING A NEW TERM SET

There are two ways to begin the process of generating a new term set, both of which use the Term Store Management Tool. Site collection administrators and owners can find the Term Store Management Tool from any site in the site collection. To begin using the Term Store Management Tool, these users select the Term Store Management link from within Site Settings, Site Administration.

Farm administrators and designated term store administrators have the ability to define term sets at the MMS instance level. To begin using the Term Store Management Tool, these users can select the Term Store Management Tool from within an MMS associated with the SharePoint farm itself.

Plan for support of Open Document Format

Prior to Microsoft Office 2007, documents were saved in binary (.doc, .xls, and so on); the introduction of Office 2007 brought a series of new document types based on an Open XML structure (.docx, .xlsx, and so on) and were quite a bit smaller from a file size standpoint. Documents saved in these formats could now be viewed and edited in other, non-Microsoft tools, such as OpenOffice.

Starting with Office 2010, Open Document Format (ODF) documents (.odt, .ods, and so on) could be viewed and edited in the Office client; SharePoint also supported the storage of these documents, but they could not be made available as a template in a single library or used in a content type. This is remedied in SharePoint 2016, which now allows users to generate documents based on these templates in a library.

> **NEED MORE REVIEW?**   For more details about configuring an ODF document as a template within a document library in SharePoint 2016, review the TechNet article entitled "Set Open Document Format (ODF) as the default file template for a library" at *https://support .office.com/article/Set-Open-Document-Format-ODF-as-the-default-file-template-for-a -library-bf30a61d-1601-486e-8fa2-924bc5ea303e*.

Plan mobile navigation

SharePoint 2016 now fully incorporates the use of HTML5 to create a fully mobile-compliant experience. Users visiting a SharePoint site or function can expect a consistent experience regardless of the screen format (phone, tablet, slate, or PC or Mac) they use to visit it.

In a hybrid configuration, a user visiting a SharePoint site is presented the opportunity to interact with both on-premises and cloud-based functionality. By using a touch-enabled interface in this configuration, a user can select to browse sites, subsites, and content right alongside apps such as Delve and OneDrive for Business. This mobile view on a device can also be switched into a full web view as would be seen from a desktop computer.

Design a logical architecture

In the previous section, we worked through the design of informational elements to be used in the SharePoint farm. The effort now shifts from planning to design, determining the layout of technical components required to implement the newly generated informational design. This section focuses on the capabilities present in Internet Information Services (IIS) and SharePoint that enable you to determine a logical design while considering storage, authentication, web applications, and other components.

Plan application pools

An application pool is a construct used to group web applications logically, based on a number of criteria such as authentication, performance, isolation, and configuration. Web applications contained in an application pool provide functionality for one or more websites in an IIS farm.

If you build a basic SharePoint farm, activate the default service applications by using the OOB Farm Configuration Wizard, and then build a site collection by using the defaults, you would see from IIS Manager that several application pools, even more web applications, and a few SharePoint-specific websites have already been created (see Figure 1-14).

Application Pools

This page lets you view and manage the list of application pools on the server. Application pools are associated with worker processes, contain one or more applications, and provide isolation among different applications.

Filter:　　　　　　　▼ 🔻 Go ▾ 🔄 Show All | Group by: No Grouping 　　▼

Name	Status	.NET CLR V...	Managed Pipel...	Identity	Applications
.NET v2.0	Started	v2.0	Integrated	ApplicationPoolId...	0
.NET v2.0 Classic	Started	v2.0	Classic	ApplicationPoolId...	0
.NET v4.5	Started	v4.0	Integrated	ApplicationPoolId...	0
.NET v4.5 Classic	Started	v4.0	Classic	ApplicationPoolId...	0
73dcd87c8a19424aac520ec9d4819798	Started	v4.0	Integrated	RC\svc_spfarm	15
Classic .NET AppPool	Started	v2.0	Classic	ApplicationPoolId...	0
DefaultAppPool	Started	v4.0	Integrated	ApplicationPoolId...	1
SecurityTokenServiceApplicationPool	Started	v4.0	Integrated	RC\svc_spfarm	3
SharePoint - tailspintoys.com80	Started	v4.0	Integrated	RC\svc_spfarm	1
SharePoint Central Administration v4	Started	v4.0	Integrated	RC\svc_spfarm	1
SharePoint Web Services Root	Stopped	v4.0	Integrated	LocalService	1
SharePoint Web Services System	Started	v4.0	Integrated	RC\svc_spfarm	1

FIGURE 1-14 Application pools supporting a SharePoint farm

Looking at Figure 1-14, you can see that there is a SharePoint – tailspintoys.com80 application pool. Filtering on this pool (by right-clicking the application pool and selecting View Applications), you can see that this application pool hosts a single root application (see Figure 1-15).

FIGURE 1-15 Root web application for the SharePoint – tailspintoys.com80 site

There is also another application pool listed that hosts a different web application, which also provides services to the SharePoint – tailspintoys.com80 site. If you filter instead on SecurityTokenServiceApplicationPool, you can see that it is linked to the SharePoint – tailspintoys.com80 site and to the SharePoint Central Administration v4 and SharePoint Web Services sites (see Figure 1-16).

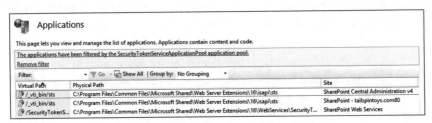

FIGURE 1-16 The SecurityTokenServiceApplicationPool and its associated sites

WEB APPLICATION POOL LIMITS GUIDANCE

Before adding a new application pool, consider whether an existing pool might be used to host your new web application. The number of pools might not initially be an issue, but as SharePoint usage grows within your organization, you might find that servers hosting the Front-end server role in your farm begin to run short of available memory resources.

CONSIDERATIONS FOR BUILDING NEW WEB APPLICATIONS

Although you want to keep the overall number of application pools low, you might find the need to build a new web application pool for any one of several reasons:

- Grouping web applications that run with the same configuration settings
- Isolating web applications that require unique configuration settings
- Providing security by running a particular group of websites under a closely monitored service account for auditing purposes
- Resource isolation
- To prevent an outage of the entire IIS application based on one or more misbehaving or failed web applications
- For Internet service providers (ISPs) to separate application pools based on customer resource needs

Before adding a new web application, consider using Performance Monitor (Perfmon.exe) to get a baseline of existing RAM usage. Monitoring a SharePoint environment is a topic that is covered in Chapter 7, "Troubleshooting and monitoring."

Plan web applications

Because there are software boundaries and limits that affect web application pools, it stands to reason that there would be metrics around the number of web applications in a SharePoint farm. For any SharePoint farm, the supported number of web applications is 20 per farm.

EXAM TIP

In the section on planning for software boundaries, you will note that the supported limit for web applications in a farm is set to 20. This is not a per-web application pool limit, but a limit for the entirety of the SharePoint farm. As with the web application pools, this limitation is memory dependent, and baseline RAM monitoring is recommended before increasing the web application count to that level.

PLANNING THE WEB APP CONFIGURATION

Several configuration items must be considered when planning web applications in a new SharePoint farm. Documenting each of these decisions as the new web application is implemented results in a streamlined, repeatable installation process.

NOTE Developing a naming standard for both your web applications and the content databases with which they interact is a key first effort at documentation, and will prevent confusion and potentially costly administration mistakes.

Determining the purpose of a web application before it is implemented guides the direction of its configuration. Defining this purpose can be as easy as developing a set of questions such as the following:

- What group of users does this application serve (intranet, extranet, Internet)?
- How are users expected to authenticate?
- What type of navigation do users expect when they visit the site or site collections in this web application?
- How will site collections be created? There are two distinct choices: host-header site collections or path-based site collections, both of which affect web application design, and are discussed later in this chapter.

AUTHENTICATION TYPES

When a new web application is created via Central Administration, there are several options available for choosing how a user will authenticate to it. More than one authentication type can be chosen for a given web application, assigned to a particular zone (we'll talk about zones shortly):

- **Windows authentication**   Integrated Windows authentication (NTLM or Kerberos)
- **Basic authentication**   Windows user name and password combination (encoded but not encrypted; password sent in clear text)
- **Forms-based authentication**   Using the ASP.NET membership and role provider
- **Trusted identity provider**   Secure Application Markup Language (SAML) token-based authentication

> **IMPORTANT**   Classic mode authentication is also technically available for a SharePoint 2016 web application, but is no longer supported and should not be used for any new user-facing web applications. In a new SharePoint 2016 farm, the only place you should encounter this authentication type is the Central Administration web application.

Each of these four authentication types uses claims-based authentication to a web application. Claims-based authentication is used for user, server-to-server, and app authentication; thus, it's recommended for use with all web applications and zones of a SharePoint 2016 farm.

Classic mode authentication is also available for a SharePoint 2016 web application, but is no longer supported and should not be used for any new user-facing web applications. If required, web applications can be configured to use classic mode (Windows classic) authentication via PowerShell. In a new SharePoint 2016 farm, the only place you should encounter this authentication type is the Central Administration web application.

> **NEED MORE REVIEW?**   For more details about authentication providers, review the TechNet article entitled "Plan for user authentication methods in SharePoint Server 2016" at *https://technet.microsoft.com/library/cc262350(v=office.16).aspx*.

ANONYMOUS ACCESS

Although not technically a form of authentication, anonymous access for a web application enables users to retrieve content without the need for a user name and password combination (in other words, they are not required to authenticate). Allowing anonymous access does not mean that content in a web application will be immediately available to users; it simply means that site administrators can enable anonymous authorization to site content.

> **IMPORTANT**   This setting should be enabled when using forms authentication mode because certain forms-aware client applications might not correctly authenticate without it.

DATABASE SERVER AND AUTHENTICATION TYPE FOR THE WEB APPLICATION

Working with your SQL database administrator (DBA) team, you should be able to determine which Microsoft SQL database server or instance should host your SharePoint content databases. The SQL DBA will let you know which type of authentication is acceptable, but it must be one of the following:

- Windows authentication (recommended)
- SQL authentication

SPECIFYING A FAILOVER DATABASE SERVER

There are currently four types of high-availability (HA) solutions provided by SQL Server; however, the only one that SharePoint is directly aware of (the others are transparent) is SQL database mirroring.

When a SharePoint database is mirrored, SharePoint must know not only the name or instance of the principal server (where the database read and write transactions are occurring) but also the name or instance of the mirror server (the read-only copy of the database). If the mirrored database is failed over, SharePoint then knows the location of the alternate name or instance.

> **IMPORTANT**   Although SQL mirroring is still supported in SQL 2012, 2014, and 2016, it has officially been deprecated, meaning that it might not be supported in future versions of SQL. If you are in the process of creating or upgrading to a new SharePoint 2016 farm, consider this an opportunity to move from SQL mirroring to SQL AlwaysOn Availability Groups. High availability and disaster recovery options are covered in Chapter 3, "Workload optimization."

SERVICE APPLICATION CONNECTIONS

SharePoint 2016 provides service application functionality (User Profile, Search, and so on) through a series of service application proxies. These proxies are usually collected into a proxy group (the first one is called "default," appropriately enough), but it is possible to connect to one or more proxies by just selecting a custom connection and selecting the check boxes of the proxies to which you want to connect the new web application.

ALTERNATE ACCESS MAPPING URLS AND WEB APPLICATION ZONES

Alternate access mapping URLs are a mechanism that allows for a single site collection to be associated to multiple URLs. Zones are logical constructs that define several different means of accessing the same web application. Each zone can have different types of authentication mechanisms based on how a user would be accessing the site. Detailed coverage of both alternate access mappings and web application zones is found later in this chapter in the "Plan zones and alternate access mappings" section.

Plan for software boundaries

Software boundaries can be interpreted as operational limitations for a system. Some limits are finite, with a maximum allowed value, whereas others exceed performance or recommended limitations. SharePoint Server 2016 has three classes of software boundaries and limits: boundaries, thresholds, and supported limits.

- **Boundaries**   A boundary is an absolute limit, meaning that the value given cannot be exceeded in the current version of SharePoint. An example of this type of limit is the number of zones in a web application; there are always five: default, intranet, extranet, Internet, and custom.

- **Thresholds** A threshold has an initial value set, meaning that the value can be modified to a maximum value (boundary). Before altering these values, consideration should be given to whether your specific infrastructure can accommodate the increased load that might be caused by this change.

- **Supported limits** A supported limit for any particular configuration parameter is a set value based on testing conducted by Microsoft. Although you can exceed supported limits, you might encounter unexpected results; these results could come in the form of diminished performance or unexpected behavior in the farm.

EXAM TIP

Reviewing boundaries and limits documentation can make for some rather dry reading. That said, don't miss reviewing this information; being able to relate software boundaries and limits effectively is one of the most important tools in your SharePoint arsenal. More important, your knowledge of these boundaries and limits can make the difference in being able to reason out the correct answer to an exam question. Concentrate on the ones that have the largest impact on the farm as a whole: those that affect RAM, storage, processor usage, and overall performance.

The current listing of software boundaries and limitations for SharePoint can be found in the TechNet article entitled "Software boundaries and limits for SharePoint 2016" at *https://technet.microsoft.com/library/cc262787(v=office.16).aspx*.

Plan content databases

SharePoint administrators often become itinerant SQL administrators as well; after all, the level of SQL familiarity required by a SharePoint implementer is often fairly significant. SQL databases constitute an entire segment of the SharePoint farm environment, so it stands to reason that a SharePoint installation's health is heavily invested in the performance and storage characteristics of the SQL environment that supports it.

SOFTWARE BOUNDARY CONSIDERATIONS

In the SharePoint software boundaries and limitations documentation, there are some boundaries given for content databases:

- 500 content databases per farm (supported limit)
- General content database size recommendations:
  - 100 GB maximum recommended
  - 200 GB supported limit for general usage scenarios
- A supported limit of 4 TB per content database for archival content databases with very little read and write access (supported limit)
- No explicit limit for content databases housing document center or record center sites

If you examine these limits for a moment, you might come to realize that an environment approaching these levels would be quite large. A farm containing 500 databases with an average content database size of 50 GB would place the SQL back-end storage requirement somewhere in the neighborhood of 25 TB.

> **IMPORTANT** In some organizations, the data tier of your SharePoint farm will be administered by one or more SQL DBAs. This team will likely be unfamiliar with the specifications and limitations for SharePoint 2016, so you will need to be able to explain the requirements from an SQL point of view.

Content databases in the range of 50 GB are quite common. Content database growth beyond this level, eventually exceeding the 100 GB limit, will cause a warning to be generated in the SharePoint Health Analyzer, stating "Some content databases are growing too large." In fact, there are two SharePoint Health Analyzer rules related to database sizing. The first, "Database has large amounts of unused space," is a daily check that reports databases with large amounts of free space (pregrowth); the second, "Some content databases are growing too large," is an hourly check that reports on content databases exceeding 100 GB in size.

SCALING A SHAREPOINT IMPLEMENTATION

A content database can house several site collections, but a site collection can reside only within a single content database. With this in mind, we begin to consider how to scale out our environment.

Before contemplating the site collection taxonomy, you might first want to consider the life cycle of site collections. Some site collections are fairly permanent, providing the structural backbone of your SharePoint environment; others might be quite temporary (a one-off collaborative site collection, for instance) and can be disposed of when no longer in use.

In an environment in which you, the SharePoint administrator, are responsible for managing growth, the initial goal is scalability. By scaling your SharePoint environment to multiple site collections, you begin to account for potential growth.

In Figure 1-17, an example content database is initially configured with five site collections:

1. Over time, one of the site collections begins to experience rapid growth and begins to cause the content database to drastically increase in size.

2. The SharePoint farm administrator recognizes this growth and moves the larger site collection into its own content database to manage growth.

   - After the content database is moved, its growth can be restricted by setting the maximum number of site collections in the database to 1.

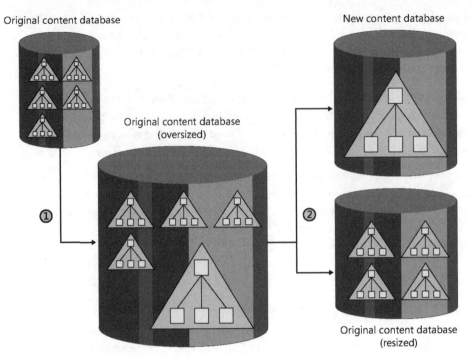

FIGURE 1-17 Moving a growing site collection into its own content database

Plan host-header site collections

This section and the later one, "Plan zones and alternate access mapping," are closely related; the two of them together result in a choice about how a user will ultimately access any particular URL within a SharePoint farm.

A LITTLE HISTORY

One of the primary reasons administrators used to build separate web applications for a SharePoint site was to enable a farm to have distinct URLs for different web applications. A business unit within an organization would request a particular URL for its function, such as *hr.yoursharepointname.com* for HR.

The farm administrator would then oblige by generating a new web application for the HR group and assigning it the *hr.yoursharepointname.com* host header. Other business units would find out about the new URL and begin to have the same requirement; soon the farm administrator could have several web applications, one for each new business unit.

If you were to build a farm and give each business unit its own web application (simply to give it a distinct URL), you might find that your farm will quickly exceed published web application limits and start to exhaust resources, particularly on the front-end servers.

USING HOST-HEADER SITE COLLECTIONS

Host-header site collections enable you to assign vanity URLs to multiple site collections contained within a single web application. In this configuration, no host header is set up in IIS Manager; host headers are assigned as part of the site collection setup process by using PowerShell. Setting up a new web application for host-header site collections requires a bit of forethought, and some basic knowledge of PowerShell.

EXAM TIP

The default behavior of the New-SPWebApplication cmdlet is to create a web application in Windows (or Classic) authentication mode. Windows authentication mode is deprecated and should not be used.

This behavior can be averted by using the -AuthenticationProvider switch. Claims Authentication should be used instead of Classic. If you forget to use the switch, PowerShell will dutifully warn you of the missing switch, but only after it runs the cmdlet and creates the web application (which you will have to delete) in Windows mode.

The Central Administration interface for creating new web applications does not provide a way to build new Host-Header Site Collection (HHSC)-based web applications. When the HHSC web application is created, a path-based root site collection should also be created. This site collection should not be available for use, nor should it have a template assigned.

Assuming that the domain name for your SharePoint farm is something like *yoursharepointname.com*, you should request that your administrators place a wildcard (*) entry in DNS and point it to the IP address of your web server. Any requests that are made to this domain will then be referred to SharePoint.

EXAM TIP

Creation of (and most of the maintenance duties for) host-header site collections is done entirely in PowerShell. Be familiar with how to create, reconfigure, and remove web applications and host-header site collections from a PowerShell perspective. Extensive coverage of this topic is available in the TechNet article entitled "Host-named site collection architecture and deployment" at *https://technet.microsoft.com/library/cc424952 (v=office.16) .aspx.*

Plan Fast Site Collection Creation

Fast Site Collection Creation is a new mechanism for quickly deploying site collections in SharePoint 2016. In SharePoint 2013 and prior versions, the creation of a new site collection was a fairly involved process, requiring multiple features to be activated after the instantiation of the site collection itself.

SharePoint 2016 improves this mechanism by allowing site collections to be created from a master copy of a site collection for an enabled template (for instance, SPSPORTAL#0 for a Collaboration Portal). The master copy is called a Site Master, and is used as the blueprint from which your new site collections are created.

The optimization for this process is that the Site Master is copied at the content database level, with all pertinent features automatically enabled and ready for use.

> **NEED MORE REVIEW?** Fast Site Collection Creation requires a working knowledge of PowerShell and some specific commands (notably Enable-SPWebTemplateForSiteMaster, New-SPSiteMaster, and the -CreateFromSiteMaster parameter for use with New-SPSite). For detailed information regarding the use of Fast Site Collection Creation, refer to the TechNet Blog article, "Fast Site Collection Creation in SharePoint Server 2016 IT Preview" at *https://blogs.technet.microsoft.com/wbaer/2015/08/26/fast-site-collection-creation-in -sharepoint-server-2016-it-preview/.*

Plan zones and alternate access mappings

Imagine for a moment that you have a web application in SharePoint that requires three different security mechanisms (discussed in Chapter 2, "Plan authentication and security") for accessing content:

- **Intranet/Internet access** Your users require access to the web application from inside your corporate network by using their regular user name and password credentials.
- **Extranet access** You have partners that require access but you need to provide another authentication mechanism, such as offering Forms Authentication (a user name and password combination that you administer).
- **Internet access** You have other partners that want to use their credentials or a trusted Identity Provider (Microsoft, Facebook, Google, and so on) account to access content.

There are five zones available in SharePoint: default, intranet, extranet, Internet, and custom. Although there is no functional difference (by default) between the zones, they provide a structure to configure access for these different user segments accessing the same web application. Each type of user can have a distinct URL and mechanism for accessing your corporate systems.

There are two ways to associate a web application with a zone.

- **Alternate access mappings** Map internal URLs to public URLs, directing users to the appropriate URLs when interacting with SharePoint 2016 sites
- **Set-SPSiteUrl** Used to add or change URL mappings for host-named site collections

> **NOTE** Every web application in your SharePoint farm should have a default zone configured. Many of the internal functions of SharePoint depend on this particular URL (including Search crawls).

When a new SharePoint web application is created, its URL is stored in the default zone. If claims authentication is to be added along with another authentication mechanism, some consideration should be given to adding claims authentication to the default zone so the same URL can be used both inside the network and from outside the network.

> **IMPORTANT** Alternate access mappings were technically deprecated in SharePoint 2013, in favor of using Set-SPSiteUrl and host-header site collections. That said, alternate access mappings must be configured for load balancing, even though alternate access mappings generally do not apply to host-header site collections. The default zone must also be configured to enable NTLM authentication for the crawl component of Search to access content.

Design a physical architecture

A key design characteristic of SharePoint Server is its scalability. An effective SharePoint design accounts for the current and expected requirements of an organization. After the initial design is implemented, the SharePoint farm can then be modified and tuned to suit the changing requirements of the business.

Design a server farm topology using MinRole

In the past, SharePoint farms have often been configured in a traditional topology, arranged in three tiers of servers: web, application, and database. Such an arrangement is quite common, but often means that the application tier servers are overcommitted, hosting all services that do not require user interaction.

In SharePoint 2016, the optimal configuration expands on the traditional topology, adding servers to create a streamlined topology. In this topology, both system performance and resources are optimized because servers are compartmentalized into roles (based on the function they perform).

This compartmentalization is further reinforced by the MinRole concept. In this concept, servers are assigned one of six possible roles:

- **Front-end** Serve user requests; optimized for low latency
- **Application** Serve back-end requests; optimized for high throughput
- **Distributed cache** Hosts only components required for a distributed cache
- **Search** Hosts only components required for searching
- **Custom** Hosts components that do not integrate with MinRole; the farm administrator has full control over which service instances can run on servers assigned to this role
- **Single-server farm** Hosts all components required for a single SharePoint server to operate in a farm configuration; this configuration should be limited use

SharePoint 2013 was quite capable of expanding to meet enterprise needs; SharePoint 2016 is no different, allowing for multiple farm types that utilize MinRole server roles. These farms meet specific requirements when federated together:

- **Content Farm**   Requires the Front-end web, Application, and Distributed cache roles; Search and Custom roles are optional

- **Shared Services Farm**   Requires only the Application and Distributed cache roles; Search and Custom roles are optional

- **Search Farm**   Requires only the Search role; Custom roles are optional

MinRole and its effect on service topologies are covered later in this chapter in the "Define service topologies" section.

> **NEED MORE REVIEW?**   More information about MinRole is discussed in the TechNet article entitled "MinRole overview" at *https://technet.microsoft.com/library/mt346114(v =office.16).aspx.*

Design Central Administration deployment

Central Administration is a specific web application where administration tasks are performed for the farm as a whole. In SharePoint 2016, Central Administration is automatically configured on the first server, and it is the only web application that does *not* use claims authentication.

Creating a new Central Administration web application is the same as it was in SharePoint 2013: Log on to the server you want to host this web app, and run the New-SPCentralAdministration PowerShell command with the desired switches. If you previously built the first server in a farm but do not want it to host Central Administration, there is a new PowerShell command designed for this use: Remove-SPCentralAdministration.

EXAM TIP

Be familiar with the process for creating and removing Central Administration from a server in your farm. For more information, refer to the TechNet article entitled "Farm cmdlets in SharePoint Server 2016" at *https://technet.microsoft.com/library/ff793362(v=office.16) .aspx.*

Design a storage architecture

SharePoint Server farms are data-intensive, requiring both large storage capacities and solid I/O storage design to ensure the best performance possible. This back-end storage is attached to the SQL (data tier) instance of the SharePoint farm.

Three storage architectures are supported within a SharePoint environment: direct-attached storage (DAS), storage area network (SAN), and network attached storage (NAS). DAS and SAN storage architectures are fully supported; NAS storage is supported only for content databases configured to use Remote BLOB Storage (RBS).

Each storage architecture has an associated set of hardware and administrative costs; the storage type you choose is often based on the hardware and administrative structure you have available within your enterprise.

DIRECT-ATTACHED STORAGE

DAS describes an environment in which each server maintains its own discrete storage without benefit of a storage network. Modern servers support two distinct types of drives: Serial Attached SCSI (SAS) and Serial Attached ATA (SATA).

STORAGE AREA NETWORK

SAN environments abstract the storage subsystem from the server hosts to which they are attached. The benefits of this abstraction are immediate: The storage subsystem can be centrally managed and expanded as desired.

The Fibre Channel connections between the storage and host are attached by using either twisted-pair copper wire or fiber-optic cables. A host connected to the SAN uses a host-based adapter to transfer small computer system interface (SCSI) commands to the storage by using the Fibre Channel Protocol (FCP) for transport.

NETWORK ATTACHED STORAGE

NAS provides file-based data storage to other devices on the network. Connectivity and I/O metrics from such a system are often subpar when compared to DAS or SAN-connected storage. As such, this type of storage is supported only for content databases that have been configured to use RBS.

EXAM TIP

All network storage connected to SharePoint is required to meet two criteria. First, the storage must respond to a ping within 1 millisecond (ms), meaning that the storage will most likely be located within the same datacenter as the host. The second criterion is that the first byte of requested data must be returned within 20 ms (this is true regardless of the disk subsystem chosen).

DISK AND RAID TYPES

The types of disks chosen can have an effect on the performance of your storage subsystem. Additionally, the redundant array of independent disks (RAID) configuration of the drives can have a dramatic effect on the performance characteristics of storage.

SharePoint 2016 supports several types of disks:

- Small computer system interface (SCSI)
- Serial Advanced Technology Attachment (SATA)
- Serial Attached SCSI (SAS)
- Fibre Channel
- Integrated drive electronics (IDE)
- Solid-state drive (SSD)

Without going into on-disk caching, rotation speed, or other in-depth storage tuning discussions, you can pretty much break down this list in terms of newer, faster drive technologies (SSD, SAS, SATA, Fibre Channel) and older technologies (SCSI and IDE). Often, the type of drive you choose will just come down to the available interface types provided by your storage subsystem.

SharePoint 2016 supports all RAID types, but the recommendation for best performance characteristics is to implement RAID 1+0 (also known as RAID 10). This RAID type configures drives in a striped set of mirrored drives—the mirroring component provides fault tolerance, and the striped component maximizes performance. In such a system, multiple drives can sustain losses, but the RAID does not fail unless a mirror loses all its drives.

> **NOTE** Resilient File System (ReFS) is a newer type of file system that was introduced with Windows Server 2012. This type of file system allows servers to have a just a bunch of disks (JBOD) storage system based on SATA or SAS without requiring specialized redundancy hardware, so this is usually configured with DAS configurations. SharePoint 2013 could not take advantage of this file system, but support for ReFS is built into SharePoint 2016.
>
> For more information about ReFS in 2012, review the TechNet article entitled "Resilient File System Overview" at *https://technet.microsoft.com/library/hh831724.aspx*.

Configure basic request management

Traditional load balancing technologies enable incoming traffic to be routed to one or more SharePoint web servers. The amount of intelligence applied to these routing actions varies in scope from the most rudimentary types of routing (such as DNS round-robin) to advanced routing as seen in dedicated load balancing solutions.

Although it is possible to configure an external load balancer to understand the specific behaviors required for a SharePoint environment, such solutions can have shortcomings:

- Changes made at the load balancer level can have dramatic effects on the SharePoint farm, resulting in inconsistencies or outages.

- Changes made within the SharePoint farm but not reflected in the load balancer configuration (such as Search crawler changes) can have a negative effect on performance.

For instance, consider a SharePoint farm that is serving both user requests and Search crawls at the same time. Enough Search requests might cause the SharePoint environment to have increased latency when serving user requests; such a situation could result in a perceived outage and irregular work stoppages.

REQUEST MANAGEMENT VERSUS THROTTLING

Earlier versions of SharePoint (prior to 2013) included the notion of HTTP request throttling, in which the current state of each web server was evaluated, and incoming requests could be throttled before a server reached a nonresponsive status. The current health of a web server could be observed in the HTTP response within a header called X-SharePointHealthScore.

Request management is a better mechanism for intelligent request routing and throttling, present in both SharePoint Server 2013 and 2016. Request management can be enabled on a per web application basis, enabling incoming requests to be evaluated against a set of rules to determine which Front-end server (if any) will respond.

DEPLOYMENT MODES

There are two deployment modes for request management: dedicated and integrated.

- Dedicated mode deployments are useful in larger environments and allow for the segmentation of request management activities away from the Front-end servers servicing the requests.

- In an integrated mode deployment, request management is handled directly on the Front-end servers, meaning that any server running the SharePoint Foundation Web Application Service also has the Request Management service instance provisioned.

> **NEED MORE REVIEW?**   Request management is a fairly complex topic with several possible configurations that are discussed in the TechNet article entitled "Configure Request Manager in SharePoint Server 2016" at *https://technet.microsoft.com/library/jj712708(v =office.16).aspx.*

Define individual server requirements

The configuration of each server in your new SharePoint farm depends greatly on the topology you choose. If you are implementing a pilot or user acceptance test installation of SharePoint 2016, you might start your design with as few as two servers, a computer running SQL server and a SharePoint server that hosts the Single-server farm MinRole.

Interestingly enough, a single-server farm installation of SharePoint requires significantly more memory and resources on the individual server than would be required on each server in a distributed server installation. The reason for this requirement is rather straightforward: A single-server farm installation combines all required services for Front-end web, Application, Distributed cache, and Search onto a single server.

SINGLE-SERVER FARM INSTALLATIONS

Single-server farm installations of SharePoint are most often used for evaluation or development environments, not production. If this approach is to be used for production, it should be used only in an environment with a limited number of users.

In such an environment, the SQL server serving as the data layer of the farm should meet at least the minimum requirements (4 GB of RAM for SQL 2014 and 2016).

The following requirements do not really address items such as the storage space required for the databases and any other services (such as Search indexes). The recommendation is to add a secondary drive for the storage of such information.

The basic requirements for a single-server SharePoint farm depend greatly on the SharePoint installation chosen and are shown in Table 1-1.

TABLE 1-1 Single-server farm requirements

Installation scenario	Deployment type and scale	RAM	Processor	Hard disk space
Single-server role that uses SQL Server	Development or evaluation installation of SharePoint Server 2016 with the minimum recommended services for development environments	12–16 GB	64-bit, 4 cores	80 GB for system drive 100 GB for second drive
Single-server role that uses SQL Server	Pilot or user acceptance test installation of SharePoint Server 2016 running all available services for development environments	16–24 GB	64-bit, 4 cores	80 GB for system drive 100 GB for second drive and additional drives

EXAM TIP

The amount of free disk space available on the system drive of a SharePoint server should never fall below two times the amount of server RAM; this limit is specifically designed to allow memory dumps to be stored on the subsystem if necessary.

MULTITIER FARM INSTALLATIONS

Because we have determined that a single server is not the preferred installation for a production SharePoint farm, you should now learn about the hardware requirements for a tiered installation. In such an environment, the web and application tier servers are separated from the SQL servers and have different hardware requirements (see Table 1-2).

TABLE 1-2 Three-tier farm requirements

Installation scenario	Deployment type and scale	RAM	Processor	Hard disk space
Web server or application server in a three-tier farm	Development or evaluation installation of SharePoint Server 2016 with a minimum number of services	8–12 GB	64-bit, 4 cores	80 GB for system drive 80 GB for second drive
Web server or application server in a three-tier farm	Pilot, user acceptance test, or production deployment of SharePoint Server 2016 running all available services	12–16 GB	64-bit, 4 cores	80 GB for system drive 80 GB for second drive and additional drives

> **NEED MORE REVIEW?** For a complete discussion of requirements for servers in a SharePoint farm, review the TechNet article entitled "Hardware and software requirements for SharePoint Server 2016" at *https://msdn.microsoft.com/library/cc262485(v=office.16).aspx.*

Define service topologies

Scaling a SharePoint 2016 installation requires planning for the distribution of service applications across the farm environment. Because each implementation differs in terms of the amount of data, services offered, and users supported, no single topology is appropriate for any given business.

It is important to note that MinRole server roles must govern the majority of service assignments within a farm (see Table 1-3 for details).

TABLE 1-3 MinRole server roles

Server Role	Description
Front-end	Service applications, services, and components that serve user requests belong on Front-end web servers. These servers are optimized for low latency.
Application	Service applications, services, and components that serve back-end requests (such as background jobs or Search crawl requests) belong on Application servers, which are optimized for high throughput.
Distributed cache	Service applications, services, and components that are required for a distributed cache belong on Distributed cache servers.
Search	Service applications, services, and components that are required for searching belong on Search servers.

Server Role	Description
Custom	Custom service applications, services, and components that do not integrate with MinRole belong on Custom servers. The farm administrator has full control over which service instances can run on servers assigned to the Custom role. MinRole does not control which service instances are provisioned on this role.
Single-server farm	Service applications, services, and components required for a single-machine farm belong on a single-server farm. A single-server farm is meant for development, testing, and very limited production use. A SharePoint farm with the Single-server farm role cannot have more than one SharePoint server in the farm.

The following topologies are by no means the only ones available, but they give guidance as a starting point for topology designs.

SMALLEST SUPPORTED FARM

In this farm type, the web and application tiers are supported by a SharePoint server by using the single-server role. The data tier is supported on a separate server. All required service applications are located on the SharePoint server, but are not fault-tolerant (see Figure 1-18).

Single-server | Database

FIGURE 1-18 Single-server farm

FOUR- AND FIVE-TIER FARMS

In SharePoint 2013, we often speak of the three-tier farm as a fairly basic production environment. The web tier (SharePoint) handles user requests, the data tier (SQL) stores the content and configuration data, and the app tier (SharePoint) handles just about everything else, including most services. Often, this requirement means that the app tier server is overcommitted from a RAM and processing standpoint, negatively affecting performance.

In SharePoint 2016, MinRole controls the assignment of services to a server based on its role in the farm. Although it might seem that you could follow the Front-end, Application, and Data server configuration, doing so would omit a key component, the distributed cache service; without this component, a farm is considered unsupported.

> **NOTE** Distributed cache service is a memory-intensive application, supporting a maximum of 16 GB of RAM. Distributed cache is required in a SharePoint farm and supports features ranging from client applications (such as OneNote) to page load performance and authentication.

Thus, a minimal MinRole-compliant configuration of SharePoint will contain four tiers (Front-end, Application, Distributed cache, and Data), as shown in Figure 1-19.

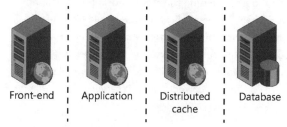

Front-end   Application   Distributed cache   Database

FIGURE 1-19 Four-tier supported farm with no search

There's one component we haven't yet considered: Search. The four-tier farm we've discussed does not incorporate any search services; we need to add one more server that holds the Search MinRole, moving us into a five-tier farm configuration (shown in Figure 1-20).

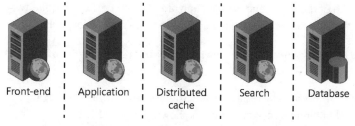

Front-end   Application   Distributed cache   Search   Database

FIGURE 1-20 Five-tier farm including Distributed cache and Search

> **NEED MORE REVIEW?** Content farms are not the only topologies that are available in SharePoint 2016. Multiple farms can be configured and then connected to one another to provide specific functionality, such as Shared Services and Search. Understanding which roles are associated with which topology will help you better understand large implementations of SharePoint. More information about MinRole is discussed in the TechNet article entitled "MinRole overview" at *https://technet.microsoft.com/library/mt346114(v=office.16).aspx.*

 Quick check

- You are the administrator of an existing SharePoint 2013 farm, with one server each in the web and application tiers. You are being required to upgrade to SharePoint 2016, but you will not be able to purchase additional servers to meet MinRole server role requirements until next quarter. How might you go about assigning server roles in SharePoint 2016 with the resources you have on hand?

Plan server load balancing

Although we discuss high availability and disaster recovery in Chapter 3, we should pause for a moment to look at what is required to provide resiliency within a SharePoint content farm, from a service point of view. Each of the server roles within SharePoint itself (let's set the SQL database tier aside for a moment) can provide an element of high availability, so long as the server count is adequate. Each of the Front-end, Application, and Search tiers will require two servers each for resiliency; the Distributed cache tier will require three servers for resiliency.

> **IMPORTANT**   There are only two valid server counts for the Distributed cache tier of a SharePoint farm: either one server or three servers.

For a SharePoint content farm to be fully resilient using MinRole server roles (excluding SQL servers), you need a total of nine servers, arranged as shown in Figure 1-21.

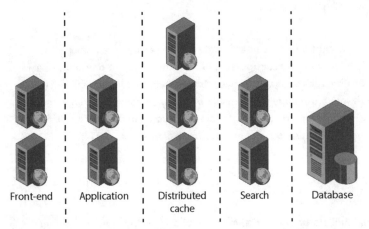

Front-end   Application   Distributed   Search   Database
                              cache

FIGURE 1-21 A fully resilient SharePoint farm (highlighted, excluding SQL servers in the data tier)

Resiliency at the data layer is discussed in Chapter 3, when we discuss the AlwaysOn options available in SQL Server.

Plan a network infrastructure

When planning the layout of a SharePoint farm, it is important to remember that the farm not only communicates with SharePoint users, but also requires communications within the farm (to each tier) and communications to other servers in the network (such as Exchange or Skype for Business servers). Effective network infrastructure planning requires that each of these connection types be considered in the overall design.

INTERSERVER AND USER-FACING COMMUNICATION

There are two distinct types of network communication present within a SharePoint farm: user-facing and interserver communication. Communications between servers within the farm can be quite intense at times; during these times, users might experience diminished performance if both types of communication take place across the same physical network interface.

NOTE The introduction of MinRole seeks to minimize intraserver network traffic.

As a result, servers in the web and application tiers of a SharePoint farm ideally will have at least two distinct network interfaces: One handles user requests, routing traffic back and forth to users, and the other handles interserver connectivity, routing traffic back and forth between the SharePoint servers (Front-end, Application, Search, and Distributed cache tiers) and the SQL data tier.

NETWORK LATENCY AND STRETCHED FARMS

Latency and bandwidth are concepts that go hand in hand. The best way to understand the relationship between these two is to imagine driving on a freeway. The speed limit (bandwidth) relates to how fast the traffic can travel on the freeway, whereas the traffic congestion present on the freeway can cause the commute time (latency) for any one car to increase.

SharePoint 2016 allows for highly available farms to be distributed or "stretched" if they meet the following criteria:

- There is a highly consistent intrafarm latency of < 1 millisecond (ms) one way, 99.9 percent of the time over a period of 10 minutes. (Intrafarm latency is commonly defined as the latency between the front-end web servers and the database servers.)
- The bandwidth speed must be at least 1 gigabit per second.

Plan for large file support

SharePoint 2013 had a hard upload and download limit of 2 GB (2,047 MB). SharePoint 2016 can be configured beyond this limit up to 10 GB, primarily due to the adoption of Background Intelligent Transfer Service (BITS), which delivers quicker and more reliable file transfer performance.

Obviously, transferring files this large into any content database should be done with an eye toward how they are to be used. Although content databases are no longer subject to the 200 GB supported limit, the fact remains that a site collection that has several hundred GB of storage will take quite a long time to back up and restore; the surface area for database corruption is also increased, making the scope of a failure potentially push both the Recovery Time Objective and Recovery Point Objective beyond organizational governance limits.

Plan an app hosting model

SharePoint 2013 once provided three different types of app hosting models: SharePoint-hosted, Autohosted, and Provider-hosted. The Autohosted model was discontinued in late 2014, and in late 2015, the terminology for the remaining hosting models changed the term App to Add-in.

In SharePoint 2016, then, we are left with two different hosting models: SharePoint-hosted and Provider-hosted. The SharePoint-hosted Add-in model is centered around SharePoint components, including lists, pages, Web Parts, workflows, libraries, and more. In this model, Add-in parts and custom actions are deployed in the host web, and all other components are deployed to the Add-in web.

The Provider-hosted model builds on the SharePoint-hosted model, allowing the use of additional remote components such as web applications, services, or databases, hosted in a separate web stack. The stack chosen is located outside the SharePoint farm and does not have to necessarily even be on a Microsoft stack (for example, it can be supported on other web hosting frameworks such as LAMP, Python, and others).

> **NEED MORE REVIEW?** Although add-in development is generally outside the realm of the IT pro (this is truly a developer topic), exactly how the environment will host Add-ins is an administrative task; therefore, understanding of these models is required. More information about hosting models is discussed in the MSDN/Office Dev Center article entitled "Choose patterns for developing and hosting your SharePoint Add-in" at *https://msdn .microsoft.com/library/office/fp179887.aspx.*

 Quick check

- You are configuring a SharePoint farm for hybrid to Office 365. This farm was originally a SharePoint 2010 farm and then was upgraded to SharePoint 2013. After a discussion with your business stakeholders and your developers, you find that there is a critical business application that is deployed via solution to the older environment. What are your options for deployment and what would the result look like for each deployment type?

Quick check answer

- Without reworking the application, your options are limited. You can choose to either have this application only available on-premises, or you might be able to rework it into a Provider-hosted model.

Skill: Plan an installation

This section reviews the configuration steps required to set up a SharePoint farm at a base level. Establishing a core infrastructure plan that is both scalable and manageable will help guide you toward the goal of a solid SharePoint installation.

This section covers how to:

- Identify and configure installation prerequisites
- Implement scripted deployment
- Plan Access Services deployment
- Implement patch slipstreaming
- Plan and install language packs
- Plan and configure service connection points
- Plan installation tracking and auditing
- Plan and Install Office Online Server
- Implement managed paths for Office 365 migrations
- Configure SharePoint hybrid cloud settings

NOTE The Plan Project Server installation skill can be found in Chapter 6, "Plan and configure cloud services."

Identifying and configuring installation prerequisites

Before SharePoint 2016 binaries can be installed on a new server, a series of installation prerequisites must be met. These prerequisites are a combination of installed software components (such as the Microsoft .NET Framework 4.6) and configuration changes to the server (such as adding the Application server and Web server roles).

NEED MORE REVIEW? The complete listing of prerequisites for SharePoint Server 2016 is extensive, covering both operating system-level roles and other software components that must be added prior to installing SharePoint Server 2016. The TechNet article entitled "Hardware and software requirements for SharePoint Server 2016" includes a listing of these requirements (and download links) in the "Minimum software requirements" section, and can be found at *https://technet.microsoft.com/library/cc262485(v=office.16) .aspx#section4*.

When the prerequisite installer is run on a Windows Server 2012 or Windows Server 2016 server, it checks to see if a prerequisite component is installed. If the installer finds a prerequisite component, the individual component installation is skipped and the installer moves to the next item in the list.

EXAM TIP

Although you should be familiar with the prerequisites for a SharePoint farm, concentrate on remembering the major components that are required, such as installing Windows Server AppFabric 1.1 or configuring Application server and Web server roles.

Installing and configuring prerequisites (online)

Prerequisites are installed as part of the SharePoint GUI install experience. When the SharePoint 2016 splash screen appears, the first item in the Install section is Install Software Prerequisites (see Figure 1-22).

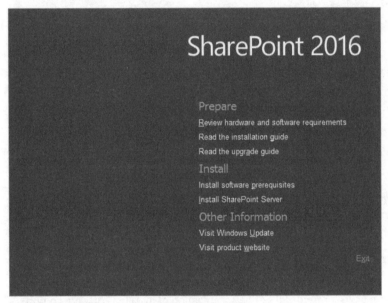

FIGURE 1-22 SharePoint 2016 installer splash screen

Clicking Install Software Prerequisites immediately activates the SharePoint 2016 Products Preparation Tool, shown in Figure 1-23.

After you click Next and accept the license terms, the tool runs through the list of items to be installed, first configuring the Application server and Web server roles, and then proceeding with the installation of the other components.

> ***NOTE*** The role installation requires a reboot of the server's operating system. After the reboot is complete, the tool resumes installation of the remaining components.

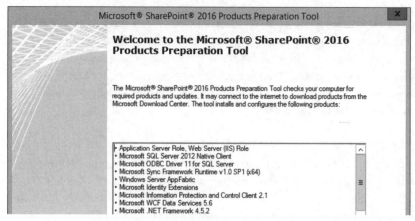

FIGURE 1-23 SharePoint 2016 Products Preparation Tool (online)

Downloading and installing prerequisites (offline)

It is also possible to install all the prerequisites with the server not connected to the Internet. Reasons for such a configuration might include corporate policies preventing servers from accessing the Internet, or you might be creating multiple servers for a farm and do not wish to have each server download its own copy of the components.

The solution is to gather the components together into a centralized location and then install the prerequisites to each server as needed. This type of installation involves two separate actions:

- Installing and configuring the Application Server role and Web Server (IIS) role to the new servers via Windows PowerShell (requires Windows Server 2012 R2 or Windows Server 2016 media)

- Creating a set of installation switches to run with the Prerequisiteinstaller.exe tool, then downloading the components to a file share that is accessible by the new server

INSTALLING THE APPLICATION AND WEB SERVER ROLES

The Application server and Web server roles can be added to a server in one of two ways: via Add Roles And Features in Server Manager or by using PowerShell. Regardless of the method you choose, this installation changes the server's configuration and will require a reboot before taking effect.

DOWNLOADING THE PREREQUISITE SOFTWARE COMPONENTS

After the server roles have been configured, you need to download each software component to a central file share location that is accessible by the new server.

CREATING AND RUNNING THE PREREQUISITE INSTALLER SCRIPT

Now that all the components have been downloaded, you can use the Prerequisiteinstaller .exe file along with some arguments to install and configure each component. Running the Prerequisiteinstaller.exe file (found at the root of your SharePoint installation media location) with the /? option displays all the available switches, as shown in Figure 1-24.

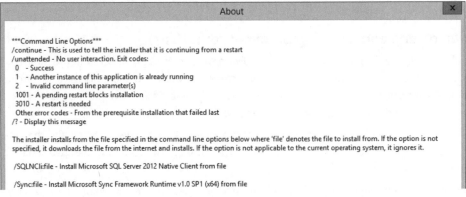

FIGURE 1-24 Command-line options for Prerequisiteinstaller.exe

Each of these installations can be run individually, but they are most often batched together into an arguments file and run all at once.

Implement scripted deployment

Installing a single-server SharePoint farm via the GUI is a pretty straightforward process. At a very high level, there are only four steps involved: download and install the SharePoint prerequisites, install all the binaries from the installation media, run the SharePoint 2016 Products Configuration Wizard, and run the Farm Configuration Wizard.

After these steps are complete, the farm will be technically up and running, but it will require further configuration to meet user needs. Additionally, it probably won't be configured to your specifications or those of your corporate IT department. For instance, running the Farm Configuration Wizard will create a series of content and service application databases. It is unlikely that the names of these databases will meet the naming convention requirements in your organization because SharePoint uses default database names that include a globally unique identifier (GUID) suffix.

Most enterprise installations require multiple servers in their SharePoint farm. The ability to reliably create, re-create, and duplicate server functionality in the farm requires you to find a better mechanism for installing and configuring SharePoint, a script.

Developing an installation script

The first step of establishing a repeatable installation pattern is to develop installation scripts to deploy the farm. If you are in a larger farm that has multiple tiers and distinct services on a certain server (assigned via MinRole), you might want to build multiple scripts that are tailored for each function.

Installation scripts can be broken down into three core segments:

1. Prerequisite installation and configuration (previously covered)
2. Farm creation and configuration of Central Administration and assignment of MinRole
3. Installing and configuring service applications (covered throughout this book)

In this section, you will review the core elements required to create and configure the farm via script, including both SQL and SharePoint configuration efforts.

Configuring the maximum degree of parallelism

For a SharePoint installation, the maximum degree of parallelism (MAXDOP) value must be set to 1, which indicates that no parallel processing activity can take place on the supporting instance, regardless of whether or not multiple processors are available. This setting needs to be made only *once* on each SQL instance that supports your SharePoint 2016 farm, and is a defining reason for SharePoint to be installed in its own SQL instance.

This value can be set via the SQL Server Management Studio (SSMS) GUI, via a T-SQL script, or via PowerShell. The thing to remember about configuring MAXDOP in your farm PowerShell scripts is that neither your SharePoint setup account nor your SharePoint farm account should have this level of permission on the SQL instance. As a result, you will most likely need the SQL DBA to configure this value on your data tier before proceeding with the rest of the scripted actions.

Preparing configuration accounts

The SharePoint Setup account will need to be created in Active Directory Domain Services. This account has four requirements: It must be a domain user, it must be a member of the local Administrators group on each SharePoint server, it must be able to log in to the SQL instance, and it must be assigned to the *securityadmin* and *dbcreator* SQL fixed server roles.

A SharePoint Farm account will also need to be created, set up simply as a user in Active Directory; the SharePoint setup process will take care of assigning required permissions to the farm account as part of the installation.

The initial farm configuration can be broken down into three major sections: creating the farm, installing farm features and services, and creating the Central Administration web application. The only real difference between SharePoint 2013 and SharePoint 2016 farm creation from a scripting perspective is the addition of the LocalServerRole switch, which specifies the server role in the farm (MinRole).

Creating the farm

The initial farm creation is accomplished while logged in as the SharePoint Setup account, and can be implemented via PSConfig.exe or via PowerShell.

USING PSCONFIG.EXE TO CREATE THE FARM

Using PSConfig.exe to create a SharePoint farm is fairly straightforward, requiring the use of a single command and quite a few switches:

```
psconfig.exe -cmd configdb -create -server <SqlServerName> -database <ConfigDbName>
-user <DOMAIN\FarmServiceAccount> -password <FarmServiceAccountPassword> -passphrase
<FarmPassphrase> -admincontentdatabase <AdminContentDbName> -localserverrole
```

```
<ServerRole> -cmd helpcollections -installall -cmd secureresources -cmd services
-install -cmd installfeatures -cmd adminvs -provision -port <PortNumber>
-windowsauthprovider onlyusentlm -cmd applicationcontent -install
```

> **NOTE** <ServerRole> in PSConfig.exe designates the required MinRole for the server you are configuring: WebFrontEnd, Application, DistributedCache, Search, Custom, or Single-ServerFarm.

In the preceding PSConfig command, notice that the installation assigns the role and then adds in modular sections like help collections, secure resources, and install features. This is similar to how the sections are added when creating the farm in PowerShell.

USING POWERSHELL TO CREATE THE FARM

Creating a farm via PowerShell is also done in a modular fashion and requires the use of a single cmdlet, New-SPConfigurationDatabase. This cmdlet allows you to specify the desired MinRole; alternately, you can remove the requirement for MinRole in your existing deployment scripts by specifying -ServerRoleOptional instead of -LocalServerRole.

> **NOTE** Just because you can, doesn't necessarily mean that you should. Prior to SharePoint Server 2016, member servers were role agnostic, relying on the farm admin to properly configure and optimize services. Although you could technically still operate in this fashion, you should instead implement MinRole server roles in your SharePoint 2016 farm, reserving the Custom role exclusively for servers hosting custom service applications, services, and components.

To begin the installation, open a SharePoint 2016 Management Shell window, running with administrative privileges. You will see a message that indicates "The local farm is not accessible. Cmdlets with FeatureDependencyId are not registered," as shown in Figure 1-25.

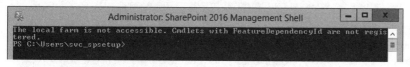

FIGURE 1-25 Farm is not accessible

This warning indicates that there is currently no farm, which is created starting with the following script.

```
# Create the Configuration Database
# ServerRole can be any of the following:
# WebFrontEnd, Application, DistributedCache, Search, Custom, or SingleServerFarm
New-SPConfigurationDatabase -DatabaseServer <SqlServerName> -DatabaseName <ConfigDbName>
-FarmCredentials <FarmServiceAccountCreds> -Passphrase <FarmPassphrase>
-AdministrationContentDatabaseName <AdminContentDbName> -LocalServerRole <ServerRole>
```

> **NOTE** The New-SPConfigurationDatabase cmdlet can take quite a bit of time to run — be patient.

Next, we must install the core components of the farm, including the help site collection files, resource security, available services, and all existing features.

```
# Install the Help Site Collection Files in the Current Farm
Install-SPHelpCollection -All
# Enforce Resource Security on the Local Server
Initialize-SPResourceSecurity
# Install and Provision Services on the Farm
Install-SPService
# Install Features from the Feature.xml file
Install-SPFeature -AllExistingFeatures
```

The last step in creating the initial farm is the creation of the Central Administration web application.

```
# Create Central Administration Web App
New-SPCentralAdministration -Port <caport> -WindowsAuthProvider "NTLM"
# Copy Shared Application Data to Existing Web Application Folders
Install-SPApplicationContent
```

> **IMPORTANT** If you look carefully at the switches available in the New-SPCentralAdminis-tration cmdlet, you will notice something interesting: Central Administration uses Windows classic authentication, as claims authentication is not used for this web app.

Plan Access Services deployment

SharePoint 2016 continues the support of Access Services via the availability of two different Service Application types: Access Services 2010 and Access Services.

Access Services 2010 is a backward-compatible service application to support the creation, editing, and updating of linked Access databases into a SharePoint Server farm; once created, these web databases can be accessed via an Internet browser, the Access 2010 client, or a linked HTML page.

Access Services is the current service application designed for the housing and presenta-tion of Microsoft Access 2013 and 2016 databases. This functionality is available both on-premises and in the cloud (Office 365) via the use of Access apps.

Core requirements

From a SharePoint administrator standpoint, there are four major steps required to config-ure Access Services for Access apps: Install and configure SQL Server 2014 SP1 (or greater), configure SharePoint Server 2016 to present SharePoint apps, configure Access Services to successfully run Access apps, and create a dedicated SharePoint site collection that will host Access apps (each Access app requires its own subsite and database).

Implement patch slipstreaming

As with any software platform, SharePoint Server 2016 is constantly being updated. These updates often include critical on-demand (COD) hotfixes, cumulative updates, and full service packs.

When new servers must be added to the existing farm, these servers must match the current update level of the existing farm to join. Although it's perfectly acceptable to install the binaries from the original media and then add each individual update, you might find this process labor-intensive and potentially error prone.

The solution, then, is to find a way to update the installation media itself. This process is called *slipstreaming*, and involves downloading each update and applying the update over the previous installation media. This media can then be used to create new servers that will join your SharePoint farm with no issues.

Preparing to slipstream updates

Slipstreaming updates requires a bit of effort. In essence, you will be building new installation media by accumulating the required updates and then applying them to your original SharePoint installation media.

If you open your SharePoint installation media in Windows Explorer, you can see that there are several subdirectories present at the root directory. One of these subdirectories is called *Updates*, and this is where you will be extracting and applying your updates, cumulative updates, and service packs (see Figure 1-26).

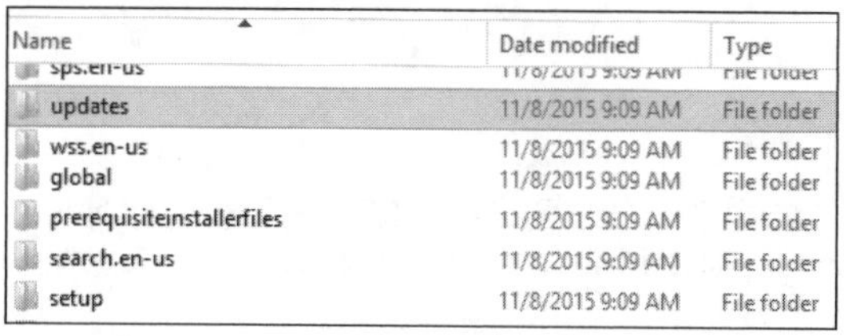

Name	Date modified	Type
sps.en-us	11/8/2015 9:09 AM	File folder
updates	11/8/2015 9:09 AM	File folder
wss.en-us	11/8/2015 9:09 AM	File folder
global	11/8/2015 9:09 AM	File folder
prerequisiteinstallerfiles	11/8/2015 9:09 AM	File folder
search.en-us	11/8/2015 9:09 AM	File folder
setup	11/8/2015 9:09 AM	File folder

FIGURE 1-26 Updates folder within the SharePoint 2016 installation media

After this directory has been populated with updates, it can be automatically installed by the SharePoint Products Configuration Wizard as part of the installation process.

EXAM TIP

Some updates are built as .exe files and must be extracted to the Updates folder. Others might be built as .msp files, which do not require extraction and can be placed directly in the Updates folder as is. Understand the required commands to expand the media for each update type and how to add it to the Updates folder; this function has not changed since SharePoint 2007. For more information, review the TechNet article entitled "Create an installation source that includes software updates (Office SharePoint Server 2007)" at *https://technet.microsoft.com/library/cc261890.aspx.*

Creating slipstream installation media

Slipstreaming SharePoint installation media gives you a robust and repeatable way to configure multiple servers from a constantly updated installation source. This source is usually a network share that will contain a combination of the original SharePoint installation media and the updates you choose to install.

To prepare the slipstream media on a network share called \\<*servername*>\SPInstall, you would do the following:

1. Copy the original SharePoint 2016 installation media to the SPInstall share.

2. Extract each update to the Updates folder in the SPInstall share, starting with the oldest update first. The update can be extracted by using the /extract switch (refer to the installation instructions for each update).

IMPORTANT The resulting installation media requires that newer updates overwrite portions of the older updates as needed. If you look at the updates media folder, don't be surprised to see individual files with different date codes and version numbers; patches are intentionally designed to be extracted and stacked one on top of the other (oldest to newest).

Plan and install language packs

SharePoint has built-in functionality that enables the use of multiple languages within a single SharePoint installation. Each language that is supported within the farm requires the download of a distinct language pack.

NOTE The current list of downloadable SharePoint 2016 language packs can be found on the Microsoft Download Center at *https://www.microsoft.com/download/details.aspx?id =49960.*

Installing a SharePoint Server 2016 language pack

Installing a SharePoint 2016 language pack is a relatively simple process, except for one detail: The installation procedure for the language pack is written entirely in the designated language. To begin the installation process, ensure that you are logged in as the SharePoint setup account, mount the .iso file for your language pack, and then run Setup.exe.

> **NOTE** You never need to download a language pack for the language in which you installed SharePoint.

In the following examples, the German language pack will be installed. The language pack installer appears in Figure 1-27, in the destination language (German).

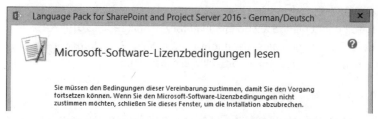

FIGURE 1-27 The Microsoft language pack license screen in German

After the installation is complete, you are offered the opportunity to run the SharePoint Configuration Wizard (Figure 1-28).

FIGURE 1-28 Configuration complete, ready to run the Configuration Wizard

EXAM TIP

There are four key items to remember regarding the installation of language packs: (1) They must be installed by using the SharePoint setup account credentials; (2) multiple language packs can be installed in the same SharePoint farm; (3) any language pack installed must be installed on all SharePoint servers in the farm; and (4) the SharePoint Configuration Wizard must be run on each SharePoint server once language pack binaries have been successfully installed.

Plan and configure service connection points

Active Directory has a marker called a service connection point (SCP) that is used by services to publish themselves in Active Directory. SCPs can be utilized as a key component of an enterprise governance strategy, intended to specifically prevent so-called rogue SharePoint installations.

After SCP functionality is correctly set up, any new SharePoint farm created in the domain will automatically register itself; the process of running the SharePoint Products Configuration Wizard causes a marker to be created and stored in the SCP container. This marker contains the address for the Application Discovery and Load Balancer Service (the Topology service application) for the individual farm, and is useful on multiple levels.

If you suspect that your environment might have many different SharePoint installs, you can use this functionality to begin building a working inventory of SharePoint 2010, 2013, and 2016 farms. If you have multiple domains that might contain SharePoint farms, you must configure the use of this marker in each domain to track these installations.

Creating and configuring the SCP container

Active Directory must be configured by using ADSIEdit to create an SCP container. After this container is built, Write and Create All Child Object permissions must be granted for SharePoint farms to automatically register themselves on installation.

> **IMPORTANT** Consider allowing all authenticated users to write and create all child objects within the SCP container; doing so enables the container to capture and track any unauthorized SharePoint installations.

1. Run ADSIEdit; from the Action menu, connect to the default naming context of your domain as shown in Figure 1-29 (in this example, 16DC.rc.local).

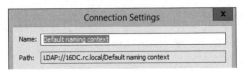

FIGURE 1-29 Default naming context in ADSIEdit

2. Expand the domain that you want to connect to, then select CN=System.

3. Right-click in the white area of the details pane to open a shortcut menu. Select New, Object (see Figure 1-30).

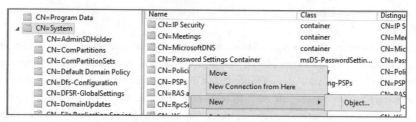

FIGURE 1-30 Creating a new object in the System container

4. Select the Container class in the Create Object box. In the Value box, type **Microsoft SharePoint Products** and then click Next. When you click Finish, your new Active Directory container should appear in the details pane (see Figure 1-31).

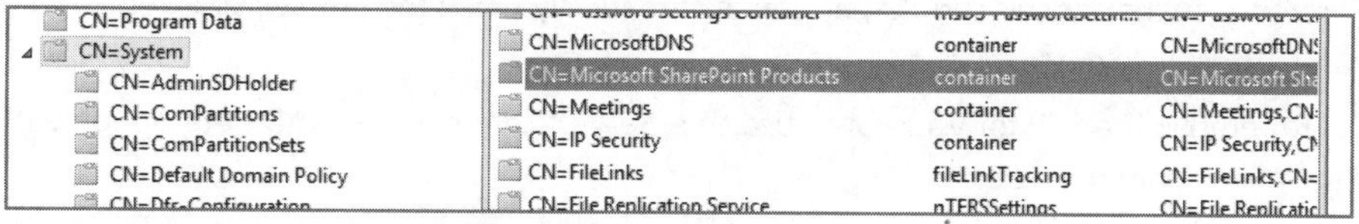

FIGURE 1-31 The Microsoft SharePoint Products container inside the System container

5. Assign permissions to the container, choosing the users you want to access the SCP container and assign them Write permissions. Alternately, you could select the Authenticated Users group and assign it Read and Write permissions (preferred).

Registering an existing farm in the SCP container

As stated previously, a new or existing farm attempts to write to the SCP container (if it exists) when the SharePoint Configuration Wizard is run. If the container is created after SharePoint products exist in the environment, there will be no record of previously existing farms in the SCP container.

To register an existing farm in the SCP container, either run the SharePoint Configuration Wizard or register the SharePoint farm in an SCP using Windows PowerShell. To create an SCP in Windows PowerShell (assuming you have the correct permissions), do the following:

1. Use Get-SPFarmConfig to see whether the farm is already registered (optional):

```
Get-SPFarmConfig -ServiceConnectionPoint
```

2. Use Set-SPFarmConfig to register the farm in the SCP container (the URL shown is the uniform resource identifier [URI] of the farm's Topology service in our example):

```
Set-SPFarmConfig -ServiceConnectionPointBindingInformation
http://16SP2016RC:32844/Topology/topology.svc
```

Deleting a farm's SCP in Active Directory

You might decide at some point that you need to remove the SCP for your farm from Active Directory. In theory, this should happen automatically when the last server is removed from a farm (effectively destroying it).

To remove the SCP for your farm, use the -ServiceConnectionPointDelete option with the Set-SPFarmConfig cmdlet:

```
Set-SPFarmConfig -ServiceConnectionPointDelete
```

Plan installation tracking and auditing

Now that the SCP infrastructure has been created, you can use this functionality to effectively audit and manage any SharePoint installations in your domain. Each time a new farm is created, the SCP container will be updated with information about that new server.

Viewing SharePoint farm SCPs in ADSIEdit

In this example, you view the Topology service content for a SharePoint 2016 farm that has registered in Active Directory. To view this information in ADSIEdit, connect to your domain and then navigate to the System container (CN=System). Once there, select the Microsoft SharePoint Products container and expand it. Entries for SharePoint farms appear with a GUID in the Name box. Right-click this GUID and select Properties. The address for the Topology service is shown (or another value if it is what you chose), as shown in Figure 1-32.

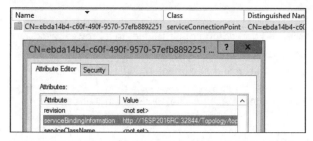

FIGURE 1-32 Topology service address within serviceConnectionPoint

Viewing the SCP for a farm via Windows PowerShell

As a SharePoint administrator, you might not have access to the ADSIEdit tool. You can re-trieve the SCP information for your farm using PowerShell:

```
Get-SPFarmConfig -ServiceConnectionPoint
```

> **NOTE** Although you might not have access to Active Directory using the ADSIEdit tool, you are likely able to run a Lightweight Directory Access Protocol (LDAP) query (read-only permissions are required) against your domain to review the registered SCPs.

Plan and install Office Online Server

Office Online Server is a companion product to SharePoint Server 2016 that replaces Office Web Apps Server 2013. Office Online Server is similar to its predecessor in that it provides functionality to instances of Exchange, SharePoint, and Skype for Business; however, it differs from its predecessor in that it replaces some on-premises functionality (such as Excel Calculation Services) while also enabling new features (such as Durable Links).

Office Online functionality

From a product line standpoint, Office Online Server supplants both Office Web Apps Server and Excel Services. By using this product, you can interact with Microsoft Office documents (Word, Excel, PowerPoint, and OneNote) from SharePoint libraries using supported web browsers on browser-enabled phones (view), smartphones (view), tablets and slates (edit), and PCs or Macs (edit).

EXAM TIP

Office Online Server only works with SharePoint web applications that use claims-based authentication.

When considering the deployment of Office Online Server, you'll need to account for three core functions: Previews and Online Viewing, Durable Links, and Excel Services.

Previews and Online Viewing

Office Online Server allows for online viewing and editing of Office files in a browser window. It also enables a preview capability that renders an initial view of a document when searching in SharePoint or a read-only view of an email-attached document in Outlook Web App.

> **NOTE** Office Online Server will not render any attachments of an IRM protected email message.

Office Online Server also provides Online Viewers, which allow a user to view Word, Excel, and PowerPoint files that are stored in file shares and other websites. Using the URL *http:// <OfficeWebAppsServername>/op/generate.aspx,* links can be generated for documents that have UNC or URL addresses.

Durable Links

Durable Links allow a document to be assigned a resource ID in Office Online Server. This ID allows a document to be moved or renamed without losing its link; for instance, a document in a draft library could be moved into a published library without losing its original link. The applicable permissions for the document would be that of the library in which it is stored (it does not retain its previous permission set), allowing for a consistent permissions governance experience.

When a user selects a link to a document, Office Online Server looks up the resource ID and returns the document to the user for presentation in Office Online Server Preview. If the document has previously been moved into a library to which the user has no permissions, the document will not be displayed, although the link is still valid.

Excel Services

Excel Services provided by Office Online Server are the next generation of those provided by Excel Calculation Services in SharePoint Server 2013. SharePoint 2016 integrates with Office Online Server (and this Excel Services), but this feature no longer exists within the bounds of the SharePoint farm proper.

This change in functionality means that additional planning is required to replace Excel Calculation Services functionality when moving content from SharePoint Server 2013 to SharePoint Server 2016. Some functionality present in Excel Calculation Services, such as trusted data providers, file locations, and data connection libraries, has been deprecated due to the change in architecture. PowerShell administration functions for Excel Services are no longer administered from within the SharePoint farm and are now applied from within the Office Online Server farm.

With this change in architecture, however, Excel Services is positioned as a modern platform capable of providing Web Parts in SharePoint while also adding current programmability features such as JavaScript Object Model (OM), User Defined Function Assemblies, Simple Object Access Protocol (SOAP), and Representational State Transfer (REST) protocol support.

Requirements for Office Online

Office Online Server is similar to Office Web Apps Server 2013 from a deployment standpoint in that it can be deployed as a single-server farm or as a multiserver, load balanced farm. If you have a high-availability requirement using a multiserver configuration, you will need to use either a hardware or software load balanced solution.

Once the farm has been created, server-to-server authentication can be set up between it and SharePoint Server 2016.

As was the case with Office Web Apps Server, server instances (either physical or virtual) that run Office Online are resource intensive. This means:

- Server applications such as Exchange, SharePoint, Skype for Business, or SQL should never be installed alongside Office Online Server.
- Office Online Server will not run on servers that run Active Directory Domain Services (domain controllers).
- Microsoft Office should never be installed on a server that is running Office Online Server.
- Don't install any services or roles that depend on the Web Server role (IIS) on ports 80, 443, or 809, as Office Online Server periodically removes web applications on these ports.

Implement managed paths for Office 365 migrations

SharePoint Server 2016 provides the ability to build custom wildcard or embedded site collections. The software boundaries and limits guidance for SharePoint 2016 provide a supported limitation of only 20 managed paths per farm; beyond this limit, system performance could suffer.

SharePoint Online does not provide a mechanism for creating new managed paths, either via the GUI or via PowerShell cmdlets. When migrating content from an on-premises SharePoint 2016 environment, /sites and /teams are the only wildcard managed paths available to store migrated site collections.

> **NOTE** **SharePoint Online has no provision for the creation of explicit managed paths.**

Configure SharePoint hybrid cloud settings

When configuring an on-premises SharePoint 2016 installation for hybrid (shown in Figure 1-33), there are three selections that should be made: My Site URL, selecting an audience, and selecting hybrid features.

- **My Site URL**   Selecting the My Site URL requires the logged in admin to sign in to Office 365 as the global admin; the My Site URL will be automatically provided.
- **Select Audience For Hybrid Features**   The SharePoint admin can choose either to make the hybrid features available to everyone, or to limit the availability of hybrid features by using one or more audiences (useful for a phased deployment of hybrid features).
- **Select Hybrid Features**   By default, hybrid OneDrive and Sites features are not enabled; admins can choose to deploy OneDrive only or both OneDrive and Sites.

cloud-driven hybrid picker

Use the hybrid settings on this page to integrate hybrid solutions with your existing SharePoint Server farm. Pick the hybrid features you want to include in your SharePoint on-premises environment, and we will configure the settings automatically.

Prerequisites

Before you can turn on hybrid OneDrive and SharePoint Sites, go to the article to set up the prerequisites

Hybrid OneDrive

Redirect OneDrive for Business to OneDrive on Office 365 so users can save and share documents from any devices. No other SharePoint on-premises features are affected.
Learn more

Hybrid SharePoint Sites

Turn on hybrid sites features.
Learn more

FIGURE 1-33 Configuring hybrid OneDrive and Sites features

Skill: Plan a hybrid cloud environment

This section reviews the configuration steps required to set up a SharePoint farm at a base level. Establishing a core infrastructure plan that is both scalable and manageable will help guide you toward the goal of a solid SharePoint installation.

Plan for deployment of Office Online

Deployment of an Office Online installation should be approached with the same care as any IT initiative. Due to the nature of the Office 365 product stack, it's likely that the Office Online rollout will be part of a larger deployment schedule. This schedule will involve staffing and expertise from the SQL, Exchange, Skype for Business, and SharePoint teams; it will also require resources from other teams, such as those responsible for Active Directory, Desktop, and Deployment services.

The deployment of Office Online will rely on a project structure, with topics such as these:

■ Determining deployment goals

■ Developing training guidelines and requirements

■ Inventorying the current environment

■ Making deployment decisions (such as product deployment order)

■ Analyzing and correcting issues that will prevent efficient deployment

■ Setting up the appropriate Office 365 services

■ Rolling out Office 365 functionality to users (phased deployment)

Configure server-to-server authentication

Server-to-server (S2S) authentication is a mechanism of establishing a trust between two server environments; once the relationship is established, resources can be securely exchanged from one environment to the other, based on user need. These trusts can be established between environments including:

■ SharePoint 2016 farms

■ Exchange farms

■ Skype for Business

■ Office Online Server

■ SharePoint Online

■ Azure Active Directory

Configure OAuth

OAuth (Open Authorization 2.0 protocol) authentication is used for S2S authentication and authorization. Usually OAuth requires an authorization server and two realms that need to communicate with each other; however, this is not always the case.

On-premises S2S authentication between two Microsoft servers does not require a third-party server. Server products such as SharePoint, Exchange, and Skype can issue and sign a security token and then communicate with other Microsoft servers.

When setting up S2S, OAuth is configured to use HTTPS by default. If you choose to use HTTP instead of HTTPS, you will need to do the following:

- Allow the use of HTTP for outbound HTTP connections from Office Online Server
- Allow the use of HTTP paths to store Office Data Connection files

Configure audiences and hybrid features

Audiences are a mechanism used in SharePoint to target content to a particular subset of users. This functionality has been available for several versions of SharePoint, although it's acquired a new use within SharePoint 2013 and 2016. Specifically, audiences are now used to determine which users receive access to hybrid services such as OneDrive for Business. Having this functionality present allows SharePoint administrators to perform a phased migration to the cloud, rather than having an all-or-nothing configuration.

Configure audiences

Audiences can be configured from Central Administration, or they can be created from PowerShell. Once created, the membership of the audience can be assigned access to hybrid features.

> **NEED MORE REVIEW?** To better understand how users can be granted access to Office 365 via audience, review the "Configure settings in Central Administration" section of the TechNet article entitled "How to redirect users to Office 365 for OneDrive for Business" at *https://technet.microsoft.com/library/dn627525.aspx*.

Configure hybrid features

Hybrid features in SharePoint Server 2016 allow users in your enterprise to have the best of both worlds: all of the local functionality present in your on-premises implementation plus the benefits of technologies that are found exclusively in Office 365. Each of the following technologies requires a baseline configuration; Office 365 must be configured to hybrid with your on-premises SharePoint Server 2016 implementation.

Additionally, SharePoint Server 2016 hybrid configurations also require the following services to be running on your farm:

- Managed Metadata Service (MMS) application
- User Profile Service application
- My Sites

EXAM TIP

Hybrid features are unavailable without first configuring your Office 365 tenant for hybrid, registering your domain, configuring User Principal Name (UPN) suffixes, and synchronizing your user accounts. Understanding and implementing this requirement should be reviewed for the test, and is detailed in the "Configure Office 365 for SharePoint hybrid" article that can be found on TechNet at *https://technet.microsoft.com/library/mt125509(v =office.16).aspx*.

Search

SharePoint Server 2016 supports two distinct types of Search configurations between on-premises and cloud installations. Cloud hybrid search is the more recent search configuration, which works both with SharePoint Server 2016 and SharePoint Server 2013 (requires the August 2015 Public Update) installations. Hybrid federated search is also supported, as was introduced in SharePoint Server 2013.

CLOUD HYBRID SEARCH

Cloud hybrid search allows crawled content from your on-premises file shares, SharePoint (2007, 2010, 2013, and 2016) and Office 365 installations to be presented by a Search index that is hosted in Office 365. Users querying content in this hybrid experience see unified search results from both installations, presented in a single search experience:

- **Enterprise Search** Search Center in SharePoint Online automatically includes results from your on-premises content. You can customize your Search Center in SharePoint Online, for example, by adding custom refiners.

- **Search verticals** Search verticals narrow search results to a specific set of content, for example, to show only videos. If you currently use a search vertical in your Search Center in SharePoint Server, you have to re-create it in your Search Center in SharePoint Online.

> *NEED MORE REVIEW?* For a better understanding of the SharePoint Online Search Center, review the Office article entitled "Manage the Search Center in SharePoint Online" at *https://support.office.com/article/Manage-the-Search-Center-in-SharePoint-Online -174d36e0-2f85-461a-ad9a-8b3f434a4213.*

Content metadata from your on-premises SharePoint 2016 implementation is securely encrypted as it's transferred to the Search index in Office 365. Search itself is configured from Office 365, except for setting up content crawls, which you do in Central Administration on your SharePoint Server farm.

Storing the Search index fully in the cloud means that users always have the most current SharePoint Online search experience possible. From an administrative point of view, you no longer have to migrate the Search index as you upgrade your on-premises installation of SharePoint; additionally, you don't have to worry about the overall size of your Search index, as it does not require any on-premises resources.

At its core, the configuration of cloud hybrid search is comprised of the following configuration steps:

1. Configure Office 365 for your SharePoint hybrid implementation.

2. Create a cloud Search service application in SharePoint Server 2016 by using the CreateCloudSSA.ps1 PowerShell script.

> *IMPORTANT* The cloud Search service application can be set up on either SharePoint 2013 or 2016; note that there can only be one cloud Search service application in a SharePoint farm.

3. Connect the cloud Search service application to the Office 365 tenant by using the Onboard-CloudHybridSearch.ps1 PowerShell script.

4.   Create (and then crawl) content sources.

EXAM TIP

Search is an essential component of most SharePoint implementations. For the test, be familiar with the roadmap provided by Microsoft for Cloud Hybrid search configuration, entitled "Configure cloud hybrid search – roadmap," which can be found on TechNet at *https://technet.microsoft.com/library/dn720906(v=office.16).aspx.*

HYBRID FEDERATED SEARCH

Hybrid federated search was introduced with SharePoint 2013 and Office 365, and is still a supported Search configuration for SharePoint 2016. In this configuration, two separate indexes are maintained: SharePoint 2016 on-premises and Office 365 in the cloud. Content from these indexes is presented together on Search results pages, but the environments are maintained separately from a search standpoint.

Hybrid federated search can be configured in inbound, outbound, or bidirectional hybrid topologies. In an Outbound configuration, users receive hybrid results when searching from the SharePoint Server 2016 Search Center, whereas in the Inbound configuration, users receive hybrid results when searching from the SharePoint Online Search Center. Bidirectional hybrid is, of course, a combination of Inbound and Outbound search configurations. All of these configurations assume that you have already set up synchronization of Active Directory to the cloud and that you have previously established your server-to-server trust with Office 365.

Displaying hybrid federated search results in the SharePoint 2016 Search Center (Inbound) requires that the following procedures be completed:

- A result source is created that defines how Search results are retrieved from SharePoint Online.
- A query rule is created to turn on hybrid Search results in SharePoint Server 2016.

Displaying hybrid federated search results in the SharePoint Online Search Center (Outbound) requires that the following procedures be completed:

- A result source is created that defines how Search results are retrieved from the on-premises deployment of SharePoint Server 2016.
- A query rule is created to turn on hybrid Search results in SharePoint Online.

Hybrid Picker tools

Hybrid Picker is a tool set found in Office 365 administration that allows you to integrate hybrid solutions with your on-premises SharePoint Server farm. This tool is used to set up one of two possible hybrid features (shown in Figure 1-34): Hybrid OneDrive for Business or Hybrid SharePoint Sites.

FIGURE 1-34 The Cloud-Driven Hybrid Picker

During activation, both of these features configure a server-to-server (OAuth/S2S) trust between SharePoint Server 2016 and Office 365. Hybrid Picker requires that the App Management, Subscription Settings, and User Profile Services are running and configured; additionally, the Search service application must be running and configured.

A series of prerequisites must be met prior to using the Hybrid Picker:

- An on-premises SharePoint Server 2013 farm requires the September 2015 Public Update; no action is necessary for SharePoint Server 2016.

- Ports 80 and 443 must be opened on the firewall for your on-premises configuration outbound to Office 365.

- You must log in to a server in the on-premises SharePoint Server farm with an account that accesses Central Administration as a Farm Administrator; from the same server, you must also log in to Office 365 as an account that is a Global Administrator.

- On-premises accounts being synchronized must have an email address, a Session Initiation Protocol (SIP) address, or a Simple Mail Transfer Protocol (SMTP) address.

EXAM TIP

At first, it would seem that you are committing your enterprise to an "all or nothing" configuration, requiring that all users are part of the hybrid options. This is actually not the case, as you can set up audiences in your on-premises SharePoint Server environment to deploy hybrid features to your users in phases. Audiences should be configured prior to running the Hybrid Picker tool; be familiar with how audiences are configured in an on-premises configuration, both from Central Administration as well as via PowerShell cmdlets.

OneDrive for Business

Hybrid OneDrive for Business is the more basic of the two Hybrid Picker options and alters your OneDrive for Business configuration to redirect users to the Office 365 version of OneDrive for Business to store their files, rather than using the on-premises variant. Users are automatically redirected to OneDrive for Business in Office 365 when they click the OneDrive link in the navigation bar.

> **IMPORTANT** As previously mentioned, audiences can be configured to allow some users to access their OneDrive for Business in Office 365 while other users access the on-premises version of OneDrive for Business.

In an exclusively on-premises implementation of OneDrive for Business, users are forced to log in via some mechanism to access their corporate storage. If this environment is available via a hybrid configuration, users can securely access their data from outside your corporate network. Information stored in this environment is still subject to governance settings that are configured from within SharePoint Server 2016.

Configuring OneDrive for Business allows you to configure Office 365 to host hybrid users' profile information, and is available in both SharePoint 2013 and 2016. Profile information is also automatically made available within Delve.

Team Sites

Team Sites (Hybrid SharePoint Sites) is a superset of OneDrive for Business, and adds both Site following and the extensible App Launcher to the user experience. Followed Team Sites from SharePoint Server 2016 and SharePoint Online are both presented on the Sites page, and are easily accessed from the Sites tile of the App Launcher.

Extensible Hybrid App Launcher

Office 365 users are familiar with the App Launcher feature in Office 365. This feature has now been extended to on-premises installations of SharePoint Server 2016, and is made available once you enable one of the two hybrid features (Hybrid OneDrive for Business or Hybrid SharePoint Sites).

Once the Extensible Hybrid App Launcher has been enabled, on-premises users of SharePoint Server 2016 can access apps such as Office 365 Delve and Video, and also access any custom Office 365 tiles. Additionally, any custom tiles pinned to the Office 365 app launcher will automatically appear in the on-premises SharePoint Server 2016 app launcher.

Summary

- External content types are used to represent data in external systems within a SharePoint site.
- Keywords, synonyms, promoted results, and managed properties heavily influence Search results.
- Durable links are a mechanism for linking documents that will survive a move or renaming action.

- DLP queries allow users to discover sensitive content in a farm, and DLP policies allow for the automated management of sensitive information.

- There are four claims-aware authentication types in SharePoint 2016: Windows authentication, Basic authentication, Forms-based authentication, and a Trusted identity provider. Classic mode authentication is not supported in SharePoint Server 2016.

- A software boundary is an absolute limit that cannot be exceeded or changed, whereas a software threshold has an initial value set that can (if required) be expanded to the boundary limit, and a software limit is a configuration value that is set based on performance testing by Microsoft.

- A site collection can be moved from one content database to another; a site cannot.

- A MinRole-compliant farm can run on as few as one SharePoint server (Single-server server role), three SharePoint servers (one server in each of the Front-end, Application, and Distributed cache tiers), or four SharePoint servers (one server in each of the Front-end, Application, Distributed cache, and Search tiers). A fully resilient MinRole-compliant farm runs on a minimum of nine servers (two each in the Front-end, Application, and Search tiers with three servers in the Distributed cache tier).

- The maximum degree of parallelism (SQL setting) for a SharePoint farm is 1.

- Server-to-server authentication is a mechanism of establishing a trust between two server environments.

Thought experiment

In this thought experiment, demonstrate your skills and knowledge of the topics covered in this chapter. You can find the answer to this thought experiment in the next section.

You are creating the first SharePoint farm at your company, and have been given guidance by your management to keep costs down. You are supporting a minimal number of users, but are supporting a large body of content that will need to be stored in SharePoint.

Answer the following questions for your manager:

1. How many servers need to be purchased (not including the data tier) to build the first production environment? What MinRole will be used?

2. How many servers need to be purchased to make the environment fully resilient (not including the data tier)? How many tiers will there need to be? What MinRoles will be used?

3. What sort of problems might you expect from an information topology standpoint?

Thought experiment answer

This section contains the solution to the thought experiment.

1. To build the smallest possible farm, you will need a single server, configured with the Single-server farm MinRole.

2. You will need to scale the farm out to a total of nine servers in four tiers with the following server roles: two Front-end servers, two Application servers, three Distributed cache servers, and two Search servers.

3. If you start with a single site collection, it will be easy to administer permissions; you might have scalability issues, depending on just how big the body of content turns out to be.

   You could consider starting with a single content database that has multiple site collections; this way, if you ever need to scale down the size of a content database, you could create a new content database, then move site collections to the new storage.

   Scaling the site collections might cause you to reconsider your navigation strategy, moving from a structural to a managed navigation structure.

## CHAPTER 2

Authentication and security

Security within a SharePoint environment is a broad-spectrum topic, requiring a clear understanding of how users will authenticate and be authorized to access content. This chapter begins with a discussion of authentication types, and then examines how authorization is carried out at the farm, application, site collection, and site levels. Additionally, we discuss security-related functionality present at the services and service application levels of the SharePoint farm.

Skills in this chapter:

- Skill: Plan and configure authentication
- Skill: Plan and configure authorization
- Skill: Plan and configure platform and farm security
- Skill: Create and configure a User Profile service application (UPA)
- Skill: Manage site and site collection security
- Skill: Provision and configure web applications

Skill: Plan and configure authentication

Authentication is a mechanism within a system that verifies the identity of the requestor as genuine against an authentication provider; this mechanism has nothing to do with the assignment of rights or permissions to a requestor. Once the requestor has been authenticated, authorization can then be granted to provide system resource access.

> **IMPORTANT** A requestor is not necessarily a human being. A requestor can be a user, an app, or another server.

SharePoint Server 2016 requires authentication for three types of interactions:

- **User authentication** A user is trying to access SharePoint resources.
- **App authentication** An installed app is trying to access SharePoint resources.
- **Site-to-site (S2S) authentication** Two-way resource access between servers in the enterprise.

When new web applications are created via SharePoint 2016 Central Administration, the authentication options available are all claims-aware. These web applications can (by default) use one of the three available authentication types: Windows authentication, Forms-based authentication, or Secure Application Markup Language (SAML) token-based authentication.

EXAM TIP

A common misconception is that SharePoint itself performs authentication; in fact, it does not. Although SharePoint prompts for authentication, the captured requestor credentials are validated against a provider such as Active Directory Domain Services (AD DS).

NEED MORE REVIEW? Understanding authentication in SharePoint is a key skill. Authentication mechanisms work the same in both SharePoint 2013 and SharePoint 2016, and are covered extensively in the TechNet article entitled "SharePoint 2013: Claims-based authentication" at *http://aka.ms/spclm*. Additionally, a video walk-through of each authentication type can be found in the TechNet article entitled "Plan for user authentication methods in SharePoint Server 2016" at *https://technet.microsoft.com/library/cc262350(v =office.16).aspx*.

This section covers how to:

- Plan and configure Windows authentication
- Plan and configure anonymous authentication
- Plan connection encryption
- Plan and configure identity federation
- Configure claims providers
- Configure site-to-site (S2S) intraserver and OAuth authentication
- Configure connections to Access Control Service
- Configure authentication for hybrid cloud deployments

Plan and configure Windows authentication

Windows authentication is the default claims authentication type used when creating a new web application. This authentication type can choose one or more of four possible Windows authentication types (Figure 2-1):

- **NTLM** A Windows integrated authentication type (one of two) requiring no additional configuration of authentication infrastructure
- **Negotiate (Kerberos)** A Windows integrated authentication type (the second of two) that requires additional configuration of Service Principal Names (SPNs) in AD DS

- **Basic authentication**   An authentication type that sends the user credentials in plain text and requires additional configuration of the web application in Internet Information Services (IIS)

- **Digest authentication**   An authentication type that sends the user credentials in an MD5 message digest and requires additional configuration of the web application in IIS

> **NOTE**   Windows integrated authentication types allow clients to authenticate without requiring a prompt for credentials.

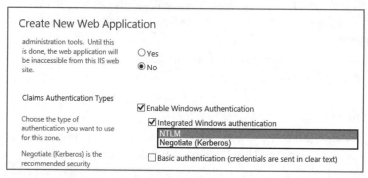

FIGURE 2-1 Windows authentication types

Integrated Windows authentication: NTLM

The NT LAN Manager (NTLM) authentication type is the simpler of the two integrated Windows authentication mechanisms to configure; no extra effort is required from a SharePoint standpoint to make NTLM function correctly.

NTLM's benefits are mostly focused on ease of use, when compared with Negotiate (Kerberos):

- NTLM authentication can still function when the computer making the request is outside the network or is a stand-alone computer.

- NTLM is much easier to set up and configure than its Kerberos counterpart.

There is, however, a price to be paid for NTLM's simplicity:

- NTLM is an older authentication type, using a challenge/response mechanism for authentication that is less secure than Kerberos.

- NTLM has a negative effect on performance, making repeated round trips between IIS and causing an increased load on domain controllers.

- NTLM does not support delegation; if a user has authenticated into a SharePoint environment and then needs to access another system through SharePoint, the request will fail.

Integrated Windows authentication: Negotiate (Kerberos)

The Negotiate (Kerberos) authentication protocol is designed for both security and efficiency. A requestor authenticating via this protocol is issued and granted a ticket from a centralized Key Distribution Center (KDC) that is used to access resources.

Kerberos authentication provides several benefits:

- Kerberos is the most secure of the Windows integrated protocols, and is an open protocol supported by multiple non-Microsoft vendors and platforms.

- Kerberos is quite efficient, minimizing the need for a client to repeatedly authenticate to a domain controller; this efficiency reduces both server and network traffic, often reducing page latency.

- Kerberos supports delegation. A user authenticated into a SharePoint environment can "double hop," directly accessing other Kerberos-configured systems through SharePoint.

Kerberos might not always be the best option:

- The proper configuration of Kerberos authentication for SharePoint requires interaction and close coordination with the Active Directory and SQL support teams.

- The security mechanisms employed by Kerberos include the ability for clients and servers to mutually authenticate one another, and clients and servers can use Advanced Encryption Standard (AES) encryption.

EXAM TIP

Although not present within Central Administration, SharePoint also supports Windows classic mode for backward compatibility. Configuration of this authentication type is done entirely in Windows PowerShell; efforts should be made to move away from this type of authentication because it does not support some SharePoint 2016 functionality (such as the SharePoint App Store).

Basic authentication

Basic authentication is by far the least secure of the four Windows authentication types. This type of authentication is fairly simple to configure by using Central Administration and IIS, but is not often used, usually because credentials (user name and password) are passed insecurely over the wire in clear text.

> ***NEED MORE REVIEW?*** If you choose basic authentication, just ensure that you do so over an HTTPS session. Secure Sockets Layer (SSL) encryption provides a fairly good level of security, encrypting the user name and password that would otherwise be transmitted over the wire in clear text. The TechNet article entitled "Configure basic authentication for a claims-based web application in SharePoint 2013" provides details on the configuration of this authentication type at *https://technet.microsoft.com//library/gg576953(v=office.16) .aspx.*

Digest authentication

Digest authentication is more secure than basic authentication, and is similar to NTLM in that it uses a challenge/response mechanism. A calculated checksum component is stored on a domain controller that must match an MD5 checksum (digest) of the user's password at logon time. If the user decides to visit more than one web application, he or she must reauthenticate (furnish user name and password) again.

> **NEED MORE REVIEW?** Digest authentication configuration is similar to that of basic configuration, requiring configuration of IIS on a per-web application basis. The TechNet article entitled "Configure digest authentication for a claims-based web application in SharePoint 2013" provides details on the configuration of this authentication type at *https://technet.microsoft.com/library/gg576966(v=office.16).aspx.*

 Quick check

- You have a requirement to provide secure pass-through authentication to your SharePoint environment. What are your options?

Quick check answer

- Integrated Windows authentication (NTLM) can be used in concert with SSL (HTTPS) connections to secure and encrypt your connections. Integrated Windows authentication (Kerberos) provides an even more secure connection than NTLM, but requires configuration efforts from your Active Directory infrastructure team.

Plan and configure anonymous authentication

Anonymous authentication enables a user to access a SharePoint web application (such as an Internet-facing website) without being challenged for user name and password credentials. As with the other types of authentication, anonymous authentication can be applied to the zone of a given web application, with each zone maintaining its own list of which authentication types can be used.

Enabling a SharePoint site to allow anonymous authentication can be done via PowerShell or Central Administration, and can be enabled at the time the web app and zone are being created (Figure 2-2), or afterward by editing the completed web app.

FIGURE 2-2 Choosing to allow anonymous authentication for a new web application

Plan connection encryption

Connection encryption is a mechanism for securing "in-flight" data as it is being transferred between SharePoint and other computers in your enterprise. In previous versions of SharePoint, either SSL 3.0 or Transport Layer Security (TLS) 1.0 cryptographic protocols could be used for secure communications; however, SSL 3.0 was later found to have vulnerabilities, making TLS 1.0 the remaining protocol available for use (SSL 3.0 could be disabled).

SharePoint 2016 now handles encryption by default by using the newer TLS 1.2 cryptographic protocol for secured connections.

> **IMPORTANT** SSL and TLS protocols are both commonly referred to as SSL in documentation, sometimes even being grouped together as SSL/TLS. Remember that when we speak of implementing SSL in this book, we mean the TLS 1.2 protocol, not SSL 3.0.

Connection encryption in SharePoint 2016 is now supported in the following situations:

- When setting up SSL bindings for a SharePoint web application
- When connecting to other systems (such as crawling websites)
- When establishing an encrypted connection to a Simple Mail Transfer Protocol (SMTP) server

Setting up SSL bindings for a SharePoint web application

As TLS 1.2 is the default for SSL in SharePoint 2016, configuration of the protocol itself is not required (we don't have to choose between SSL and TLS protocols as we did in the previous implementations of SharePoint). All that remains, then, is to add SSL to a web application, and there are two ways to do that: either on or after the creation of the web application.

The optimal mechanism for configuring SSL with a SharePoint web application is to specify that SSL is to be used while the web application is being created (Figure 2-3), and then add and bind the certificate to IIS. This ensures that, as your farm grows, the configuration database configures any newly added front-end servers with the same SSL-enabled web application configurations.

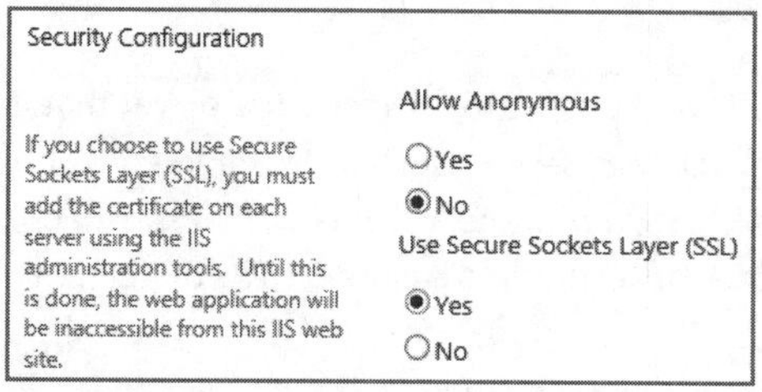

Security Configuration

Allow Anonymous

If you choose to use Secure
Sockets Layer (SSL), you must
add the certificate on each
server using the IIS
administration tools. Until this
is done, the web application will
be inaccessible from this IIS web
site.

○ Yes
◉ No

Use Secure Sockets Layer (SSL)

◉ Yes
○ No

FIGURE 2-3 SSL setting within Security Configuration

The provisioning and configuration of web applications is covered later in this chapter.

Connecting to other systems

SharePoint 2016 farms are capable of connecting to other systems such as Exchange 2016, Skype for Business 2016, Azure Workflow Service, other SharePoint farms, and SharePoint Server 2016 running in Office 365 via the use of S2S authentication. This connectivity is established by using the OAuth protocol, which is also used for app authentication in SharePoint 2016.

Establishing an S2S connection via OAuth requires the involvement of three parties: an authorization server and the two realms that need to connect to each other. In the case of Microsoft servers such as SharePoint, Exchange, and others, they can assume the role of the authorization server and one of the two realms to connect; the authorization server verifies the trusts between the two realms by issuing security tokens via the Security Token Service.

When a SharePoint 2016 user needs to access functionality present in another server farm, an S2S token requests access to the resource, acting on the part of the user.

EXAM TIP

It should be noted that a logon token is *not* part of this process; the S2S token contains information about two things: the server requesting access and the user for whom the server is acting.

When the OAuth connection is established between realms, the implementer has a decision to make regarding encryption, specifically to encrypt or not to encrypt. By default, these connections are established via HTTPS, but the administrator has the option of overriding this behavior and allowing unencrypted HTTP connections in PowerShell.

> **NEED MORE INFORMATION?**   Separate processes exist for establishing relationships between SharePoint farms and other server farms, both on-premises and in the cloud. For a better understanding of the mechanisms involved, visit the TechNet article entitled "Plan for server-to-server authentication in SharePoint Server 2016" at *https://technet.microsoft.com/library/jj219546(v=office.16).aspx*.

Establishing SMTP encryption

Connection encryption is also available between a SharePoint 2016 farm and the server that it uses to provide SMTP functionality for outgoing email. Mail servers such as Exchange provide the ability to require encryption via the use of STARTTLS, a protocol command that is issued by the client (SharePoint) to request an upgrade of an insecure to a secure SMTP connection by using TLS or SSL cryptographic protocols.

Although STARTTLS itself is capable of supporting both TLS and SSL protocols, SharePoint 2016 does *not* allow the use of SSL 2.0 or 3.0 when negotiating connection encryption with an SMTP server; the only protocols supported are TLS versions 1.0, 1.1, and 1.2.

For SharePoint to securely connect to an SMTP server, the server must have STARTTLS enabled and have a valid server certificate installed, with a name that matches that provided to SharePoint during the configuration for outbound SMTP.

> **IMPORTANT** If an encrypted connection is specified by SharePoint to the SMTP server, there is no fallback support for unencrypted connections.
>
> Starting with Exchange 2013, STARTTLS (also known as Opportunistic TLS) is enabled automatically. Exchange 2013 and later versions also create a self-signed certificate that is used to secure the encrypted connection.

Configuring secure outgoing email in SharePoint can be set up on the Outgoing E-Mail Settings page under Central Administration, System Settings (Figure 2-4). Alternately, secure outgoing email can be set up via the Set-SPWebApplication PowerShell cmdlet and the -SMTPServer switch. You can optionally use the -DisableSMTPEncryption switch if the SMTP server doesn't allow connection encryption.

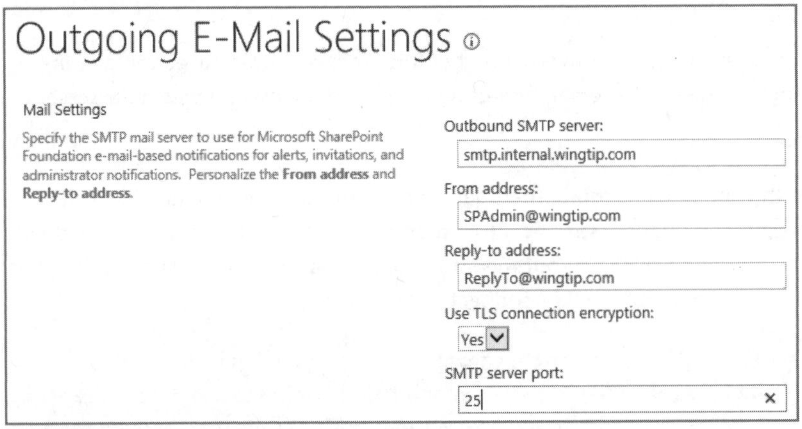

FIGURE 2-4 Configuring Outgoing E-Mail Settings

Quick check

- You are given a requirement from your infrastructure team to configure a secure connection from your SharePoint farm to the SMTP server. What options do you have available?

Quick check answer

- SMTP connection encryption is available, by using TLS 1.2 (not SSL 3.0). Additionally, you could work with your mail administrators to use a nondefault TCP port (instead of TCP port 25).

Plan and configure identity federation

As an organization's business needs change, it often becomes necessary to extend the use of an application such as SharePoint 2016 to outside users or partners. Businesses often respond to this requirement by extending their internal authentication mechanism, issuing user names and passwords to partner organization personnel.

This sort of arrangement is not without its share of headaches:

- The organization's IT staff are now responsible for maintaining both internal and external user accounts, often within two different authentication structures (Forms-based authentication, Active Directory).

- Users from the external party must now keep track of one more set of credentials and authenticate more than once.

- Special arrangements must be made to expose the authentication mechanism to the Internet, posing a security risk and requiring extra maintenance effort.

Discussions about claims-based authentication often quickly extend into user requirements for identity federation. Applications that were once exclusively held within a particular enterprise now can be extended to the cloud and into other partner enterprises.

This federation provides two major benefits for IT admins:

- Extra authentication mechanisms such as Forms-based authentication or separate Active Directory structures are no longer required to provide resources or applications to external business partners.

- Users traveling or working outside the enterprise network are able to work with no special arrangements, acting in the cloud much as they would on premises.

Users taking advantage of identity federation are required to maintain only one set of credentials, authenticating within their own environment to an Identity Provider Security Token Service (IP-STS), such as Active Directory Federation Services (AD FS) or Azure Access Control Service (ACS). Once users have authenticated, they receive an SAML token, which can then be used to access applications in their organization, in partner organizations, and in the cloud.

> **NEED MORE REVIEW?** In addition to AD FS and ACS, an alternative identity provider can also be used, but it must support the WS-Federation standard. For a better understanding of how AD FS and ACS work, see the articles entitled "Configure SAML-based claims authentication with AD FS in SharePoint 2013" at *https://technet.microsoft.com/library/hh305235(v=office.16).aspx*, "Federated Identity with Microsoft Azure Access Control Service" at *https://msdn.microsoft.com/library/hh446535.aspx*, and "Authenticate your SharePoint website users with Facebook" at *http://blogs.technet.com/b/meacoex/archive/2013/12/25/authenticate-your-sharepoint-website-users-with-facebook.aspx*.

In addition to acting as an identity provider (IdP), both ACS and AD FS can instead act as federation providers (FPs). By using this functionality, you can configure either to trust any number of IdPs such as Microsoft account (Windows Live ID), Facebook, Google, Twitter, and Active Directory itself, allowing external users to authenticate using these IdPs. Additionally, you should note that the use of more than one IdP is supported.

EXAM TIP

Either of these technologies can be used in your organization to federate users from another organization, federate with an external authentication mechanism to nonpartner organization users, or both, if needed. Remember that users always authenticate to the IdP to receive an SAML token.

Configure claims providers

Connecting to either AD FS or ACS requires a brief discussion about application proxies. Regardless of which option you choose, you will need to deploy and configure the matching application proxy. This functionality acts as a reverse proxy for web applications, allowing users to authenticate to published web applications, and also as a proxy for authenticating users.

> **IMPORTANT** Application Proxy is a feature that is unavailable in the free edition of Azure Active Directory. If you want to use Application Proxy, upgrade to either the Basic or Premium edition of Azure Active Directory.

Choosing a provider

Either AD FS or Azure ACS can be used for on-premises deployments of SharePoint. If you already have an AD FS installation within your network, you are ready to configure external or federated claims access to your internal applications, including SharePoint.

If, on the other hand, you have not yet deployed AD FS but do have an Azure subscription, you can instead choose to deploy the Application Proxy functionality present in Azure AD. This proxy works by installing a new Windows service (called a Connector) inside your on-premises network, then registering the Connector with your Microsoft Azure AD tenant subscription.

> **NEED MORE REVIEW?** The configuration and deployment of AD FS or ACS must be customized to your organization's specific needs. Because this configuration affects more than SharePoint, there might be some functionality available to you that requires coordination with your Active Directory infrastructure team, such as using ExpressRoute to connect your SharePoint 2016 environment directly to Azure.
>
> For a better understanding of how AD FS and ACS (and their associated proxies) work, see the article entitled "Connect to Applications and Services from Anywhere with Web Application Proxy" at *https://technet.microsoft.com/library/dn280942.aspx* for AD FS and "Enabling Azure AD Application Proxy" at *https://azure.microsoft.com/documentation /articles/active-directory-application-proxy-enable/* for ACS.

Configure S2S intraserver and OAuth authentication

SharePoint 2016 uses the Open Authorization 2.0 (OAuth) protocol to establish *server-to-server* or *site-to-site* (S2S) connections between a SharePoint farm and another SharePoint Server farm, an Exchange installation, a Skype for Business installation, or SharePoint Online. Users in SharePoint can then retrieve information from these other environments. This configuration is unchanged from SharePoint 2013 to SharePoint 2016.

EXAM TIP

By default, S2S relationships are carried out over HTTPS, which is always a best practice. Establishing an S2S relationship over HTTP is technically possible (but not secure) and should be done only in a nonproduction environment.

Configuring S2S between two SharePoint 2016 farms

Server-to-server requests in SharePoint farms are configured so that one server farm may provide resources or functionality to another on behalf of a user. These configurations come in one of two types:

- A trust relationship to a farm that has web applications
- A trust relationship to a farm that has no web applications

Configuration for each type happens from the perspective of the farm that will be receiving the S2S requests (aptly named the "receiving" farm). Although the S2S functionality is the same, configuration of the trusts differs greatly between the two types.

The configuration of S2S on a receiving farm (having web applications) requires that the New-SPTrustedSecurityTokenIssuer cmdlet be used to configure the trust, specifying the JavaScript Object Notation (JSON) metadata endpoint of the sending farm.

```
New-SPTrustedSecurityTokenIssuer –MetadataEndpoint "https://<HostName>/_layouts/15/
metadata/json/1" –Name "<FriendlyName>"
```

Configuring S2S on a receiving farm (with no web applications) obviously excludes the ability to use a JSON metadata endpoint; this configuration is a bit more involved, requiring the admin to accomplish several tasks:

1. Export the SharePoint Security Token Service certificate (.cer) without the private key from the receiving farm, then store it in an accessible location (usually a secured file share).

2. Retrieve the NameIdentifier field of the receiving farm.

3. On the trusting SharePoint farm, add the SharePoint STS of the receiving SharePoint farm as a trusted security token issued by using the following PowerShell cmdlet.

   ```
   New-SPTrustedSecurityTokenIssuer -name <hostname> -Certificate "<CERLocation>"
   -RegisteredIssuerName "00000003-0000-0ff1-ce00-000000000000@<NameID>"
   -Description "<FriendlyName>" -IsTrustBroker:$false
   ```

> **NEED MORE REVIEW?** The configuration process for setting up S2S gets more complex based on the number of farms being interconnected and the way in which these connections are made. For more information about this process, see the TechNet article "Configure server-to-server authentication between SharePoint 2013 farms" at *http://technet.microsoft.com/library/jj655400.aspx*.

Configuring S2S between SharePoint Server 2016 and Exchange Server 2016

S2S authentication between these two environments requires coordination between the administrators of each because the configuration of each system must be modified for SharePoint and Exchange to share resources.

There are three major steps involved in completing this configuration:

- Configure the SharePoint server to trust the Microsoft Exchange server by using a JSON endpoint located on the Exchange server.

- Configure permissions on the SharePoint server for S2S.

- Configure the Exchange server to trust the SharePoint server by using the Configure-EnterprisePartnerApplication.ps1 PowerShell script.

EXAM TIP

Be familiar with the three distinct processes that go into establishing the relationship between these two environments. As usual, these configuration efforts take place in Windows PowerShell and require the use of SSL for communication between server environments.

> **NEED MORE REVIEW?** The trust that is shared between these two environments is not web-app-specific. Establishing the trust from Exchange 2013 to one of the SharePoint 2013 web apps establishes a trust with all the web apps in the entire farm. For a better understanding of this configuration, visit the TechNet article "Configure server-to-server authentication between SharePoint 2013 and Exchange Server 2013" at *http://technet.microsoft.com/library/jj655399.aspx*.

Configuring S2S between SharePoint 2016 and Skype for Business Server 2015

S2S authentication between these two environments requires coordination between the administrators of each because the configuration of each system must be modified for SharePoint and Skype to share resources.

There are only two steps involved in completing this configuration:

- Configure the SharePoint server to trust the Skype for Business server by using a JSON endpoint located on the Exchange server.

- Configure the Skype for Business server to trust the SharePoint server as a new partner application.

These configuration efforts take place in Windows PowerShell and require the use of SSL for communication between server environments.

> **NEED MORE REVIEW?** If you want to know more about the process of connecting these two environments, visit the TechNet site "Assign a server-to-server authentication certificate to Skype for Business Server 2015" at *https://technet.microsoft.com/library/jj205253.aspx*.

Configure connections to the Access Control Service

The Azure Access Control Service (ACS) is a mechanism that enables users to access an application while removing the authentication and authorization burden from the design of the application.

> **IMPORTANT** There have been two versions of this service. The latest, ACS 2.0, is free for use and is the only supported version.

ACS enables applications such as SharePoint 2016 to integrate with both enterprise directories (such as Active Directory) and IdPs in the cloud such as Windows Live ID, Google, Yahoo!, and Facebook.

Using ACS for SharePoint authentication

Partner organizations that host both AD FS installations can set up trusts between their environments to allow users to access resources from either environment. A lot of configuration work and coordination between IT organizations is required to connect these environments.

Extending this concept, a growing organization could soon find itself needing to connect to multiple partner organizations. Requiring the IT organizations from each of these organizations to agree on how they will federate could become cumbersome.

ACS provides a way for organizations to connect their SharePoint farm (and other farms, including Exchange and Skype) to a cloud-based Active Directory tenant. From here, relationships can be established with other partner organizations, or IdPs such as Facebook, Live, Google, and others can be used to authenticate into an organization's SharePoint infrastructure.

Another benefit of using ACS is the ability to extend an organization's SharePoint installation into the cloud for any of the following reasons:

- Setting up development and test environments
- Providing disaster recovery SharePoint environments in Azure
- Providing Internet-facing sites using SharePoint functionality not available in Office 365 and SharePoint Online
- Creating app farms to support either on-premises or Office 365 SharePoint environments

> **NEED MORE REVIEW?** Multiple Azure architecture types exist for SharePoint 2016 installations. Understanding which can be used to meet the needs of your organization is a critical component to any Microsoft-based cloud architecture. Detailed information on these architectures can be found in the TechNet article entitled "Microsoft Azure Architectures for SharePoint 2013" at *https://technet.microsoft.com/library/dn635309(v=office.16).aspx*.

Configure authentication for hybrid cloud deployments

The configuration story for hybrid cloud deployments in SharePoint 2013 could be quite complex and confusing to understand. Several options were available for use, each of which was configured individually:

- **DirSync**   A tool that copies the local Active Directory, propagating to an Azure AD instance

- **FIM + Azure AD Connector**   Synchronized identity information from Forefront Identity Manager 2010 R2 to Azure AD

- **Azure AD Sync**   Replaced both DirSync and FIM + Azure AD Connector

Hybrid implementations varied between these different tool offerings based on the authentication goals and when the project was carried out. Some organizations chose to just implement DirSync, and others chose to fully carry out a single sign-on (SSO) implementation by using one of the other options.

EXAM TIP

Each of these three technologies has been deprecated (most recently the AADSync toolset). As you will see momentarily, Azure AD Connect has replaced each of these tools; however, there is a good chance that you will encounter one or more of these older implementations in existing hybrid environments. Be familiar with each of these types (particularly DirSync and AADSync) and how it was implemented in SharePoint 2013. For detailed information about these tools, review the MSDN article entitled "Directory Integration Tools" at *https://msdn.microsoft.com/library/azure/dn757582.aspx*.

Azure Active Directory Connect

Although the previous technologies are still supported to connect to Azure AD, the configuration path for implementing these technologies can be daunting. Microsoft recently introduced a tool called Azure AD Connect, which simplifies the implementation of hybrid cloud deployments.

As with any other deployment wizard, it is possible to run the tool and accept the express settings; however, the true value of this tool can be found in the custom settings, which allow you to accomplish tasks such as these:

- Deploy multiforest topologies.
- Deploy a pilot environment, that uses just a few users in a group.
- Configuration without deployment (also known as Staging mode).
- Sign on by using federation.
- Enabling Azure AD premium features, such as the ability to write back passwords and devices from the cloud.
- Synchronizing custom Active Directory attributes from your on-premises implementation to your Azure AD tenancy.

Within Azure AD Connect, there are two configurations available: Password Sync and AD FS for SSO.

PASSWORD SYNC

Password Sync resembles the earlier DirSync tool in functionality, and is the most commonly chosen option. In such an environment, SSO is not the main goal, although this configuration can be used as a backup for federation, allowing for a quick failover.

From a security standpoint, on-premises passwords are never transferred to Azure AD. The on-premises password hash is itself hashed before being transferred to the cloud, protecting passwords against "pass-the-hash" attacks; the lack of access to a local hash prevents unauthorized access to on-premises resources.

AD FS FOR SINGLE SIGN-ON

The more advanced of the two configurations, federation with AD FS is used to implement a true SSO environment. Azure AD Connect can either use your existing AD FS or assist in the creation of an AD FS implementation.

With the inclusion of AD FS in this solution, advanced SSO options become available, such as these:

- The ability to deploy desktop SSO from domain-joined machines on the corporate network, including the use of multifactor authentication
- Soft account lockout or Active Directory password and work hours policy enforcement
- Provisioning conditional access for resources, both on premises and in the cloud

> ***NEED MORE REVIEW?*** Azure AD Connect is a one-stop shop for setting up authentication in a hybrid implementation, combining both basic and advanced configurations in a single tool set. Information surrounding the setup, configuration, and maintenance of a hybrid authentication environment can be found in the article entitled "Integrating your on-premises identities with Azure Active Directory" at *https://azure.microsoft.com /documentation/articles/active-directory-aadconnect/*.

 Quick check

- Your manager requests that you work with your infrastructure teams (Active Directory, Exchange, Skype) to come up with a way to connect to Azure AD, requiring the least amount of configuration effort. After you review multiple websites, the options that come up are DirSync, FIM + Azure AD Connector, Azure AD Sync, and Azure AD Connect.

Skill: Plan and configure authorization

After a user has been authenticated, he or she can then be validated attempting to interact with resources in a web application; this validation process is called *authorization*.

This section covers how to:
- Plan and configure SharePoint users and groups
- Plan and configure People Picker
- Plan and configure sharing
- Plan and configure permission inheritance
- Plan and configure anonymous access
- Plan web application policies

Plan and configure SharePoint users and groups

After users have been authenticated to a web application, they need to access the site collections contained within the web app. This access is granted via a series of permission levels that can be assigned to individual users or to SharePoint groups.

The optimal assignment of the permission structure goes something like this:

1. Individual permissions are assigned to a permission level.
2. One or more permission levels are assigned to a SharePoint group.
3. Users are assigned to the SharePoint group, receiving access based on the individual permissions.

EXAM TIP

It is not uncommon to see a user added to more than one group within a SharePoint site collection. As an example, consider a user who belongs to both the Visitors (Reader permissions) and Members (Contributor permissions) SharePoint groups for a site. This person will receive the greater of the two permission sets, thus having the permissions that are assigned to the Contributor permission level.

Individual permissions

SharePoint 2016 has a total of 33 individual permissions that control how a user interacts with a SharePoint site. These permissions are broken into three distinct levels:

- **List permissions (12)**   Apply only to lists and libraries
- **Site permissions (18)**   Apply to a particular site
- **Personal permissions (3)**   Apply to specialized objects such as personal views and personal Web Parts

Permission levels

As a SharePoint site is created, a series of permission levels are also created. The number and type of permission levels may vary, depending on the type of site created (for instance, there are a total of seven created for a Team Site, whereas there are 10 created for a Publishing Portal).

> **NEED MORE REVIEW?**   For a complete list of permission levels and individual permissions, see the TechNet article "User permissions and permission levels in SharePoint 2013" at *http://technet.microsoft.com/library/cc721640.aspx*.

These permission levels are nothing more than an aggregation of the individual permissions available within the site collection. To view the permission levels on a site and the individual permissions assigned to each level, select the Permissions Levels icon from Site Permissions. When the Permission Levels screen appears, you see the individual permission levels available and their descriptions (see Figure 2-5).

Home

Permissions › Permission Levels ⓘ

🗔 Add a Permission Level | ✖ Delete Selected Permission Levels

Permission Level	Description
Full Control	Has full control.
Design	Can view, add, update, delete, approve, and customize.
Edit	Can add, edit and delete lists; can view, add, update and delete list items and documents.
Contribute	Can view, add, update, and delete list items and documents.
Read	Can view pages and list items and download documents.
Limited Access	Can view specific lists, document libraries, list items, folders, or documents when given permissions.
View Only	Can view pages, list items, and documents. Document types with server-side file handlers can be viewed in the browser but not downloaded.

FIGURE 2-5 Selecting the Permission Level icon

Selecting an individual permission level will allow you to see the list of permissions that make up that permission level. The creation and alteration of permissions levels is covered in the section "Manage site and site collection security" later in this chapter.

> **IMPORTANT** Although you can alter the permission levels that are defined when you create a site, it is not a good idea to do so. Copy the permissions level to a new permissions level and then alter the copy to have the distinct permissions you desire. If you don't need a permission level or don't like how it's configured, you don't have to delete it; just don't use it.

SharePoint groups

When a site is created via the SharePoint web interface and configured to use its own permissions, three groups are automatically created:

- **Visitors** Assigned the Read permissions for the site (view pages and list items, download documents)

- **Members** Assigned the Contribute permissions for the site (view, add, update, and delete list items and documents)

- **Owners** Assigned the Full Control permission level for the site (full control)

> **IMPORTANT** When Windows PowerShell is used to create a new site collection (New-SPSite) or site (New-SPWeb), the resulting site has no SharePoint groups created. You can either create new groups by using the Windows PowerShell interface as part of your site creation script, or just use the mechanism that SharePoint uses to provision groups on a new site. Just append _layouts/15/permsetup.aspx to the end of the site's URL (http://sitename), and the default group creation screen will appear.

Plan and configure People Picker

People Picker is a web control that is used to find and select users, groups, and claims to grant permission to items (lists, libraries, and sites) in SharePoint 2016. For web applications using claims authentication, this control uses claims providers to list, resolve, search, and determine the "friendly" display of users, groups, and claims.

The People Picker control can be tailored to the authentication mechanism used for each zone of a web application. As each zone is created, different authentication types (and People Picker properties) can be applied.

For instance, if you have users who were being authenticated over a Forms-based authentication interface, you might choose to exclude Active Directory accounts from appearing in the People Picker. Users authenticating via a different Active Directory authenticated zone would see these accounts in their People Picker.

Configuring People Picker properties

In previous versions of SharePoint, administration of the People Picker web control can be configured by using the STSADM command (along with getproperty to retrieve values and setproperty to apply new values). The preferred mechanism for administering People Picker is via PowerShell, however, as STSADM is deprecated.

If you were to execute the STSADM -help setproperty command, you would find a total of nine property names that can be used to administer the People Picker web control. These property names are listed beneath the SharePoint virtual server properties section, and all begin with the "peoplepicker" prefix. These property name and property value pairs map directly to PowerShell properties and values for a web application zone (Table 2-1).

TABLE 2-1 People Picker properties in STSADM and PowerShell

Property Name (STSADM)	Property Name (POWERSHELL)	Description
Peoplepicker-activedirectorysearchtimeout	ActiveDirectorySearchTimeout	Configures the time out when a query is issued to AD DS
Peoplepicker-distributionlistsearchdomains	DistributionListSearchDomains	Restricts the search of a distribution list to a specific subset of domains
Peoplepicker-nowindowsaccountsfornonwindows authenticationmode	NoWindowsAccountsForNon WindowsAuthenticationMode	Specifies not to search Active Directory when the current port is using Forms-based authentication
Peoplepicker-onlysearchwithinsitecollection	OnlySearchWithinSiteCollection	Displays only users who are members of the site collection
Peoplepicker-peopleeditoronlyres olvewithinsitecollection	PeopleEditorOnlyResolveWithin SiteCollection	Displays only users who are members of the current site collection
Peoplepicker-searchadcustomfilter	ActiveDirectoryCustomFilter	Enables a farm administrator to specify a unique search query
Peoplepicker-searchadcustomquery	ActiveDirectoryCustomQuery	Permits the administrator to set the custom query that is sent to Active Directory
Peoplepicker-searchadforests	SearchActiveDirectoryDomains	Permits a user to search from a second one-way trusted forest or domain
Peoplepicker-serviceaccountdirectorypaths	ServiceAccountDirectoryPaths	Enables a farm administrator to manage the site collection that has a specific organizational unit (OU) setting as defined in the Setsiteuseraccountdirectorypath setting

Retrieving property values in PowerShell is only slightly more involved than it was in STSADM. For instance, to retrieve the current property value for the Active Directory Search Timeout, you would run PowerShell code looking something like this:

```
$webApp=Get-SPWebApplication http://www.contoso.com
$webApp.PeoplePickerSettings.ActiveDirectorySearchTimeout
```

Changing property values in PowerShell is a very similar process. Setting the Active Directory Search Timeout property value to 45 seconds instead of the default of 30 seconds might look like this:

```
$webApp.PeoplePickerSettings.ActiveDirectorySearchTimeout="00:00:45"
$webApp.Update()
```

> **NEED MORE REVIEW?** There are many different scenarios for configuring the People Picker, most having to do with either configuring it for a particular authentication type or restricting the number and type of results shown. In either event, the TechNet article "Configure People Picker in SharePoint 2013" details a lot of these options (and some LDAP magic). This article can be found at *http://technet.microsoft.com/library/gg602075.aspx*.

Plan and configure sharing

Site owners might not be familiar with every user who accesses the site. Perhaps the team member is in the next office, but it is just as likely that he or she could be located half a world away in a different regional office.

Users in remote offices often change roles without the site owner's knowledge. Allowing users to request access for themselves or others allows the site owner to administer, not select, which users require access to a SharePoint site. Personnel in the remote office can now "share" content in SharePoint 2016, recommending that a person be able to access information by using one of the site's permission groups (Visitor, Member, and so on). Users can also request access on their own.

When the request is made, the site owner is notified of the request and can then choose whether to approve or reject the permission request from Site Settings, Access Requests.

Prerequisite configuration

For the sharing functionality to work, outbound email must be properly configured in Central Administration so access requests can be routed and acknowledgments sent via email.

> ***NEED MORE REVIEW?*** **Outgoing email configuration was covered earlier in this chapter. For more information about the configuration of outgoing email in SharePoint, refer to the TechNet article entitled "Configure outgoing email for a SharePoint 2013 farm" at *https://technet.microsoft.com/library/cc263462.aspx.***

Sharing interface improvements

SharePoint 2016 improves on the default sharing behaviors found in SharePoint 2013, particularly Sharing hints, One-Click Sharing, and Create and Share.

SHARING HINTS

Menu items such as Share and Follow now have mouse-over hint behaviors, helping users better understand the function of each menu item (Figure 2-6).

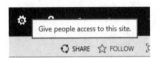

FIGURE 2-6 Hint for the Share menu item

ONE-CLICK

Users who cannot themselves share information from a site can request that the admin share content. The administrator can approve or deny this response by just clicking within the email itself.

CREATE AND SHARE

Users creating a new folder within a document library are presented with the option to invite people to access this site. Selecting this link changes the Create A Folder page, allowing the user to specify the people with whom they are sharing the content, indicate what permissions the users can have (can edit, can view), and send an email invitation, all in a single set of actions (see Figure 2-7).

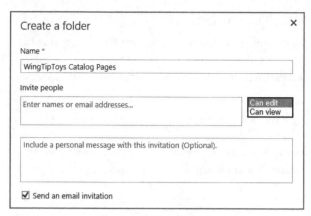

FIGURE 2-7 Expanded Create A Folder page

Configuring a site for access requests

For sharing to take place within a site, it must be configured to enable access requests. On the Site Permissions page, a site owner can allow users to share the site, files, or folders, and also allow access requests (on the Access Requests Settings page, shown in Figure 2-8).

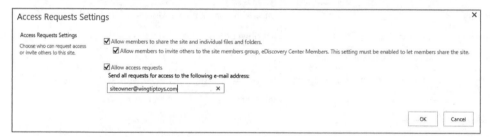

FIGURE 2-8 Selecting access request settings

EXAM TIP

If you have not yet configured outgoing email settings for your farm, the Access Requests Settings page will display a warning indicating that the server is not configured to send email and you should contact your server administrator for assistance. Once this configuration has been set, the Allow Access Requests check box will be enabled.

Once Sharing has been enabled, users can then share either the entire site or particular lists and libraries from the site.

Plan and configure permission inheritance

Permission inheritance is often a sensitive subject. On the one hand, you want to provide the best security for the objects within a site collection; on the other, you want to ease the administrative burden by making the permission structure as flexible as possible while still providing effective permissions.

EXAM TIP

Breaking permission inheritance does not immediately change the effective permissions on the site, list, or library. A copy of the parent's permissions is made and applied to the object before permissions are split.

Common permission inheritance

Consider the objects in Table 2-2 and their permission inheritance structure. Some of these sites and libraries are sensitive in nature, and should receive unique permissions.

TABLE 2-2 Common permission inheritance

Securable Object	Description	Permissions
Intranet	Intranet home page	Unique
Intranet/ManagementTeam	Sensitive group	Unique
Intranet/ManagementTeam/BonusStructure	Sensitive data	Unique
Intranet/ManagementTeam/EmployeeSurveys	Nonsensitive data	Inherits from ManagementTeam
Intranet/NewsArticles	Intranet news	Inherited
Intranet/NewsArticles/DailyUpdates	Nonsensitive data	Inherited
Intranet/FieldGroup	Field team site	Inherited
Intranet/FieldGroup/ShopNotes	Nonsensitive data	Inherited
Intranet/FieldGroup/Clients	Sensitive data	Unique

Permissions in this series of objects are assigned to promote ease of maintenance:

- The NewsArticles and FieldGroup sites inherit permissions from the parent site (Intranet).
- The DailyUpdates and ShopNotes libraries also inherit this permissions structure.
- The EmployeeSurveys list inherits its permissions from the ManagementTeam site.

Several items, however, require unique permissions and are to be separated from the overall permissions structure:

- The ManagementTeam site and its lists and libraries
- The Clients list under FieldGroup

Administration of this environment will be fairly straightforward because most levels inherit from their parent objects. No fine-grained permissions are required, easing administrative overhead.

Fine-grained permissions

Permissions in the series of objects shown in Table 2-3 are more complex because the document libraries in the FieldGroup and ManagementTeam sites now have documents that must be individually secured.

TABLE 2-3 Fine-grained permissions

Securable Object	Description	Permissions
Intranet	Intranet home page	Unique
Intranet/ManagementTeam	Sensitive group	Unique
Intranet/ManagementTeam/DocLibrary	Sensitive and nonsensitive data	Inherited; employee surveys must be individually secured
Intranet/NewsArticles	Intranet news	Inherited
Intranet/NewsArticles/DailyUpdates	Nonsensitive data	Inherited
Intranet/FieldGroup	Field team site	Inherited
Intranet/FieldGroup/DocumentLibrary	Sensitive and nonsensitive data	Inherited, but client documents must be individually secured

At first, this would not seem to be much of a problem. A new sensitive document (bonus structure or client document) could be individually secured, right? Absolutely; but the problem occurs when the document isn't secured properly or permissions for that series of documents change.

> **IMPORTANT** It is important to remember that Search in SharePoint 2016 is pervasive. Unless it has been configured to do otherwise, Search indexes all the documents in the farm; only the Search result is trimmed. When users search for a keyword, their permissions level is checked; if a sensitive document (say, an executive's payroll and bonus structure) were unsecured and the user searches for the word *"performance,"* Search would dutifully return this document in the query result, thus revealing sensitive information.

More in-depth details for implementing permission levels and inheritance are provided in the section "Manage site and site collection security" later in this chapter.

Plan and configure anonymous access

After a web application zone has been configured to enable anonymous authentication, the site owners within that application can then decide what level of authorization to grant to anonymous users.

Enabling anonymous access to a site

Enabling anonymous access to a site enables users to view the site without being challenged for a user name and password combination. All subsites, lists, and libraries that are configured to inherit permissions enable this level of access as well.

Anonymous site access is configured through the Site Permissions interface. Just click the Anonymous Access icon to begin the process (Figure 2-9).

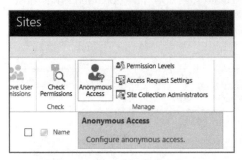

FIGURE 2-9 Anonymous Access icon

EXAM TIP

If the Anonymous Access icon does not appear in the Manage Permissions interface, anonymous access has not been enabled at the web application level.

Control of which items can be accessed anonymously is shown on the next page. By default, nothing can be accessed; you can choose instead to provide access to only lists and libraries or to the entire website (Figure 2-10).

FIGURE 2-10 Anonymous Access settings, with Lists And Libraries selected

Altering this setting (in this example, allowing access to lists and libraries) results in the newly assigned anonymous access being listed on the Manage Permissions page (Figure 2-11).

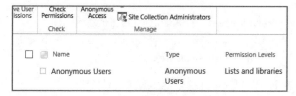

FIGURE 2-11 Anonymous Users Permission Levels on the Manage Permissions page

Enabling anonymous access to a list or library

Enabling anonymous access to a list or library enables users to view only the particular list or library within the site. This means that anonymous users have to know the explicit URL to directly access the list or library content (there is no navigation available).

EXAM TIP

Authentication relies on the presence of a user name and password challenge. Credentials are never requested from anonymous users unless they attempt to access a location that is secured or choose to sign in to the SharePoint farm.

If a library is to be given anonymous access (but the site it is on does not allow anonymous access), then it will need to have its permissions inheritance broken from its parent site. With this change made (and anonymous access granted from a web application and site perspective), the library can be shared from its Permissions page (Figure 2-12).

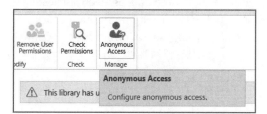

FIGURE 2-12 Anonymous Access icon within the library

Enabling anonymous access at the list or library level allows you to select the permission levels you wish to grant (Figure 2-13).

FIGURE 2-13 Anonymous access permissions

IMPORTANT There are differences in anonymous access behavior for a list versus a library. A list enables an anonymous user to add, edit, delete, or view items; a library enables an anonymous user to only view items (this is a security measure).

Altering this setting (in the example, assigning View access to this library) results in the newly assigned anonymous access being listed on the Manage Permissions page (Figure 2-14).

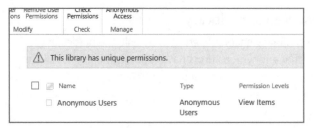

FIGURE 2-14 View Items permissions for Anonymous Users on the Manage Permissions page

Plan web application policies

Web application policies are a way to effectively control access for a web application from a global standpoint. This control can be used to assign or deny permissions to all content within the web application.

There are three web application policies that can be configured on a per-web application basis: user policy, anonymous policy, and permission policy (see Figure 2-15). These policies are configured in the Application Management (Manage Web Applications) section of Central Administration.

FIGURE 2-15 User, Anonymous, and Permission policies for a web application

---

EXAM TIP

Know what the effect will be of altering each of these policies within a SharePoint farm, particularly those that deny users access.

Permission policy

Permission policies are used to specify the permission options available in user policy. You can think of them as permission groups that are scoped at the web application level. Selecting the Permission Policy icon shows the permission policy levels that are created OOB, as shown in Figure 2-16.

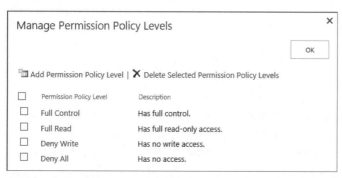

FIGURE 2-16 Permission policy levels

If you need a different policy level than what's available OOB, you can click the Add Permission Policy Level link and create one that meets the needs of your organization.

> **IMPORTANT** As with permission levels within a site collection, it's not a good idea to alter these stock permission levels; consider creating a new one if required.

User Policy

Imagine that you have a legal requirement to enable an auditor access to review all content contained within a web application, regardless of the permissions assigned at the site collection or site levels. This sort of access can be provided within the user policy, granting Read permissions to the auditor at the user policy level for the web application (on a temporary basis, of course).

Within the user policy, you can choose to alter the access of one or more users at the web application level (see Figure 2-17). The users specified can be assigned permissions that you specify within the permission policy for the web application.

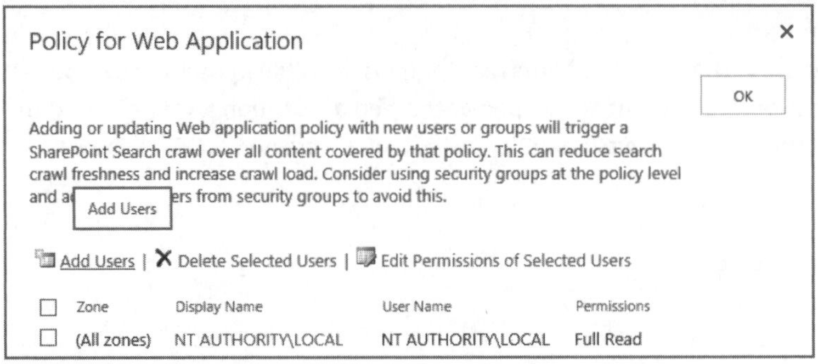

FIGURE 2-17 Managing the user policy for a web application

As indicated by the warning shown in Figure 2-17, changing the policy for a web application *immediately* kicks off a SharePoint search crawl, which could result in diminished performance for your users. Consider waiting until off-peak hours to alter a web application policy.

> **IMPORTANT** By default, the Search crawling account has been granted Full Read access to the web application. This permission level is required for the account to crawl content in each SharePoint web application. It is not recommended to alter this access in any way, including granting the account Full Access, which would expose draft and unpublished documents, which should not appear within Search results.

Anonymous policy

As another example, consider an organization that has a governance policy that states that no unauthenticated users can be allowed to upload or change content within a site, but still has a requirement to provide anonymous access to content on a read-only basis.

In the previous section, you saw that enabling anonymous access allowed site owners to enable access to add, edit, and delete list items, which would be against policy. By using the anonymous policy, you can choose on a zone-by-zone basis whether anonymous users can be prevented from writing changes across a web application (Deny Write) or whether they have any access at all (Deny All). These options are shown in Figure 2-18.

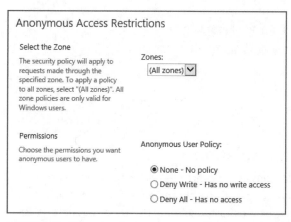

Anonymous Access Restrictions

Select the Zone

The security policy will apply to requests made through the specified zone. To apply a policy to all zones, select "(All zones)". All zone policies are only valid for Windows users.

Zones:
(All zones) ▾

Permissions

Choose the permissions you want anonymous users to have.

Anonymous User Policy:

⦿ None - No policy

○ Deny Write - Has no write access

○ Deny All - Has no access

FIGURE 2-18   Managing the anonymous policy for a web application

EXAM TIP

Anonymous access restrictions override any permissions previously granted at the site or list and library level.

Skill: Plan and configure platform and farm security

Securing a SharePoint environment requires a significant amount of coordination between the networking, data, and SharePoint teams at your organization. Configuration efforts vary in scope from altering core settings on your SharePoint web tier servers to altering SQL settings at the data tier, and enabling or disabling firewall configurations at the networking level. All these changes combine to form a more secure SharePoint implementation. Therefore, this skilll focuses on securing the farm from intrusion and data corruption from external sources. In addition, this skill focuses on how to secure the farm from the inside, assigning the appropriate administrative permissions and creating policies that help secure assets contained within the SharePoint infrastructure.

This section covers how to:

- Plan and configure security isolation
- Plan and configure services lockdown
- Plan and configure antivirus settings
- Plan and configure certificate management
- Plan for Kerberos support for service applications
- Plan and configure Information Rights Management

- Plan and configure delegated farm administration
- Plan and configure delegated service application administration
- Plan and configure managed accounts
- Plan and configure blocked file types
- Plan and configure Web Part security

Plan and configure security isolation

SharePoint is positioned in most organizations as the central nexus (or hub) for the presentation and aggregation of business knowledge. Content can be maintained within the SharePoint 2016 farm, or can just as easily be maintained in separate line-of-business (LOB) applications and then presented by SharePoint.

Regardless of the content's original context, the fact that it can be presented in SharePoint has its pros and cons. On the one hand, information that was once stored in distinct, siloed systems is now readily available for use; on the other, information that might have been improperly secured in these disparate systems can be inadvertently exposed.

EXAM TIP

One of the key balances to be struck in defining isolation is between security and utility. Know not only the benefits of each isolation type, but its drawbacks as well.

Security isolation requirements

This, then, is not so much a technical issue as a business process and legal issue. Dependencies such as how your business is organized, who the stakeholders are, and what your business purpose is can have far-ranging effects on the design outcome for your SharePoint farm.

For instance, if the SharePoint system being designed will be used to store medical information, knowledge management processes must be followed to comply with legal mandates. Failure to follow these mandates or to comply with auditing requirements could result in monetary and licensing penalties.

Even if your business does not have to comply with a heavy regulatory burden, you probably don't have to go that far within your business to find reasons for considering security isolation. If you have employees, trade secrets, legal, or other boundaries, you might want to consider these design factors:

- **Farm architecture** Do you require more than one SharePoint farm to fully segregate the presentation of your data? Are there legal requirements for separating the data stores that support your SharePoint farm?

- **Web application layout**   Legal, auditing, and human resources departments might require the creation of separate application pools for the appropriate segmentation of data.

- **Creating more than one search application**   Your business could be penalized for exposing information via search that is improperly secured. Recall from Chapter 1 that data loss prevention (DLP) searches are quite effective in reviewing your farm for content that is sensitive.

Physical isolation

In highly secure environments, you might want to secure a particular SharePoint farm at a separate site. This SharePoint site would participate in business operations, but would probably maintain its own web, application, and data tier servers.

Due to the nature of the data being stored in this environment, disaster recovery to a remote location might be required, making this environment immediately available in the case of a business continuity event. These events range in scope from an extended network outage event (in which the data services provider experiences a large-scale outage) to a flat-earth event (in which the site no longer exists or is irreparably damaged for the foreseeable future).

From an Information Rights Management point of view (covered later in this chapter), this environment should be configured to restrict rebroadcast (email) and hard copy (printouts) for most users, requiring that auditing be fully enabled to track access to the data.

Users accessing this environment would likely be required to provide multiple layers of authentication, and this environment would be heavily secured from both physical and virtual (networking) points of view.

Service application isolation

SharePoint 2010 introduced the idea of service applications, which were the direct replacement for shared service providers. Each service application provides a connection (or proxy) that can be used by a web application to "subscribe" to the functionality provided by the particular service application.

A common example of this isolation is the separation of search information. Users who are privy to sensitive information, such as salaries and personal identification information, still require the use of Search. In fact, Search might be the key mechanism with which they can get work accomplished.

Creating a different search application for these folks enables them to use a particular search index in a web application without the exposure risk associated with sharing a search application with other users in the farm.

Application pool isolation

An application pool can be used to host one or more URLs within a SharePoint environment. Each application pool can be configured to run as a distinct service account, meaning that you can allow this application to participate in the farm and still be compliant with many regulatory requirements.

This type of isolation is particularly useful in environments in which the application pool retains credentials from and access to sensitive line of business (LOB) systems on premises and in the cloud.

Web application and zone isolation

A distinct web application starts with a single URL, presented in the default zone. It is possible to extend this web application up to four more times, each time assigning a new URL and zone.

With zones now defined, the authentication mechanism for each zone in the web application can be chosen. Additionally, web application policies can be specified that will allow for administrative control over user access in each zone.

Data isolation

If supporting multiple physical environments is not feasible (or possible) within your organization, you might have to support distinct data tiers. Separating these data tiers could enable distinct teams to support environments that are more sensitive or require a higher level of availability.

Data isolation is particularly applicable to environments in which service level agreements and recovery time objectives differ based on the type of data being accessed from within a single SharePoint farm.

> **NEED MORE REVIEW?** Security isolation is applicable at every level of a SharePoint design; both logical and physical considerations must be made to tailor the implementation to a particular need. In-depth coverage of logical architectures is provided in the TechNet article "Plan logical architectures for SharePoint 2013" at *https://technet.microsoft.com/library/ff829836.aspx*. Additionally, technical diagrams for logical architectures can be found in the TechNet article "Technical diagrams for SharePoint 2013" at *https://technet.microsoft.com/library/cc263199(v=office.15).aspx#architecture*.

Plan and configure services lockdown

As the SharePoint Server platform has matured, it has become better suited for use not only as an intranet and extranet platform, but also for Internet use. The array of publishing features, ease of use, and scalability present in the platform provide a versatile website experience.

SharePoint has become a bigger security target as a result of this exposure and popularity. With detailed documentation readily available describing all of SharePoint's components and how they interact with one another, it falls to the administrator to secure Internet-facing SharePoint sites from external attacks.

Using the Limited-Access User Permission Lockdown Mode feature

When configuring a SharePoint Server site for access via the Internet, you will need a mechanism for effectively locking down the SharePoint site. In this case, locking down SharePoint just means that users in a "limited access" role will be unable to access application pages, thus minimizing the attack footprint on a SharePoint site.

Fortunately, there is a feature developed specifically for this task, called the Limited-Access User Permission Lockdown Mode, available in both SharePoint 2016 and in SharePoint Online. By using this feature, you can allow your authenticated users to log on to a SharePoint site while still securing application pages in your environment.

EXAM TIP

If you decide to configure lists and libraries for anonymous access, you might run into a situation in which anonymous users cannot access lists and libraries, even though the correct permissions have been granted at the site or list and library level. This situation usually occurs when an administrator has activated the Limited-Access User Permission Lockdown Mode feature. This feature is a prerequisite for other features (such as the Publishing feature). If you need to share a site with this feature enabled, make sure to share individual files (not folders), or the entire site collection or subsite.

Be familiar with how to enable and disable this feature from the site collection and via PowerShell.

Plan and configure antivirus settings

Most organizations deploy antivirus software to their client workstations; some also apply server-specific antivirus software to their back-end systems as an extra protective measure. As one of these back-end systems, SharePoint 2016 provides for integration of third-party antivirus software and its configuration within the Central Administration website.

SharePoint presents an interesting challenge to the designers of antivirus software because documents uploaded to a SharePoint instance are not directly stored on a file system; instead, they are stored within SQL tables as a Binary Large Object (BLOB).

The direct manipulation of SharePoint databases from SQL is not supported; this prevents the direct scanning of SharePoint content databases. Instead, Microsoft provides a SharePoint Virus Scan (VS) API, which enables third-party software to interact with SharePoint content databases.

Standard antivirus software typically scans documents in two ways:

- As a document is being copied to the system, it is checked for evidence of any malicious code.
- The file system is scanned on a periodic basis to ensure that all existing documents remain free of malicious code.

SharePoint allows for similar functionality via third-party antivirus solutions:

- As a document is being uploaded to or downloaded from SharePoint, it can be checked for evidence of any malicious code.
- Existing files contained within SharePoint content databases can be scanned on a periodic basis to ensure that all existing documents remain free of malicious code.

Implementing SharePoint antivirus solutions

Configuring virus scans for your SharePoint installation is a fairly straightforward process, unchanged from SharePoint 2013. Few options require configuration (shown in Figure 2-19), most of which have to do with controlling the performance impact of antivirus scans within your farm.

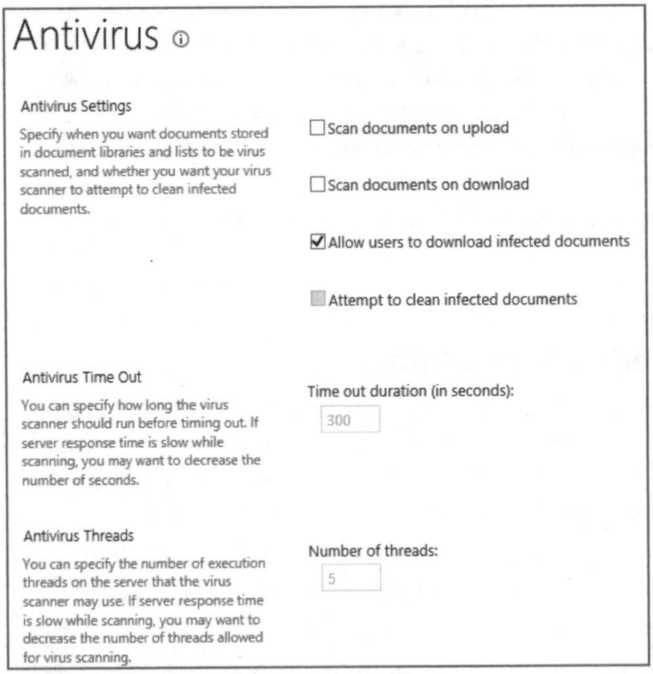

FIGURE 2-19 SharePoint antivirus settings

On the Antivirus page within Central Administration, Security, you can control three major settings:

- **Antivirus Settings**   Control when documents are scanned (on upload or download), whether users can download infected documents, and whether or not the antivirus solution should attempt to clean infected documents.
- **Antivirus Time Out**   Control how long (in seconds) the virus scanner should run before timing out.
- **Antivirus Threads**   Control the number of execution threads on the server that the virus scanner can use.

The Allow Users To Download Infected Documents check box is selected by default, and enables users to download infected documents; this setting is most often enabled to trouble-shoot virus-infected documents already in SharePoint BLOBs within a content database. It is recommended that when you enable an antivirus solution (for upload, download, or both), you clear this check box until required.

The Attempt To Clean Infected Documents check box enables the third-party antivirus solution to clean infected documents automatically. Bear in mind that, if this sufficiently changes a file within a content database (particularly one that has been customized from its template), the file might need to be replaced from a backup with an uninfected copy, should the cleaning be ineffective.

When configuring the Antivirus Time Out Duration setting, you can specify the amount of time that can be spent before the virus scanner times out (the default setting is 300 seconds). Decreasing this setting can result in a performance increase in a slower SharePoint environment, as scanning documents can be resource intensive.

The Antivirus Threads section is somewhat related to the Antivirus Time Out Duration section, in that the number of threads (5 by default) indicates the number of processing resources that are spent on antivirus processing. As with the time out duration, decreasing this setting can also result in a performance increase in a slower SharePoint environment.

EXAM TIP

SharePoint-aware virus scanning software should be installed on all front-end servers within the farm; failure to do so causes the antivirus settings within Central Administration to be ineffective.

Plan and configure certificate management

Up to this point, the use of certificates in a SharePoint farm has been largely optional. In many installations, SharePoint farms were intranet-facing, Central Administration was not configured by using SSL, connectivity between servers was not encrypted, and no external services were required (Azure, SharePoint Store).

This situation has changed dramatically. SSL certificates are being used for many different configurations, including:

- Internal and external client connectivity
- Connections between environments (Exchange, SharePoint, Skype for Business) via OAuth
- Connections between SharePoint and Office Online Server/Office Web Apps
- Connections to Microsoft Azure Workflow Manager

In the case of external client connectivity, you will most likely purchase a certificate from a well-known SSL certificate provider; but in the other cases, you need to know the essentials for exporting, copying, and importing SSL certificates correctly.

EXAM TIP

Know the different types of certificates that are required to secure interfarm communications and how to generate each type.

In the following example, you will interact with the certificates used by two SharePoint farms as the relationship between them is established. This example shows you how to export and import both root and security token service (STS) certificates in an interfarm setting.

Setting up for the trust creation

A trust relationship must be established between SharePoint farms that share service application functionality. In this relationship, one SharePoint farm (the publisher) publishes a service application that can then be consumed by a different SharePoint farm (the consumer).

This relationship is established in a secure fashion via the use of three distinct certificates:

- A root certificate, which is exported from the consuming farm.
- An STS certificate, which is exported from the consuming farm.
- Another root certificate, which is exported from the publishing farm.

Exporting a root certificate (consuming farm)

Logging in to what will be the consuming farm, we begin the process of exporting the root certificate via PowerShell and the Get-SPCertificateAuthority cmdlet, exporting (in this case) to C:\ConsumingFarmRoot.cer:

```
$rootCert = (Get-SPCertificateAuthority).RootCertificate
$rootCert.Export("Cert") | Set-Content "C:\ConsumingFarmRoot.cer" -Encoding byte
```

Running the Get-SPCertificateAuthority cmdlet by itself will return the certificate details, including an expiration date that is set far in the future (Figure 2-20).

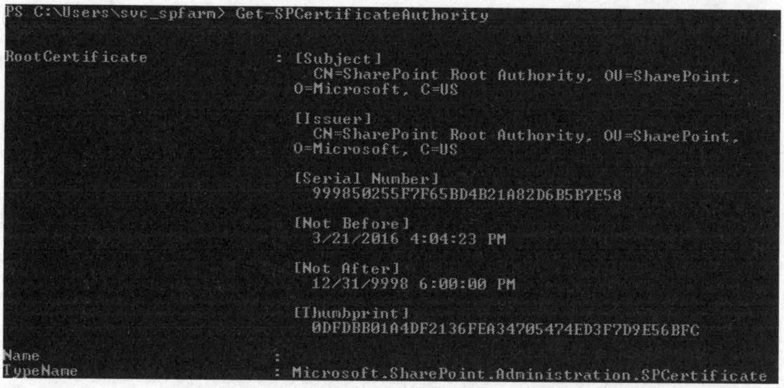

FIGURE 2-20 Partial details of the SharePoint root certificate (consuming farm)

Exporting an STS certificate (consuming farm)

Next up is exporting the STS certificate, again from the consuming farm. As with the root certificate, this certificate can be exported by using Windows PowerShell 3.0, this time with the Get-SPSecurityTokenServiceConfig cmdlet; we'll export it to C:\ConsumingFarmSTS.cer:

```
$stsCert = (GetSPSecurityTokenServiceConfig).LocalLoginProvider.SigningCertificate
$stsCert.Export("Cert") | Set-Content "C:\ConsumingFarmSTS.cer" -Encoding byte
```

Exporting a root certificate (publishing farm)

Finally, we'll retrieve another root certificate, this time from the publishing farm. The process of exporting the root certificate on the publishing farm is identical to that on the consuming farm (with the exception of the file name, of course). We'll export the certificate to C:\PublishingFarmRoot.cer:

```
$rootCert = (Get-SPCertificateAuthority).RootCertificate
$rootCert.Export("Cert") | Set-Content "C:\PublishingFarmRoot.cer" -Encoding byte
```

Preparing to establish the trust

To prepare for establishing the S2S farm trust:

- Copy the *ConsumingFarmRoot.cer* and *ConsumingFarmSTS.cer* files from the consuming farm to the publishing farm.
- Copy the *PublishingFarmRoot.cer* file from the publishing farm to the consuming farm.

Establishing the trust

Establishing the S2S farm trust is a three-part process. First, we'll create a trusted root authority on the consuming farm, then we'll establish the trust from the publishing farm, and finally, we'll create a trusted service token issuer.

CREATING A TRUSTED ROOT AUTHORITY (CONSUMING FARM)

Establishing the trust requires that we first create a new trusted root authority on the consuming farm, by using the publishing farm's root certificate and the New-SPTrustedRootAuthority cmdlet. To create the new trusted root authority called "PublishingFarmRA":

```
$trustCert = Get-PfxCertificate "C:\PublishingFarmRoot.cer"
New-SPTrustedRootAuthority "PublishingFarmRA" -Certificate $trustCert
```

Confirm the creation of the trusted root authority by using the Get-SPTrustedRootAuthority command.

CREATING A TRUSTED ROOT AUTHORITY (PUBLISHING FARM)

Next, we'll need to create a new trusted root authority, this time on the publishing farm; this requires that we use the consuming farm's root certificate and the New-SPTrustedRootAuthority cmdlet. We'll call the new trusted root authority "ConsumingFarmRA":

```
$trustCert = Get-PfxCertificate "C:\ConsumingFarmRoot.cer"
New-SPTrustedRootAuthority "ConsumingFarmRA" -Certificate $trustCert
```

Confirm the creation of the trusted root authority by using the Get-SPTrustedRootAuthority command.

CREATING A TRUSTED SERVICE TOKEN ISSUER ON THE PUBLISHING FARM

The last step in this process is to create a trusted service token issuer (establishing the trust), importing the STS certificate from the consuming farm. We'll call the token issuer "ConsumingFarmSTS".

```
$stsCert = Get-PfxCertificate "c:\ConsumingFarmSTS.cer"
New-SPTrustedServiceTokenIssuer "ConsumingFarmSTS" -Certificate $stsCert
```

 Quick check

- What certificates do you need to establish a trust between consuming and publishing farms?

Quick check answer

- Three certificates are required for this configuration: A root certificate from the consuming farm, an STS certificate from the consuming farm, and a root certificate from the publishing farm.

Plan for Kerberos support for service applications

Kerberos is often used to secure client-facing web applications in SharePoint farms. Although the infrastructure configuration can be daunting, requiring collaboration with the Active Directory team in your environment, there are several benefits for running in this configuration:

- Kerberos is the strongest integrated Windows authentication protocol, capable of enterprise-grade encryption and mutual authentication between clients and servers.

- Kerberos allows for the delegation of credentials, enabling clients to authenticate into an environment and then allow that environment to connect to other servers or services on their behalf.

- Kerberos heavily reduces the amount of network authentication traffic to AD DS domain controllers.

> **NEED MORE REVIEW?** Kerberos requires a certain amount of focus to properly configure; it is quite easy to misunderstand the relationship between clients, servers, services, delegation types, and other topics. Microsoft has produced several articles that discuss Kerberos, among them the TechNet blog article "Kerberos for the Busy Admin" at *https://blogs .technet.microsoft.com/askds/2008/03/06/kerberos-for-the-busy-admin/*, and the heavily detailed TechNet article "How the Kerberos Version 5 Authentication Protocol Works" at *https://technet.microsoft.com/library/4a1daa3e-b45c-44ea-a0b6-fe8910f92f28*.

In SharePoint 2016, we have the ability to use Kerberos in two ways:

- **Basic Kerberos delegation**   Can cross domain boundaries within the same forest, but cannot cross a forest boundary
- **Kerberos constrained delegation**   Cannot cross domain or forest boundaries, except when using Windows Server 2012 or greater domain controllers (DCs)

Service applications often require Kerberos delegation to allow SharePoint users to access external, non-SharePoint resources. These service applications quickly divide into two groups, depending on the Kerberos delegation required.

Service applications that are less restrictive, supporting either basic or constrained Kerberos delegation, include the following:

- Business Data Connectivity Services
- Access Services
- SQL Server Reporting Services

Other service applications require the translation of claims-based credentials to Windows credentials, and use Kerberos constrained delegation only. These include:

- PerformancePoint Services
- InfoPath Form Services
- Visio Services

Plan and configure Information Rights Management

Active Directory Rights Management Services (AD RMS) protect the intellectual capital of an enterprise. Built on Active Directory, these services enable the author of a document to determine its intended use, and prevent any unauthorized distribution or reproduction of the document's contents. This form of Information Rights Management (IRM) is supported by a server running the AD RMS role.

The RMS client is installed by default along with all the other SharePoint Server 2016 components, making the configuration and integration with RMS that much easier.

When implementing IRM, you have three choices for specifying the location of Windows RMS, found on the Configure Information Rights Management menu beneath the Security section of Central Administration:

- **Do Not Use IRM On This Server** The default selection, this prevents the use of IRM on this server.
- **Use The Default RMS Server Specified In Active Directory** Enable the use of RMS within this SharePoint implementation.
- **Use A Particular RMS Server** This allows you to select a particular RMS server for use with SharePoint Server 2016.

There is an additional selection check box on this page, allowing tenants of this SharePoint farm (in a multitenancy configuration) to configure their own IRM settings (Figure 2-21).

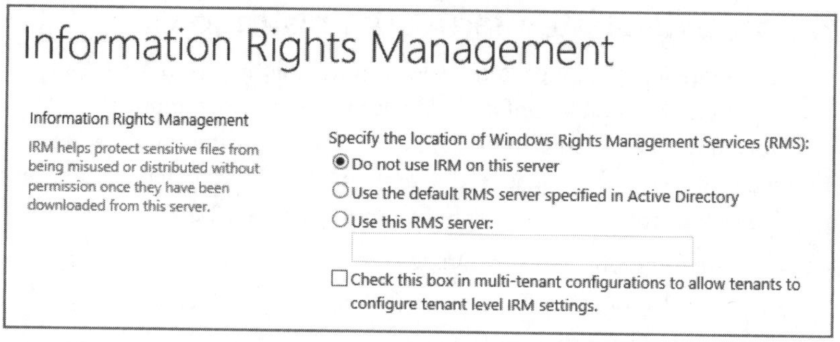

Information Rights Management

Information Rights Management

IRM helps protect sensitive files from being misused or distributed without permission once they have been downloaded from this server.

Specify the location of Windows Rights Management Services (RMS):

◉ Do not use IRM on this server

○ Use the default RMS server specified in Active Directory

○ Use this RMS server:

☐ Check this box in multi-tenant configurations to allow tenants to configure tenant level IRM settings.

FIGURE 2-21 Configuring Information Rights Management options

Selecting the Check This Box In Multi-tenant Configurations To Allow Tenants To Configure Tenant Level IRM Settings check box allows Windows PowerShell cmdlets to be used for enabling, disabling, and configuring IRM for each individual tenant, also allowing for the selection of a desired RMS server.

> **IMPORTANT** Clicking OK at this point (to save your IRM selections), you might receive this error: The Required Active Directory Rights Management Service Client MSIPC.DLL Is Present But Could Not Be Configured Properly. If this is the case, the RMS server is probably not configured to enable the SharePoint web servers to access its ServerCertification. asmx page (found within the *C:\Inetpub\Wwwroot\ADRMS_Wmcs\Certification* file path on the RMS server). Contact your RMS administration team and have them grant both (a) Read and Execute on this file for each web server in your SharePoint farm, and (b) Read and Execute for the AD RMS service group of the RMS server.

Alternately, Windows PowerShell administration for on-premises RMS deployments is carried out via a total of four cmdlets:

- **Get-SPIRMSettings**   Returns the IRM settings
- **Get-SPSiteSubscriptionIRMConfig**   Returns the IRM settings for a specified tenant within the farm
- **Set-SPIRMSettings**   Sets the IRM settings
- **Set-SPSiteSubscriptionIRMConfig**   Sets the IRM settings for a specified tenant within the farm

> **NEED MORE REVIEW?** Although the configuration of RMS within SharePoint 2016 provides no option for the SharePoint admin to control AD RMS integration with AD FS, this is nonetheless an option for larger organizations that regularly exchange sensitive information with partner companies. For more information about how this is configured, review the TechNet article entitled "Deploying Active Directory Rights Management Serviceswith Active Directory Federation Services" at *https://technet.microsoft.com/library/Dn758110 .aspx.*

Plan and configure delegated farm administration

As your SharePoint implementation continues to grow in size, you might soon realize that having only one or two people responsible for farm administration becomes impractical. Rather than employ three shifts of coverage (24 hours) of Tier 3 support, enterprises often choose to delegate some of the core maintenance of SharePoint to the members of a support team, some of whom are available on a 24 hours a day, seven days a week basis.

Setting up delegated administration means two things:

- Less experienced admins become familiar with individual components and can have their responsibilities expanded as their skills mature.
- More experienced admins do not have to be continuously on call to perform rudimentary maintenance tasks.

Up to this point, it is likely that a small group of individuals have had access to the server farm account and they have been using it to accomplish administrative tasks. Although this might not have caused an issue (yet), allowing several people to have access to this credential set is just not a good idea and does not comply with any sort of auditing requirements. Simply put, if everyone logs in with the same account, then it's impossible to determine who makes which changes in the farm.

The SharePoint farm account:

- Has full access to each of the databases in the SharePoint infrastructure (and the permission to create and delete more).
- Serves as the application pool identity for the Central Administration website.
- Is the process account for the Windows SharePoint Services Timer Service.

IMPORTANT With this kind of administrative power, a compromised farm account could quickly result in the corruption or destruction of a SharePoint farm environment. Use of this secured account should be heavily restricted and audited because it has access to literally every component of a SharePoint farm, including securityadmin rights on the SQL instance supporting the farm.

To begin the process of delegating administration, you must first decide whether the user being delegated needs to be a Farm or a Shared Services Administrator.

NEED MORE REVIEW?   Knowing what privileges are assigned at which level of farm administration is a key skill in successfully deploying a SharePoint installation. Information about the administrative permission levels can be found in the TechNet article entitled "Choose administrators and owners for the administration hierarchy in SharePoint 2013" at *https://technet.microsoft.com/library/cc263291.aspx.*

Farm level administrators

Two groups exist that provide permissions to administer the SharePoint Farm:

- The Farm Administrators group
- The Windows Administrators group

Members of the Farm Administrators group have Full Control permissions to all servers in the farm and can be responsible for their general upkeep. Users in this group administer all the items they see in Central Administration: delegating service application permissions; administering managed accounts; and creating, deleting, and editing application pools, databases, and site collections. Backups and restores are possible, even to the extent of backing up content databases without having to interact directly with SQL Server through SQL Server Management Studio (SSMS).

> **IMPORTANT** Members of the Farm Administrators group have no local logon privileges to servers in the SharePoint farm. The extent of their administrative privilege stops at the Central Administrative level, as they also cannot perform activities at the Windows PowerShell level (by default).

Members of the Windows Administrators group on the local server can act as farm administrators, because the BUILTIN\Administrators group is added to the SharePoint Farm Administrators group (by default). These administrators can log on locally to the server, and have console-level access to install binaries to the farm, create new websites, and administer services. As is the case with the Farm Administrators, they have no default access to site content.

SHELL ACCESS

To approximate the permissions held by the original SharePoint farm account, Farm Administrators must also be added to the SharePoint_Shell_Access role via PowerShell. This Shell Admin role can allow the logged on admin to interact with the farm configuration database only, or a combination of the farm configuration, Central Administration content, and individual content databases.

> **NEED MORE REVIEW?** Shell Admins have Farm Administrative permissions plus the ability to interact directly with databases in the farm. By using the Add-SPShellAdmin cmdlet, these users can be selectively given administration over one or more content databases in the farm, making their permissions level roughly equivalent to those held by the SharePoint farm account. For more information, see the TechNet article "Add-SPShellAdmin" at *http://technet.microsoft.com/library/ff607596.aspx*.

EXAM TIP

By default, the local Windows Administrators group on a SharePoint server has administrative privileges to the SharePoint farm. In fact, they have more privileges than Farm Administrators because they can install and configure items from the command line (but are still subject to the Shell Admin limitations). Don't remove this group, but be sure that you know who in your organization is assigned to this group from an access auditing standpoint.

Plan and configure delegated service application administration

As with the farm administration group, each service application can have users added to allow distributed management of functionality within the farm. These users will be assigned one of two roles: Service Application Administrator or Feature Administrator.

Service Application Administrators

Farm Administrators can designate new administrators (known as Service Application Administrators) for individual service applications within a farm. These users cannot create new service applications or perform actions within their service application that affects farm-level change.

For instance, although a Search service application administrator can freely make changes to the functionality present in the service application, he or she cannot make changes to the topology of Search, assigning or removing Search roles to a server in the farm.

> **NEED MORE REVIEW?** For a clearer understanding of how to assign administrators to a particular service application within a SharePoint farm, review the TechNet article entitled "Assign or remove administrators of service applications in SharePoint Server 2016" at *https://technet.microsoft.com/library/ee704546(v=office.16).aspx.*

Feature Administrators

Feature Administrators can be considered a subset of the Service Application Administrators. Essentially, these administrators can only administer a portion of a service application, as given by the Service Application Administrator.

EXAM TIP

Become familiar with the different administrative levels in the more common service applications for delegation, such as the User Profile service application (UPA), Search service, and Managed Metadata Service (MMS).

Plan and configure managed accounts

In early versions of SharePoint (SharePoint 2007 and earlier), it was difficult to keep SharePoint-specific service accounts in compliance with enterprise password standards. Changing service account passwords on a regularly scheduled basis was an incredibly difficult task, often requiring farm outages (even brief ones) to accomplish.

SharePoint 2016 continues the concept of managed accounts first introduced in SharePoint 2010. A managed account is an Active Directory account (usually used as a service account) with a password that is maintained within the bounds of SharePoint itself. If configured to do so, this account is capable of automatically changing its password in accordance with your organization's security governance strategy.

> **IMPORTANT**   Managed service accounts in Active Directory and managed accounts in SharePoint are not the same thing. If your organization uses the managed service account functionality found in Active Directory, it is imperative that SharePoint-specific managed accounts be excluded from this policy, as the account password must be maintained from within the SharePoint farm to function correctly.

A SharePoint managed service account enables you to change the account credentials from within Central Administration. These passwords can be changed either manually (by an administrator) or automatically (by SharePoint) on a timed interval.

If your infrastructure team enables a password change policy for your enterprise, SharePoint managed accounts can be configured to observe these changes, thus keeping your farm in compliance with the enterprise password policy.

Registering a new managed account

Registering a new managed account requires little effort, but a bit of forethought to answer questions like these:

- Should the service account be able to change its own password?
- Is there already a password policy in place, and how far in advance should my farm change the password?
- Should the Farm Administrators receive advance notice of this change, and when should they be notified?

With the answers to these questions, you are now able to register a new managed account from Central Administration, Security, Register Managed Account. Initially, you will specify credentials (an initial user name and password) for the service account, and then configure the Automatic Password Change settings (Figure 2-22).

The interface for this functionality is a bit cluttered; the Weekly and Monthly options are not for email notifications, but for how often the password should change and what the window of opportunity is for changing the password, in accordance with your governance policies.

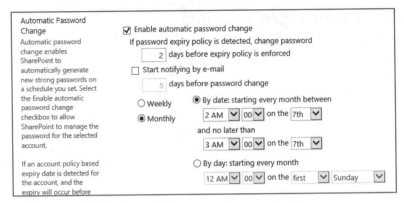

FIGURE 2-22 Automatic Password Change configuration settings

NEED MORE REVIEW? For a clearer understanding of what managed accounts are and how they are able to change their own passwords, see the TechNet article entitled "Configure automatic password change in SharePoint Server 2016" at *https://technet .microsoft.com/library/ff724280(v=office.16).aspx*.

EXAM TIP

Because SharePoint service accounts are also Active Directory accounts, a distributed Active Directory team might not know to avoid automatically changing passwords on your SharePoint service accounts. If this happens, know how to take the new credentials and apply them by editing the managed accounts.

 Quick check

- Your manager has just received a series of requirements for service password governance. She's heard that you have the ability to configure managed accounts and requests that you work with your Active Directory team to allow them to create Active Directory managed accounts. Can you meet the requirements within your SharePoint farm, and should you use Active Directory managed accounts?

Quick check answer

- Active Directory managed accounts cannot be used with SharePoint 2016 farms. Managed accounts in SharePoint are controlled by SharePoint, but are capable of obeying Active Directory-issued password change requirements; as the password nears expiration, the account can be configured to automatically change its own password.

Plan and configure blocked file types

SharePoint 2016 enables an administrator to block certain file types from being uploaded into a SharePoint farm. In fact, there are several file extensions that are already disallowed on the Blocked File Types page of Central Administration.

> **NEED MORE REVIEW?** For the current list of file types blocked by default, review the TechNet article entitled "Manage blocked file types in SharePoint 2013" at *https://technet .microsoft.com/library/cc262496(v=office.16)*.

There are several scenarios that might define a reason for a file type to be disallowed. For instance, if your organization has a media server that streams MP4 video files, you might want to prevent these files from being uploaded into SharePoint document libraries. Certain file types might also be disallowed just because they can contain malicious code (as an example, .exe files are disallowed by default).

Files are blocked by just examining the file extension to determine the type; if you were to change an extension from a forbidden to an acceptable type (from .mp3 to .txt, for instance), the file would be allowed to upload into SharePoint.

The configuration of blocked file types is done on a per-web app basis to accommodate design choices you make for representing data within your SharePoint farm. To add or remove a new blocked file type (Figure 2-23), go to the Security menu of Central Administration and then select Define Blocked File Types from within the General Security section.

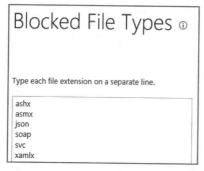

FIGURE 2-23 Blocked File Types page (Central Administration)

On this page, you can do the following:

- Select an extension and delete its entry to unblock it.
- Add a new file extension in and it will be blocked. It is not required to add a new entry in alphabetical order, as it will be reordered automatically.

EXAM TIP

Newly blocked file types will have no effect on existing files already stored within a SharePoint web application. For instance, if there are already .mp3 files present in a given web application, blocking this file type prevents only the addition of new .mp3 files to document libraries within the web application.

Plan and configure Web Part security

Although Web Part security is a topic that heavily affects SharePoint developers, SharePoint administrators should be familiar with the security protocols in place for Web Part development and implementation.

The SharePoint Web Part infrastructure is a direct extension of the ASP.NET Web Part infrastructure; therefore, security guidelines that apply to ASP.NET are applicable to SharePoint development as well, because SharePoint is built on top of ASP.NET.

> **NEED MORE REVIEW?** SharePoint Web Parts represent a significant portion of its functionality, enabling functional elements to be added to a SharePoint webpage by users without requiring any technical expertise. A development primer for learning SharePoint Web Part development can be found on the MSDN site at *http://msdn.microsoft.com /library/ee231579.aspx.*

Security for Web Part Pages is controlled from within Central Administration, Security, General Security. These settings directly control what abilities are given to users within that web application to configure, connect, and modify Web Parts (Figure 2-24).

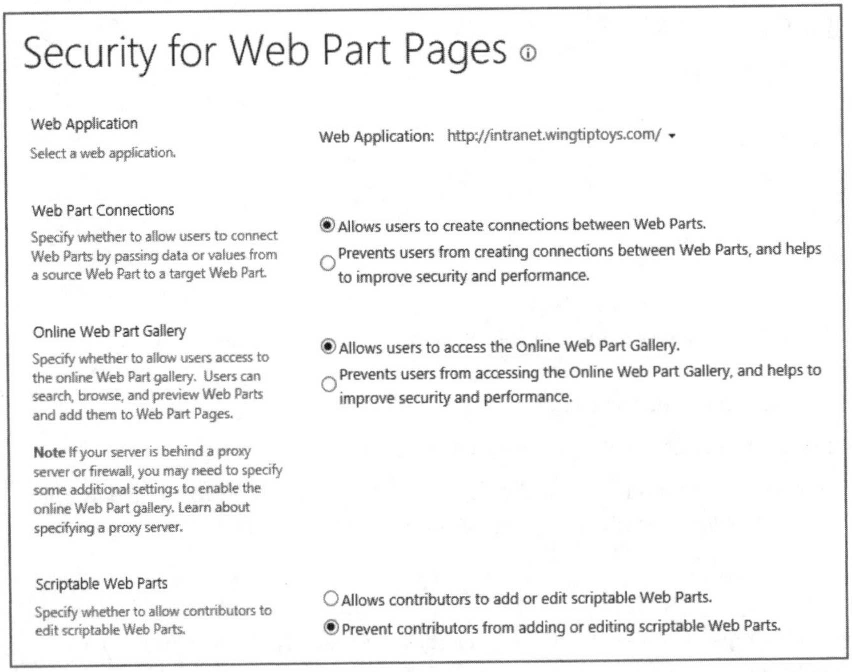

Security for Web Part Pages ⓘ

Web Application
Select a web application.

Web Application: http://intranet.wingtiptoys.com/ ▾

Web Part Connections
Specify whether to allow users to connect Web Parts by passing data or values from a source Web Part to a target Web Part.

● Allows users to create connections between Web Parts.
○ Prevents users from creating connections between Web Parts, and helps to improve security and performance.

Online Web Part Gallery
Specify whether to allow users access to the online Web Part gallery. Users can search, browse, and preview Web Parts and add them to Web Part Pages.

● Allows users to access the Online Web Part Gallery.
○ Prevents users from accessing the Online Web Part Gallery, and helps to improve security and performance.

Note If your server is behind a proxy server or firewall, you may need to specify some additional settings to enable the online Web Part gallery. Learn about specifying a proxy server.

Scriptable Web Parts
Specify whether to allow contributors to edit scriptable Web Parts.

○ Allows contributors to add or edit scriptable Web Parts.
● Prevent contributors from adding or editing scriptable Web Parts.

FIGURE 2-24 Configuring Security for Web Part Pages

Within the context of administration, SharePoint Web Part security can be configured in three ways:

- Connections between Web Parts can be allowed or disallowed.
- Access to the Online Web Part Gallery can be allowed or disallowed.
- Web Parts that host JavaScript can be allowed or disallowed.

EXAM TIP

Security for Web Part Pages is assigned on a *per-web application* basis. There are no exceptions to these settings in the affected web application, so work with your user base and consider carefully which are and are not needed before making any changes.

Web Part Connections

This selection just allows users (by default) to establish connections between Web Parts. Although this is an integral part of Web Parts, allowing users to do things like retrieve information in one Web Part and then use another Web Part to actively filter the content returned, this functionality might not be suitable for sites like a publishing portal, and so on. A page hosting significant numbers of these connections can have a diminishing effect on the performance of the site.

Online Web Part Gallery

This selection (allowed by default) is a legacy component carried over from earlier versions of SharePoint, and is provided for backward compatibility. The Online Web Part Gallery was a precursor to today's SharePoint App Store; although primitive by comparison, it did have a series of useful Web Parts that were hosted by Microsoft.

IMPORTANT If you haven't heard of a need for this gallery, or you aren't upgrading a very old installation of SharePoint, you can safely disable this gallery. In fact, from a security and a performance standpoint, preventing access to this gallery is recommended.

Scriptable Web Parts

This selection (disabled by default) controls the ability of users to insert JavaScript into Web Parts. It is important to evaluate whether your users should be able to add JavaScript to a SharePoint site versus adopting a more formal development of those requirements. Altering this setting applies to all scriptable Web Parts in the pertinent web application.

Skill: Create and configure a User Profile service application (UPA)

The User Profile service application (UPA) is a collection of databases and functionality focused on individual users in a SharePoint 2016 installation. This functionality can be limited in scope to a single farm or made available to multiple SharePoint farms in the enterprise.

This service application is used to provide user profiles, profile synchronization with enterprise directory services, audiences, the My Site host and individual My Sites, and social notes and tagging.

> **This section covers how to:**
> - Configure a UPA application
> - Configure social permissions
> - Plan and configure sync connections of MIM 2016 synchronization
> - Configure profile properties
> - Configure claims integration with UPA

Configure a UPA application

Configuring the UPA can be accomplished from either the Central Administration interface or Windows PowerShell cmdlets. Both configurations result in a series of three databases that are created along with the service application:

- **Profile database** Stores information about users, such as a profile picture, the organization the users belong to, and so on.
- **Social database** Stores social tags and notes associated with individual users' profile IDs.
- **Synchronization database** Stores configuration and staging data for use when profile data is being synchronized with directory services such as Active Directory.

> **NEED MORE REVIEW?** For a better understanding of the different databases used in SharePoint 2016, review the TechNet article entitled "Database types and descriptions in SharePoint Server 2016" at *https://technet.microsoft.com/library/cc678868(v=office.16) .aspx*.

Configuring the UPA from Central Administration

Configuring the UPA from Central Administration will try to automatically associate the UPA with the default proxy group of the farm, and requires that you specify values for:

- Naming the UPA and specifying its Application Pool and Credentials.

- The Server, Name, Authentication Type, and Failover Server (mirroring only) for the Profile, Synchronization, and Social Tagging databases.
- The My Site Host URL and Managed Path.
- The Site Naming format, and whether or not to resolve naming conflict automatically.
- The Default Proxy Group.
- Yammer Integration (choosing whether to use Yammer or on-premises SharePoint social functionality for social collaboration).

Configuring the UPA from Windows PowerShell

Configuring the UPA from Windows PowerShell requires the use of two Windows PowerShell cmdlets:

- **New-SPProfileServiceApplication**   Enables you to specify the service application pool name and databases that you want to use for the new service application.
- **New-SPProfileServiceApplicationProxy**   Enables you to create a service application proxy or connection for use with the service application; this proxy is usually associated with the default proxy group.

EXAM TIP

Know how to specify a proxy group (including the default proxy group) in Windows PowerShell for a new service application.

Configure social permissions

As in previous versions, a fully configured installation of SharePoint 2016 automatically provides full use of the personal and social features to everyone in the organization. These features are broken into three major permissions sets that can be assigned to Active Directory groups:

- Create Personal Site (required for personal storage, newsfeed, and followed content)
- Follow People and Edit Profile
- Use Tags and Notes

If you want to alter these permissions, you can do so by managing the UPA application itself from Services Applications in Central Administration (Figure 2-25).

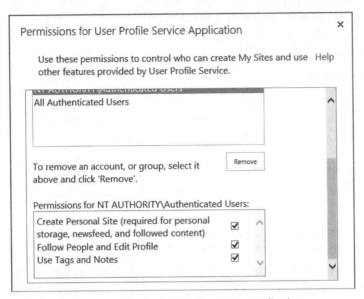

FIGURE 2-25 Permissions for the User Profile service Application

Configure settings for hybrid OneDrive for Business

As your SharePoint 2016 environment moves into a hybrid configuration, one of the first things you might consider deploying to the cloud is OneDrive for Business. This technology can fully replace your on-premises My Site storage functionality, redirecting requests to your Office 365 tenant. If desired, you can also choose to only redirect a portion of your users to the cloud, by specifying an audience to which they will belong (Figure 2-26).

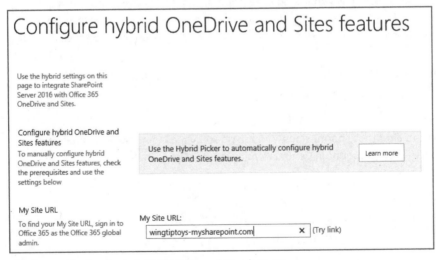

FIGURE 2-26 Configuring hybrid OneDrive and Sites features

Configuration of these settings can be done either automatically or manually. Automatic configuration is done via the Hybrid Picker in SharePoint Online, and requires that the person running the picker be:

- A member of the Farm Administrators group
- A Service Application Administrator (Full Control) for the UPA
- Either an Office 365 Global Administrator or a SharePoint Online Administrator
- Logged in to both Office 365 and SharePoint Server from a server in the SharePoint farm

IMPORTANT It goes without saying that the automatic configuration requires that the SharePoint server have a direct connection to the Internet while this configuration is taking place. If this is not available, you will need to manually configure the hybrid OneDrive and Sites features.

Manual configuration of these features only requires that you be able to determine the URL of your My Sites URL in Office 365, determine if any audiencing is required, and select the appropriate hybrid features. To determine the appropriate My Sites URL, look for the site collection in your Office 365 configuration that looks like *<domain>-mysharepoint.com*.

Plan and configure sync connections of MIM 2016 synchronization

Two mechanisms exist for importing user profiles in SharePoint 2016: Active Directory Import and Microsoft Identity Manager (MIM) server integration. The configuration options for each vary in complexity, and provide different benefits based on your enterprise requirements for profile synchronization.

Active Directory Direct Import

Considered the lighter weight option for importing user profiles, the Active Directory Direct Import option (most often referred to simply as Active Directory Import) requires no configuration on the part of your Active Directory administrator. This operation is read-only and unidirectional in nature, pulling information from Active Directory and populating it in the SharePoint UPA application.

Active Directory Import, although not as complex or as powerful as MIM synchronization, does cause the import to be significantly faster, but at a cost:

- It imports with a single Active Directory forest only; multiforest configurations are not supported.
- It does not import user photos automatically.
- It supports nothing but Active Directory Lightweight Directory Access Protocol (LDAP).

- The lack of bidirectional functionality precludes this option from being useful for adding metadata about users from SharePoint profiles to Active Directory (such as phone numbers, addresses, and so on).

CONFIGURATION OPTIONS

Active Directory Import is familiar to administrators who have configured and maintained profile imports in previous versions of SharePoint Server (except SharePoint Server 2010). An import can be configured from within the Synchronization, Configure Synchronization Connections menu of the User Profile service Application (Figure 2-27).

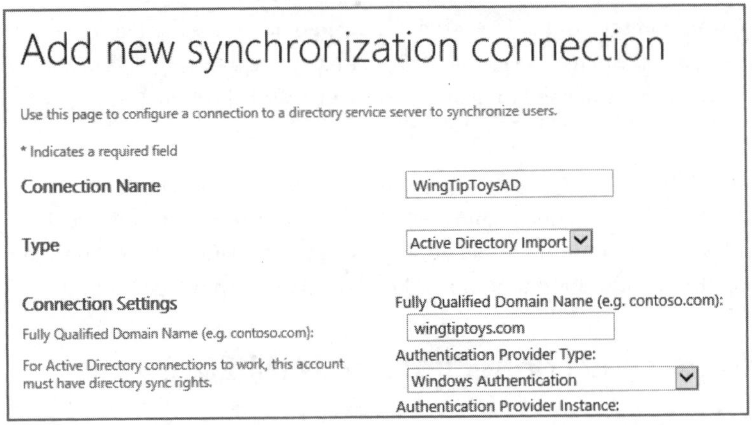

Add new synchronization connection

Use this page to configure a connection to a directory service server to synchronize users.

* Indicates a required field

Connection Name
WingTipToysAD

Type
Active Directory Import ▼

Connection Settings
Fully Qualified Domain Name (e.g. contoso.com):

For Active Directory connections to work, this account must have directory sync rights.

Fully Qualified Domain Name (e.g. contoso.com):
wingtiptoys.com

Authentication Provider Type:
Windows Authentication ▼

Authentication Provider Instance:

FIGURE 2-27 Adding a new synchronization connection (Active Directory Import)

From this page, a new connection can be established with Active Directory, requiring the following information:

- **Connection Name** The friendly name for your Active Directory connection.
- **Type** Active Directory Import (the only option for this configuration).
- **Connection Settings** Requires several different types of information, including:
  - The Fully Qualified Domain Name (FQDN).
  - Authentication Provider Type, either Windows Authentication, Forms Authentication, or Trusted Claims Provider Authentication.
  - Authentication Provider Instance, used for Forms or Trusted Claims Provider Authentication only.
  - The Account name and Password of the account that will retrieve the profile information.
  - The TCP Port (defaults to 389, for LDAP).
  - Options including whether or not to use an SSL-secured connection, Filter out disabled users, and another option for Filtering in the LDAP syntax.
- **Containers** Selecting Populate Containers allows the user to specify which container in Active Directory is to be synchronized in this connection.

Microsoft Identity Manager

MIM 2016 replaces the functionality that had previously been offered by the SharePoint-integrated version of Forefront Identity Manager (FIM). This configuration requires the use of an external MIM server.

Two options exist for integrating MIM with SharePoint 2016: Convert from FIM or New MIM deployment:

CONVERT FROM FIM

Converting from a FIM installation in SharePoint 2013 as part of the upgrade to SharePoint Server 2016 requires two steps to implement: converting the Sync service XML files to a format usable by MIM, and importing the Sync service XML files by using the MIM Synchronization Service Manager. This process is full fidelity, allowing customizations to your sync configuration in FIM to work in MIM 2016, after the conversion has taken place.

To convert the Sync service XML files, use the following process:

- Export the server configuration from Miisclient.exe (your FIM management console in the SharePoint 2013 farm) and save this to a location that will be available to the MIM server.

- Convert the exported file by using the ConvertTo-SharePointEcma2 PowerShell cmdlet on the MIM server.

- Open the Synchronization Service Manager by using the Start-SynchronizationServiceManager cmdlet on your MIM server.

IMPORTING THE CONVERTED FILES

This is the easier of the two tasks. All that is required is to run the MIM Synchronization Service Manager (Miisclient.exe) and then click Import Server Configuration (Figure 2-28).

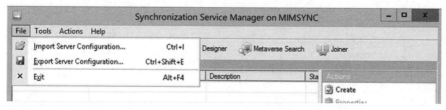

FIGURE 2-28 Importing a server configuration from Miisclient

Connection information (usually just the password) will be required for each management agent used in the configuration of your MIM installation.

NEW MIM DEPLOYMENT

As stated previously, MIM server is installed separately from your SharePoint Server 2016 farm, and can be used to support multiple SharePoint farm installations. Configuring a new deployment of MIM for your organization's SharePoint infrastructure requires only two major steps: installing MIM itself, and installing the SharePoint Management Agent.

> **NEED MORE REVIEW?** Configuring MIM will likely be a joint effort among the SharePoint, SQL, and Active Directory Infrastructure teams. Multiple configuration options are available during the deployment process for MIM, meant for expanding this functionality beyond a single server. Detailed configuration for both upgrading and installing MIM server (specifically pertaining to SharePoint 2016) can be found in the UserProfile.MIMSync ReadMe file on GitHub at *https://github.com/OfficeDev/PnP-Tools/tree/master/Solutions /UserProfile.MIMSync* and in the TechNet article "Deploy a new Microsoft Identity Management (MIM) server for User Profile Sync in SharePoint 2016" at *https://technet .microsoft.com/library/mt637055(v=office.16).aspx*.

Configure profile properties

The UPA application functionality is highly extensible; everything from custom code to Business Connectivity Services (BCS) can be used to both input and output information from this component. As part of this extensibility, profile properties can be altered (and even added), providing much more detail about users in the enterprise.

Properties in a user profile

There are dozens of properties that describe each user in SharePoint 2016; information contained in these properties varies in scope from system-required fields (security identifier [SID], account, claims, and other pieces of information) to more user-friendly metadata about users, such as their names and phone numbers. A sample user profile is shown in Figure 2-29.

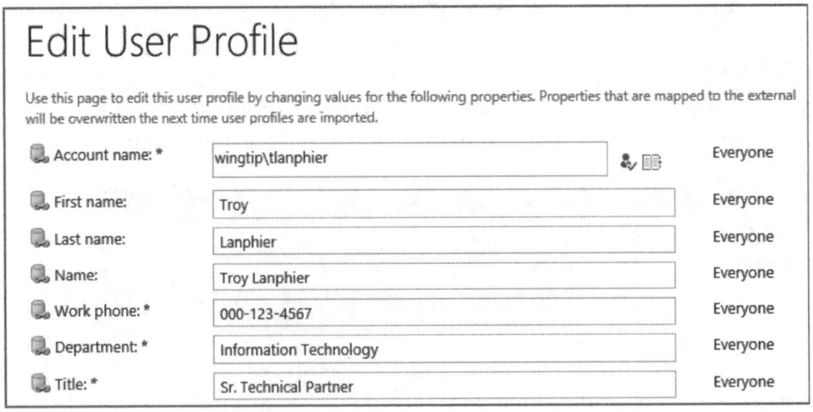

FIGURE 2-29 User profile properties

In this profile, you can see the following:

- Property fields (Name, Work Phone, Department, and so on)
- Active Directory mappings (indicated by the cylinder and link icon)
- Show To field (Everyone, for the fields shown)

This last field, Show To, chooses one of two social levels that can be allowed to view a field (Only Me, Everyone). The selection of a social level enables or disables the field to be shown to people in your organization, and also controls the feed events for that field (a setting of Only Me shuts it off, a setting of Everyone turns it on).

Configuring profile properties

By using the Edit User Profile Property menu item from within Manage User Properties, you can change several property settings for each profile item. Fortunately, because there are dozens of choices and dozens of profile properties, several of these values are already pre-configured OOB, or have been completed as a result of profile import (Figure 2-30).

Manage User Properties

Use this page to add, edit, organize, delete or map user profile properties. Profile properties can be mapped to Active Directory or LDAP compliant directory services. Profile properties can also be mapped to Application Entity Fields exposed by Business Data Connectivity.

New Property | New Section | Manage Sub-types | Select a sub-type to filter the list of properties: Default User Profile

Property Name	Change Order	Property Type	Mapped Attribute	Multivalue	Alias
> **Basic Information**	⌄	Section			
Id	⌃⌄	unique identifier			
SID	⌃⌄	binary			
Active Directory Id	⌃⌄	binary			
Account name	⌃⌄	Person	<Specific to connection>		✔
First name	⌃⌄	string (Single Value)			
Phonetic First Name	⌃⌄	string (Single Value)			
Last name	⌃⌄	string (Single Value)			

FIGURE 2-30 Managing and configuring user properties in Central Administration

Profile properties are also able to be configured independently or for use with Active Directory. If there is a custom property in the Active Directory schema for your organization that makes sense to have in a user profile, then it's fairly straightforward to include this as a custom property in SharePoint.

Profile properties are broken into sections:

- Basic Information (name, work phone, title)
- Contact Information (work email, mobile phone, home phone)
- Details (past projects, skills, interests)

- Delegation (empty by default)
- Newsfeed Settings (email notifications, people I follow)
- Language and Region (time zone, define your work week, and so on)
- Custom Properties (enables you to add new properties)

To alter a profile property, just select Edit from its drop-down menu. Most often, the items you will interact with are the mapping to Active Directory and the Policy Setting, which determines whether a user can change the setting and what the default privacy setting is.

> **IMPORTANT** All of these properties are (or can be) added to the index, and thus become searchable (and security trimmed) within SharePoint, enabling the enterprise to track specific information such as individual certifications, status, and so on about a staff member.

Configure claims integration with UPA

SharePoint farms are often implemented without any need for S2S authentication. Within a single farm, a user is claims authenticated, and these claims have no issues whatsoever being resolved to a specific SharePoint user.

When a SharePoint infrastructure extends beyond the scope of an initial farm, the question of user identity rehydration comes into play. S2S infrastructures allow two SharePoint farms to connect, whether on premises or in the cloud. With this in mind, we must consider how claims integration works in such an arrangement.

Let's take two SharePoint farms as an example. A user is authenticated into the first farm but requires access to the other. The second SharePoint farm server has to accomplish two tasks to provide the resource:

- It has to be able to resolve the request to a specific SharePoint user.
- It has to determine the set of role claims that are associated with the user (rehydrate the user's identity).

SharePoint Server 2016 takes claims from the incoming security token and resolves this to a specific SharePoint user by using the UPA. To rehydrate the user's identity, one of the following four key user attributes must be current in user profiles:

- The Windows Security Identifier (SID).
- The Active Directory Domain Services (AD DS) user principal name (UPN).
- The Simple Mail Transfer Protocol (SMTP) address.
- The Session Initiation Protocol (SIP) address.

> **IMPORTANT** SharePoint expects that only one matching entry will be found for a user in a query based on these attributes. If multiple results are returned, SharePoint will return an error stating that multiple user profiles were found.
>
> Both user profile and relevant group memberships must be mapped for Windows Claims to work properly, as both are used to provide access to a resource.

Skill: Manage site and site collection security

Securing a SharePoint installation can involve several different configuration levels. These levels vary in complexity from just granting or removing access to a single item to decid-ing what applications should be run on a web application or what content can be displayed within a site.

This section covers how to:

- Manage site access requests
- Manage app permissions
- Manage anonymous access
- Manage permission inheritance
- Configure permission levels
- Configure HTML field security

Manage site access requests

As new users are added to the business, site collection administrators are not always kept informed of who needs access to a site or site collection. Additionally, permissions are not always granted to the appropriate sites.

Most often, new users network with their peers to find out what components of the SharePoint environment are used for their work. When users visit a site to which they do not have permissions, they often see the message shown in Figure 2-31.

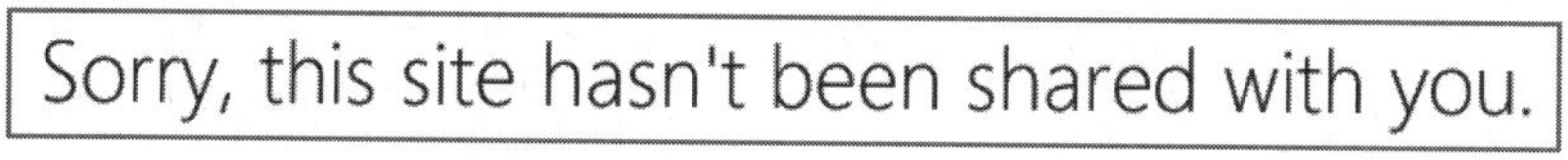

Sorry, this site hasn't been shared with you.

FIGURE 2-31 We truly are sorry …

Although this message is concise and to the point, it is not of much value to the person who needs access to the site: no phone number, no IM, not even an email address to figure out just exactly who should be contacted to grant access to the site.

Fortunately, SharePoint administrators can make the user's interaction with this site a bit more practical by enabling access requests for the site, resulting in the user being able to ask permission to access the site.

Enabling site access requests

The first thing that is required for site access requests to work is outgoing email; if this is not yet set up in your farm, you have to set it up before proceeding to configure site access requests.

After the outgoing email is configured, access requests can be configured in Site Settings, Site Permissions, Access Requests Settings (Figure 2-32).

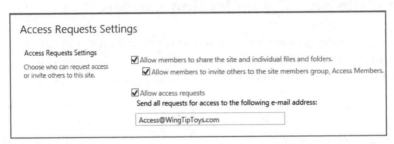

FIGURE 2-32 Allowing access requests from Access Requests Settings

EXAM TIP

Access requests are some of the few email interactions that are not sent directly to a site collection administrator (by default). These email messages are often sent to a group email box because you can choose only a single email address.

Managing site access requests

When a user visits the site now, the lack of permissions presents a different experience (see Figure 2-33).

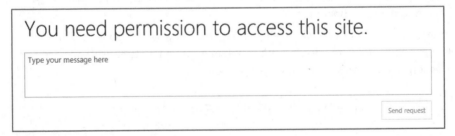

FIGURE 2-33 Sending a message requesting permission for access

An administrator visiting the permissions page for the site sees a pop-up warning (see Figure 2-34).

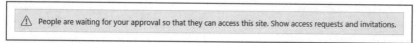
⚠ People are waiting for your approval so that they can access this site. Show access requests and invitations.

FIGURE 2-34 Pop-up for access requests

The admin can either click the link in the pop-up warning or select the Access Requests And Invitations link in Site Settings. The submitted access requests now show in the library and can be acted on (see Figure 2-35).

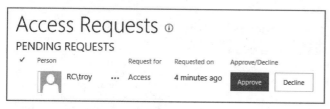

FIGURE 2-35 Pending requests for access

Manage app permissions

Apps from the SharePoint Store can be installed directly to your SharePoint farm. If you've ever installed an app to your phone or tablet device, you are familiar with this process:

1. Find an app that would be useful in your SharePoint environment.

2. Purchase (they are sometimes free), download, and install the app to your environment.

3. Note the permission levels the app is requesting; decide whether to trust the app to possess those permissions.

4. Use the app on your SharePoint site.

EXAM TIP

Depending on the security considerations for your SharePoint farm, you might want to make the SharePoint Store available for users to view but review and approve any app before it is installed.

App permission requests

When an app is installed to your SharePoint farm, it requests one of four permission levels available in your farm (shown in Table 2-4).

TABLE 2-4 App permission levels

Permission Request	Description	Permissions Included
Read-Only	Enables apps to view pages, list items, and download documents	View Items Open Items View Versions Create Alerts Use Self-Service Site Creation View Pages
Write	Enables apps to view, add, update, and delete items in existing lists and document libraries	Read-Only permissions, plus: Add Items Edit Items Delete Items Delete Versions Browse Directories Edit Personal User Information Manage Personal Views Add/Remove Personal Web Parts Update Personal Web Parts
Manage	Enables apps to view, add, update, delete, approve, and customize items or pages within a website	Write permissions, plus: Manage Lists Add and Customize Pages Apply Themes and Borders Apply Style Sheets
Full Control	Enables apps to have full control within the specified scope	All permissions

App permission request scopes

An app permission request can be assigned at any of four possible scopes within your SharePoint farm:

- SPSite defines the app permission request scope as a SharePoint 2013 site collection (site).
- SPWeb defines the app permission request scope as a SharePoint 2013 website (web).
- SPList defines the app permission request scope as a SharePoint 2013 list.
- Tenancy defines the app permission request scope as a tenancy.

These scopes are hierarchical in nature: If an app is assigned permissions at one level, all levels that inherit from the parent also provide the same permissions. For example, if an app is granted permission to the SPSite scope, it also has the same permissions at the SPWeb and SPList scopes.

Scope types are expressed as uniform resource identifiers (URIs); the first three URIs begin with the *http://sharepoint/content* string. This URI indicates that these permissions are assigned to a content database within a SharePoint farm.

Each scope appends its type to the end of the URI (except Tenancy):

- SPSite appends the */sitecollection/* string to the end of the URI (*http://sharepoint /content/sitecollection/*)

- SPWeb appends the */sitecollection/web* string to the end of the URI (*http://sharepoint /content/sitecollection/web*)

- SPList appends the */sitecollection/web/list* string to the end of the URI (*http:// sharepoint/content/sitecollection/web/list*)

- Tenancy follows the URI structure (*http://<sharepointserver>/<content>/<tenant>/*)

App authorization policies

To use an app requires two distinct permission sets: user and app. Depending on the policy assigned to the app, a policy that designates one or both of these sets must be assigned to the app for it to access a content database.

There are three distinct authorization policies available:

- User and app policy requires that both the permissions of the user and app be evaluated before authorization is granted to the content database.

- App-only policy requires that only the permissions of the app be evaluated before authorization is granted to the content database. This setting is used when the app does not act on behalf of the user.

- User-only policy requires that only the permissions of the user be evaluated before authorization is granted to the content database. This setting is used when users are accessing their own resources.

Manage anonymous access

Anonymous access is controlled at multiple levels within a SharePoint 2013 farm. As previously discussed, a web app must be configured in IIS to allow anonymous access before any site collections, sites, or content within the web application can be allowed to be accessed anonymously.

Enabling anonymous access at the web application level in SharePoint provides no access to any of the content within the web application; it merely allows users to pass through to the web app (anonymous isn't truly authentication, per se, so it bypasses a prompt for user name and password). To actually access content contained within the web app, anonymous access needs to be added at the site collection, site, or list and library level.

Manage permission inheritance

Permission inheritance is a means of simplifying the administration of permissions on a site collection, site, list, or individual item. Instead of having to designate permissions on each and every item, you can configure inheritance (enabled by default) within a site or site collection.

Breaking permissions inheritance

By default, sites inherit their permissions structure from the *site collection* in which they are contained, whereas lists and libraries inherit permissions from the *site* in which they are contained. More often than not, you will find yourself breaking permissions inheritance rather than enabling it.

1. To stop permissions inheritance, select Site Setting, Users And Permissions, and then click the Site Permissions link.

2. Before proceeding, have a look at the permissions—they do not change. When you stop inheriting permissions from the parent, a copy of the permissions is applied directly to the child site.

3. On the ribbon, note the Manage Parent icon, indicating that the permissions that apply to this child site are set at the parent level. Click the Stop Inheriting Permissions icon to break inheritance (see Figure 2-36).

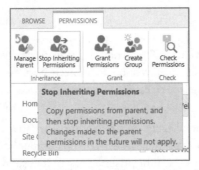

FIGURE 2-36 Stop Inheriting Permissions icon

4. A pop-up window appears, notifying you that you will soon be creating unique permissions for this site and its subsites. Click OK to proceed and set up groups.

5. The next page allows you to set up groups for this newly separated site, and offers you the chance to create new visitors (read privileges), members (change privileges), and owner (full privileges) groups for this site (Figure 2-37).

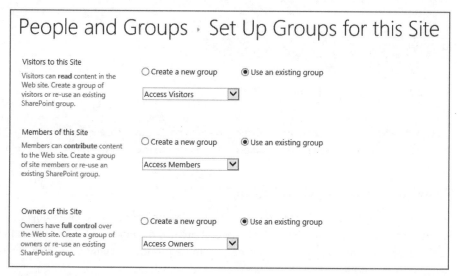

FIGURE 2-37 Setting up new groups

6. You can choose to either create a new group or use existing groups as provided within the site collection, but most often you will create new members and owners, leaving the parent's visitors group (team site visitors) able to read the site.

Deleting unique permissions

At some point in the future, you might decide to reinherit permissions from the parent site. This is done by using the Delete Unique Permissions icon on the Permissions tab of the Site Permissions page.

EXAM TIP

It is very important to note that the act of reinheriting permissions not only affects this site, but also affects all sites beneath this level that inherit permissions from this site. You might inadvertently expose content if you apply these changes incorrectly.

Permissions are reinherited from the Site Permissions link under Site Settings, Users And Permissions. Prior to reverting the permissions to the parent, it's best to have a look at the permissions present (and potentially document them).

When you are ready to delete the unique permissions, select the Delete Unique Permissions icon (Figure 2-38).

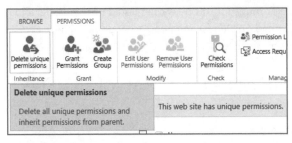

FIGURE 2-38 Deleting unique permissions

> **IMPORTANT** If you created any specific groups as part of the "stop inheritance" process, these groups remain in the site collection until you delete them.

Configure permission levels

Earlier in this chapter, we discussed the inheritance of permissions and showed how these permissions related to groups within a SharePoint site (from a high level). This section takes the discussion step further, showing how each of these groups is assigned a permission level that, in turn, is assigned a group of more granular permissions.

Default permission levels within a SharePoint site aggregate a series of permissions within each site collection; these permission levels can then be assigned to an individual or group. There are several OOB permission levels, including those shown in Table 2-5.

TABLE 2-5 App permission levels

Permission Level	Users and Groups with this Permission Level
Full Control	Have full control.
Design	Can view, add, update, delete, approve, and customize.
Edit	Can add, edit, and delete lists; can view, add, update, and delete list items and documents.
Contribute	Can view, add, update, and delete list items and documents.
Read	Can view pages and list items and download documents.
Limited Access	Can view specific lists, document libraries, list items, folders, or documents when given permissions.
View Only	Can view pages, list items, and documents. Document types with server-side file handlers can be viewed in the browser but not downloaded.

Although these permission levels tend to cover most needs, SharePoint administrators are occasionally called on to alter existing permission levels or configure new permission levels within a site collection.

Adding a new permission level

It is a fairly common request to build a permission level similar, but not identical to, one of the OOB permission levels. In this example, we view and document the existing rights of the Contribute permission level, starting at the top of the site collection.

Begin by viewing the granular permissions present in the Contribute permission level:

1. In Site Settings, under Users And Permissions, click the Site Permissions link, then click the Permissions tab and click the Permission Levels icon and link (see Figure 2-39).

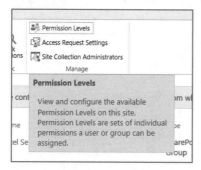

FIGURE 2-39 Permission Levels icon

> **IMPORTANT** If you do not see the Permission Levels icon, you are not at the top site in the site collection.

2. The Permission Levels page displays a series of permission levels. Click the Contribute link to view the individual permissions present.

3. The individual permissions that are present in each permission level are broken into three major groups:

    - **List Permissions**   Control a user's interaction with lists and libraries on the site.
    - **Site Permissions**   Control a user's interaction with the site.
    - **Personal Permissions**   Control a user's personal view of lists and Web Part pages.

Obviously, it might take you a while to document each of these permissions by hand; fortunately, you won't have to. Scrolling down to the bottom of the page and clicking Copy Permission Level allows you to copy this permission level.

In this example, we copy the Contribute permission, but remove the users' ability to delete an item; appropriately enough, we call the new permission level Contribute (No Delete), as shown in Figure 2-40.

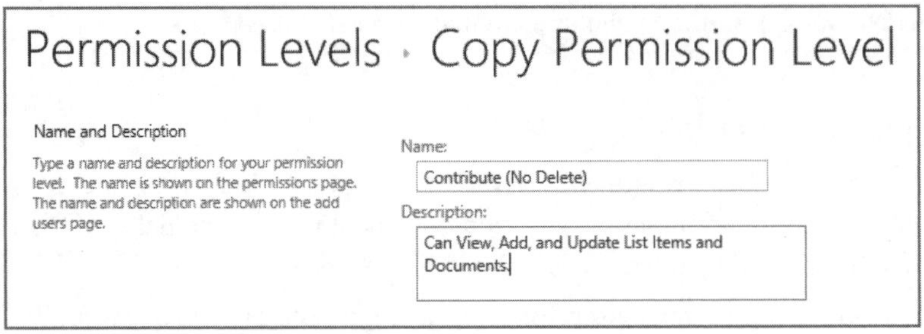

FIGURE 2-40 Copying the Contribute permission level, Contribute (No Delete)

Removing the Delete capabilities present in the original permission level is now just a matter of clearing the Delete Items and Delete Versions permission check boxes (see Figure 2-41).

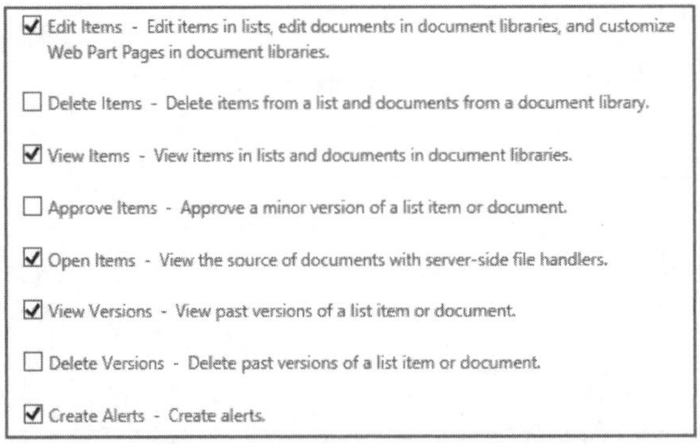

FIGURE 2-41 Delete Items and Delete Versions check boxes cleared

Scrolling to the bottom of the page and clicking Create will commit your changes. Your new permission level is now ready for use (see Figure 2-42).

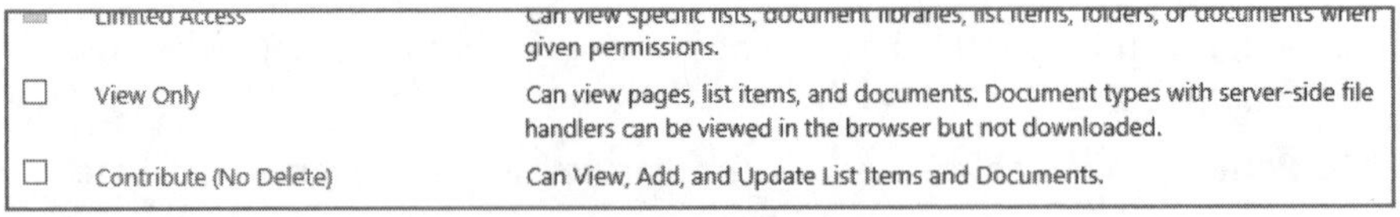

FIGURE 2-42 The new permission level, Contribute (No Delete)

Configure HTML field security

SharePoint 2016 enables you to embed inline frames (iframes) into SharePoint sites that represent external web content. Within Site Settings, as shown in Figure 2-43, you can choose one of three HTML field security levels:

- Do Not Permit Contributors To Insert Iframes From External Domains Into Pages On This Site (default)
- Permit Contributors To Insert Iframes From Any External Domain Into Pages On This Site
- Permit Contributors To Insert Iframes From The Following List Of External Domains Into Pages On This Site (selected for this example)

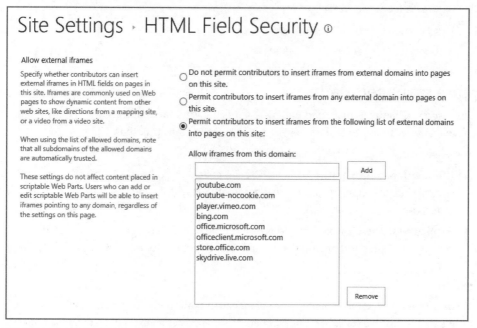

FIGURE 2-43 HTML Field Security options

EXAM TIP

It is possible (although not very likely) to cause a security breach by having an iframe represent content in a site that has been compromised. Choosing to limit your users to a particular subset of external domains is the best way to strike a balance between showing external content and showing none at all.

The last option enables you to determine the domains from which you allow iframes to be chosen. A sample listing of iframes is already chosen for you, including those from YouTube, Vimeo, and Microsoft. You can also add other domains of your choosing.

Skill: Provision and configure web applications

The web applications that support your SharePoint installation are the first component that your users encounter. An incorrectly configured web application can vary in experience from being entirely nonfunctional (misconfigured authentication mechanisms) to being functional but inconsistent (in the case of poorly configured alternate access mappings).

Configuring efforts at this level of the farm implementation form your first effort at maintaining effective security and governance mechanisms.

> **This section covers how to:**
> - Create managed paths
> - Configure alternate access mappings
> - Configure SharePoint Designer settings

Create managed paths

As discussed in Chapter 1, managed paths are a mechanism that enables you to create a uniform navigational structure that relates multiple site collections together.

There are two distinct types of managed paths:

- **Wildcard managed paths**   Enable one site collection to be the "implied" parent of several site collections by using a wildcard path value (for example, *http://URL/path /Site1, http://URL/path/Site2*).

- **Explicit managed paths**   Enable one and only one site collection to be nested directly beneath another within a navigational structure (for example, *http://URL/Site1*).

EXAM TIP

There are a supported maximum number of managed paths per web application (20). Although it is possible to exceed this number, doing so places an extra processing load on the web-tier servers in your farm.

Managed path creation varies based on whether you will be using path-based site collections (PBSC) or host-header site collections (HHSC). Managed paths created for HHSC are defined at the farm level rather than at the web application level, and cannot be created or administered from Central Administration. They are also shared among all HHSCs in the farm; for example, adding /americas as a managed path on *http://intranet.wingtiptoys.com/americas* would also add it to *http://backoffice.wingtiptoys.com/americas*.

Creating managed paths (Central Administration)

Managed paths for path-based site collections (PBSCs) are defined on a per-web application basis and created from Central Administration in a few steps:

1. From the Application Management page, Manage Web Applications, select the web application for which you want to create a managed path. When the ribbon activates, click the Managed Paths icon.

2. The Defined Managed Paths page appears, showing all existing paths. In the Add A New Path section, specify the name of a new managed path (see Figure 2-44).

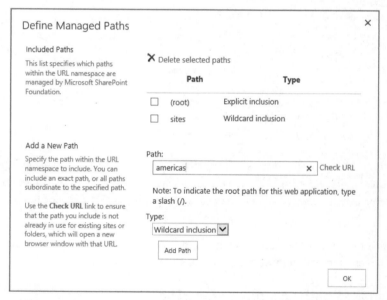

FIGURE 2-44 Creating a managed path

3. Finally, select whether the new link is to be a wildcard inclusion (selected in this example) or an explicit inclusion and then click Add Path.

Remove a PBSC managed path (Central Administration)

Removing a managed path from Central Administration is a fairly simple task, by using the same Define Managed Paths page on which managed paths are created.

> **IMPORTANT** Before removing a managed path, ensure that the site collections nested within it or beneath it have either been moved to a new location or removed altogether.

1. From the Application Management page, Manage Web Applications, select the web application for which you want to create a managed path. When the ribbon activates, click the Managed Paths icon.

2. The Defined Managed Paths page appears, showing all existing paths. Select an existing managed path and click Delete Selected Paths (see Figure 2-45).

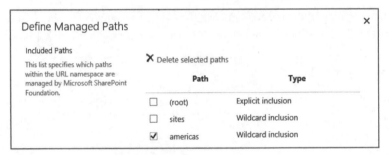

FIGURE 2-45 Deleting a managed path

> **IMPORTANT** When configuring managed paths via the interface, the Add Path button and the Delete Selected Paths link act in the same manner; that is to say, they have no confirmation action. After you have made your selection, that's it: The change is made.

3. The Define Managed Paths page now shows the existing managed paths, with the americas managed path removed. Click OK to close the window.

Create a managed path (Windows PowerShell)

By using Windows PowerShell cmdlets, you can create new managed paths quickly. This Windows PowerShell path creation works for web applications that host both path-based and host-named site collections.

Creating the "americas" managed path in a PBSC web application only requires a couple of lines in PowerShell:

1. Start by assigning a variable for your web application by using the Get-SPWebApplication cmdlet:

```
$webApp = Get-SPWebApplication -identity http://intranet.wingtiptoys.com
```

2. Use the New-SPManagedPath cmdlet with the web application variable to build the managed path (note that if the -explicit switch is not specified, this cmdlet will build a wildcard inclusion):

```
New-SPManagedPath "americas" -WebApplication $webApp
```

Remembering that managed paths for an HHSC web application are defined at the farm level, we find that creating the "americas" managed path would be even easier, requiring only one line of PowerShell (no reference to a web application is required):

3. Use the New-SPManagedPath cmdlet without the web application variable, but with the -hostheader switch (note that if the -explicit switch is not specified, this cmdlet will build a wildcard inclusion).

```
New-SPManagedPath "americas" -HostHeader
```

EXAM TIP

If the web application you are configuring creates PBSCs, don't forget to specify the -WebApplication switch. If the web application you are configuring creates HHSCs, don't forget to specify the -HostHeader switch.

Removing a managed path (Windows PowerShell)

By using Windows PowerShell cmdlets, you can also remove managed paths in two simple steps. This Windows PowerShell path removal works for web applications that host both path-based and host-header site collections.

To remove the "americas" managed path in a PBSC web application also requires a couple of lines in PowerShell:

1. Again, start by assigning a variable for your web application by using the Get-SPWebApplication cmdlet:

```
$webApp = Get-SPWebApplication -identity http://intranet.wingtiptoys.com
```

2. Use the Remove-SPManagedPath cmdlet with the web application variable to delete the managed path:

```
Remove-SPManagedPath -identity "americas" -WebApplication $webApp
```

Removal of the "americas" managed path on an HHSC web application requires only one line of PowerShell (no reference to a web application is required):

1. Use the Remove-SPManagedPath cmdlet without the web application variable, but with the -hostheader switch.

```
Remove-SPManagedPath "americas" -HostHeader
```

> **NEED MORE REVIEW?** Managed path creation and removal is a fairly straight-forward process, unchanged from SharePoint 2013. Refer to the TechNet articles "New-SPManagedPath" at *https://technet.microsoft.com/library/ff607693.aspx* and "Remove-SPManagedPath" at *https://technet.microsoft.com/library/ff607707.aspx* for information about the creation and deletion of managed paths in a SharePoint 2016 implementation.

 Quick check

- You hire a new administrator and assign this admin a task to create a new managed path for a host header web application in your SharePoint farm environment. The admin does not have shell access to the farm. Can they complete the task?

Quick check answer

- Unfortunately, no. Admins must create managed paths for HHSCs via PowerShell; thus, the admin requires shell access to the farm before they can complete this task.

Configure alternate access mappings

Alternate access mappings are deprecated in SharePoint 2016, as they are specifically geared toward path-based site collections (host-named site collections are recommended). Nonetheless, alternate access mappings are still present in SharePoint 2016 to provide backward compatibility, and they are also required to meet the needs of certain hardware-based load balancer and reverse proxy configurations.

Three major activities are involved in the configuration of alternate access mappings in SharePoint 2016:

- Editing public URLs
- Adding internal URLs
- Mapping to external resources

Internal and public URLs

Each alternate access mapping collection has an associated grouping of public URLs, which are associated with internal URLs. Internal URLs are the URL of the web request as it is received by SharePoint, which are then mapped to Public URLs. Public URLs are how SharePoint formats links corresponding to requests that match one of the internal URLs on that zone when returning a response. In other words, it's the base URL that is used on the pages returned to a requesting user.

External resource mappings

External resource mappings enable you to present non-SharePoint content utilizing the alternate access mapping functionality present in SharePoint 2016. This mapping is presented as an alternate access mapping collection at the same peer level as the other alternate access mapping collections within your SharePoint Server 2016 environment.

Configuring SharePoint Designer settings

SharePoint Designer 2013 is a client application that allows for the creation and modification of SharePoint sites, pages, and workflows within a SharePoint 2016 environment. This version of the tool will not be upgraded to a 2016 version, but is fully supported for use in SharePoint Online, SharePoint 2013, and SharePoint 2016 environments.

Administrative control of SharePoint Designer is controlled on a per-web application basis and enables four distinct configuration options:

- Allowing or preventing SharePoint Designer to be used in a given web application.
- Allowing or preventing Site Collection Administrators to detach or customize pages from the site template, which can result in performance loss.

- Allowing or preventing Site Collection Administrators to customize individual master and layout pages, a key requirement for customizing most SharePoint installations.

- Allowing or preventing Site Collection Administrators to inspect and modify the URL structure of their website.

IMPORTANT Each of these options is enabled by default in a newly created SharePoint web application.

Configuration changes for these four options are carried out by selecting Application Management, Manage Web Applications in Central Administration and then selecting the General Settings, SharePoint Designer menu item for an individual web application.

Summary

- Anonymous authentication isn't technically authentication at all, but is an option for SharePoint web applications.

- Connection encryption in SharePoint 2016 does not use SSL 3.0, instead preferring TLS 1.2.

- Identity federation can use AD FS or Azure ACS.

- SharePoint 2016 uses the OAuth 2.0 protocol to establish server-to-server connections; this can happen over HTTPS (default) or HTTP.

- Azure AD Connect has replaced DirSync, FIM+Azure AD Connector, and Azure AD Sync to implement hybrid cloud deployments.

- SMTP outgoing email has to be configured for access requests to work properly.

- Web application policies include user policy, anonymous policy, and permission policy.

- S2S trust relationships require a root certificate from the consuming farm, an STS certificate from the consuming farm, and a root certificate from the publishing farm.

- Managed accounts can be configured to automatically follow a defined password policy, but are not the same as Active Directory managed accounts.

- A User Profile service application has three databases: profile, social, and synchronization. It can be configured to do an Active Directory import only or be configured to integrate with MIM.

- Hybrid OneDrive for Business settings can be configured manually or via the use of the Hybrid Picker.

- One of the following four attributes must be used for the user's identity to rehydrate in a claims integration with UPA: the Windows Security Identifier (SID), the AD DS user principal name (UPN), the SMTP address, or the SIP address.

- App permissions levels include Read-Only, Write, Manage, and Full Control; app permission request scopes include SPSite, SPWeb, SPList, and Tenancy.

- Managed paths for path-based site collections can be created via Central Administration or PowerShell, whereas managed paths for host-header site collections can only be created via PowerShell.

Thought experiment

In this thought experiment, demonstrate your skills and knowledge of the topics covered in this chapter. You can find answers to this thought experiment in the next section.

You are looking to extend your SharePoint farm installation to external users, and are evaluating the different authentication mechanisms for both partners and users who would authenticate by using Google and Windows Live.

Answer the following questions for your manager:

1. What sort of mechanisms could you use if you do not prefer any sort of cloud connection?

2. How might your organization federate with partner organizations?

3. What sort of changes might you need to make to allow trusted party authentication?

Thought experiment answer

1. Users could authenticate by using forms authentication, which would require you to configure an SQL database for the storage of credentials. You could also work with your Active Directory team to set up AD FS, giving external users the ability to log in to accounts that are maintained within your Active Directory infrastructure.

2. Your organization could use Azure AD to authenticate users, either by synchronizing accounts or by using SSO (AD FS). Partner organizations could establish federation through an AD FS trust or preferably could connect to the Azure AD with a trust.

3. Trusted party authentication would assume the use of Azure AD connected to a trusted authentication provider such as Google or Windows Live. You would likely need to add one or more fields to your Active Directory schema for claims authentication.

Workload optimization

This chapter focuses on day-to-day administrative tasks and architecture, as seen from the SharePoint administrator's perspective. Understanding these concepts provides insight into the current farm configuration, the flow of daily operations, and forecasting for the future state of the farm as a whole.

Skills in this chapter:

- Skill: Create and maintain site collections
- Skill: Plan SharePoint high availability and disaster recovery
- Skill: Plan backup and restore
- Skill: Plan and configure social workload
- Skill: Plan and configure a Web Content Management (WCM) workload
- Skill: Plan and configure an Enterprise Content Management (ECM) workload

Skill: Create and maintain site collections

The creation and maintenance of site collections in a SharePoint farm is part of the daily activities associated with being a Farm Administrator. Some of the concepts in this section are familiar to SharePoint 2010 and 2013 administrators, but others have to do with new functionality introduced in both SharePoint Server 2016 and hybrid implementations with SharePoint Online. Having an understanding of these new concepts will speed the deployment of sites in your enterprise and reduce the data footprint and scale of your site collections.

> **This section covers how to:**
> - Configure Fast Site Collection Creation
> - Configure host header site collections
> - Configure self-service site creation
> - Maintain site owners
> - Maintain site quotas

- Configure site policies
- Configure a team mailbox
- Plan Sites page pinning

Configure Fast Site Collection Creation

SharePoint 2016 introduces the concept of Fast Site Collection Creation, allowing for a significant reduction in the time required to deploy new site collections from a SharePoint template. By using this functionality, a Site Master (or copy of the fully created site collection) can be created for each individual SharePoint template in your environment. This Site Master is then stored in a content database, and copies are made when the New-SPSite cmdlet is issued, immediately creating a complete site collection that has all features activated (no activation of features happens after the site is created, by default).

Creating the Site Master

Creating the Site Master is a two-step process. First, the SharePoint template must be enabled for use with a Site Master, and then the Site Master must be created from the template:

```
<# Enable the Template for use with a Site Master #>
Enable-SPWebTemplateForSiteMaster -Template <TEMPLATENAME> -CompatibilityLevel 15
<# Create the new Site Master from the enabled Template #>
New-SPSiteMaster -ContentDatabase <CONTENTDB> -Template <TEMPLATENAME>
```

> **IMPORTANT** The Site Master and the created site collection can exist in different content databases; additionally, the Site Master can be used in multiple content databases, including those associated with a different web application (if required).

> **NEED MORE REVIEW?** For a complete listing of the PowerShell cmdlets associated with Fast Site Collection Creation (and some other useful cmdlets), review the TechNet article entitled "Use Windows PowerShell cmdlets to manage sites in SharePoint Server 2016" at *https://technet.microsoft.com/library/ee890106(v=office.16).aspx.*

Creating a new site collection using the Site Master

Creating a new site collection using a Site Master uses the same PowerShell cmdlet as creating one without the Site Master; the only difference is the use of the -CreateFromSiteMaster switch:

```
<# Create a new site collection using the Site Master #>
New-SPSite http://wingtiptoys/sites/<SITE> -Template <TEMPLATE> -ContentDatabase
<CONTENTDB> -Compatibility Level 15 -CreateFromSiteMaster -OwnerAlias <OWNER>
```

> **IMPORTANT** If you develop customizations that are feature-based for your on-premises
> SharePoint environment and require these features to reference the current site collec-
> tion's information, then you will need to mark your features to be activated postcopy for
> use with Fast Site Collection Creation; this step ensures that the additional features activate
> only after the site collection is created.

Configure host header site collections

Traditionally, there are three ways to host more than one website on a server:

- Issue a unique IP address to each website.
- Designate a nonstandard TCP port number (for instance, *http://<website>:10800*).
- Create a host header.

Host headers allow Internet Information Services (IIS) to assign more than one fully qualified domain name (FQDN) on a server to a single IP address. In DNS, each of these FQDNs
might be configured as an A record; requests going to each different FQDN would all route
to the same IP address on a web server, requiring that the web server itself be configured to
know which site is being referenced by each host header.

> **IMPORTANT** Documentation sources within both TechNet and MSDN refer to this func-
> tionality alternately as either host header site collections or host-named site collections.
> The current exam listing for 70-339 refers to host header site collections; thus, this is how
> they are referred to throughout this book.

SharePoint 2016 has no issue with this arrangement, allowing you to build a single web
application from Central Administration and then specify a single host header (FQDN) used
by IIS to route user requests. These requests could come to the top-level site collection itself
(*http://sitename.com*) or could use a managed path to specify a site collection further within
the URL (*http://sitename.com/sites/siteone*).

Site collections created and arranged in this manner are known as path-based site collections, due to the fact that either exclusive or wildcard managed paths (*/sites* in the preceding
path) are required to group more than one site collection beneath a host header URL.

In such a configuration, an application pool and site is created in IIS. A binding is assigned
to the site that specifies the host header and the TCP port, as shown in Figure 3-1.

FIGURE 3-1 The newly created application pool and site, and its associated site binding

Comparing path-based and host header site collections

What's not available in such a configuration is a mechanism for creating multiple site collections within the same web application, while assigning a unique FQDN for each. For instance, if you wanted to have a URL pattern that would allow you to specify business units (*home. wingtiptoys.com, hr.wingtiptoys.com, accounting.wingtiptoys.com*), you would need to create three web applications from Central Administration by using path-based site collections.

As it is recommended to minimize the number of web applications, both from a resourcing and administrative overhead standpoint, there has to be a better way, and there is. Within SharePoint, host header site collections can be created; this allows an administrator to build the application pool and site in IIS, but not specify the host header in the binding, choosing instead to allow this information to be stored within SharePoint itself (see Figure 3-2).

FIGURE 3-2 The newly created application pool and site (for host header site collections), no site bindings

> **IMPORTANT** The web application containing multiple host header site collections should never have a host header or host name of its own in the site bindings.

Creating host header site collections

Once the decision has been made to move to host header site collections, all administrative efforts should as a necessity move to PowerShell. Limited administration potential exists from within Central Administration for host header site collections; they can be viewed from Application Management, View All Site Collections (see Figure 3-3).

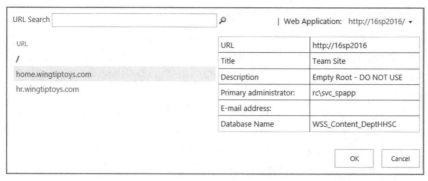

FIGURE 3-3 Host header site collection, as viewed from within Central Administration

Only a few steps are required to configure a web application and the associated host header site collections:

1. Create the Host Header web application by using the New-SPWebApplication cmdlet, ensuring that you do *not* use the *-HostHeader* switch.

2. Do an *IISRESET /noforce* on each server in the farm.

3. Create an empty path-based root site collection in the web application.

4. This site collection is used for crawling content and must be present; it should never be assigned for use by users.

5. Create new host header site collections by using the New-SPSite cmdlet and the *-HostHeaderWebApplication* switch.

EXAM TIP

For Search and other components to work effectively, there must be a root site collection in a host header web application. This site collection should be created and left unused.

NEED MORE REVIEW? The creation and administration of host header site collections requires a bit of practice, as the administration of the site collections, managed paths, zones, and other specifics can all be administered from PowerShell. It is important to note that host header site collections don't necessarily preclude the use of managed paths and path-based site collections; in fact, they work together just fine. For a better understanding of how to administer host header site collections, visit the TechNet article entitled "Host-named site collection architecture and deployment" at *https://technet.microsoft.com /library/cc424952.aspx*. For a more in-depth review of host header site collections and their applications, see the MSDN blog article "What Every SharePoint Admin Needs to Know About Host Named Site Collections" at *https://blogs.msdn.microsoft.com/kaevans/2012 /03/27/what-every-sharepoint-admin-needs-to-know-about-host-named-site-collections/*.

Configure self-service site creation

One of the key collaborative functionalities present in SharePoint is the ability to quickly add new sites for use by individuals and teams. This flexibility can be further extended by allowing users themselves the option of creating a site on an ad hoc basis, a feature known as self-service site creation.

With this flexibility come questions surrounding the life cycle of a SharePoint site, from creation to eventual disposition. The ability to create new sites (and subsites, for that matter), often leads to rapid organic growth. Users, excited about the new tool set, create sites at will to match an expected structure; if the structure isn't suitable, then these sites are just as quickly abandoned.

> **IMPORTANT** Self-service site creation cannot currently be activated inside a host header site collection.

Site creation governance

In earlier versions of SharePoint, the lack of site governance often meant that this powerful feature was either (a) implemented and then retracted, or (b) never implemented at all. Without the ability to create new sites, users often would nest sites beneath other sites, sometimes several layers deep.

Fortunately, the options for self-service site creation governance in SharePoint 2016 are significant in scope. When enabled, these options can:

- Be created in a specific managed path within a web application.
- Have effective site quotas assigned, controlling growth metrics.
- Allow for the use of a custom form (perhaps to control intradepartmental billing for resources).
- Specify the required or optional use of site classification settings.
- Require a secondary contact for the newly created site.

EXAM TIP

Although it is important to understand how to enable self-service site creation, it's probably just as important to have a good grasp on the site quota and site classification features that make this functionality a reasonable option for many IT organizations.

Activating self-service site collections

Once governance and billing questions have been addressed, it's possible to enable self-service site collections on a per-web application basis. Within Application Management, Site Collections, select Configure Self-Service Site Creation to begin the activation process (shown in Figure 3-4).

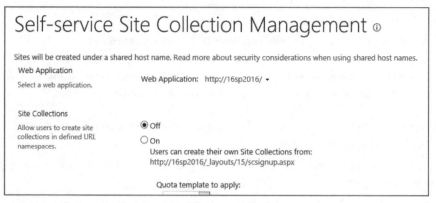

FIGURE 3-4 Managing self-service site collections (partial view)

On the Self-Service Site Collection Management page, you can control five selections:

- **Web Application** Allows you to select the appropriate web application.
- **Site Collections** Allows you to enable or disable self-service site collection creation and select a site quota.
- **Start a Site** Allows you to configure the Start A Site link.
    - Hide the link from users.
    - Prompt the users to create a team site under a particular URL.
    - Prompt users to create a site collection under any managed path.
    - Display a custom form (and provide a location for the form).
- **Site Classification Settings** Choose whether to hide, make optional, or make required.
- **Require secondary contact** Choose whether or not to enable a secondary contact for the site collection.

> **NEED MORE REVIEW?** For a better understanding of what's required for a successful self-service site creation implementation, visit the TechNet article entitled "Plan self-service site creation in SharePoint 2013" at *https://technet.microsoft.com/library/cc263483.aspx*.

Maintain site owners

Each site collection within SharePoint 2016 has the capability to specify multiple site collection administrators. These administrators are the de facto owners of the site collection and are responsible for the administration of their site collection from a resourcing and permissioning standpoint.

EXAM TIP

It is possible to add individuals to the administrators from within a site collection; additionally, you can designate someone as an owner of an individual site. However, neither of these people is responsible for receiving notifications about site status and resourcing; that role is only for the primary and secondary administrators of a site collection.

Viewing and changing the site collection administrators is done through the same interface in Application Management, as follows:

1. On the Application Management page in Central Administration, click the Change Site Collection Administrators link.

2. When the Site Collection Administrators page appears, ensure that you have the correct site collection selected and then assign the Primary Site Collection Administrator and Secondary Site Collection Administrator values (see Figure 3-5).

FIGURE 3-5 Selecting site collection administrators

IMPORTANT If more than two site collection administrators are to be set for a particular site collection, this must be set up from Site Settings, Users And Permissions, Site Collection Administrators within the site collection itself.

Maintain site quotas

Site quotas (mentioned earlier in our discussion about self-service site creation) enable a SharePoint 2016 administrator to control the disk resource usage of site collections in a SharePoint farm. A site collection is allotted a particular amount of resources, and the administrator of that site is notified when the site has grown to consume a significant percentage of the overall resource allotment.

EXAM TIP

Users do not receive reminder emails if the SharePoint farm does not have outgoing email configured and functional. Ensure that this service is available before placing any quota restrictions within your farm.

There are only two resources measured within a site quota:

- The overall disk space consumed
- The number of points consumed by sandboxed solutions with code

Site quota templates

Site quotas are assigned as new site collections are being created. Although it is technically possible to assign quotas on an individual basis to site collections in the farm, it is much easier to manage growth of a site by making multiple site quota templates available.

These templates would decide how much space is made available for a particular site collection, by default. For example, you might choose to have project sites with a maximum storage limit quota setting of 25 GB, whereas departmental portal sites might possess a maximum storage limit quota setting of 100 GB.

Site quotas are set from the Specify Quota Templates link within Application Management, Site Collections. On the Quota Templates page, you can control three items:

- **Template Name**   Specify a new template name (and optionally, an existing template from which to start).
- **Storage Limit Values**   This setting allows you to limit the overall site storage maximum limit as well as allowing you to send a warning email when a certain size threshold is reached. Note that both of these values are set in MB, not GB.
- **Sandboxed Solutions With Code Limits**   As solutions are developed and deployed to the site collection, they consume sandbox resources, which are a number representing memory and processing cycles. You can limit the maximum usage (on a daily basis) to a certain number of points and then set the warning email to be sent out as you pass a certain resource value.

IMPORTANT   A good rule of thumb is that the warning emails should be sent when limits reach 80 percent of the total storage or points maximum values.

The completed quota template can now be assigned to site collections (Figure 3-6).

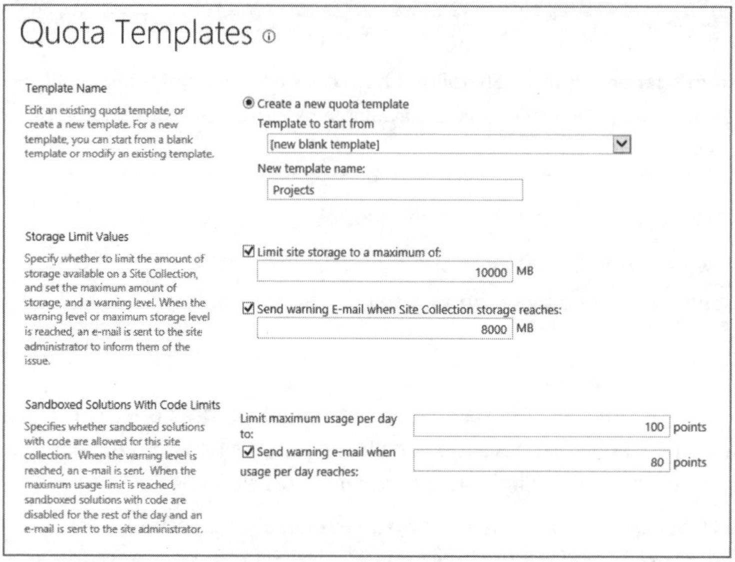

Quota Templates ⓘ

Template Name

Edit an existing quota template, or create a new template. For a new template, you can start from a blank template or modify an existing template.

⦿ Create a new quota template
Template to start from

[new blank template] ▾

New template name:

Projects

Storage Limit Values

Specify whether to limit the amount of storage available on a Site Collection, and set the maximum amount of storage, and a warning level. When the warning level or maximum storage level is reached, an e-mail is sent to the site administrator to inform them of the issue.

☑ Limit site storage to a maximum of:

10000 MB

☑ Send warning E-mail when Site Collection storage reaches:

8000 MB

Sandboxed Solutions With Code Limits

Specifies whether sandboxed solutions with code are allowed for this site collection. When the warning level is reached, an e-mail is sent. When the maximum usage limit is reached, sandboxed solutions with code are disabled for the rest of the day and an e-mail is sent to the site administrator.

Limit maximum usage per day to:

100 points

☑ Send warning e-mail when usage per day reaches:

80 points

FIGURE 3-6 Quota Templates page, showing the completed quota template

> **NEED MORE REVIEW?** For a better understanding of quota templates, including how to assign them via PowerShell, visit the TechNet article entitled "Create, edit, and delete quota templates in SharePoint 2013" at *https://technet.microsoft.com/library/cc263223.aspx.*

Assigning a quota to a site collection

After you have a series of quota templates built, assigning them to existing site collections is a straightforward process from Central Administration. To assign a site quota template to a site collection, follow these steps:

1. On the Application Management page, in the Site Collections section, click *Configure Quotas And Locks*.

2. Select the appropriate site collection.

3. Choose the lock status for the site.

   - **Not Locked**   Site collection is available for use.

   - **Adding Content Prevented**   Site collection cannot have any new content uploaded.

   - **Read-Only**   Site collection cannot have any content changed or added; either the site collection administrator or the Farm Administrator can control this lock.

   - **No Access**   No one can access content in this site collection.

4. Site Quota Information allows you to either select an existing quota template (also displays these values) or specify bespoke limits for this site collection.

Once these values are accepted, the site collection to which they are assigned now has some level of control for resources allotted (Figure 3-7).

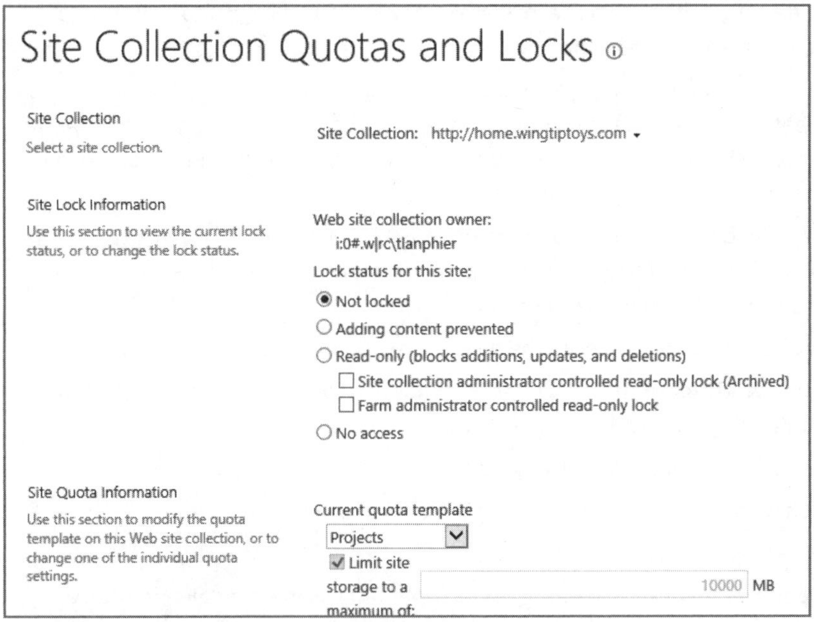

Site Collection Quotas and Locks ⓘ

Site Collection
Select a site collection.

Site Collection: http://home.wingtiptoys.com ▾

Site Lock Information
Use this section to view the current lock status, or to change the lock status.

Web site collection owner:
   i:0#.w|rc\tlanphier
Lock status for this site:
◉ Not locked
○ Adding content prevented
○ Read-only (blocks additions, updates, and deletions)
   ☐ Site collection administrator controlled read-only lock (Archived)
   ☐ Farm administrator controlled read-only lock
○ No access

Site Quota Information
Use this section to modify the quota template on this Web site collection, or to change one of the individual quota settings.

Current quota template
[Projects ▾]
☑ Limit site
storage to a   [10000] MB
maximum of:

FIGURE 3-7 Configuring the Site Collection Quotas and Locks page

> **NEED MORE REVIEW?** For a better understanding of quota locks, including how to assign them via PowerShell, visit the TechNet article entitled "Manage the lock status for site collections in SharePoint 2013" at *https://technet.microsoft.com/library/cc263238.aspx*.

Configure site policies

If you have been involved with SharePoint for any length of time, you might have run into sites within a particular site collection that have been abandoned. As mentioned previously, there are several reasons this can happen:

- The subsite was created along an organization structure that no longer applies.
- The subsite was created for a discontinued project and was abandoned along with the project.
- The subsite was left in place, but now hosts information that is out of date and no longer of value.

Any way you cut it, a site that is not in use or is not useful as an archive should eventually be removed. This trimming effort is made possible by the use of site policies. These policies are set within the confines of a site collection.

Site closures and deletions

In early versions of SharePoint, the only disposition of a site from an automated standpoint was its eventual deletion. Although a site in SharePoint 2016 can still be automatically deleted, it can also be set to a closed state.

A closed site is marked for eventual deletion, but its users can still modify the site and its content. A site that is in closed status no longer appears in locations that aggregate sites such as Outlook. If a site is closed, but the owner wants it to remain in use, he or she can go into the site settings menu and reopen the site.

Creating a new site policy is done within the bounds of a site collection, specifically from within the Site Policies menu of Site Collection Administration. Once there, clicking the Create link allows the SCA to configure the settings of the policy:

- **Name And Description**   Specify the name of the policy and describe its purpose.
- **Site Closure And Deletion**   Describes what happens to the site (and its subsites) as a result of this policy. The options available are as follows:
  - Do not close or delete site automatically.
  - Delete sites automatically, specifying the deletion event date.
  - Close and delete sites automatically.
- **Site Collection Closure**   In addition to the options available for deleting sites, applying this policy to the root site in the site collection sets the site collection to closed, making the root site and all subsites read only.

EXAM TIP

Closing a site is very different from deleting a site. A site owner or site collection administrator can reopen a closed site by going to the Site Closure And Deletion page under Site Administration.

NEED MORE REVIEW?   If you define site policies within a content type hub, they can be published across multiple site collections. For a more detailed understanding of site policies in SharePoint 2016, review the TechNet article entitled "Overview of site policies in SharePoint 2013" at *https://technet.microsoft.com/library/jj219569.aspx*.

Configure a team mailbox

A team mailbox (also known as a site mailbox) is a convenient feature that allows users in a SharePoint site to collaborate from a mail standpoint. This mailbox can be used to share important email messages, gather important team conversations, or share important documents by email.

From an IT perspective, this arrangement is optimal because the newly created mailbox resides in Exchange rather than being hosted inside SharePoint. SharePoint uses a site feature (appropriately named Site Mailbox) to provision the necessary components.

Configuring site mailboxes

Although SharePoint 2016 servers come with the Site Mailbox Site feature installed, this feature has a dependency on a Site Collection feature that is not available in an OOB SharePoint 2016 installation (also called Site Mailboxes). This is because a fair amount of configuration work is required to enable this particular functionality. Prerequisites include the following:

- User Profile Synchronization must be enabled in the farm.
- The App Management Service Application must be configured in the farm.
- SSL must be configured on the SharePoint servers hosting the default zone of web applications configured for server-to-server authentication and app authentication.
- The administrator performing the configuration must be part of the SharePoint and Exchange Server administrator groups; additionally, the Exchange server must be configured and providing mailboxes for users.

Once the prerequisites are in place, only a few more steps remain for the configuration to be complete:

- The Exchange Web Services API must be installed (SharePoint web-tier servers).
- IIS must be reset (SharePoint web-tier servers).
- OAuth Trust and Service Permissions must be set (SharePoint Server farm).
- OAuth Trust and Service Permissions must be set (Exchange Server farm).

NEED MORE REVIEW? For more detail on this configuration, including PowerShell scripts required for each configuration, visit the TechNet article entitled "Configure site mailboxes in SharePoint Server 2013" at *https://technet.microsoft.com/library/jj552524.aspx*.

Creating the team mailbox

Initializing the site mailbox from within a team site is quite simple, requiring little technical ability. After a team site has been created, there is an extra tile in the Getting Started banner titled *Keep Email In Context*. Selecting this tile (see Figure 3-8) activates the Site Mailbox feature.

FIGURE 3-8 Keep email in context

Plan Sites page pinning

Users browsing SharePoint sites in a hybrid SharePoint environment have the ability to follow a site by selecting Follow (Figure 3-9).

FIGURE 3-9 The Follow option for a SharePoint site

In a hybrid environment, this information is promoted to an individual's SharePoint tile (also called the Sites tile in some tenancies). This page shows four groupings of sites (shown in Figure 3-10):

- Promoted Sites
- Followed Sites
- Recent Sites
- Recommended Sites

FIGURE 3-10 The SharePoint/Sites page in a hybrid deployment

Once a user has followed a site, it appears in the Followed Sites area of the SharePoint/Sites page. If the user follows several different sites, then the list of sites might be a bit hard to navigate, especially when visiting followed sites that are regularly in use. These sites can be "pinned" to the top of the Followed Sites section by selecting a site's ellipsis and then selecting Pin To Top (Figure 3-11).

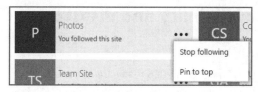

FIGURE 3-11 Selecting a site to pin to the top of the Followed Sites section

From an administrative standpoint, it is possible to alter the sites that are viewed by all in the organization within the Promoted Sites section of the SharePoint/Sites page. Selecting Manage in the Manage The Promoted Sites Below dialog box causes the tiles to change appearance, showing a new tile, Add A Promoted Site (Figure 3-12).

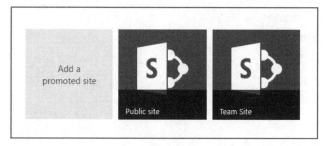

FIGURE 3-12 Add A Promoted Site tile

Selecting Add A Promoted Site allows you to specify the Title, Link Location, Description, and Background Image Location for the newly promoted site (Figure 3-13).

FIGURE 3-13 Assigning the Promoted Sites values

Skill: Plan SharePoint high availability and disaster recovery

High availability and disaster recovery concepts in SharePoint 2016 really are not that much different than they were in earlier versions. Some of these concepts have been deprecated by Microsoft (for example, SQL AlwaysOn Mirroring), but are provided by SharePoint for backward compatibility.

This section covers how to:

- Plan for service distribution
- Plan for service instance configuration
- Plan for physical server distribution
- Plan for network redundancy
- Plan for server load balancing
- Plan for SQL Server aliases
- Plan for SQL Server clustering
- Plan for SQL Server AlwaysOn Availability Groups
- Plan for SQL Server Log Shipping
- Plan for storage redundancy
- Plan for login replication

Plan for service distribution

In previous installations, you would often find that SharePoint follows a three-tier topology, with web servers, application servers, and database servers. This configuration is often referred to as a *traditional topology*.

Compare this topology to that found in a MinRole-compliant farm, and you will quickly see that the configuration becomes more distributed, with front-end, application (batch), distributed cache, and search servers replacing those found in a traditional topology. This configuration is built around the notion of minimizing network traffic between servers in the farm while maximizing the system resources of the individual server hardware and processing requests from the individual server. Such a configuration is called a *streamlined topology*.

> ***NEED MORE REVIEW?*** These two topology approaches are really nothing new, having been present in SharePoint 2013, but with the streamlined topology not having the extra MinRole health and governance technology to assist. For an understanding and comparison of how services are distributed between these two models, visit the TechNet article

entitled "Plan service deployment in SharePoint 2013" at *https://technet.microsoft.com /library/jj219591.aspx*. Each of these models has a corresponding Services on Server Install Worksheet; the Streamlined Topology worksheet closely echoes the configuration of services in a MinRole-compliant 2016 farm.

Plan for service instance configuration

When discussing the concept of a highly available MinRole-compliant farm, it becomes obvious that quite a few servers will be involved. At the Front-end, Application, and Search tiers of the farm, at least two of each server are required, and three servers are required for Distributed cache to be highly available (Figure 3-14).

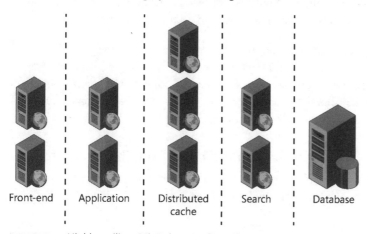

Front-end   Application   Distributed   Search   Database
cache

FIGURE 3-14 Highly resilient MinRole-compliant SharePoint 2016 farm

Add in the number of SQL servers required at the database level to provide high availability by using an AlwaysOn Cluster or AlwaysOn Availability Groups (2), and then the number of servers in the farm quickly escalates to a minimum of 15.

In smaller environments, you might find that the licensing, infrastructure, and maintenance costs for such an installation are prohibitive. If this indeed turns out to be the case, then a clearer understanding of what services each MinRole provides is in order.

Scaling services in a smaller, non-MinRole-compliant SharePoint farm

Creating a SharePoint 2016 farm with limited resources can be challenging. If you start with a single server, then it's obvious that you will wind up creating a single-server farm that is MinRole compliant. But what happens when you are only able to add another one, two, or three servers to the SharePoint farm?

In general, you would choose the most logical MinRole and apply it first to the farm, specifying that the other servers in the farm become Custom role servers. For instance, if you had four servers total, you might choose to have two of the servers be Front-end MinRole compliant (to efficiently serve pages) and have the other two servers use the Custom role, hosting all other necessary services.

> **IMPORTANT**   In such a configuration, you might choose to have only one Distributed cache server because this topology requires that you must decide to have either one Distributed cache server or three Distributed cache servers.

In such a configuration, it becomes paramount that you closely monitor the performance of servers that are using the Custom role because they could become overcommitted depending on user load. Prior to configuring the Custom role servers in this farm, you should have a solid understanding of which services are required on these servers.

> **NEED MORE REVIEW?**   Understanding which services are maintained on which MinRole servers isn't much different than planning services on previous SharePoint 2013 farms. For a better understanding of how these services are assigned by MinRole, visit the TechNet article entitled "Description of MinRole and associated services in SharePoint Server 2016" at *https://technet.microsoft.com/library/mt667910.aspx*.

Scaling services in a smaller, fully MinRole-compliant SharePoint farm

If your farm is to remain fully MinRole compliant, then it's required that no service applications be created until the farm has at least one server in each of the following roles:

- Front-end
- Application
- Distributed cache
- Search (optional)

Scaling services in a MinRole-compliant farm, then, just requires that you create the required MinRole servers at the appropriate level. For instance, if you require resiliency for the Front-end, Application, or Search components of your farm, you would just add a server with the appropriate MinRole at the appropriate level in the farm. If the Distributed cache role needed to be expanded, then you would add two additional servers to enable full resiliency.

Plan for physical server distribution

Servers in a SharePoint high availability and disaster recovery configuration have the ability to be installed in separate physical locations. This configuration is obviously not without its very own set of rules, which must be observed to keep the resulting SharePoint installation in a supported state. These rules are different, depending on the need: high availability only, disaster recovery only, or both.

Creating a stretched farm across two datacenters

As we discussed previously, each of the SharePoint MinRoles is capable of resiliency, requiring a minimum of two servers. By using DNS or a hardware load balancer, it is possible to split the installation down the middle for the purposes of high availability, installing hardware in two datacenters that are located near one another. This has the added benefit of allowing one center to fail without suffering a complete outage in the farm.

This configuration is described as a *stretched* farm implementation, and only has two requirements from a SharePoint standpoint to be fully supported:

- Connections within the SharePoint farm between servers (in particular, the Front-end and Database servers) must exhibit a latency of less than 1 ms, 99.9 percent of the time over a period of 10 minutes.

- The bandwidth connecting these two SharePoint installations must be maintained at a speed of at least 1 gigabit per second (Gbps).

> ***NEED MORE REVIEW?*** It's important to understand that high availability and disaster recovery are often addressed together but are not the same thing. Understanding high availability configurations, particularly those that use multiple datacenters, is a fairly advanced topic, and requires an understanding of networking, servers, SharePoint, and SQL topics. For a detailed understanding of high availability in SharePoint 2016, review the TechNet article "Create a high availability architecture and strategy for SharePoint 2013" at *https://technet.microsoft.com/library/cc748824.aspx*.

Creating a SharePoint disaster recovery environment across two datacenters

A SharePoint disaster recovery environment really isn't a single SharePoint environment, but rather two environments, one of which is in use (and sometimes configured for high availability use itself) and another that is built as a standby. Choosing which SharePoint disaster recovery configuration is used tends to be influenced by cost and implementation complexity, resulting in the need to choose one of three possible options:

- **Cold Standby Recovery** This environment type is the slowest to recover, and requires that backups of servers from the production datacenter be restored to physically different servers in the DR datacenter.

- **Warm Standby Recovery** This environment type is faster to recover, and involves regular restores of full and incremental backups from the production datacenter to physically different servers in the disaster recovery datacenter.

- **Hot Standby Recovery** This environment type is by far the quickest to recover, often requiring seconds to minutes for the recovery to take place.

This last option, Hot Standby Recovery, requires further explanation. In such a configuration, a complete SharePoint farm is installed at the Primary (production) and Secondary (disaster recovery) locations. Each farm maintains its own separate Configuration database and Central Administration website content database.

Each of these farms must receive all customizations and updates in a synchronous fashion (deployment and maintenance scripts are recommended for consistency). Finally, from a back-end standpoint, content databases must be replicated from the primary to secondary farms on a regular basis by using one of three supported technologies:

- **SQL Log Shipping**   A mechanism that allows for the automatic transmission of transaction log backups from a primary database instance to a secondary server instance.

- **Asynchronous AlwaysOn Mirroring**   A mechanism that replicates changes from a per-database standpoint from a primary database instance to a secondary server instance. This configuration is known as High-Performance Mode, and it implies that transactions do not have to synchronously commit on the primary and secondary instances.

- **Asynchronous AlwaysOn Availability Groups**   A mechanism that replicates changes in a grouping of SQL content databases, from the primary instance to the secondary instance.

EXAM TIP

Although AlwaysOn Mirroring is still supported for legacy SQL installations, it has also been deprecated and should not be used going forward.

Regardless of which of these replication strategies is used, it's important to note that they can occur over hundreds or thousands of miles, without affecting the primary farm.

NEED MORE REVIEW?   Choosing a disaster recovery strategy requires quite a bit of coordination among the server infrastructure, SQL, networking, and SharePoint teams. It is unlikely that you, as the SharePoint administrator, will get to configure each of these options; that said, it's important to understand the tools that are available to ensure continuous availability of your SharePoint farm. For more detailed information concerning DR strategies, review the TechNet article "Choose a disaster recovery strategy for SharePoint 2013" at *https://technet.microsoft.com/library/ff628971.aspx*.

Plan for network redundancy

Although discussions of network redundancy are technically outside the purview of the SharePoint administrator, it is important nonetheless to consider the availability of the networks to which your SharePoint farms connect. SharePoint farms are dependent on consistent network connectivity to provide intrafarm communication between servers in the SharePoint topology as well as communications to and from the respective users of the SharePoint farms.

Any SharePoint high availability design must be able to ensure that a network failure cannot single-handedly take down the farm. For instance, a connectivity break between cache hosts for the distributed cache service in the farm could result in a failure of the built-in cache cluster.

Network resiliency

Just as multiple servers in a SharePoint farm provide resiliency for services and roles, redundancy from a network standpoint can provide resiliency for farm connectivity. This resiliency might only be necessary for a single location (such as a high availability farm), or might also be necessary for disaster recovery site connections or connections to the cloud for hybrid implementations.

Factors that can affect network resiliency include the following:

- **Power blackouts and brownouts**   Easily addressed via backup generators and multiple power distribution unit (PDU) connections.

- **NIC failures on member servers**   Most modern servers provide redundant network interface cards (NICs), which may each be connected to a separate virtual local area network (VLAN; an isolated or partitioned section of your local area network).

- **Router and switch failures**   Maintaining redundant VLANs is usually accomplished across multiple routers, preventing a network failure due to the loss of a single router in the datacenter.

- **Network services failures**   Most enterprises have multiple Domain Name System (DNS) and Dynamic Host Configuration Protocol (DHCP) servers, specifically created to provide resiliency.

- **Upstream provider failures**   A disaster recovery environment is only as good as the network that connects it. Selecting redundant routes (or perhaps, redundant providers) allows you to ensure wide area network (WAN) connectivity to your disaster recovery environment.

Plan for server load balancing

Load balancing at the Front-end level of a SharePoint farm allows the SharePoint administrator to scale the inbound load from a user standpoint. As the number of users in a SharePoint farm increases, more Front-end servers can be added to a pool of servers to better distribute the load.

There are two useful mechanisms for load balancing a SharePoint farm:

- **Using the Network Load Balancing feature**   This feature in Windows Server allows for two or more servers to be assigned as a virtual cluster. If one server fails, inbound requests can automatically be directed to the remaining nodes.

- **Using a hardware load balancer**   Dedicated load balancers are often quite sophisticated, and capable of not only performing basic load balancing, but also assessing the health of servers in a server pool. For instance, if a network card failed on a server pool, the load balancer would simply reassign requests to the remaining servers in the pool.

Plan for SQL Server aliases

When you configure a SharePoint server farm, you are asked to provide the name of the SQL server (and perhaps a server instance, if you are not using the default). The name of the SQL server becomes part of the farm's configuration.

From both an operational and disaster recovery standpoint, this can be less than optimal. What happens if the SQL server fails or is irreparably damaged? How quickly would you be able to set up a replacement server and then restore SharePoint services?

SQL Server aliases are a mechanism that allows you to quickly disconnect one SQL back-end server instance and replace it with another. This is done by assigning an alias name by using a tool called the SQL Server Client Network Utility, or CLICONFG. CLICONFG (note the spelling; there is no second "i") is found on every Windows server, and is fairly straightforward to configure.

> **IMPORTANT** The CLICONFG utility is found on most Windows servers at *C:\Windows \System32\cliconfg.exe*.

Creating an SQL Alias

Configuring an SQL alias is done on every SharePoint server being configured in your farm and requires only a few steps. First, TCP/IP must be enabled (see Figure 3-15).

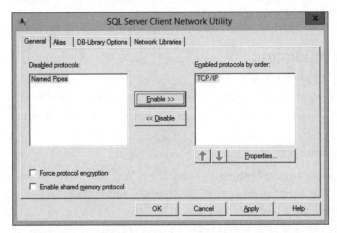

FIGURE 3-15 Enabling TCP/IP

Next, click the Alias tab and click Add to configure the alias itself. Specify three things: the network library (TCP/IP), the server alias (Northwind, in this example), and the server name

(16SQL, in this example). Optionally, you can choose to either dynamically determine the TCP port used by SQL, or select a particular port (the default is 1433). Figure 3-16 shows the alias being configured.

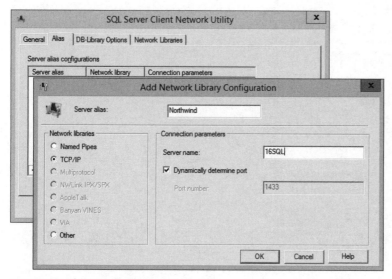

FIGURE 3-16 The SQL alias being added

Click OK in the Add Network Library Configuration dialog box and then click OK in the SQL Server Client Network Utility dialog box to enable the newly created SQL alias.

Verify the SQL alias

Verifying the SQL alias is simple. Create a text file on your desktop (use ANSI coding), saving it with a .udl extension (this example uses SQLAlias.udl). Open the text file, and type the SQL alias name. Select Use Windows NT Integrated Security, and click the Select The Database On The Server drop-down list (shown in Figure 3-17). If everything is configured correctly in the SQL alias (and you have permissions to the SQL server), you should be able to see all the SQL databases associated with your farm. No changes need to be made, so click Cancel after you've verified connectivity (Figure 3-17).

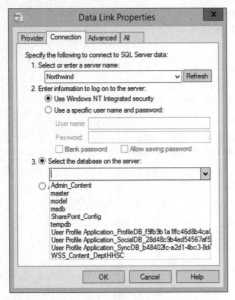

FIGURE 3-17 Verifying the SQL alias connectivity

Plan for SQL Server clustering

SQL Server clustering is part of the AlwaysOn family of high availability and disaster recovery technologies. Also known as AlwaysOn Failover Cluster Instances, this technology relies on the underlying Windows Server Failover Clustering (WSFC) functionality at the server level.

An SQL Server Failover Cluster Instance (FCI) is a single instance of SQL Server that is installed across multiple nodes. In more recent editions, this functionality has been expanded to allow the FCI to exist on nodes that occupy multiple subnets, allowing for network resiliency in the cluster.

Multiple nodes in the SQL FCI present themselves to the network as a single SQL instance. Failover between these nodes is transparent to the user, and generally takes seconds to accomplish.

Requirements for SQL Server clustering

SQL Server clustering has requirements at the server and storage levels specifically focused on maintaining the cluster itself. Hardware at these levels must be supported by the underlying Server Operating System level and must be certified for use with clustering, particularly in the case of storage based on storage area networks (SANs).

Plan for SQL Server AlwaysOn Availability Groups

SQL Server AlwaysOn Availability Groups were introduced in SQL Server 2012, and use portions of the functionality found in SQL mirroring (deprecated), SQL clustering, and SQL log shipping. The result is the ability to group databases together (an Availability Group), and replicate it synchronously (high availability) and asynchronously (disaster recovery) to the respective environments.

Implementing SQL Server AlwaysOn Availability Groups is a process similar to the deployment of SQL Server clustering with one notable exception: SQL itself does not have to be clustered. Instead, individual SQL instances can be installed on cluster nodes and then configured to present what looks like a SQL instance to network clients.

This configuration is particularly useful in a full high availability and disaster recovery configuration. Multiple Windows servers can be configured with clustering at both the primary (production/high availability) and secondary (disaster recovery) environments. The servers clustered in each of these environments do not necessarily have to be part of the same cluster. You could have one high availability cluster in the primary environment and a single-server disaster recovery cluster in the secondary environment.

Even though these two environments are not related from a cluster standpoint, the primary environment can maintain an AlwaysOn synchronous-commit availability group configuration for the high availability production environment, replicating databases by using an AlwaysOn asynchronous-commit availability group for the disaster recovery environment. At this site, a separate SharePoint environment could be configured (different Configuration database, different Central Administration database, and other different configuration items) to use the replicated data in a read-only fashion.

Plan for SQL Server Log Shipping

SQL Server Log Shipping is one of the oldest disaster recovery mechanisms in use today. This configuration is relatively straightforward to set up and requires no special hardware. As recovery technologies go, SQL Server Log Shipping can be used to create a warm standby location, copying Transaction Log backups from the primary to secondary locations. As is the case with SQL AlwaysOn, the SharePoint installation at the secondary site will be created separately and only share certain databases with the primary site.

From a functional point of view, SQL Server Log Shipping is a simple process:

1. The Transaction Log is backed up at the primary server instance.
2. The Transaction Log file is then copied ("shipped") from the primary to the secondary server instance.
3. The Transaction Log file is restored at the secondary server instance.

Failover for such a configuration is always a manual proposition, and data copied from the source is usually current to within a matter of minutes (compared with seconds in an AlwaysOn Availability Groups configuration). This environment can optionally be created with a Monitor server, which looks at the Transaction Logs being shipped and can provide information about the process and generate alerts as required.

> **NEED MORE REVIEW?** More information regarding the configuration and maintenance of SQL Server Log Shipping can be found in the MSDN article "About Log Shipping (SQL Server)" at *https://msdn.microsoft.com/library/ms187103.aspx*.

Plan for storage redundancy

Thus far, we've worked through power, networking, and server redundancy. The storage layer of a high availability system has to be able to meet the same redundancy requirement as all the other components. This redundancy is available at two levels: the storage media itself and the communication channels within the storage array.

Storage media redundancy

At the disk level (whether rotational or solid-state media), the individual disk is not capable of any sort of redundancy. In rotational media, the interface, motor, and sometimes the chemical composition of the platters themselves can fail. In solid-state media, similar issues can present themselves at the interface and component levels.

The only way, then, to provide redundancy in the media itself is to increase the number of individual storage devices. Doing so statistically decreases the overall effect on the storage subsystem by way of RAID technology. Redundant array of inexpensive or independent disks (RAID) is a mechanism whereby a failure of one or more member storage devices can be covered by the remaining devices in the array.

RAID has several standard levels (0–6), with RAID 0 (Striping), RAID 1 (Mirroring), and RAID 5 (Block Level Striping with Distributed Parity) being the most common. On modern storage subsystems, nested or hybrid RAID solutions are generally in use, either RAID 0+1 (a mirror set composed of two striped sets) or RAID 1+0 (a stripe set composed of two mirrored sets).

> **IMPORTANT** Media redundancy can be either software- or hardware-based in Windows Server systems. Windows Server can take a series of attached disks and make them into a set, relying on the operating system itself to handle the maintenance of parity and other items. Although this is functional, it nonetheless requires additional resources from a processor and memory standpoint. Hardware-based solutions, by comparison, are available from a number of vendors and have their own controllers in the array to handle the computational tasks required to maintain a RAID subsystem.

> **NEED MORE REVIEW?** For a better understanding of RAID levels as they pertain to Windows systems, review the TechNet article "Comparing Different Implementations of RAID Levels" at *https://technet.microsoft.com/library/ms178048(v=sql.105).aspx.*

Storage array redundancy

Moving beyond single and multiple groups of disk media, we come upon two types of enterprise storage, network-attached storage (NAS) and storage area network (SAN). Both of these storage types make use of arrays of media storage (RAID) for internal redundancy.

NETWORK ATTACHED STORAGE

Network-attached storage (NAS) is a term that describes a specialized computer presenting a series of drives for use over a network connection. These environments generally can be configured for hardware redundancy within the NAS itself, but are dependent on multiple external connections for redundancy in the same way servers require multiple connections.

STORAGE AREA NETWORK

SAN, or *storage area network,* is a term that describes a more advanced grouping of storage and hardware into an expandable environment from both an internal connectivity and storage standpoint. Interfaces to this environment sometimes require dedicated hardware on each server, tend to be faster than those presented by an NAS environment, and can be made available to servers by using a series of protocols including Fibre Channel, iSCSI, ATA over Ethernet, and others.

Plan for login replication

As you might imagine, the databases being copied between environments require a certain amount of configuration from a login standpoint. The logins themselves are not replicated with data in either an AlwaysOn Availability Groups or Log Shipping DR solution, leaving us to find a way to replicate or re-create them.

There are a couple of ways to handle this requirement:

- If you happen to know the user names and passwords for the accounts accessing SQL, then you can re-create the credentials within SQL at the secondary site (manual solution).
- You can create a script to replicate these credentials between environments by using a stored procedure (semiautomatic solution).
- You can create an SQL Server Integration Services (SSIS) job that transfers logins between instances of SQL Server (fully automatic solution).

> **NEED MORE REVIEW?**   Microsoft provides a T-SQL script for replicating credentials between environments in the Knowledge Base article entitled "How to transfer logins and passwords between instances of SQL Server" at *https://support.microsoft.com/kb/918992*. For information on how to set up fully automated login replication, visit the MSDN article "Transfer Logins Task" at *https://msdn.microsoft.com/library/ms137870.aspx*.

Skill: Plan backup and restore

Whereas the previous skill was about keeping the farm available for as much of the time as possible, this skill is primarily concerned with how to recover it in the event of a failure. These failures can exist at many possible levels: hardware, software, database, power, and others; the purpose of this skill is to assist you in planning how your environment will be recovered when (not if) something goes wrong.

This section covers how to:

- Establish a SharePoint backup schedule
- Establish an SQL Server backup schedule
- Plan a nonproduction environment content refresh
- Plan for farm configuration recovery
- Plan for service application recovery
- Plan for content recovery
- Configure a recovery solution by using SQL Database running in Azure and other Azure backup solutions

Establish a SharePoint backup schedule

SharePoint 2016 backup schedules are built by using the Backup and Restore section of Central Administration. Backups run from Central Administration actually create SQL Server backups of the SharePoint farm environment, and can be configured at several levels:

- **Farm-level backups**   Can include both content and configuration data.
- **Web application**   Can back up an individual web application configuration (including IIS settings) and one or more content databases.
- **Services and service applications (not shared)**   Can back up both the settings and any associated databases.
- **Proxies for service applications (not shared)**   Backed up separately from their associated service applications.
- **Shared services**   Can back up both the service application and the service application proxy.

Backups created in Central Administration require a location for the completed backups to be stored. This location must be a network share on a file server and shared with Full Control permissions to the SQL service account, Timer service account, and the Central Administration application pool identity account.

> **IMPORTANT**   SharePoint backups do not capture configuration changes made at the file level or changes made outside of SharePoint Central Administration or PowerShell. In particular, things like Web.config files, custom graphics installed at the file level (without a solution or feature), and other modifications will not be captured.

Search backups

The effective backup of the Search topology is a special case, particularly because the topology can be spread across multiple servers in the SharePoint farm. This backup is conducted in SQL Server and includes the Search administration, crawl, and property databases, as well as the index partition files.

Configuration-only backups

SharePoint Backup can create what's known as configuration-only backups. These backups contain settings information, such as those affecting email, antivirus software, and Information Rights Management (IRM).

The ability to back up the configuration of a particular SharePoint farm has several applications:

- This configuration can be applied across multiple farms for the purposes of standardization.
- Configurations can be replicated from production to a development or staging environment.

Scheduling a SharePoint backup

Oddly, there is no provision in the Backup and Restore section of Central Administration for regular backups. If you want to use SharePoint backups on a scheduled basis (you can set up both full and differential backups), then you will need to build a backup script by using PowerShell and schedule the backups.

> **NEED MORE REVIEW?** SharePoint backups from Central Administration are discussed in the TechNet article "Overview of backup and recovery in SharePoint 2013" at *https://technet.microsoft.com/library/ee663490.aspx*. For more information on how backups are created from a PowerShell perspective, review the TechNet article entitled "Backup and re-covery cmdlets in SharePoint 2013" at *https://technet.microsoft.com/library/ee890109.aspx*.

Establish an SQL Server backup schedule

For environments with a supporting SQL administration team, it's often preferable to allow the SQL team to gather backups of SharePoint configuration and content databases directly from the SQL instance itself. These backups have the benefit of (usually) being part of an overarching enterprise-level backup system, and they can be scheduled and easily monitored; some of the SQL backups (content databases) can be used directly from SharePoint because database restores can be directly mounted and their content can be extracted to a site collection.

Determining an SQL backup schedule

Although it's likely that the SQL team will have input into the overall backup schedule, you will likely need to determine how often you want the farm or its components backed up. This requirement will definitely be driven by both recovery point objectives (where we must restore to) and recovery time objectives (when the restore should be completed).

> **NEED MORE REVIEW?** Although SQL backup and restore operations aren't part of day-to-day SharePoint administration, understanding how these operations are carried out could be an important skill. For more information, review the MSDN article "Back Up and Restore of SQL Server Databases" at *https://msdn.microsoft.com/library/ms187048.aspx*.

Plan a nonproduction environment content refresh

Now that you have an effective mechanism for capturing all or a portion of a production SharePoint farm, it's time to put it to good use. Having a nonproduction environment that closely resembles the production environment from a configuration and limited content standpoint can be a valuable tool for testing configuration and operational changes such as:

- Testing updates you want to add to your production farm.
- Evaluating third-party tool sets, such as administration, backup, antivirus, and others.
- Performing backup and restoration tests.

If desired, you can completely segregate these environments from production altogether, placing them in their own environment from an Active Directory, SQL, and Exchange standpoint. This is an effective way to virtualize development environments to fully test code interactions with external infrastructure systems.

Moving limited content

Occasionally, a select portion of content in an SQL database is all that's required to test a piece of code. In such a case, it's a simple matter to place a copy of the restored content database on the local SharePoint file system and temporarily mount it from within Central Administration. Once the database is mounted, site collection content can be selectively retrieved and restored to the nonproduction environment.

Plan for farm configuration recovery

Central Administration backups include the ability to back up and restore only the SharePoint farm configuration. Farm configurations are always done via a full backup, and can be restored from Central Administration or PowerShell, depending on need.

Restoring a farm configuration backup only overwrites from values present in the backup itself. If the destination farm has a configuration value defined (say, the name of an email server) and the backup being restored does not have the same value defined, it will leave the previous value unchanged.

If you need to recover a farm configuration from a backup and overwrite the existing farm configuration, this action should happen only during a system outage window because the farm will be unavailable until the configuration has been completely restored. Never stop, pause, or restart a farm configuration restore operation because this action will likely cause the farm to become damaged or unstable.

> **NEED MORE REVIEW?** For detailed information concerning the restoration of a farm configuration, refer to the TechNet article "Restore farm configurations in SharePoint 2013" at *https://technet.microsoft.com/library/ee428326.aspx.*

Plan for service application recovery

The restoration of service applications from either a full backup or a full and differential backup combination is a more granular version of the full farm recovery. A backup containing the service application configuration is selected and then restored. During this process, the service application is unavailable for use; thus, it is recommended that this restoration type also be performed during an outage window.

When recovering a service application, the service application type can affect the steps required for restoration from a backup. These restorations can be implemented via Central Administration, PowerShell, or partially (for databases only) by using SQL Server tools:

- **Shared service application**   Only requires the restoration of a single service application.

- **Nonshared service application**   Could include either the restoration of the service application or the restoration of both a service application proxy and the related service application.

- **User Profile service application**   Will restore the entire configuration, including the associated User Profile service databases.

- **Search service application**   Might require the restoration of a separately backed up thesaurus file (not included in a farm backup). The restoration of the Search application itself restores the entire configuration, including the associated Search databases, but requires that the Search application be started after the restoration has completed because the service is restored in a "paused" state.

- **Secure Store service**   Will restore the entire configuration. Once the restoration is complete, the passphrase will need to be refreshed by using the Update-SPSecureStoreApplicationKey cmdlet.

> *NEED MORE REVIEW?*   The backup and restoration of SharePoint farms is heavily dependent on whether or not a third-party utility is used. Instructions in this book and on TechNet are more concerned with backup and restore operations that can be used in Central Administration, PowerShell, or SQL Server tools. For an in-depth understanding of the restoration processes used throughout this chapter, review the TechNet articles under the "Restore (SharePoint 2013)" article at *https://technet.microsoft.com/library/ee428303 .aspx*.

Plan for content recovery

Backed up content in a SharePoint configuration can take several forms, ranging from granular restorations on a per site collection basis to full farm restorations that restore configuration and content information. The type of recovery you wish to perform will in turn specify the type of backup that you will use for the restoration.

The good news here is that SharePoint content can be restored in a remarkably granular fashion in at least three different ways:

- Recovering a SharePoint content database.

- Recovering content from an unattached SharePoint content database.

- Recovering content from an attached, read-only content database.

Recovering a SharePoint content database

A SharePoint content database can be recovered by using either Windows PowerShell cmdlets, Central Administration, or SQL Server tools. The mechanism you choose will determine the appropriate steps for restoration.

In the case of a farm that has an existing content database that will be overwritten, access to the database will need to be released before the restoration can take place. Content databases being restored by using either the Restore-SPFarm cmdlet or Central Administration automatically causes SharePoint to free up access to the content database before the restoration takes place. Content databases being restored from SQL Server tools have to follow a different restoration path, with the following requirements:

- The account doing the restoration should have the sysadmin fixed server role.
- The Windows SharePoint Services Timer service should be stopped on all SharePoint servers, allowing the running stored procedures to finish. This will take several minutes to complete.
- All full, differential, and transaction logs should be applied. As you are restoring the database, don't forget to select the Overwrite The Existing Database option.
- Once the database backups and logs have been restored, the Windows SharePoint Services Timer service can be started on all SharePoint servers.

> **NEED MORE REVIEW?** For detailed instructions concerning the restoration of content databases in SharePoint 2016, visit the TechNet article entitled "Restore content databases in SharePoint 2013" at *https://technet.microsoft.com/library/ee748604.aspx.*

Recovering content from an unattached SharePoint content database

In an enterprise setting, users will occasionally delete content (and sometimes, complete site collections). In earlier SharePoint versions, an entire content database would need to be restored to simply restore an individual site collection.

Fortunately, this situation has changed greatly. SharePoint site collections, sites, and even lists can be restored by using either PowerShell cmdlets or Central Administration. If the latter is used, you have the ability to browse content in the unattached content database, which can be selected for one of two partial actions:

- Back up a site collection.
- Export site or list (don't forget to select Export Full Security and select the correct version).

EXAM TIP

This recovery mechanism is by far the most regularly used in an enterprise setting. Be able to explain and perform recovery of content from an unattached content database.

NEED MORE REVIEW? For in-depth instructions concerning the restoration of content from an unattached SharePoint content database, visit the TechNet article entitled "Restore content from unattached content databases in SharePoint 2013" at *https://technet.microsoft.com/library/hh269602.aspx*.

Recovering content from an attached, read-only content database

This option is focused directly on environments that have one of two configurations: a dedicated, read-only disaster recovery environment, or a temporary, read-only updating environment that is used while the primary environment is being upgraded. This restoration can only be completed by using PowerShell cmdlets (this restoration cannot be done via Central Administration).

For this restoration to take place, the person executing the restoration should have:

- The Securityadmin fixed server role on the SQL Server instance
- The db_owner fixed database role on all databases that will be updated
- Membership in the Administrators group on the SharePoint server where the PowerShell cmdlets will be performed

IMPORTANT Depending on your role in the organization, you might not have the appropriate shell admin credentials within the SharePoint farm. If this is the case, the farm Setup Administrator can assign shell access via the Add-SPShellAdmin PowerShell cmdlets. Once these permissions have been assigned, the database can be mounted via the Mount-SPContentDatabase cmdlet.

NEED MORE REVIEW? For a better understanding of how to attach read-only content databases, review the TechNet article entitled "Attach and restore a read-only content database in SharePoint 2013" at *https://technet.microsoft.com/library/ee748633.aspx*.

Configure a recovery solution by using SQL Database running in Azure and other Azure backup solutions

Up to this point, we've discussed SharePoint recovery from a high availability standpoint (at the primary datacenter) and from a disaster recovery standpoint (at the secondary datacenter). One option has yet to be discussed: setting up a disaster recovery solution in Azure.

As is the case with standard disaster recovery sites, three recovery environments can be created by using Azure Infrastructure Services:

- **Hot standby recovery** A fully configured farm is provisioned, updating, and running in standby mode (read only).
- **Warm standby recovery** A farm has been created, but might require additional effort such as scaling and content database and service application configuration.

- **Cold standby recovery**   A farm has been created, but all the relevant virtual machines are in a stopped state.

The selected recovery configuration will meet two pertinent metrics: recovery objectives and operational costs. The environment that you select will have to meet both the recovery point and recovery time objectives as defined by the business; conversely, the environment selected will also need to meet operation cost forecasts.

Costs for recovery environments in Azure are based on memory, processor, and storage usage. As you move across the options from hot to cold standby recovery, the costs tend to reduce dramatically, but need to be weighed fairly against the costs of maintaining an offsite disaster recovery location.

> **NEED MORE REVIEW?**   Specific considerations for each recovery type (hot, warm, and cold) are thoroughly covered in the TechNet article entitled "SharePoint Server 2013 Disaster Recovery in Microsoft Azure" at *https://technet.microsoft.com/library/dn635313(v =office.15).aspx*.

Skill: Plan and configure social workload

One of the key drivers in SharePoint 2013 was the introduction of large-scale social networking. SharePoint 2016 further advances the integration of enterprise social features in day-to-day collaboration. Users in SharePoint 2016 can now firmly take advantage of these features both on premises and in the cloud, thanks to effective hybrid integration design.

> **This section covers how to:**
> - Plan communities
> - Plan My Sites
> - Plan OneDrive redirection
> - Plan social permissions
> - Plan user profiles
> - Plan activity feeds
> - Plan connections
> - Configure Yammer settings

Plan communities

Communities are part of the social computing platform within SharePoint 2016, and coordinate collaboration between large groups of users in the enterprise. From a comparison standpoint, communities are to SharePoint hierarchies what folksonomies are to a taxonomy; that is to say, they allow people to collaborate outside of their traditional hierarchy and related navigational structure within a SharePoint 2016 installation.

Community types can vary based on the membership of the community and the desired visibility of the community within the enterprise:

- **Private communities**   These communities are the least discoverable in a SharePoint farm and are purposely shared with only a limited number of members who contribute content.

- **Closed communities**   These communities are viewable to everyone in the SharePoint installation, but only approved members can contribute content. Visitors can request access, but not join the site automatically.

- **Open communities (with explicit membership)**   These communities are viewable to everyone in the SharePoint installation, and a visitor can automatically join as a member to contribute content.

- **Open communities**   These communities are viewable by everyone in the SharePoint installation, and all users can contribute by default.

Required services and service applications for communities

Three services and service applications should be configured for the use of communities within a SharePoint 2016 farm:

- **User Profile service**   Integrates with community sites by updating mentioned users and hash tags in users' activity feeds on their My Site.

- **Managed metadata**   Allows users to include hash tags in their discussions and replies. Users can also create new tags and add them to the term store, helping to generate a corporate taxonomy.

- **Search service**   Allows users to search within discussions and community sites; it also populates the Community Portal page with links to community sites.

EXAM TIP

For the test, be familiar with which services and service applications are needed for the proper operation of community sites and portals; also be acquainted with the permission levels required for each different community implementation type.

NEED MORE REVIEW?   A complete discussion on the planning required for community implementations is available in the TechNet article "Plan for communities in SharePoint Server 2013" at *https://technet.microsoft.com/library/jj219489.aspx.*

Plan My Sites

My Sites in a SharePoint enterprise are individual, personal sites that are available for a single user. This is an alternate, on-premises arrangement to using the OneDrive functionality present in a hybrid arrangement with Office 365.

My Sites are the result of several distinct configuration efforts, and consist of the underlying web application hosting both the My Site host site collection (used to generate individual My Sites) and requiring the use of several SharePoint service applications such as Managed metadata, Search, and the User Profile service application.

> **IMPORTANT** Although we still refer to this functionality as My Sites from an administration standpoint, it is important to note that users will see this functionality as OneDrive for Business in SharePoint 2016, even though this is an on-premises implementation.

Enabling individual sites for users in the enterprise can be a contentious discussion with management and with entities such as human resources and legal departments. At first glance, it seems that this is a waste of resources, and could potentially cause a governance headache; nothing could be further from the truth.

By default, My Sites have site quotas to control the overall size of the individual's storage space. They also have a built-in workflow that defines the disposition of the individual's site collection, should the individual leave the company.

Without My Sites, two major functions are completely lost:

- **People search** Enterprises continuously struggle with keeping contact information for individuals up to date, but My Sites allow for users to update their own information. The selection of fields to be updated is entirely under the control of the SharePoint administrator and any governance or regulation that applies to the enterprise. The resulting system allows for an easy mechanism to locate a user, see their free and busy schedule for meetings, send emails, and have conversations via phone or Skype for Business.

- **Expertise search** Enterprises also struggle with keeping an individual's skills and certifications up to date. Having this information available in a searchable index allows the organization to easily and quickly locate people of a certain expertise level or skill set.

EXAM TIP

Understanding the particulars of how a My Site host is configured and how supporting services and service applications are configured will likely be on the exam.

> **NEED MORE REVIEW?** To gain an understanding of the planning and configuration required for My Sites, visit the TechNet article "Plan for My Sites in SharePoint Server 2016" at *https://technet.microsoft.com/library/cc262500(v=office.16).aspx*.

Plan OneDrive redirection

In SharePoint hybrid deployments, users can be redirected to use the OneDrive in Office 365 functionality. This redirection can be narrowed in scope, allowing some users to use hybrid OneDrive for Business while others still use the on-premises version of OneDrive for Business (My Sites).

Requirements for OneDrive redirection

To successfully redirect licensed users to OneDrive in Office 365, a handful of configuration changes will need to be made:

- **Permissions** As is the case for on-premises OneDrive for Business users, hybrid OneDrive for Business users requires two permissions to be enabled in the User Profile service application:
  - Create Personal Site, which is required for personal storage, newsfeeds, and followed content
  - Follow People and Edit Profile
- **Audiencing (optional)** You might want to phase in the availability of OneDrive for Business in a hybrid configuration. Adding a selection of users to an audience allows you to grant access to only those users while potentially allowing others to access OneDrive for Business on premises. This configuration is made in the Configure Hybrid OneDrive And Sites Features menu within Office 365 in Central Administration.
- **Configuration of hybrid OneDrive and Sites features** In Central Administration, you can specify a My Site URL present in your Office 365 tenancy, select an audience as required, and then choose to enable OneDrive only.

> **NEED MORE REVIEW?** More information about the configuration of OneDrive for Business redirection can be found in the TechNet article entitled "How to redirect users to Office 365 for OneDrive for Business" at *https://technet.microsoft.com/library/dn627525 .aspx.*

Plan social permissions

Whether speaking of My Sites on-premises or OneDrive for Business in the cloud, the permissions structure for individual users is the same.

Three types of social permissions exist in the User Profile service:

- **Create Personal Site** Enables users to create personal sites to store documents, newsfeeds, and followed content.
- **Follow People and Edit Profile** Enables users to follow people from OneDrive for Business and edit their personal profile.
- **Use Tags and Notes** Enables users to use the Tags and Notes feature from earlier versions of SharePoint. This setting is enabled by default.

> **IMPORTANT** It is recommended that existing permissions in the User Profile service not be altered because making changes can have unintended consequences.

Plan user profiles

At a core level, a user profile is a collection of metadata and properties that describes an individual user. From a SharePoint standpoint (and within Active Directory), a user is unique, and properties can be assigned to provide information about the user.

An example of this might be a user's contact information within a company. Each user has an associated name, address, phone number, email, manager, job title, and other information within their distinct user profile. This user profile can be populated manually, but it's often better to import these properties from an external system, such as Active Directory; this function is profile synchronization, and is controlled from Central Administration.

Extending a user profile

Although the information found in Active Directory is useful, it does not fully describe an individual. For instance, other information about a user can be manually added or populated by different systems (or the user themselves), such as:

- Customers
- Products
- Sales leads
- Expertise
- Certifications
- Hobbies

Granted, some of this information might seem trivial (and perhaps unnecessary); after all, what does an individual's interest in a particular hobby have to do with the business? Individual information often forms the basis of community, and this community comprises the workforce. As understanding improves between individuals, barriers fall, and users collaborate more freely.

Property policies

Laws concerning individual privacy vary by location. The ability to configure and control the properties associated with an individual user can be controlled from within Central Administration, and allow you to specify the following:

- Whether a property is included in user profiles
- Whether the property is required
- Whether users can change the privacy setting on an individual property
- Who in the organization can view the property (role based)

NEED MORE REVIEW? User profiles can be simple to configure, but require quite a bit of forethought regarding the privacy and use of information gathered about an individual. More information about how the properties can be implemented can be found in the TechNet article entitled "Plan user profiles in SharePoint Server 2013" at *https://technet .microsoft.com/library/ee721054.aspx*.

Plan activity feeds

Activity feeds are known in SharePoint as *microblogging*. This feature is wholly dependent on the availability of the distributed cache service, and allows users to have short, public conversations, very similar to those found on public social websites.

A microblog allows a user to post messages that can include text, URLs, pictures, and videos. A post is limited to a maximum of 512 characters; once posted, it is immediately seen in a feed. Hash tags (#Tag) and mentions (@Mention) are a way to capture the attention of users, who can then follow (and potentially "like") the conversation.

If you've used the Yammer online functionality present in Office 365, it's likely that this feature might seem redundant. The reason for this apparent redundancy is that activity feeds are available solely in an on-premises installation, replaced in a hybrid installation by Yammer.

NEED MORE REVIEW? Although activity and newsfeeds are largely superseded by Yammer, some organizations are not willing to maintain their social interactions in a cloud-based forum. Understanding how to configure this on-premises feature is covered in two TechNet articles, "Overview of microblog features, feeds, and the Distributed Cache service in SharePoint Server 2013" at *https://technet.microsoft.com/library/jj219700.aspx*, and "Plan for feeds and the Distributed Cache service in SharePoint Server 2013" at *https:// technet.microsoft.com/library/jj219572.aspx*.

Plan connections

As mentioned previously, user profiles in SharePoint provide metadata and properties about a user. This information is generally captured from two types of sources: Directory services and business systems.

Directory service integration

Users represented in profiles within SharePoint Server 2016 must have a profile in a supported directory service. These services include Active Directory, Sun Java System Directory Server, Novell eDirectory, and IBM Tivoli. A connection must be configured and an import sync done to retrieve users from one or more directory services.

SharePoint 2016 supports Active Directory Import without the need for any external functionality, but has limitations such as the inability to support more than one forest, import user photos, or export attributes back to Active Directory. If the required directory service integration cannot support these limitations, then an external MIM server can be configured.

By using MIM, connections to external, non-Active Directory systems can be configured to import data to user profiles. This technology also eclipses the OOB sync tool, allowing bidirectional flow of profile properties and attributes, the use of multiple Active Directory forests, and the automatic import of user profile photos.

> **NEED MORE REVIEW?**   Guidance for selecting an import mechanism (Active Directory Import vs. MIM) is available in the TechNet article entitled "Install Microsoft Identity Manager for User Profiles in SharePoint Server 2016" at *https://technet.microsoft.com/library/mt627723(v=office.16).aspx*.

Business services integration

Business services connectivity requires the use of external content types that are backed by Business Connectivity Services (BCS). BCS established a one-way, read-only connection to the respective business service, then a field (or fields) in the external content type can be mapped to corresponding properties in a user profile.

> **IMPORTANT**   Connections to both of these types of external systems should be carefully evaluated and planned. Microsoft provides planning worksheets that include directory services and business services connectivity at *https://www.microsoft.com/download/details.aspx?id=35404*.

Configure Yammer settings

Yammer is an online-only social tool that is available in two versions: Yammer Basic and Yammer Enterprise. Yammer Basic is free, and intended for the consumer market, whereas Yammer Enterprise provides additional tools and resources to assist administrators in configuring a social environment within SharePoint 2016.

Connecting SharePoint on premises to Yammer

SharePoint 2016 on premises can use one of two mechanisms for connecting to Yammer:

- **AAD Connect**   A mechanism for allowing users to use their Active Directory Domain Services (AD DS) credentials with Yammer by synchronizing their on-premises accounts to the cloud.

- **Single-sign on**   A mechanism for allowing users to use their AD DS credentials with Yammer via a federated identity provider.

These mechanisms should seem familiar by now because these are also the mechanisms for establishing a hybrid connection between SharePoint on premises and other Office 365 functionality (such as OneDrive and My Sites).

Once the connection mechanism is in place, connecting the SharePoint environment to Yammer is pretty straightforward, requiring only that you click a button in Central Administration, Office 365, Configure Yammer (Figure 3-18).

Yammer Configuration

Yammer Integration

Yammer is Microsoft's recommended tool for
social collaboration.

Activate Yammer to make Yammer the primary
social experience for everyone in your
organization. You can switch back anytime.

Activate Yammer

FIGURE 3-18 Activating Yammer

EXAM TIP

Be familiar with the processes available for configuring the connection between SharePoint Server 2016 and Office 365, including those required for activating Yammer in the enterprise. More information about this activation process can be found in the TechNet article entitled "Integrate Yammer with on-premises SharePoint 2013 environments" at *https://technet.microsoft.com/library/dn270535.aspx*.

Displaying the Yammer feed inside SharePoint sites

Reviewing documentation, you might see a reference to a Yammer App, which was used to display Yammer information within a SharePoint site. This app has since been deprecated and replaced by Yammer Embed.

Yammer Embed allows you to display one of several feeds on your SharePoint site:

- **My Feed**   Shows each user their personal feed with relevant items
- **Group Feed**   Shows the latest conversations in a specific Yammer group
- **Topic Feed**   Shows all posts having to do with a specific topic

- **User Feed**   Shows all posts participated in by a particular user
- **Open Graph Feed**   Allows you to start a discussion about an object (for example, a webpage)

These feeds are displayed by cutting and pasting an HTML script from Yammer into a SharePoint Script Editor Web Part.

> **NEED MORE REVIEW?**   For more information about how to configure Yammer feeds in SharePoint 2016 sites, visit the Yammer Developer article entitled "Embed Feed" at *https://developer.yammer.com/v1.0/docs/embed*.

Skill: Plan and configure a Web Content Management workload

Web Content Management (WCM) is concerned with the creation and deployment of content from a publishing standpoint; that is to say, a few people generate content that is then consumed by a far greater number of users. This skill develops an understanding of the features in SharePoint 2016 that support this effort, extending content to desktop, tablet, and mobile clients alike.

> **This section covers how to:**
> - Plan and configure channels
> - Plan and configure product catalog and topic pages
> - Plan and configure Design Manager
> - Plan and configure content deployment
> - Plan and configure display templates
> - Plan and configure variations

Plan and configure channels

In the modern world, we expect websites to render content appropriate to the screen format of the device we are using. One approach to meeting this expectation is to brand SharePoint by using a responsive design. Although this solution works without issue, the amount of content being sent from the web server to the client (cascading style sheets [CSS], images, and other data) can be significant.

SharePoint 2016 (and previous versions) can be configured to change the response (and thus the amount of downloaded data) depending on the type of device requesting the web content; this functionality is called design channels.

Design channels tailor the response by using multiple sets of master pages and CSS, each designed specifically for the device making the request. One response type can be created for smartphones (with 4- to 5-inch screens) and another is created for tablets with larger screens (8 to 10 inches). A total of 10 device channels can be created in an on-premises installation of SharePoint 2016.

EXAM TIP

Although it's not likely that device channels will be on the exam, you should know two things. First, device channels are only available on publishing sites (or those with the Publishing feature enabled), and second, each type of device identifies itself by using an alias; testing the alias requires that you append *?DeviceChannel=alias* to the URL.

The act of configuring a device channel is not terribly complex (although the generation of appropriate master pages and CSS definitely can be). To configure a device channel, you must specify the following settings:

- **Name (required)**   The name used to identify the channel being created
- **Alias (required)**   A unique name that can be used in code to refer to the channel
- **Description**   An optional description of the channel
- **Device Inclusion Rules (required)**   One or more user agent substrings (how SharePoint identifies a particular device type) that determine the devices that will use this channel
- **Active**   A check box that activates this channel for use

NEED MORE REVIEW?   Device channels require quite a bit of design work for each set of master page, CSS, and image combinations, and are described in the MSDN article entitled "SharePoint 2013 Design Manager device channels" at *https://msdn.microsoft.com/library /office/jj862343.aspx*.

Plan and configure product catalog and topic pages

SharePoint 2013 introduced a new type of publishing site called a product catalog. Despite the name, a product catalog site (Figure 3-19) can be used to surface lists and libraries (catalogs of information) via Search. Any series of lists and libraries can be surfaced in this template for use in cross-site publishing.

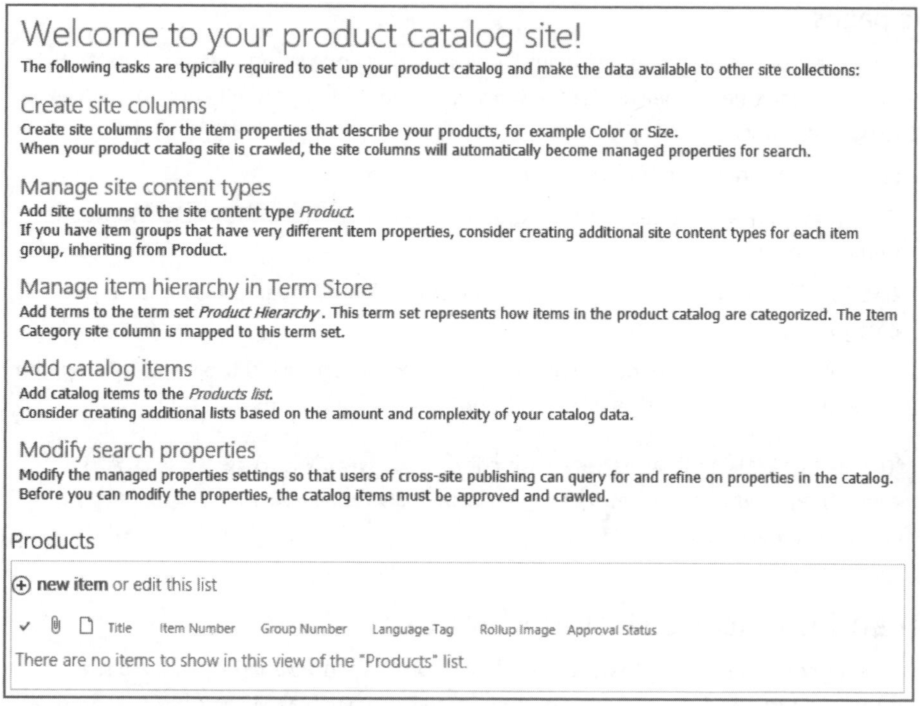

FIGURE 3-19 A newly created product catalog site

A newly created product catalog site guides you through the process and steps necessary to fully configure the site and its catalogs. These steps are broken down into five major activities, as shown in Figure 3-19:

- **Create Site Columns**   Columns with descriptive metadata that can be reused and describe the products in a catalog.

- **Manage Site Content Types**   Adding the newly created site columns to a content type (such as Product).

- **Manage Item Hierarchy In Term Store**   Adds individual terms to the product hierarchy term set, representing how items from the product catalog are categorized.

- **Add Catalog Items**   Allows individual items to be added to the Products list.

- **Modify Search Properties**   Used to modify managed properties settings so that cross-site publishing can query for and refine on properties in the catalog.

EXAM TIP

Because the product catalog sites use both the Term Store and Search properties, they are heavily dependent on the Managed Metadata Service and Search service application, respectively.

Topic pages

Although these pages can be used with any publishing site consuming managed metadata, topic pages are nonetheless heavily associated with a SharePoint product catalog, and are effective ways of providing navigation based on a term set.

There are two distinct types of topic pages:

- **Category pages**   A category page displays a single term that describes individual items.
- **Catalog item pages**   A catalog item page displays individual terms beneath the category term.

An example of these topic pages might be having a category called tools and catalog item pages for items such as screwdriver, saw, drill, and lathe.

> **NEED MORE REVIEW?**   Topic pages are described in the TechNet article entitled "Assign a category page and a catalog item page to a term in SharePoint Server 2013" at *https:// technet.microsoft.com/library/jj884105.aspx.*

Plan and configure Design Manager

Design Manager is a publishing feature that allows you to brand a SharePoint 2016 site without the need to develop solutions in a coding platform such as Microsoft Visual Studio. Branding a SharePoint implementation then draws closer to the toolsets and experiences required to brand standard websites. The resulting design can be copied to publishing sites and activated to instantly achieve a uniform branding experience.

Implementing a design by using Design Manager

Often, website design is carried out on a number of third-party tools. The resulting output of these tools (the design) can include:

- HTML files (which will be converted to SharePoint Master Pages)
- CSS files
- JavaScript files
- Site images

> **IMPORTANT**   To use Design Manager, you must possess at least the Designer permission level on your site in SharePoint 2016.

After the HTML file is automatically converted to a Master Page, a relationship is established between the HTML file and Master Page. Further revisions should not be applied to the Master Page, but to the HTML file itself; SharePoint will automatically update the Master Page.

Snippets

When you are deciding how you wish the site to appear, you might decide that you need to add SharePoint-specific functionality; after all, it's unlikely that the third-party design tool knows or cares that the resulting output will be used in SharePoint. Thus, the completed HTML page will need to add the SharePoint functionality via Snippets.

Step 4 of the overall Design Manager process calls for you to edit Master Pages; this is the point at which an HTML file will be converted to a Master Page. Selecting a Master Page (only its HTML, really) opens the Master Page in a separate browser window. At the top right corner of this window, you will see the Snippets link (Figure 3-20).

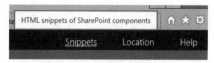

FIGURE 3-20 The Snippets link

Clicking Snippets opens a series of menu items specific to SharePoint functionality. Selecting an item (such as Top Navigation) causes the HTML for that tag to be shown. This HTML can be applied at the correct location in your HTML file, and it will automatically be added to the resulting Master Page.

> **NEED MORE REVIEW?**   For a better understanding of how you might use Design Manager in SharePoint 2016, review the MSDN site entitled "Overview of Design Manager in SharePoint 2013" at *https://msdn.microsoft.com/library/office/jj822363.aspx*.

Plan and configure content deployment

Within SharePoint 2016, it is possible to generate content in one site and deploy the content to another site. This functionality, often referred to as cross-site publishing, can be useful, particularly in regulatory, business, or legal situations that require that the content being generated be physically separated from the location to which it is published.

> **IMPORTANT**   In previous versions of SharePoint (2010 and before), content deployment could be carried out by using the Content Deployment Source feature, which only deploys content such as webpages, document libraries and lists, and other web design files, such as images and style sheets. This deployment mechanism is intended *solely* for backward compatibility. As a result, it is incompatible with a series of other SharePoint 2016 features, such as ratings, managed navigation, blog sites, slide libraries, social sites, and others.

If you are updating a content deployment solution based on the Content Deployment Source feature, then you have three options for content deployment:

- Author in place or use cross-site publishing by using the built-in security model.
- Use a disaster recovery solution such as SQL Server Log Shipping or Availability Groups to replicate content between source and destination farms.

- Make a backup copy of the site, restore it to a separate content database, and then work on the site. Once the site is ready for use, change the alternate access mappings URL to point at the new site.

Plan and configure display templates

Probably one of the most useful components related to Search in SharePoint Server 2016, display templates are Web Parts that control which properties appear in a Web Part and how the properties appear in the Web Part.

Each display template is made up of two distinct components:

- An HTML version of the display template
- A .js file

These files are combined in a Search Web Part to produce the expected functionality.

Configuring a display template

The process for creating a new display template really boils down to four major steps:

1. Map and open a connection to the Master Page gallery. This location can be found in Step 3 of Design Manager, Upload Design Files, and in general is the URL of the site collection you are working on, appended with *_catalogs/masterpages*.

2. Open the Display Templates folder.

3. Copy the HTML file for an existing display template that is similar to the template you want to create.

4. Modify the HTML for your copy in an editor.

> **IMPORTANT** There's really no need to reinvent the wheel here: Copying an existing template as a basis for the change you want to make really is the fastest way to generate a new display template.

EXAM TIP

Display templates are a key functionality in SharePoint 2016. Understand (at least at a high level) the differences in display template types, how each can be altered, and how new ones can be implemented. More information on display templates can be found in the MSDN article entitled "SharePoint 2013 Design Manager display templates" at *https://msdn.microsoft.com/library/office/jj945138.aspx*, and reference information about display templates can be found in the TechNet article "Display template reference in SharePoint Server 2013" at *https://technet.microsoft.com/library/jj944947.aspx*.

Plan and configure variations

Variations are a mechanism for presenting multiple versions of the same page that are based on different human languages (such as English, Russian, or Japanese). The individual's browser settings are used to identify their native tongue, and the SharePoint server responds with the correct language variant of the content.

Variation labels

Each language that can be installed in SharePoint has an associated two-character variation label; for instance, EN for English, FR for French, and DE for German. This variation label is used to present the appropriate variation of the original site.

If you had a SharePoint site at *https://home.wingtiptoys.com* and wanted to enable these three variations, users visiting this site would be routed to the appropriate variation:

- *https://home.wingtiptoys.com/EN* for English
- *https://home.wingtiptoys.com/FR* for French
- *https://home.wingtiptoys.com/DE* for German

As each of these variations is created, a navigation term set is created for its variation label. The term set for the source variation label is named Variations Navigation; this is further expanded when a variations label is created for the language, appending the variations label to the source variation label, such as Variations Navigation (en-us) for U.S. English.

> **NEED MORE REVIEW?** The proper configuration of languages and variations within SharePoint can be quite complex. When translation services are added (to allow for third-party translators to create the language-specific pages), the end result is a globally ready content management system. Variations are covered on TechNet in the article entitled "Variations overview in SharePoint Server 2013" at *https://technet.microsoft.com/library/ff628966.aspx*.

Skill: Plan and configure an Enterprise Content Management workload

Enterprise Content Management (ECM) is concerned with the sheer number of documents that are created in a collaborative setting by users across the enterprise. This content is subject to a series of business process and legal requirements that prevent personally identifiable information and other types of sensitive content from being deployed into publicly available SharePoint sites.

This section covers how to:

- Plan and configure eDiscovery
- Plan and configure document routing
- Plan and configure co-authoring
- Plan and configure durable links
- Plan and configure record disposition and retention
- Plan large document repositories
- Plan and configure software boundaries
- Plan and configure data loss prevention
- Plan and configure in-place holds and document deletion features

Plan and configure eDiscovery

Legal departments in many enterprise environments are feeling increasing pressure on two fronts:

- The ability to quickly locate and place holds on content
- The ability to create both scheduled and ad hoc searches for sensitive content in the enterprise

This pressure results in a need for users in these departments to easily and reliably search for content across three distinct systems of record: SharePoint Server, Exchange Server, and Skype for Business Server. There are three major activities involved in connecting these systems of record: Connecting Skype for Business to Exchange, Configuring Skype for Business Server to use Exchange Server archiving, and Connecting Exchange to SharePoint.

Establishing connectivity between Skype for Business and Exchange

Connecting Skype for Business to Exchange involves the creation of a server-to-server (S2S) relationship between these two systems; this relationship requires that each environment be configured as a partner application to the other:

- **Skype for Business to Exchange**   Requires that the appropriate server certificates be installed; then the use of the *Configure-EnterprisePartnerApplication.ps1* PowerShell script will establish connectivity.

- **Exchange to Skype for Business**   Requires that the appropriate server certificates be installed; then the use of the New-CSPartnerApplication PowerShell cmdlet will establish connectivity.

> *NEED MORE REVIEW?*   Although neither Skype for Business nor Exchange Server are core elements of understanding needed for the exam, an understanding of how these two environments can be configured as partner applications will lead to a better understanding of

the infrastructure required to enable eDiscovery. Detailed information about this configuration can be found in the TechNet article entitled "Configure partner applications in Skype for Business Server 2015 and Microsoft Exchange Server" at *https://technet .microsoft.com/library/jj688151.aspx.*

Configuring Skype for Business to use Exchange Server archiving

The action of archiving Skype for Business conversations to Exchange Server requires a maximum of three steps:

1. Enable Exchange archiving by modifying your Skype for Business Server archiving configuration settings (required for all deployments).

2. Enable archiving for internal communications, external communications, or both for your users (required for all deployments).

3. Configure the *ExchangeArchivingPolicy* property for each user (only required if Skype for Business Server and Exchange are located in different forests).

Connecting Exchange to SharePoint

If at all possible, SharePoint Server should be connected to Exchange for the purposes of eDiscovery. Once this connection has been established, SharePoint Search can be used to retrieve and place holds on information across both enterprise systems.

EXAM TIP

Be very familiar with the process of establishing S2S connectivity between SharePoint and Exchange Server systems. This configuration is described in the TechNet article "Configure server-to-server authentication between SharePoint Server 2013 and Exchange Server 2013" at *https://technet.microsoft.com/library/jj655399.aspx.*

Dependency on Search

eDiscovery in SharePoint Server 2016 is heavily dependent on the correct configuration of the Search service application. As both ad hoc and scheduled eDiscovery queries rely on the Keyword Query Language (KQL), the Search index must be populated and in good working order.

IMPORTANT Although we've mentioned the Search service application, up to this point, we've not yet configured one. If you are configuring eDiscovery for use, you'll need to do so, and this is covered in Chapter 5, "Search."

Navigating the eDiscovery Site Collection

The final step in this effort is to create an eDiscovery Center site for use in building new eDiscovery cases (shown in Figure 3-21).

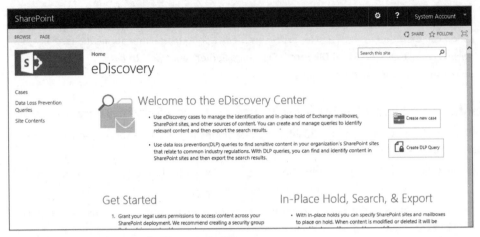

FIGURE 3-21 The newly created eDiscovery Center

Once the eDiscovery site has been created (its creation is no different than that of any other site), you can create a site for your first case:

1. Click Create New Case.

2. Enter a Title and Description for your new site.

3. Enter a name for the new site in the Website Address section.

4. Under the Template Selection, select eDiscovery Case.

5. At this point, you can choose to Use The Same Permissions As The Parent Site or to create and Use Unique Permissions.

6. Finally, you can choose whether you want this site on the Quick Launch of the eDiscovery site, and whether you want the case site to use the Top Link bar from the eDiscovery site.

Plan and configure document routing

Document routing addresses a fundamental problem from a user administration standpoint; that is, a user uploading content to a folder on a file share can (most often) see documents created and uploaded by others. Although this usually isn't an issue, some documents are more sensitive than others and should not be exposed to view.

It is possible in SharePoint to permission a document library so that the user can do a "blind drop" or "mail slot" document upload (where they cannot see the document they just uploaded); this is an improvement but still doesn't allow the person receiving the content to make much use of it without establishing a workflow to route the document from library to library.

Using Content Organizer

SharePoint provides a feature known as Content Organizer for just this purpose. This feature can automatically perform a series of tasks:

- **Route documents to different libraries or folders**   Content Organizer can route an uploaded document to a library or folder, based on a series of rules. This includes the ability to route documents to a different document library altogether.

- **Upload all documents to a Drop Off Library**   Content Organizer can be used to place all uploaded documents in a Drop Off Library, where metadata can be entered and a submission process completed.

- **Manage folder size**   Content Organizer can be used to monitor the number of items in a folder and ensure that no folder contains more than a specified number of items (2,500 by default). When this number is exceeded, a new folder is created.

- **Manage duplicate submissions**   When the same document is uploaded twice, Content Organizer can be used to either configure versioning or change the file name by adding unique characters.

- **Maintain audit logs**   Content Organizer can maintain audit logs about a document stored with the document after it is routed.

To enable the use of Content Organizer, just activate the Content Organizer site feature in the site you are using. Once this is complete, you will need to create new Content Organizer rules and then configure the appropriate Content Organizer settings. Both of these options are found within the Site Administration section of Site Settings.

> **NEED MORE REVIEW?**   More information about Content Organizer, including how to set it up at a basic level, can be found in the support.office.com article "Create Content Organizer rules to route documents" at *https://support.office.com/article/Create-Content-Organizer-rules-to-route-documents-1E4D37A3-635D-4764-B0FC-F7C5356C1900*.

Plan and configure co-authoring

How is collaboration accomplished in your organization? Traditionally there are a couple of ways this is done, even after deploying SharePoint:

- A document is emailed to other users, asking for their input; the author then has to take this information and transfer it back from the altered copies to the original document.

- A document could be uploaded to SharePoint; then by using check-in and check-out, could be altered in an orderly fashion.

It's fairly obvious that neither of these solutions is perfect for a document that is heavily edited by multiple users; the email solution is just not workable, and the SharePoint check-in and check-out solution works great until someone leaves the document checked out and goes on vacation.

Fortunately, there's something better: co-authoring. This functionality within SharePoint allows for multiple users to *simultaneously* edit a document. Editing a document in this fashion requires a certain amount of training from a user standpoint, but is fairly straightforward to learn.

Planning considerations for co-authoring (documents)

Several factors should be considered before deploying co-authoring:

- **Permissions** Users participating in co-authoring should have Edit rights in the appropriate document library.
- **Versioning** Either major or major and minor versioning can be used.
- **Versions retained** Retaining a large number of versions can become unwieldy over time, resulting in increased storage requirements. Consider restricting the number of major and minor versions in a library.
- **Versioning period** This period is specifically for use with co-authoring and specifies how often a version of a document being co-authored should be captured.
- **Check out** The Require Check Out feature should never be activated for libraries that host co-authored documents.

Planning considerations for co-authoring in Microsoft OneNote

OneNote brings its own considerations to co-authoring, particularly related to the way it stores content in a SharePoint library:

- **Minor versioning** Absolutely, positively, do *not* enable minor versioning in a document library that hosts OneNote notebooks. Minor versioning will cause the OneNote notebook to stop allowing co-authoring and could result in corruption.
- **Versions retained** OneNote is a famously chatty application, regularly committing data to its notebooks. It is recommended that the number of versions retained be specified at a reasonable level, to ensure that the supporting document library does not become too large.

> **IMPORTANT** Consider creating new OneNote notebooks in their own, dedicated document library. This way, you will ensure that no one inadvertently makes configuration changes that are disagreeable or cause corruption in OneNote notebooks.

> **NEED MORE REVIEW?** For a clearer understanding of how co-authoring is configured and used in SharePoint 2016, visit the TechNet article entitled "Co-authoring administration in SharePoint 2013" at *https://technet.microsoft.com/library/ff718235.aspx*.

Plan and configure durable links

Durable links is a feature in SharePoint 2016 that allows a document to be moved within a site collection without changing its resource URL. This is particularly useful for documents that are commonly used (and thus bookmarked) by users. As this document is moved around (perhaps by a workflow), the user can always reference the document by its bookmark, even though the document itself has changed location.

Office Online Server requirement

The durable links feature is not available in a core, OOB SharePoint 2016 installation. SharePoint relies on Office Online Server to handle the assignment of a resource-based ID link for Web Application Open Platform Interface (WOPI) protocol documents. The resource ID assigned to individual documents is stored inside the content database, and is related to the source document.

When a user selects a document link, SharePoint Server 2016 looks up the file by Resource ID and then opens it in Office Online Server.

Document movement considerations

Although the document might move from location to location, its permissions do not. No provision is available for per-item permissioning of documents that use durable links. If a document is moved to a location where a user does not have permissions, the durable link will still be functional, but the user will not be able to access the document.

EXAM TIP

From an exam point of view, the configuration of durable links is firmly intertwined with the configuration of Office Online Server (and its trust with SharePoint 2016). Review the TechNet article entitled "Configure Office Online Server for SharePoint Server 2016" at *https://technet.microsoft.com/library/ff431687(v=office.16).aspx.*

Plan and configure record disposition and retention

Compliance officers in a SharePoint Server environment work with SharePoint administrators to define the life cycle of documents in the enterprise. Not every document becomes a declared record in the enterprise, but the management of those that do becomes of paramount importance.

Records in an enterprise are often held for a period of several years based on the type of document they are. For instance, the priority and life span of a legal contract or other enterprise document might far exceed that of a budget workbook or memorandum (even if these documents were placed on hold for a legal case).

Disposition and retention of documents often has to do with a number of deciding questions:

- What is the legal responsibility of the enterprise to retain or destroy a document?
- What is the physical capacity of the system that stores the data?
- How capable is the Search subsystem of capturing large amounts of data and retaining them in an index? Would it make sense to maintain these long-lived records in a different index?

SharePoint 2016 has the ability to not only provide for the disposition of individual documents, but also to control the life span and eventual disposition of an entire site (and all its associated data and libraries).

Defining site policies

SharePoint 2016 allows for site policies to be created at the root of a site collection. This functionality can also be configured to apply to multiple site collections (including self-service site creation sites) by deploying the policies at a site collection that also happens to be a content type hub.

A site policy captures three sets of data (Figure 3-22):

- The Name And Description of the newly created site policy
- What happens from a Site Closure and Deletion standpoint when the policy has been activated:
  - Do Not Close Or Delete Site Automatically.
  - Delete Sites Automatically.
  - Close And Delete Sites Automatically.
- What happens at a Site Collection Closure (whether or not the site collection will be set to read-only status)

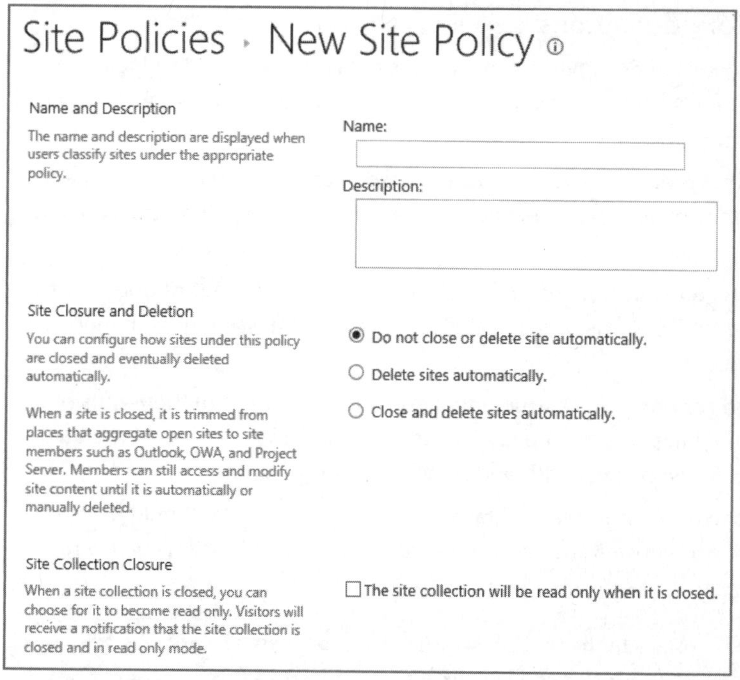

Site Policies · New Site Policy ⓘ

Name and Description

The name and description are displayed when users classify sites under the appropriate policy.

Name:

Description:

Site Closure and Deletion

You can configure how sites under this policy are closed and eventually deleted automatically.

When a site is closed, it is trimmed from places that aggregate open sites to site members such as Outlook, OWA, and Project Server. Members can still access and modify site content until it is automatically or manually deleted.

◉ Do not close or delete site automatically.

○ Delete sites automatically.

○ Close and delete sites automatically.

Site Collection Closure

When a site collection is closed, you can choose for it to become read only. Visitors will receive a notification that the site collection is closed and in read only mode.

☐ The site collection will be read only when it is closed.

FIGURE 3-22 Creating a new site policy

Plan large document repositories

SharePoint lists and libraries are quite capable of storing up to 30 million items in a list or library. That said, a great deal of configuration work is required to ensure that the environment storing these documents is capable of supporting this workload.

Guidance from Microsoft on TechNet (see *https://technet.microsoft.com/library /hh395916(v=office.14).aspx*) defines a set of tests to determine the proper configuration of your farm (particularly the SQL back end) for large document repositories:

- Document upload test
- Document upload and route test
- Document download
- Access document library
- Access home page with Content Search Web Parts
- Managed metadata fallback query (return more than 5,000 results)
- Managed metadata selective query (return fewer than 5,000 results)
- Content type fallback query (return more than 5,000 results, filtering by content type)

Document repository definitions

To effectively service millions of documents to a user base from an archival standpoint, some boundaries must be placed around the configuration of which documents live in a library and how the files are accessed.

- **Unstructured document library**   An unstructured library (hundreds of documents) has no document manager, and allows for high read transactions, with balanced adds and updates.

- **Collaborative large list or library**   A large list or library (thousands of documents) might have some subject owners, and allows for high read transactions with more updates than adds.

- **Structured large repository**   A structured large repository (tens of thousands of documents) should have an assigned content steward, and allows for very high read transaction numbers with fewer adds and significantly fewer updates.

- **Large-scale archive**   A large-scale archive (millions of documents) should have an assigned team of content stewards, and allows for very high adds with very few reads and updates.

> **NEED MORE REVIEW?**   It falls to the SharePoint administration team to work with the records management group to architect and implement a portion of the SharePoint environment that will be suitable for long-term records storage. Part of this conversation will have to do with server resources and design, as this type of document load needs to perform well. For a better understanding of these requirements, visit the TechNet article "Estimate capacity and performance for compliance and eDiscovery for SharePoint Server 2013" at *https://technet.microsoft.com/library/dn169053.aspx*.

Plan and configure software boundaries

In designing a SharePoint solution, the designers must address farm characteristics such as the number of servers, their memory and storage configuration, and how SharePoint itself should be architected from an internal standpoint.

To this end, Microsoft provides guidance based on performance testing that's been done with SharePoint 2016. This guidance comes in the form of software boundaries and limits, including:

- **Boundaries**   Static limits that cannot be exceeded by design.
- **Thresholds**   Configurable limits that may be exceeded to accommodate specific requirements.
- **Supported limits**   Configurable limits that have been set by default to a tested value.

Understanding software boundaries

These boundaries can be interpreted as operational limits for a system. Some limits are finite, with a maximum allowed value, whereas others exceed performance or recommended limitations. To better understand these boundaries, consider a new car. This car might have the following specifications:

- Four doors (a boundary)
- A maximum weight recommendation (occupants and cargo) of 1,000 pounds (a threshold)
- A maximum number of engine rotations per minute (RPM) limitation as given by the tachometer (a limit)

The number of doors that the car possesses is a value that cannot be changed without significantly altering the car's design. Exceeding the weight recommendation probably won't cause the car to stop functioning, but will significantly affect both its performance and economy. Finally, exceeding the maximum RPM limitation is entirely possible, but the engine could fail and would surely not be warranted by the manufacturer.

Two sets of limits exist for a SharePoint farm: hierarchy limits and feature limits.

Hierarchy limits

Hierarchy limits define boundaries, thresholds, and supported limits that affect the logical hierarchy of the farm, including limits on web applications, SharePoint servers, content databases, site collections, lists and libraries, columns, pages, and security.

Feature limits

Feature limits define boundaries, thresholds, and supported limits affecting individual SharePoint features, including limits on Search, User Profile services, content deployment, blogs, Business Connectivity Services, workflow, Managed Metadata Term Store (Database), Visio Services, PerformancePoint, Word Automation, Machine Translation Service, Office Online Service, Project Server, SharePoint apps, distributed cache service, and others.

EXAM TIP

Although you're not likely to be able to (or want to) memorize all the different boundaries and limits in SharePoint 2016, having a solid grasp on major limitations such as the maximum amount of RAM available to a distributed cache server host or perhaps the number of content databases per SharePoint farm might come up on the test. Spend some time reading through the article "Software boundaries and limits for SharePoint Server 2016" on TechNet at *https://technet.microsoft.com/library/cc262787(v=office.16).aspx.*

Plan and configure data loss prevention

As we covered in Chapter 1, data loss prevention (DLP) queries allow users managing sensitive content to locate content that might not belong in certain SharePoint sites, in accordance with corporate governance policies. This sensitive content is defined by a series of sensitive information types, available in both SharePoint 2016 and Exchange 2016.

Two different mechanisms exist for locating and managing content in a SharePoint farm: DLP queries from an eDiscovery Center and automated DLP policies, found in a Compliance Policy Center.

Data Loss Prevention Queries

One-off DLP queries can be run from the eDiscovery Center, referred to earlier in this chapter. Running a new DLP query presents you with a series of predefined sensitive information types, which can then be searched for in the enterprise (Figure 3-23).

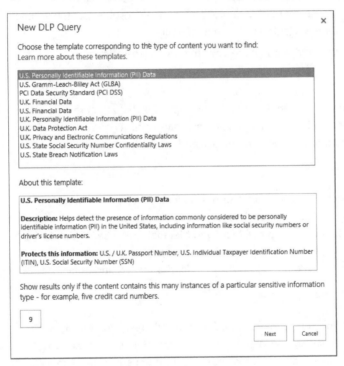

FIGURE 3-23 Running a new DLP query

The query being run allows you to specify a name for the query, start and end dates for the query, who the author or sender might be (remember, this can search Exchange and Skype content as well), and possible sources. You can also use Export to create an Electronic Data Reference Model file, used in accordance with industry standards (visit *www.edrm.net* for details).

Compliance Policy Center

By creating a Compliance Policy Center, you can automate the life cycle of site collections in the enterprise. Additionally, you can run automated DLP queries and assign DLP policies to site collections, as shown in Figure 3-24.

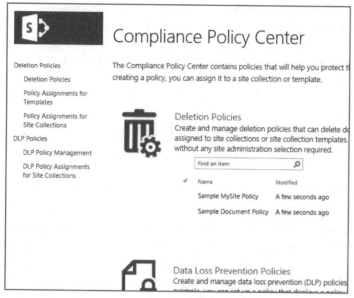

FIGURE 3-24 A newly created Compliance Policy Center

Five options exist in the Compliance Policy Center:

- **Deletion Policies**   Allow for creation of different deletion policies.

- **Policy Assignments For Templates**   Allow for the assignment of deletion policies to different site templates.

- **Policy Assignments For Site Collections**   Allow for the assignment of deletion policies to specific site collections. These assignments override any template assignment previously given.

- **DLP Policy Management**   Allows for the creation of DLP policies, sending incident reports to the compliance manager. Optionally, users can be notified with a policy tip warning them not to use sensitive information types. Content can also be blocked if desired.

- **DLP Policy Assignments For Site Collections**   Allows for the assignment of DLP policies to different site collections in the enterprise.

EXAM TIP

DLP integration in SharePoint is a key functionality, enabling SharePoint to abide by industry standard eDiscovery and compliance practices. An understanding of these technologies can be gained by visiting the *support.office.com* article entitled "Create a DLP query in SharePoint Server 2016" at *https://support.office.com/article/Create-a-DLP-query-in-SharePoint-Server-2016-c0bed52d-d32b-4870-bcce-ed649c7371a3*, and by visiting the TechNet article entitled "Sensitive Information Types in SharePoint Server 2016 IT Preview" at *https://blogs.technet.microsoft.com/wbaer/2015/08/26/sensitive-information-types-in-sharepoint-server-2016-it-preview/*.

In-place holds and document deletion features

Documents in SharePoint can be placed on hold for a period of time, to meet business regulation and compliance standards. The time period specified for a document can be assigned when the document is first created (relative to created date) or last modified (relative to last modified date).

Users of the document are not necessarily made aware of the hold, and can continue to interact with the document; this is done by creating a copy of the content, which is retained in the original location.

Two types of hold exist: eDiscovery in-place holds, and time-based in-place holds. eDiscovery in-place holds are generally used by the legal team to fulfill requests by the court for document evidence, whereas time-based in-place holds are crafted to meet with retention standards put in place by a content management team.

Holds can be created and managed from the In-Place Hold Policy Center. This site must be created (Figure 3-25), just as you already created the Compliance Policy Center and the eDiscovery center.

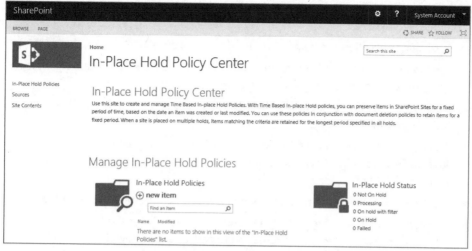

FIGURE 3-25 A newly created In-Place Hold Policy Center

Once a document is no longer on hold, a timer job cleans up a hidden preservation hold library on the site, deleting the previously retained content.

> **NEED MORE REVIEW?** Documentation describing the hold process exists on support. office.com in the article entitled "Overview of in-place hold in SharePoint Server 2016" at *https://support.office.com/article/Overview-of-in-place-hold-in-SharePoint-Server-2016 -5e400d68-cd51-444a-8fe6-e4df1d20aa95*.

Summary

- Fast Site Collection Creation involves the generation of a SharePoint Site Master template, which is then used to quickly deploy new site collections from within SQL Server itself.

- Host header site collections allow for the creation of multiple, host-named site collections within a single web application, and do not require a host headentry from an IIS standpoint.

- Site policies allow the SharePoint site owner or site collection administrator to generate policies that govern the instantiation and deletion of site collections and subsites; these policies can be made available for use across site collections by a content type hub.

- Team mailboxes are a way of capturing emails and attached documents concerning a project without storing them in the SharePoint site; they are maintained within an Exchange mailbox tailored to the SharePoint site.

- Service distribution in a SharePoint farm can follow either a traditional or a streamlined topology; SharePoint 2016 supports the latter via the use of MinRoles.

- SQL Server AlwaysOn Availability Groups can provide both high availability and disaster recovery services.

- SQL Login Replication can be provided either manually, via T-SQL script, or via SSIS.

- Cold, warm, and hot standby recovery can be performed from SQL databases in Azure just as they can be by using standard colocation services.

- Communities provide collaboration between large groups of people in a SharePoint 2016 on-premises installation.

- Connections provided to User Profiles can come from both Directory Services and Business Services; full connectivity to a Directory Service (Microsoft or otherwise) is available with MIM.

- Display templates are used to format and present content from a Search standpoint.

- Document routing by using Content Organizer is an effective way of performing routing by using a series of rules, versus having to generate workflows for the task.

- Durable links are a mechanism for retaining a resource URL to a document that changes location, and is dependent on Office Online Server to function.

- Software boundaries support boundaries (limits that cannot be exceeded), thresholds (configurable limits that can be exceeded if necessary), and supported limits (set to a default by a tested value).

- Data loss prevention allows users maintaining sensitive content to locate content that might not belong in certain SharePoint sites by using a DLP query.

Thought experiment

In this thought experiment, demonstrate your skills and knowledge of the topics covered in this chapter. You can find the answer to this thought experiment in the next section.

You are designing a large-scale document management system in SharePoint 2016, particularly used by representatives of the legal and compliance teams.

1. What site templates might you find yourself using to meet the needs of DLP, compliance, and document and site management?

2. What guidance might you seek from Microsoft regarding the proper configuration of your SharePoint farm's resources and limitations?

3. Rather than keep all documents in a single location, what might you propose as an alternative solution?

Thought experiment answer

This section contains the solution to the thought experiment.

1. It's likely that you will need at least three distinct sites for your legal and compliance teams: an eDiscovery Center (for ad hoc DLP searches and management of holds), a Compliance Policy Center (for generating formal DLP queries and enforcement), and an In-Place Hold Policy Center.

2. You might consider evaluating the boundaries, thresholds, and limits documentation available from Microsoft to vet your proposed solution from a supportability standpoint.

3. Depending on the scale and function of the solution, you might also consider document routing by using the built-in SharePoint Content Organizer feature.

## CHAPTER 4

Productivity solutions

This chapter shifts the focus away from the purely technical aspects of the farm, moving instead toward SharePoint farm users. Each of the solutions covered can comprise a major portion of the user's day-to-day interaction with SharePoint, including upgrade methods, customizations, and functionality provided within the farm itself to improve productivity and business process.

Skills in this chapter:

- Skill: Evaluate content and customizations
- Skill: Plan an upgrade process
- Skill: Create and configure app management
- Skill: Create and configure productivity services
- Skill: Create and configure a Business Connectivity Services (BCS) and Secure Store application
- Skill: Manage SharePoint solutions and applications

Skill: Evaluate content and customizations

Implementing a successful migration from one version of SharePoint to another requires a great deal of planning and coordination on the part of the SharePoint administration team. This planning effort will concentrate on the roles and responsibilities required to carry out the four upgrade stages:

- Creating the SharePoint 2016 farm
- Copying databases to the new farm
- Upgrading service applications
- Upgrading the content databases and site collections

The coordination effort concentrates on (1) what other systems will be affected by the upgrade (for example, SQL, Storage, Exchange, Skype, and Infrastructure), and (2) what steps are required to communicate with each of these teams. The level of interaction required with these teams is greatly influenced by how much integration SharePoint 2013 previously had with each of these environments (for instance, existing server-to-server (S2S) protocol trusts, authentication mechanisms, high availability and disaster recovery (HADR), and User Profile service application (UPA) configurations with Active Directory).

This skill pays particular attention to the documentation and verification of the existing farm's suitability for upgrade, concentrating on the health of the databases, authentication mechanisms, and file systems of the servers themselves.

This section covers how to:

- Perform migration precheck tasks
- Analyze content database test results
- Configure web application authentication for upgrade
- Resolve orphan objects
- Resolve missing file system components
- Resolve configuration conflict issues

Perform migration precheck tasks

Before beginning the process of migrating or upgrading the SharePoint 2013 environment, the existing environment must be assessed. This assessment should concentrate on documentation and evaluation efforts.

Documenting the existing farm

When SharePoint implementations are first carried out, documentation that describes the initial state of the farm is usually included. As time passes and farm requirements change, configuration and functional changes are often not captured in updated documentation.

The documentation created for the upgrade effort should be able to capture the current state and interactions of the existing farm, including:

- Server topology and the resulting configuration of service applications and roles
- The resiliency capability at each layer or service of the farm
- Existing S2S relationships with other server types (SharePoint, Exchange, Skype, Office 365)
- Configuration and capacity metrics for web applications and content databases

NEED MORE REVIEW? The upgrade from SharePoint Server 2013 to 2016 uses the same database attach method that was used to upgrade from SharePoint Server 2010 to 2013. Reviewing and documenting the existing SharePoint environment prior to an upgrade requires quite a bit of time, but can be expedited by using a planning worksheet, such as the "Upgrade worksheet for SharePoint 2013," which can be found at *https://www.microsoft .com/download/details.aspx?id=30370*.

Evaluating the existing farm

With the documentation effort complete, the results can now be evaluated for upgrade suitability. The evaluation effort allows the upgrade team to determine the current health and upgrade potential of the existing farm, including:

- Current patch state of the farm and content databases
- Orphaned items in content databases
- Compatibility level of site collections in content databases
- Alignment with published boundary, threshold, and supported limits

The eventual result of this effort should be a remediation plan that details steps required to get from the existing farm state to that of a prepared farm migration environment.

Introducing Test-SPContentDatabase

One mechanism for comprehensive evaluation of a content database is to use the Test-SPContentDatabase PowerShell cmdlet. This cmdlet is used to evaluate each content database for use with SharePoint Server 2016 prior to upgrade.

> **NEED MORE REVIEW?** Over the next few sections, we will repeatedly refer to the Test-SPContentDatabase cmdlet. For a complete listing of the optional switches available for use, review the TechNet article entitled "Test-SPContentDatabase" at *https://technet .microsoft.com/library/ff607941(v=office.16).aspx*.

Evaluating a content database for upgrade is always done from the destination system (SharePoint 2016, in this case), and requires the following steps:

- **From SQL Server Management Studio**
  - Back up a copy of the SharePoint 2013 content database and restore it to the SQL instance used with SharePoint 2016.

- **From SharePoint 2016 farm**
  - Create a new web application and supporting content database.
  - Match the authentication mode of the SP2013 content database, either classic or claims-mode.
  - Discard the supporting content database (we won't be using it).
  - Run the Test-SPContentDatabase cmdlet, specifying the SP2013 content database to be tested against the web application. Output the test results to a text file.

> **IMPORTANT** Although Test-SPContentDatabase makes no changes in a content database, it nonetheless can cause a significant server load. If you already have users on your SharePoint 2016 farm, it is recommended that this test be carried out after hours or during times of minimal load.

As we progress through this chapter, understand that Test-SPContentDatabase cmdlet can indicate (but not correct) issues with the SharePoint 2013 content databases. These corrections are usually carried out on the farm to be migrated (SharePoint 2013) prior to being migrated, although some (such as authentication) can be remedied in the destination environment (SharePoint 2016).

Analyze content database test results

Upgrades to SharePoint 2016 are directly dependent on the state of the underlying content databases; as a result, each content database must be inspected and tested prior to upgrade.

Version status

The version of the SharePoint content database should be inspected from within the SharePoint 2013 environment. When a content database is attached to a SharePoint 2016 environment, the environment reviews the attached content database to obtain its version status. If the version status is not up to the minimum upgradable status, the attachment of the content database will be blocked outright.

EXAM TIP

All content databases to be migrated must be first upgraded to a minimum level of 15.0.4481.1005, or Service Pack 1 and the March 2013 PU. If the farm was originally installed by using combination SharePoint 2013 and Service Pack 1 media, then the content databases are already at this updated level.

Checking a content database for its version status is a fairly straightforward (but commonly overlooked) process, involving only three steps:

1. Determining the farm patch level.
2. Determining if one or more content databases has not upgraded.
3. Determining what the actual schema of the content database is.

IMPORTANT Don't confuse the configuration database version with the version of a content database. It's entirely possible to have a farm that is patched to a higher level (configuration database) with a content database that has not fully upgraded.

From Central Administration on the original SharePoint environment, from System Settings, select Manage Servers In This Farm. The Farm Information items (Figure 4-1) show the configuration database version (the patch level applied to the configuration database, and perhaps the entire SharePoint farm), as well as the configuration database server and name.

NEED MORE REVIEW? The Configuration database version is not always a certain indication of the current update level within the farm, but can quickly point you in the right direction. This number should be compared with the individual patches shown in the Check Product And Patch Installation Status menu of Upgrade and Migration, to get a clear

Servers in Farm

Farm Information

Configuration database version: 15.0.4551.1508
Configuration database server: WingtipDB01
Configuration database name: SP2013_SharePoint_Config

FIGURE 4-1 The Servers In Farm page

Now that the update level for the configuration database has been captured, it can be compared to that of an individual content database. Selecting Review Databases Status from Upgrade and Migration in Central Administration presents the Manage Databases Upgrade Status page. On this page, you will see the content databases (indicated in blue text and hyperlinked) and their current status, as well as the configuration and service application databases.

Note that the screenshot shown in Figure 4-2 shows a status of Database Is In Compatibility Range And Upgrade Is Recommended for the WSS_Content_MeasureMe database, indicating that this database is not currently upgraded to the same level as the other content databases and the configuration database.

Manage Databases Upgrade Status ⓘ

SQL Instance	Database	Type	Status
WingtipDB01	SP2013_SharePoint_AdminContent	Content Database	No action required
WingtipDB01	WSS_Content	Content Database	No action required
WingtipDB01	WSS_Content_MeasureMe	Content Database	Database is in compatibility range and upgrade is recommended
WingtipDB01	MMS_TEMP	MetadataWebServiceDatabase	No action required
WingtipDB01	SP2013_SharePoint_Config	Configuration Database	No action required
WingtipDB01	SP2013_SVC_appmanagement	App Management Database	No action required

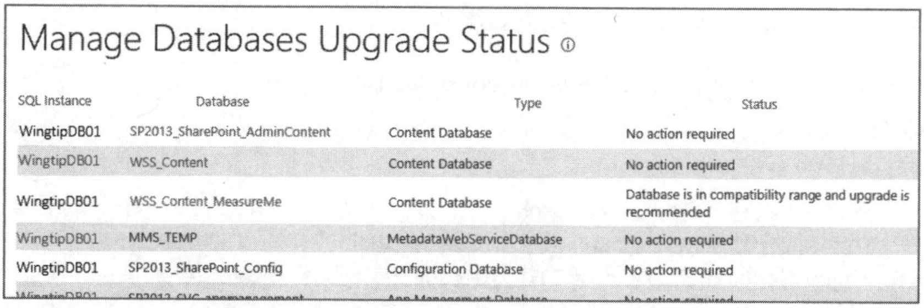

FIGURE 4-2 Manage Databases Upgrade Status page

Selecting the content database on the Manage Databases Upgrade Status page allows us to inspect the update levels. When the Manage Content Database Settings page opens (partially shown in Figure 4-3), the last line under Database Schema Version indicates two values:

- **Microsoft.SharePoint.Administration.SPContentDatabase Current Schema Version** This value represents the current SharePoint database schema version for the selected content database.

- **Maximum Schema Version** Also known as the Maximum SharePoint Database Schema Version, this indicates the current update level of the farm or configuration database.

A current schema version that is lower than the maximum schema version indicates that this content database has not successfully upgraded to the current update level of the farm, whereas a match between these two values indicates that the database has been successfully made current.

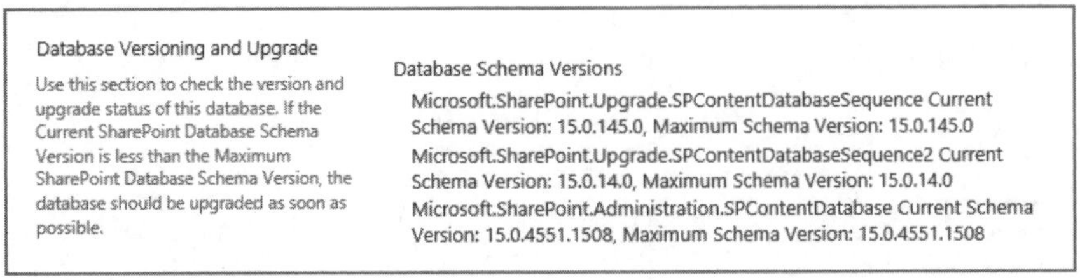

Database Versioning and Upgrade

Use this section to check the version and upgrade status of this database. If the Current SharePoint Database Schema Version is less than the Maximum SharePoint Database Schema Version, the database should be upgraded as soon as possible.

Database Schema Versions

Microsoft.SharePoint.Upgrade.SPContentDatabaseSequence Current Schema Version: 15.0.145.0, Maximum Schema Version: 15.0.145.0
Microsoft.SharePoint.Upgrade.SPContentDatabaseSequence2 Current Schema Version: 15.0.14.0, Maximum Schema Version: 15.0.14.0
Microsoft.SharePoint.Administration.SPContentDatabase Current Schema Version: 15.0.4551.1508, Maximum Schema Version: 15.0.4551.1508

FIGURE 4-3 Partial view of the Manage Content Database Settings page, showing values in the Database Versioning And Upgrade section

SharePoint 2010 site collections

During the process of upgrading to SharePoint 2016, content databases will also be inspected to see if they have any SharePoint 2010 mode site collections (compatibility level 14) requiring upgrade. If these site collections are not upgraded to SharePoint 2013 mode (compatibility level 15), the content database attach will be blocked and not upgraded to SharePoint 2016.

SharePoint 2010 site collections can be identified by using the Get-SPSite PowerShell command and inspecting the compatibility level:

- To test all site collections in a farm:

```
Get-SPSite -Limit All | ? { $_.CompatibilityLevel - eq 14 }
```

- To test site collections within a specific content database:

```
Get-SPSite -ContentDatabase <database name> -Limit All | ? {
$_.CompatibilityLevel -eq 14 }
```

IMPORTANT Shortly, we'll be covering the Test-SPContentDatabase command, which also checks for the presence of SharePoint 2010 site collections in a content database. Unfortunately, there's no way to upgrade these site collections from the SharePoint 2016 environment, so it's simply easier to locate and correct these site collections in SharePoint 2013 (prior to beginning the upgrade test process).

Configure web application authentication for upgrade

In Chapter 1, "Infrastructure," we discussed the different authentication modes, types, and methods. The authentication types (Windows authentication, forms-based authentication, and Secure Application Markup Language [SAML] token-based authentication) and methods (for Windows authentication only: NTLM, Kerberos, Digest, and Basic) are unchanged from SharePoint 2016.

Authentication mode

The largest change in SharePoint 2016 with regard to authentication has to do with the authentication mode. As was the case with the upgrade from SharePoint 2007 to SharePoint 2010, the upgrade from SharePoint 2010 to SharePoint 2013 didn't *necessarily* require that you alter the authentication method in a web application from classic-mode authentication to claims-mode. Unfortunately, this means that there are still SharePoint farm environments in use that do not use claims-mode authentication, even though this configuration is not recommended going forward.

EXAM TIP

Windows classic-mode authentication is no longer supported in SharePoint Server 2016. Prior to upgrade, examine the Health Analyzer in the SharePoint 2013 farm being upgraded; provided the rule hasn't been suspended or removed, there is a daily timer job that indicates web applications that are still using classic-mode authentication.

If your environment happens to be among those still using classic-mode authentication and you are planning for the upgrade to SharePoint 2016, you will need to make the conversion from classic-mode to claims-mode authentication to configure the new farm in a supported state.

> **IMPORTANT** As you are preparing to run Test-SPContentDatabase, don't forget to match the authentication mode from your SharePoint 2013 environment when creating the SharePoint 2016 environment. If the 2013 web application was set to classic mode, set the 2016 mode to classic when creating the new web application (and vice versa for claims mode).

Converting a web app from classic-mode to claims-mode authentication

Although the process for converting to claims mode isn't terribly difficult, you have two options to consider. Either:

- Convert SharePoint 2013 classic-mode web applications to claims-based authentication in the SharePoint 2013 farm, then attach copies of these content databases to SharePoint 2016 claims-mode web applications,

or

- Configure SharePoint 2016 classic-mode web applications, attach copies of the SharePoint 2013 classic-mode content databases, and then convert the SharePoint 2016 classic-mode web applications to claims-based authentication.

EXAM TIP

Perform a backup before proceeding with this conversion; after you convert a web app to claims-based authentication, you cannot revert it back to classic-mode authentication.

Resolve orphan objects

Orphaned objects are items in a database that are lacking a hierarchical relationship; for instance:

- Child sites without a reference to a parent site
- Lists or libraries without a site reference
- Apps that are not accessible within a content database

These orphans can be created by any number of causes, including site collections failing to fully provision, incomplete or halted restore operations, features not deploying properly, and so on. Orphans in the content database cannot be reassigned to a reference; thus, they should be deleted from the affected content database.

IMPORTANT Ensure that you have a full backup of the content database prior to correcting issues with orphans, in case there are issues with removing orphaned items.

SharePoint 2013 has two built-in Health Analyzer Rule Definitions (in the Availability category) that help identify these issues prior to upgrade, one of which looks for orphaned apps, and one that looks for all other orphan types. Both of these rules are run on a monthly basis, although you can run them ad hoc before copying a content database.

IMPORTANT When the orphan rules are run against a content database, the resulting notice gives you the option to simply Repair Automatically. Although this can be a reasonable solution to removing orphans, the fact remains that it places a significant load on the SharePoint content databases and can take quite a bit of time to run (on large content databases).

An alternate solution to allowing the health rule to repair content databases is to use PowerShell cmdlets. This allows you to repair one content database at a time, providing for finer control of this process.

1. Get the content database, assigning it to a variable.

   ```
   $cdb = Get-SPContentDatabase -Identity <content database name>
   ```

2. Inspect the content database to see if repairs are needed.

   ```
   $cdb.repair($false)
   ```

   At this point, you should receive output from the SharePoint PowerShell console (Figure 4-4). If the OrphanedObjects count is zero, then the database is ready for upgrade. If there are orphaned objects in the content database, a full backup of that database should be completed before proceeding.

FIGURE 4-4 Verifying that there are no orphaned objects in a content database

3. (Optional) If the content database has orphaned objects, then these must be removed.

`$cdb.repair($true)`

Regardless of why these orphans exist, the fact remains that their existence in content databases can prevent the upgrade of a content database from SharePoint 2013 to SharePoint 2016.

Resolve missing file system components

Missing file system components won't necessarily prevent an upgrade to SharePoint 2016, but they will gladly replicate existing errors and issues found in your SharePoint 2013 farm. Although missing file system components appear on occasion within the Unified Logging Service (ULS) logs of the SharePoint 2013 farm, they are not usually viewed in a group until Test-SPContentDatabase is run from the SharePoint 2016 farm.

Essentially, missing file system components are those needed by solutions, branding, Add-ins (apps), and other components that are referenced in the content database. These file system components are expected on the local drives of the individual SharePoint farm servers, and are obviously missing.

Correcting missing files

A first best effort at correcting these issues is ensuring that solutions, assemblies, and third-party products have been installed in the newly configured SharePoint 2016 farm. Remember that it's not only possible but sometimes necessary to run the Test-SPContentDatabase cmdlet several times, each time capturing the output of what files a content database is expecting but not receiving.

> **NEED MORE REVIEW?** It's quite possible that Add-in functionality was added to the SharePoint 2013 environment and could have been installed or removed improperly, leaving artifacts behind in the content database. Add-in removal is detailed in the TechNet article entitled "Remove app for SharePoint instances from a SharePoint 2013 site" at *https://technet.microsoft.com/library/fp161233.aspx*.

Removing solutions and features

Solutions and features that are not necessary (or available) in the new SharePoint 2016 environment should be removed prior to copying the SharePoint 2013 content database. This action can have severe consequences in the SharePoint 2013 environment, so a backup of the farm is recommended (including the web applications) prior to the removal of any solution.

> **NEED MORE REVIEW?** The removal of solution functionality is not something that SharePoint administrators do every day. As a result, review is often needed for this activity before proceeding. Essentially, a solution must first be uninstalled and then removed, all from within PowerShell. The Uninstall-SPSolution and Remove-SPSolution cmdlets are reviewed within the TechNet article "Features and solutions cmdlets in SharePoint 2016" at *https://technet.microsoft.com/library/ee906565(v=office.16).aspx.*

Resolve configuration conflict issues

The discussion of configuration conflicts takes us all the way back to the beginning of this section. Documentation that describes the existing SharePoint 2013 environment and its configurations suddenly becomes the focus of our efforts.

This documentation forms the framework that describes the SharePoint farm integration topics such as these:

- **Server-to-Server (S2S) connectivity** Interactions between the SharePoint 2013 farm and other farms might have resulted in a significant arrangement of trusts between farms on premises (and potentially in the cloud). Each of these S2S relationships will need to be re-created between the new SharePoint 2016 farm and its counterparts.

- **Authentication mechanisms** Changes in the authentication architecture for the SharePoint 2016 farm might negate the need for certain authentication types. For instance, are external users going to continue to log in via Forms or are they being moved to an Active Directory Federation Services (AD FS)-connected authentication mechanism?

- **On-premises secure configurations** If your current SharePoint 2013 farm is part of a larger Business Intelligence (BI) infrastructure, it's likely that Kerberos has been implemented. If this is the case, Service Principal Names (SPNs) must be created in the new environment that allow the existing BI infrastructure to be implemented.

- **Moving away from Excel Calculation Services** Many organizations make regular use of Excel Calculation Services within their SharePoint 2013 configuration. Excel Calculation Services functionality has been moved away from being a service application and into the Office Online Server configuration (which is an on-premises server product outside SharePoint, superseding existing Office Web Application functionality).

- **Business Connectivity Services** Any existing Business Connectivity Services (BCS) connections must be re-established within the new environment, including the creation of the appropriate external content types. This configuration might be affected by plans for utilizing BCS services available in Office 365.

■ **User profile services and application changes**   In SharePoint 2013, user profile information can be pushed from the SharePoint farm to Active Directory by way of the Forefront Identity Manager (FIM) component found within SharePoint 2013. In SharePoint 2016, this component is replaced by Microsoft Identity Manager 2016 (MIM). It might be desired to move the configuration of the FIM server into MIM to maintain functionality previously available in the SharePoint 2013 farm.

■ **Load balancer configuration**   External hardware load balancers are commonly in use with SharePoint 2013 farms. The configuration for the SharePoint 2016 farm will involve re-creating the SharePoint 2013 load balancer configuration, but could change based on the architecture chosen; for instance, changes in topology from traditional to streamlined (MinRole) might affect the configuration.

Skill: Plan an upgrade process

Now that we've covered some of the planning and evaluation required for a SharePoint 2016 farm upgrade, we can begin to discuss how the actual implementation might proceed. Consideration at this point should be given to resourcing and which team members might be involved in the creation and migration efforts going forward.

> **This section covers how to:**
> ■ Plan removal of servers in rotation
> ■ Configure a parallel upgrade
> ■ Configure read-only access for content
> ■ Configure upgrade farms
> ■ Measure upgrade performance
> ■ Plan an installation sequence
> ■ Migrate SharePoint on-premises to SharePoint Online or a hybrid topology

Plan removal of servers in rotation

As more and more users are moved between SharePoint environments (from 2013 to 2016), the user load on the SharePoint 2013 environment will decrease and increase on the SharePoint 2016 environment. Combining this fact with the potential change in topology and need for resiliency, it becomes likely that some SharePoint 2013 servers might be repurposed as members in the SharePoint 2016 farm, if for no other reason than economy.

Prior to removing a server from any SharePoint 2013 farm, it's a good idea to see what role(s) and services the individual server is hosting. Part of the documentation you are doing for the actual migration comes in handy here, allowing you to ask questions like these:

- What role(s) did the server host (Front end, batch, and so on)?
- Can the availability requirements for certain tiers in the farm be reduced while the migration is taking place?
- Is there more than one server in this tier? If so, how many? Are they configured identically from a services perspective?
- Are there any specialized services or service applications in this tier that require PowerShell configuration before servers can be removed?

As users are migrated, a careful review of performance at each tier (along with answers to the preceding questions) will determine which servers (if any) can be removed from the SharePoint 2013 farm and repurposed.

Specialized services and service applications

At first blush, removing a server from the SharePoint farm might seem straightforward because all you'd have to do is run the configuration wizard and unjoin it from the farm. This most often is not the case, however, as removing the role of the server in the farm might require extra steps to reconfigure:

- **Search servers** To remove a server from the search topology, you must first clone that topology, remove the server from the cloned topology, and then make it the active topology. Search servers often exist in both the web and application tiers of a traditional topology.

> *NEED MORE REVIEW?* Altering the search topology in SharePoint 2016 isn't a difficult task, but if done incorrectly, it can cause the loss of the current search index or a failure in SharePoint Search. Prior to making any topology changes, review the TechNet article "Manage the search topology in SharePoint Server 2013" at *https://technet.microsoft .com/library/jj219705.aspx*.

- **User Profile servers** Two services are associated with the User Profile service application: User Profile Service and User Profile Synchronization Service. The latter "Sync" service is only installed on one server in the farm, and thus cannot be removed (unless you move this function to a different server in the farm).

> *NEED MORE REVIEW?* As a SharePoint farm administrator, you might not often have the requirement to interact with or alter the User Profile Services or User Profile service application. Reviewing the TechNet article "Overview of the User Profile service application in SharePoint Server 2013" at *https://technet.microsoft.com/library/ee662538.aspx* will reacquaint you with the concepts required to alter these servers.

- **Servers in the distributed cache cluster**   A single server can provide distributed cache services in a SharePoint farm. A cluster of these servers (*3–16* per farm, a two-server installation is not allowed) can also exist. If you have multiple servers in the farm and wish to remove them from the cluster, you can do so via PowerShell. You cannot simply shut down this service from Services on Server, as this does not remove the server from the cluster and will render your farm in an unsupported state.

> **NEED MORE REVIEW?**   Removing a server from the distributed cache cluster is done via PowerShell, and can result in a nonfunctioning or unrecoverable configuration if performed improperly. Two major steps are required: Perform a graceful shutdown of the distributed cache service and then remove a server from the cache cluster. Carefully review and understand the TechNet article "Manage the Distributed Cache service in SharePoint Server 2013" at *https://technet.microsoft.com/library/jj219613.aspx* before proceeding with any change.

- **Workflow Manager servers**   Workflow Manager servers may exist either inside or outside of the SharePoint farm itself. These servers would not be a good option for removal until the farm is being shut down. If you must remove a Workflow Manager server, ensure that the server is made to leave a farm before proceeding.

> **NEED MORE REVIEW?**   Workflow Manager is maintained outside the realm of the SharePoint Server farm, although it might exist on a SharePoint server (depending on your existing configuration). Information on how to remove a Workflow Manager server from a farm can be found in the MSDN article "Leaving a Farm" at *https://msdn .microsoft.com/library/jj193527(v=azure.10).aspx*.

- **Office Web App servers**   If you have multiple Office Web Apps servers in your existing SharePoint 2013 farm, these are optimal servers for refit into Office Online servers for use in your 2016 farm. As these servers are likely behind a load balancer, each could be removed from the load balancer configuration before being removed from the Office Web Apps server farm and then shut down, as only one server is required in the Office Web Apps farm for it to be used with SharePoint (watch your performance characteristics as you remove each server).

EXAM TIP

Two PowerShell cmdlets exist for use in removing Office Web Apps functionality, Remove-OfficeWebAppsHost and Remove-OfficeWebAppsMachine. Only the latter removes the current server from an Office Web Apps server farm.

Configure a parallel upgrade

Close coordination with your SQL administration team can provide opportunities for improving the SharePoint upgrade process. Working with the storage, storage area network (SAN), and network attached storage (NAS) teams, the SQL admins might be able to provide configurations that provide more processing, I/O, and storage resources. For example, they might be able to temporarily move the storage of your new farm over to a faster set of disks (say, from standard hard drives to solid-state drives [SSD]) to improve upgrade speed.

Upgrading the SharePoint farm, then, is directly dependent on the performance levels of the underlying SQL configuration. It could be that you have a constrained window of time in which to perform your upgrades, so it stands to reason that you take advantage of every possible optimization strategy.

It is likely that, while your SharePoint and SQL environments are upgrading a single content database, they are not fully utilizing the processing, memory, or I/O performance available in the farm. Fortunately, it is entirely possible (and fully supported) to attach and upgrade more than one content database at a time, a concept known as *parallel upgrades*.

There is no particular configuration requirement for performing parallel upgrades; however, there are a handful of recommendations.

- **PowerShell sessions**   Use a separate PowerShell session to run each content database upgrade, giving you the opportunity to monitor each separately (and monitor the performance levels of the SQL and SharePoint servers performing the upgrade).

- **Start times**   Separate the start time for each new database upgrade session by several minutes, especially when connecting multiple content databases to a single web application. This is necessary to avoid temporary locking, which will cause an error in the upgrade session.

> **NEED MORE REVIEW?**   Parallel upgrades are only a small portion of an overall content database migration strategy. More detailed information can be found in the TechNet article entitled "Upgrade content databases to SharePoint 2013," which can be found at *https://technet.microsoft.com/library/cc263299.aspx*.

EXAM TIP

Using SharePoint Central Administration to attach a content database is not supported for upgrading. Be familiar with the Mount-SPContentDatabase cmdlet and the available options used for upgrading content databases.

Configure read-only access for content

It could be that your organization has a requirement for allowing users read access to content in your SharePoint 2013 system while you are upgrading to SharePoint 2016. This is actually not a limiting factor, but additional effort will be required to coordinate upgrade schedules with the site collection administrators and business stakeholders associated with a particular content database.

If this configuration is required for your organization, then it's entirely possible to set an originating (SharePoint 2013) content database to read-only mode, copy it to the SharePoint 2016 environment, and then mount and upgrade the content database.

> **IMPORTANT**   At this point, we are not talking about setting a content database to read-only status from within SharePoint Central Administration. The content database will be set to read-only from within SQL Server Management Studio (SSMS) prior to copy.

Prior to the read-only and copy activities, verify the following:

- The account used to copy the databases has access to SSMS on both the SharePoint 2013 and SharePoint 2016 environments (data tier), and has access to a network location accessible by both environments.

- The account used to set the databases to read-only or read-write is a member of the db_owner fixed database role on the content databases that you are upgrading.

- The content databases to be upgraded have been checked for database consistency errors (and repaired, if required).

- The appropriate service pack or cumulative update (CU) has been applied (and the update verified in the content databases) to the SharePoint 2013 environment.

> **NEED MORE REVIEW?**   Although the process of setting a content database to read-only, backing up the database, and restoring the database is specifically an SQL skill, a SharePoint administrator might be called on to either specify the particular actions or carry them out in SSMS. To gain a better understanding of this process, review the TechNet article entitled "Copy databases to the new farm for upgrade to SharePoint 2016" at *https://technet.microsoft.com/library/jj839720(v=office.16).aspx*.

Configure upgrade farms

Although there were three versions of SharePoint 2013 (Foundation, Standard, and Enterprise), SharePoint 2016 only comes in two distinct versions: SharePoint Server 2016 Standard and SharePoint Server 2016 Enterprise. The upgrade path chosen for SharePoint 2016 will depend on the current version of SharePoint in use within your organization.

- **SharePoint 2010 and previous**   SharePoint only allows an upgrade from the immediately preceding version. If your organization is upgrading from an older version of SharePoint to SharePoint 2016, you have two options: perform a step upgrade through previous versions (for example, upgrade to SharePoint 2013 and then upgrade again to SharePoint 2016), or use a third-party tool to extract information from your existing SharePoint environment and restore this information to your new environment.

- **SharePoint Foundation 2013** There is no similar product in the SharePoint 2016 product line, so you will use a content database attach upgrade to either a SharePoint 2016 Standard or Enterprise farm.

- **SharePoint 2013 Standard** Use a content database attach upgrade to SharePoint 2016 Standard and then optionally upgrade the license to SharePoint 2016 Enterprise farm.

- **SharePoint 2013 Enterprise** Use a content database attach upgrade to a SharePoint 2016 Enterprise farm. Although technically possible, it's not recommended to migrate from **SharePoint** 2013 Enterprise to **SharePoint** 2016 Standard, due to expected solution and feature functionality used in the content databases.

> **NEED MORE REVIEW?** SharePoint is not the only component in your farm. When you are considering upgrade paths, don't forget to plan for other components such as Office Web Apps, Workflow Manager, and Project Server. In particular, a Project Server upgrade (Project Server is an additional functionality that can be activated in a SharePoint 2016 farm) requires a specific upgrade path, which is described in the TechNet article "Upgrade to Project Server 2016" at *https://technet.microsoft.com/library/gg502590(v=office.16) .aspx*.

Measure upgrade performance

If you've installed SharePoint in an enterprise on-premises setting, it's likely that you've built more than one SharePoint instance (development, staging, production). These environments are used to vet new development efforts, evaluate third-party solutions, and to test configuration and performance changes intended for production.

When it's time to evaluate an upgrade scenario, you might decide to repurpose the staging environment as a test environment for the new SharePoint farm. This environment usually has the same specifications as its production counterpart, and should be identical from a per-server processor, RAM, and I/O standpoint. If this option is chosen, you might want to add servers to this environment to more accurately reflect the MinRole configuration that will be used in the SharePoint 2016 production environment.

Whether you choose to repurpose or reconfigure the existing staging environment or build a new test environment for your SharePoint 2016 upgrade plans, the fact remains that the resulting environment should perform identically to the eventual SharePoint 2016 production farm.

> **IMPORTANT** The test environment does not require the same resiliency levels as its production counterpart (no high availability, disaster recovery or load balancing), but affords you the opportunity to practice evaluating performance levels and estimating upgrade times.

Storage evaluation

In addition to being memory- and resource-intensive, a SharePoint upgrade can require a significant amount of space. This space is manifested in two separate components:

- **Content database growth** A content database usually grows in size while the upgrade is taking place, causing growth of the database itself.
- **Transaction log growth** The matching transaction log can grow significantly during the upgrade process, as backups will likely not yet be configured.

> **IMPORTANT** During the process of copying and restoring a content database, consider "pregrowing" the content database file in SSMS to reduce the amount of time SQL spends trying to add space for the upgrade process. Additionally, consider altering the growth rate for the transaction logs well beyond the default of 10 percent, so as to avoid a time-out during the content database upgrade.

Performance evaluation

Upgrade performance should be evaluated for the entire test farm; however, some metrics will be captured explicitly from the SQL server (data tier), as it commits most of the effort from a resourcing standpoint to the upgrade effort. Environmental and database factors will both heavily influence the captured performance metrics.

Environmental factors that affect the performance of database and site collection upgrades have to do with the physical configuration of servers in the farm, and include the following:

- **Simultaneous (parallel) upgrades** As we discussed previously, every content database being upgraded requires resources from the SQL server attached to the farm.
- **SQL Server disk IOPS** The number of input/output operations per second (IOPS) provided by the storage layer to the SQL server has a direct correlation to the upgrade speed of the farm as a whole.
- **SQL Server database to disk layout** Multiple content databases may occupy the same physical set of disks; optimally, these disks will be spread across multiple I/O channels and sets of disks, thus minimizing the amount of load on any particular set of disks.
- **SQL Server temporary database optimizations** The TempDB database on the SQL database server itself should be optimized, with the correct number and size of TempDB files.
- **SQL Server CPU and memory characteristics** Sometimes the SQL data layer servers are on their own server, but sometimes the SQL layer is but a single instance of SQL on a larger SQL database server. The amount of processing power and memory available to the instance has a direct bearing on how transactions are carried out (and databases are upgraded).

- **Web server CPU and memory characteristics**   The rest of the servers in a SharePoint installation have an influence (albeit a great deal smaller) on upgrade performance. As is the case within SQL, the processor and memory characteristics should be configured so as to not bottleneck performance (and slow or halt the upgrade process).

- **Network bandwidth and latency**   While the upgrade is occurring, there will be a considerable amount of communication between the different tiers of the SharePoint server farm. If possible, consider having the intrafarm communications exist on a different virtual local area network (VLAN).

Database factors that affect the performance of database upgrades have to do with information contained within the content database itself, and include the following:

- **Site collections**   Each site collection is itself upgraded as part of the content database upgrade process; if the upgrade of a single database will take too long, consider building another content database in the SharePoint 2013 environment prior to upgrade and move a portion of the site collections to the new database.

- **Subwebs**   As site collections are subject to upgrade, the number of webs contained within the site collection has a direct effect on the upgrade speed for the site collection.

- **Lists**   Lists within SharePoint can contain hundreds, thousands, or more individual items that are part of the upgrade process. Consider working with the site collection administrator to clean large lists if possible.

- **Rowspan within lists**   Lists with a significant number of columns (known as *wide lists*) cause a phenomenon known as *rowspan* within the underlying SQL content database.

- **Document versions (number and size)**   Although this is not as significant an issue as when upgrading from SharePoint 2010, upgrades from SharePoint 2013 to SharePoint 2016 nevertheless have to address each major and minor version of a document to be upgraded. Versions retained can be configured via the GUI or via the object model.

- **Documents**   Documents within a SharePoint library can be fairly significant in size and number. Work with your site collection administrator and users to see about removing any outdated or discarded documents. Don't forget to empty the Recycle Bin for the library itself.

- **Links**   Links function identically to lists, and are subject to the same corrective actions.

> ***NEED MORE REVIEW?***   Several pieces of guidance exist on TechNet, specifically addressing upgrade performance and how to clean up an existing environment. For performance planning, review the TechNet article "Plan for performance during upgrade to SharePoint 2013" at *https://technet.microsoft.com/library/cc262891.aspx*. For tips on SharePoint environmental cleanup, review the TechNet article "Clean up an environment before

an upgrade to SharePoint 2013" at *https://technet.microsoft.com/library/ff382641.aspx*. Testing and troubleshooting information specific to SharePoint 2016 can be found in the TechNet article "Test and troubleshoot an upgrade to SharePoint Server 2016" at *https://technet.microsoft.com/library/ff382642(v=office.16).aspx*.

Plan an installation sequence

The installation process for a new SharePoint farm is largely unchanged from previous versions. Essentially, the order of installation starts with the data tier and works its way up (even in a MinRole farm):

1. **SQL servers**   This environment is technically configured separately from the rest of a SharePoint environment, but sets the tone for the performance and operation of the entire farm. Items addressed at this level are high availability data recovery efforts and Business Intelligence Services.

2. **Application servers**   Once the SQL server is ready to present a database instance to SharePoint, the next step is to set up application servers. The first server set up in a SharePoint 2016 farm is the de facto Central Administration server (easily changed later if required).

3. **Distributed cache servers**   A SharePoint farm is not valid without at least one distributed cache server present. Remember that if you required resiliency at this tier that a farm with two distributed cache service boxes is not supported, so you must have a minimum of three (or up to 16 total).

4. **Search servers**   Although this MinRole is optional, this grouping of servers should be put in place prior to the Front-end servers if Search is to be required in the farm. The search topology can be configured after the Front-end servers have been configured.

5. **Front-end servers**   The Front-end servers require the least amount of interaction for setup, and would be the last servers required to complete the SharePoint farm.

Migrate SharePoint on-premises to SharePoint Online or a hybrid topology

So far, we've been discussing the effort required to upgrade from SharePoint 2013 to SharePoint 2016 on premises. It might be that part of your upgrade strategy is to move portions of the environment to SharePoint Online and leave portions on premises, or you could decide that the entire environment should be moved to the cloud.

This conversation becomes important when talking about migrating an on-premises environment wholly to the cloud, because there might be custom functionality that is not supported by SharePoint Online or Office 365. If this is the case, the good news is that you can host the "custom" part of the environment in Azure; configuration and upgrade functions are identical for this environment to what they are on premises.

The remaining functionality can be hosted in SharePoint Online, and must be migrated from an on-premises environment by some means. This is the same effort as is required for moving certain hybrid content to the cloud.

> **IMPORTANT** We are not really talking about My Sites or OneDrive for Business sites here. These are the standard, ordinary collaboration and publishing sites that we have consistently hosted in the on-premises SharePoint environment.

Content migration mechanisms

Although we could task users with moving content manually (by using Sync for their libraries, and so on), this might not be efficient in the long run, either from an efficiency or accuracy standpoint. Instead, we have a series of migration methods to put content in the cloud:

- **Microsoft FastTrack** This is a service intended to help push content to the cloud by engaging a Microsoft Partner.

- **SharePoint Online Migration API** By using the object model, content can be moved from file shares and SharePoint Server sites to SharePoint Online and OneDrive Migration.

- **Windows PowerShell cmdlets** By using PowerShell cmdlets, content can be moved from file shares and SharePoint Server sites to SharePoint Online and OneDrive Migration.

> **NEED MORE REVIEW?** The SharePoint Online Migration API and Windows PowerShell cmdlets are both covered as part of the TechNet article "SharePoint Online and OneDrive Migration Content Roadmap," at *https://technet.microsoft.com/library/mt203955.aspx*.

The SharePoint Online Migration API and PowerShell options are intended for importing files to Office 365 by network upload. Depending on the amount of data, both of these options might be inadequate for an efficient transfer to the cloud.

> **IMPORTANT** Guidance from Microsoft suggests that you should consider shipping drives (versus uploading data) if you have more than 10 TB of data that will ultimately live in SharePoint Online. See "Import SharePoint data to Office 365" at *https://support .office.com/article/Import-SharePoint-data-to-Office-365-ed4a43b7-c4e3-45c8-94c8 -998153407b8a* for more details.

If this is the case, there is another mechanism available: importing files to Office 365 by shipping drives. There are few requirements for this mechanism, specifically the types of drives and adapters and the requirement for BitLocker encryption.

This mechanism requires a connection to SharePoint Online to gather information and prepare the migration.

1. Download and install the drive preparation tool.

2. Download the SharePoint Online Management Shell.

3. Connect to the SharePoint Online tenant.

4. Get the storage account key.

5. Create a SharePoint Online Migration package manifest and data.

6. Prepare the drives.

7. Prepare a mapping file.

8. Upload the drive files and mapping file.

9. Ship the drives.

10. Enter shipping information in the Office 365 admin center.

Once this effort is complete and Microsoft has received the drive, information can be transferred to your Office 365 tenancy.

> **NEED MORE REVIEW?**   This is not a terribly difficult process, but it requires that the steps be carefully followed. More information about this process (including the required steps and the associated PowerShell cmdlets) can be found in the *support.office.com* article entitled "Import SharePoint data to Office 365," found at *https://support.office.com/article /Import-SharePoint-data-to-Office-365-ed4a43b7-c4e3-45c8-94c8-998153407b8a*. Note that this document shows steps for both network and drive upload mechanisms.

> **EXAM TIP**
>
> Although Office 365 is not necessarily part of the SharePoint test, it is important nonetheless to be familiar with the PowerShell cmdlets that allow these migrations to take place.

Skill: Create and configure app management

In earlier versions of SharePoint, custom code and functionality were created and deployed via full trust solutions in the SharePoint farm. Although this was (and is) a valid way to add new functionality, this mechanism is being superseded by SharePoint apps and add-ins.

One reason for this change is simply that the apps can be created and deployed to both on-premises and cloud solutions. This reusability means that customizations can be developed once and deployed somewhat uniformly to both environments.

> **IMPORTANT**   The nomenclature for SharePoint (and Office) apps is currently changing; instead of Apps for SharePoint, they are now referred to as SharePoint Add-ins. App Parts and App Webs are also changing nomenclature, named Add-in part and Add-in web, respectively.
>
> Regardless of how they are named, the functionality is the same; as the user interface still refers to these as Apps (Apps for Office, Apps for SharePoint, and so on), we will use the term *App* when called for in the interface but use the more current designation of Add-in when talking about the individual functionality.

> **This section covers how to:**
> - Configure DNS entries
> - Configure wildcard certificates
> - Create and configure subscriptions
> - Create and configure the App Store
> - Configure marketplace connections

Configure DNS entries

To configure Add-ins with SharePoint 2016, you will need to accomplish two tasks in Domain Name Services (DNS): creating a DNS zone for your Add-in domain, and creating a wildcard alias for the new domain name.

Creating a DNS zone for the Add-in domain

By using the DNS console, you will need to create a new DNS zone (such as *http://www .wingtiptoysaddins.com*). The new DNS zone should be created as a forward lookup zone, and should not be a subdomain of the existing domain that hosts the SharePoint sites (such as *http://www.addins.wingtiptoys.com*), as this poses a potential security risk (such as cross-site scripting).

This zone is created by using the DNS console on a domain controller, and requires the user creating the zone to be a domain administrator.

Creating a wildcard alias for the domain name

Once the DNS entry for the Add-in domain has been created, the next task is to create a wildcard alias record that points to the SharePoint domain. This record can be created as an Address (A) record, but is more often created as a Canonical Name (CNAME) record.

Using the previous example, you would create a record for **.wingtiptoysaddins.com* and point to this by using a CNAME to the SharePoint domain (for example, *sharepoint .wingtiptoys.com*).

EXAM TIP

Although DNS configuration is not necessarily a core skill for effective SharePoint administration, it is nonetheless a good idea to understand how to create the appropriate DNS entries required for your add-in domain.

If at all possible, practice the steps required to both create the forward lookup zone and the CNAME entry by using the DNS console. If this is unavailable, it is strongly suggested that you be familiar with how to start the DNS console and make these entries.

NEED MORE REVIEW?   The steps for creating the forward lookup zone for the app domain as well as those required to create the wildcard entry are shown in the TechNet article entitled "Configure an environment for apps for SharePoint (SharePoint 2013)" at *https://technet.microsoft.com/library/fp161236.aspx*.

Configure wildcard certificates

It's technically possible to avoid using Secure Sockets Layer (SSL) with the Add-in functionality in SharePoint, but this is not a recommended configuration, particularly if either of the following is true:

- Existing SharePoint sites are using SSL.
- Any of the Add-ins to be used connect to data located external to SharePoint sites.

Requesting a wildcard certificate

A new wildcard certificate can be requested from the Internet Information Server (IIS) console and then imported to the SharePoint web application where the App Catalog will be located. When the certificate is imported, it's important that the Friendly Name entry includes the asterisk character (*), indicating the wildcard (for example, *.wingtiptoys.com*).

EXAM TIP

Be familiar with the process of requesting a new certificate from the IIS console. In particular, remember that this certificate must be installed in IIS for each Front-end server of the farm.

NEED MORE REVIEW?   The processes for both requesting and installing a new wildcard certificate are shown in the TechNet article entitled "Configuring Internet Server Certificates (IIS 7)" at *https://technet.microsoft.com/library/cc731977(v=ws.10).aspx*.

Create and configure subscriptions

Prior to the creation of the Add-in Catalog, two service applications must be configured in the SharePoint Server 2016 farm:

- **App Management**   This service application is responsible for storing and providing SharePoint Add-in licenses and permissions, including those downloaded from the SharePoint and Office Store.
- **Subscription Settings**   This service application enables the sharing of stored setting data within a set of site collections.

Creating these two new service applications is a bit different in a MinRole-compliant SharePoint 2016 environment than it was in SharePoint 2013. Particularly, the supporting services for each service application (App Management Service and Microsoft SharePoint Foundation Subscription Settings Service) are automatically provisioned and started in servers holding the Front-end and Application roles within the SharePoint 2016 farm (Figure 4-5). No manual start and stop is required.

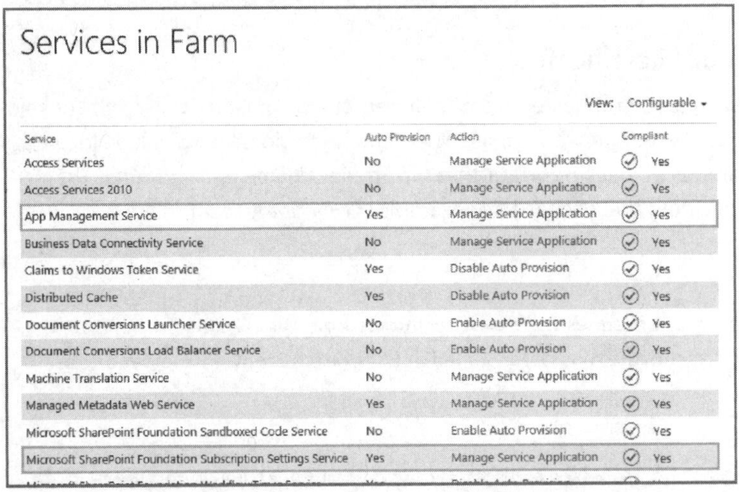

Services in Farm

View: Configurable ▾

Service	Auto Provision	Action	Compliant
Access Services	No	Manage Service Application	✓ Yes
Access Services 2010	No	Manage Service Application	✓ Yes
App Management Service	Yes	Manage Service Application	✓ Yes
Business Data Connectivity Service	No	Manage Service Application	✓ Yes
Claims to Windows Token Service	Yes	Disable Auto Provision	✓ Yes
Distributed Cache	Yes	Disable Auto Provision	✓ Yes
Document Conversions Launcher Service	No	Enable Auto Provision	✓ Yes
Document Conversions Load Balancer Service	No	Enable Auto Provision	✓ Yes
Machine Translation Service	No	Manage Service Application	✓ Yes
Managed Metadata Web Service	Yes	Manage Service Application	✓ Yes
Microsoft SharePoint Foundation Sandboxed Code Service	No	Enable Auto Provision	✓ Yes
Microsoft SharePoint Foundation Subscription Settings Service	Yes	Manage Service Application	✓ Yes

FIGURE 4-5 Newly started services in the SharePoint 2016 farm

Configuring the Add-in URLs for use

The last step in the subscription process is to create the App domain prefix and the tenant name to use for Apps in this SharePoint environment. Within the Apps section of Central Administration, select Configure App URLs (under App Management, shown in Figure 4-6).

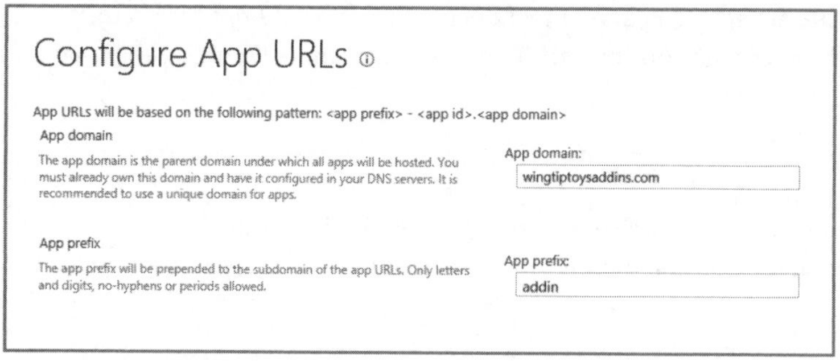

Configure App URLs ⓘ

App URLs will be based on the following pattern: <app prefix> - <app id>.<app domain>

App domain

The app domain is the parent domain under which all apps will be hosted. You must already own this domain and have it configured in your DNS servers. It is recommended to use a unique domain for apps.

App domain:

wingtiptoysaddins.com

App prefix

The app prefix will be prepended to the subdomain of the app URLs. Only letters and digits, no-hyphens or periods allowed.

App prefix:

addin

FIGURE 4-6 Configuring the App URLs

> **NEED MORE REVIEW?** Configuration of the Add-in URLs is detailed in the TechNet article "Configure an environment for apps for SharePoint (SharePoint 2013)" at *https://technet .microsoft.com/library/fp161236.aspx*.

Create and configure the App Store

Apps for SharePoint (now called SharePoint Add-ins) are self-contained extensions of SharePoint websites (on premises or online) that are created without the need for custom code on the SharePoint server farm. Two types of these Add-ins exist:

- **SharePoint-hosted**   Used for creating functionality scoped to a single-site collection, created entirely in JavaScript.
- **Provider-hosted**   Used for more complex business requirements, this functionality can be used to reach across multiple sites and line-of-business apps, and does not necessarily have to be created in JavaScript.

These Add-ins can be developed in house or can be purchased from the Office Store, within the SharePoint Add-Ins section.

> **IMPORTANT**   The nomenclature can get a bit confusing here; since its inception, the ability to incorporate Add-ins and Apps to SharePoint has been provided both on premises in the App Catalog and Add-in Catalog. The online location for sourcing these Add-ins is currently referred to in Central Administration as simply SharePoint and Office Store; throughout different documentation efforts, you might also hear this location referred to as the SharePoint MarketPlace, App Store, or SharePoint Store.

SharePoint Add-ins and the App Catalog

Before SharePoint Add-ins can be installed to a SharePoint farm, an App Catalog must be configured for use. This catalog hosts both locally created Add-ins as well as those hosted within SharePoint and Office Store (also known as the App Store).

Apps in the catalog site are stored in one of two document libraries: Apps for SharePoint or Apps for Office. As the administrator, you can choose which of these libraries can be utilized by your user base.

EXAM TIP

An App Catalog site is scoped to a single web application within SharePoint; as a result, farms that maintain multiple web applications can have distinct, matching App Catalog sites.

A new App Catalog can be created simply by selecting the Apps within Central Administration and then selecting Manage App Catalog. Once there, you can choose to either create a new App Catalog site (no different than creating a standard SharePoint site) or enter a URL for an existing App Catalog site.

> **IMPORTANT**   As we will cover in the section about configuring DNS entries, the site collection that hosts the App Catalog should be set up with its own fully qualified domain name (FQDN); additionally, this FQDN should not be a subdomain (for example, *apps .wingtiptoys.com*). The reason for using an FQDN is because newly added Add-ins have a unique URL, which is composed of the app domain name plus a prefix and an Apphash (a unique identifier for each app for use with SharePoint). Using a subdomain presents a security risk due to exposing information found in cookies.

Configure marketplace connections

Connections to the SharePoint Marketplace (now known as the Office and SharePoint Store) are configured in two distinct locations within Central Administration: SharePoint Store Settings and Application Management.

SharePoint Store Settings

The first configuration that is required is to decide on a per-web-app basis whether users will be able to select SharePoint Apps, Office Apps, both, or neither for use within the SharePoint farm.

This selection is made within the SharePoint Store Settings page of the Apps section in Central Administration, and is configured on a per-web-app basis (shown in Figure 4-7).

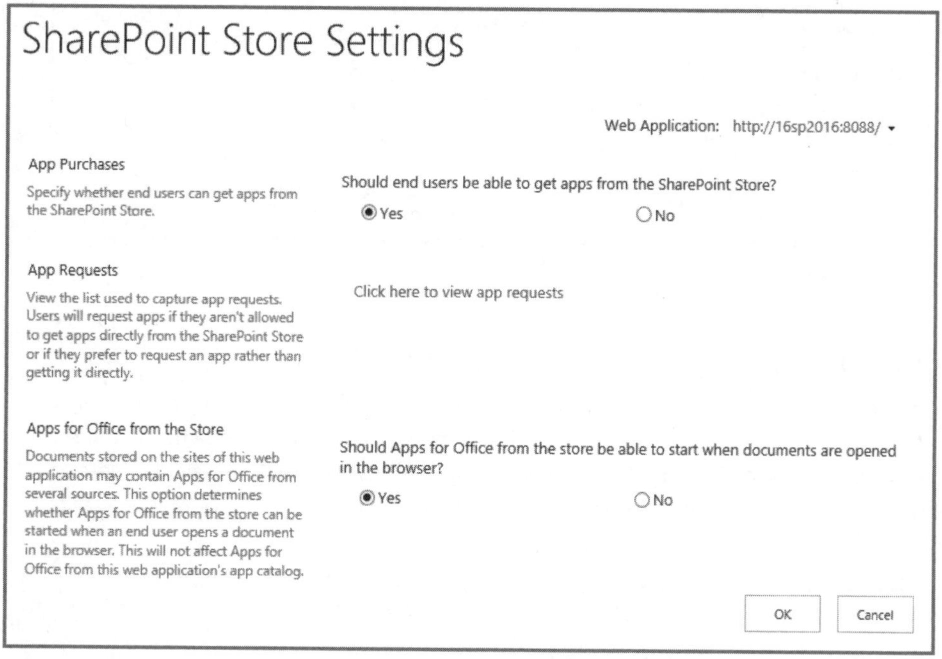

SharePoint Store Settings

Web Application: http://16sp2016:8088/ ▾

App Purchases

Specify whether end users can get apps from the SharePoint Store.

Should end users be able to get apps from the SharePoint Store?

◉ Yes   ○ No

App Requests

View the list used to capture app requests. Users will request apps if they aren't allowed to get apps directly from the SharePoint Store or if they prefer to request an app rather than getting it directly.

Click here to view app requests

Apps for Office from the Store

Documents stored on the sites of this web application may contain Apps for Office from several sources. This option determines whether Apps for Office from the store can be started when an end user opens a document in the browser. This will not affect Apps for Office from this web application's app catalog.

Should Apps for Office from the store be able to start when documents are opened in the browser?

◉ Yes   ○ No

[OK]   [Cancel]

FIGURE 4-7 SharePoint Store Settings page

Selecting the appropriate web application then allows the admin to choose from three settings:

- **App Purchases**   Choose whether users should be able to get apps from the SharePoint Store.
- **App Requests**   View any pending app requests.
- **Apps For Office From The Store**   Allow Apps for Office to start when users interact with documents in a web browser.

Application management

If sites in a web app are configured to allow Internet-facing endpoints, you can turn on the Internet-facing endpoints feature to allow the use of Add-ins that support this functionality; otherwise, these Add-ins are unavailable in the SharePoint Store.

Selecting the web app and then selecting Manage Features (Figure 4-8) allows you to activate the feature called Apps That Require Accessible Internet Facing Endpoints. This can be useful when your users are unable to access the SharePoint Store with the message Sorry, We Can't Seem To Connect To The SharePoint Store.

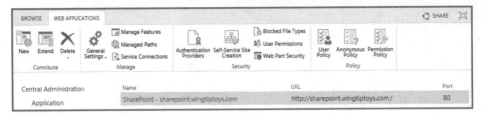

FIGURE 4-8 Manage Applications page, Web Applications tab, showing the Manage Features and Service Connections icons

Service connections

Depending on how your environment was configured, you might have more than a single App Management service application. If this is the case, you might need to choose the service application connections used for your web application; in our case, we are concerned that we select the correct connection group and then select the App Management Service Application Proxy (see Figure 4-9).

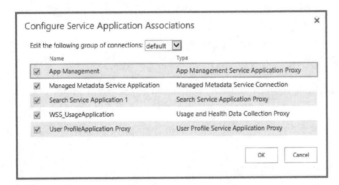

FIGURE 4-9 Ensuring that the App Management Service Application Proxy is selected

Skill: Create and configure productivity services

Beyond the core services and service applications of a SharePoint farm lie the productivity services, which extend different features out to users in the farm. These features range in scope from MS Office centric (Access, Visio, Word, PowerPoint, and so on) to hybrid components (OneDrive and the App Launcher), and finally to the newly introduced management components within the SharePoint Insights and Telemetry feature set.

Create and configure Office Online Server and optional SharePoint services

Extensible functionality is available in (but not fundamental to) the setup and creation of a SharePoint Server 2016 farm. Some of this functionality is provided by service applications, whereas other functionality exists in the form of an external, non-SharePoint environment.

This functionality is provided by:

- **Office Online Server** Office Online Server is an on-premises server (not a SharePoint farm server) that delivers browser-based versions of Office applications (such as Microsoft Word). This functionality can be provided to Exchange Server 2016, Skype for Business Server 2015, Lync Server 2013, and SharePoint environments.

- **Microsoft Access Services** Access Services enables the creation and customization of Access add-ins for SharePoint.

- **Microsoft Visio Services** Visio Services allows users to share and view Visio diagrams in a SharePoint site. These diagrams can be configured to be updated by using information from various data sources.

- **Microsoft Word Automation Services** Word Automation Services provides unattended, server-side conversion of documents into formats supported by Microsoft Word.

- **Microsoft PowerPoint Conversion Services** PowerPoint Conversion Services (also known as PowerPoint Automation Services) allows for the conversion of PowerPoint files (.pptx and .ppt) to a number of different formats, including .pptx, .pdf, .xps, .jpg, and .png.

- **Microsoft Translation Services** Translation Services allows for the automatic machine translation of files and sites. This is accomplished by sending these files to the Microsoft Translator cloud-hosted machine translation service, also used by the Office, Skype, Yammer, and Bing translation features.

Office Online Server

- In Chapter 1, we discussed the planning and installation of Office Online Server. This server is an on-premises solution, exists out of the bounds of the SharePoint server farm, and can be configured to provide services to SharePoint, Skype for Business, and Exchange Server environments.

Configuration steps for this farm are largely unchanged from those required to set up Office Web Apps Server (replaced by Office Online Server), and can be broken down into three major groupings: installing prerequisites, installing Office Online Server binaries, and configuring the connection between Office Online Server and the SharePoint Server 2016 farm.

- **Install prerequisites** Once the physical servers have been built for Office Online Server, additional components and configuration are required before the Office Online Server components can be installed.
    - Install .NET Framework 4.5.2.
    - Install the supporting operating system features required by Office Online Server.
    - Reboot the Office Online Server server(s).
- **Install Office Online Server** This installation requires that you download Office Online Server binaries from the Volume License Service Center.
    - On the Office Online Server servers, run Setup.exe.
    - Obtain and install SSL certificates. If you are running split DNS, you will only need a single certificate; if you have different internal and external FQDNs, you will need two different certificates.
    - Configure DNS to point to the appropriate FQDNs.
    - Use the New-OfficeWebAppsFarm PowerShell cmdlet to build the new Office Online Server farm.
- **Configure SharePoint 2016** The newly created Office Online Server environment must be connected to SharePoint.
    - Use the New-SPWOPIBinding cmdlet to bind the two environments together.
    - Use the Set-SPWOPIZone cmdlet to configure the zone that the SharePoint will use to navigate the browser to Office Online Server.
    - Configure Office Online Server to allow HTTP OAuth connections (if required, *not* recommended for a production environment).

EXAM TIP

Installing Office Online Server isn't terribly difficult. The items that should be studied for the test are the prerequisites for installation, and the PowerShell cmdlets for configuration, along with their optional switches.

NEED MORE REVIEW? Detailed information concerning the installation and configuration of Office Online Server (including how to connect it to SharePoint, Exchange Server, and Skype for Business Server) can be found in the TechNet Wiki article "Install & Configure Office Online Server" at *http://social.technet.microsoft.com/wiki/contents /articles/34289.install-configure-office-online-server.aspx.*

Microsoft Access Services

As was the case with SharePoint 2013, SharePoint 2016 hosts two service applications that provide Access Services functionality:

- **Access Services** Access add-ins for SharePoint allow you to build databases in Access 2016 and then share them with other users as an add-in for SharePoint in a web browser.

- **Access Services 2010** Access Services 2010 is still provided for backward compatibility, and provides the ability to view and edit web databases that were previously created by using Access 2010 and SharePoint Server 2010.

EXAM TIP

Although SharePoint 2016 allows for the presentation and editing of Access Services 2010 databases, new web databases cannot be added to SharePoint 2016. Instead, you must use the newer Access Services functionality.

Access Services in SharePoint 2016 provides a series of add-in features, including the following:

- Cascading controls
- Datasheet filter improvements
- Related Item Control enhancements
- Image storage and performance improvements
- Office Add-ins integration with Access web apps
- Additional packaging and upgrade functionality for Access web app packages
- On Deploy macro action for upgrade scenarios
- Lock tables from editing functionality
- Download in Excel feature for datasheet views

The configuration of Access Services on a SharePoint server requires that a series of SQL Server Components be added to the SharePoint servers that host the Front-end role.. Once these components have been added to the SharePoint servers, Access Services configuration requires only five major configuration steps:

1. Configure the SharePoint Server farm for Add-ins (covered in the last section).
2. Configure SQL Server, used to store Access Add-in content.
3. Create a Secure Store service application (covered in the next section).
4. Create the Access Services service application (from either Central Administration or PowerShell).
5. Configure Security.

NEED MORE REVIEW?   At the time of publication for this Exam Ref, detailed instructions for configuring Access Services in a SharePoint 2016 environment had not yet been
released. Fortunately, SharePoint 2016 documentation on TechNet is maintained alongside
the SharePoint 2013 documentation, and will be introduced in the TechNet article "Plan for
Access Services in SharePoint Server 2013" at *https://technet.microsoft.com/library
/ee683869(v=office.16).aspx*.

Microsoft Visio Services

Prior to use, Visio Services requires that both a service application and the associated proxy
be created. As is the case with many other service applications in SharePoint Server 2016, it is
not necessary to attempt to start the Visio Graphics service prior to the creation of the actual
Visio Graphics service application and proxy, due to MinRole service controls. When the Visio
Graphics service application has been configured, the Visio Graphics service is activated automatically on SharePoint servers that host the Front-end role.

CREATING THE VISIO GRAPHICS SERVICE APPLICATION

Creating a service application and proxy for the Visio Graphics service is fairly straightforward,
requiring only that you select New, Visio Graphics Service on the Service Applications screen
in Central Administration (alternately, you could use PowerShell for a scripted configuration).

Only four pieces of information are required to complete this process:

- **Name**   The name of the Visio Graphics service application.
- **Application Pool And Credentials**   Choose whether to reuse an existing application
  pool or create a new application pool, providing the managed account for security
  credentials.
- **Partitioned Mode**   Choose whether or not to run in partitioned mode; this is used in
  multitenancy environments.
- **Add To Default Proxy List**   Choose whether or not to add the service application's
  proxy to the farm's default proxy list.

CONFIGURING THE VISIO GRAPHICS SERVICE APPLICATION

The Visio Graphics service allows you to configure two distinct sets of items: Global Settings
and Trusted Data Providers. Configuring these items can influence both the performance and
security of this service.

- **Global Settings**   This menu allows for the management of performance, security, and
  data connection refresh rates.
  - **Maximum Drawing Size**   The maximum size in MB (default is 25) of a web draw-
    ing that can be rendered.
  - **Minimum Cache Age**   The minimum number of minutes (default is 5) that a web
    drawing is cached in memory.

- **Maximum Cache Age**   The number of minutes (default is 60) after which cached web drawings are purged.

- **Maximum Recalc Duration**   The number of seconds (default is 60) before data refresh operations time out.

- **Maximum Cache Size**   The maximum cache size in MB (default is 5,120) that can be used.

- **External Data**   Allows the administrator to assign the target Application ID used to reference Unattended Service Account Credentials.

- **Trusted Data Providers**   A listing of trusted data providers available for use with Visio Graphics service, which includes SQL Server, Oracle, IBM, SharePoint, and Excel Web Services.

> *NEED MORE REVIEW?*   The use of Visio within SharePoint Server 2016 can range from very simple (rendering Visio drawings in the browser) to very complex (rendering Visio drawings that connect to external data sources). For a better understanding of this service application, review the TechNet article entitled "Visio Graphics Service administration in SharePoint Server 2013" at *https://technet.microsoft.com/library/ee524059(v=office.16) .aspx.*

Microsoft Word Automation Services

Word Automation Services is configured in a similar manner to Visio Services, requiring that both a service application and the associated proxy be created. Note that it is not necessary to attempt to start Microsoft Word Automation Services prior to the creation of the actual Word Automation service application and proxy, due to MinRole service controls.

When the Word Automation service application has been configured, the corresponding Word Automation service is activated automatically on SharePoint servers that host the application role (as this application runs a batch process).

CREATING A WORD AUTOMATION SERVICE APPLICATION

Creating a service application and proxy for the Microsoft Word Automation service is a fairly standard SharePoint service application install, but does also require a supporting database.

To begin creating this service application, select New, Word Automation service from the Service Applications page in Central Administration (alternately, you could use PowerShell for a scripted configuration).

Five pieces of information are required to complete this process:

- **Name**   The name of the Word Automation service application.

- **Application Pool And Credentials**   Choose whether to reuse an existing application pool or create a new application pool, providing the managed account for security credentials.

- **Partitioned Mode**   Choose whether or not to run in partitioned mode; this is used in multitenancy environments.

- **Add To Default Proxy List**   Choose whether or not to add the service application's proxy to the farm's default proxy list.

- **Database**   Specify the Database Server, Database Name, and Database authentication credentials.

CONFIGURING A WORD AUTOMATION SERVICE APPLICATION

The Word Automation service provides several options having to do with both the document formats that can be converted by this service and tuning the performance (and service load) on the SharePoint farm.

- **Supported File Formats**   Which file formats can be opened by the service application.
  - Open XML Documents (such as .docx, .docm, .dotx, .dotm).
  - Word 97-2003 (binary) documents (such as .doc, .dot).
  - Rich Text Format (.rtf).
  - Webpage (.htm, .html, .mht, .mhtml).
  - Word 2003 XML Document (.xml).
- **Embedded Font Support**   Allows the choice of supporting embedded fonts in a document.
- **Maximum Memory Usage**   The maximum percentage of system memory (default is 100 percent) made available in the service application.
- **Recycle Threshold**   The number of documents (default is 100) converted by a conversion process before it is restarted.
- **Word 97-2003 Document Scanning**   Word 97-2003 documents are a binary format, and can carry hidden payloads; this setting decides whether or not these documents should be scanned prior to conversion.
- **Conversion Processes**   Specifies the number of conversion processes (default is 1) created on each server available to the service application.
- **Conversion Throughput**   Determines both the frequency in minutes (default is 15) with which conversions are started and the number of conversions to start (default is 300) per conversion process.
- **Job Monitoring**   Specifies the length of time before conversions are monitored (default is 5) and potentially restarted.
- **Maximum Conversion Attempts**   Specifies the maximum number of times a conversion is attempted (default is 2) before its status is set to Failed.
- **Maximum Synchronous Conversion Requests**   Specifies the maximum number of synchronous conversion requests (default is 25) that can be processed at a time on each server available to the service application.

Microsoft PowerPoint Conversion Services

PowerPoint Conversion Services is very similar to Word Automation Services in concept. It is a service application that is responsible for taking content of one type (in this case, .ppt and .pptx PowerPoint files) and converting it into one of several formats.

From a creation point of view, PowerPoint Conversion Services is quite a bit different than the Word Automation or Visio Graphics services, as it must be configured in PowerShell. It does, however, require that both a service application and the associated proxy be created.

EXAM TIP

There is no mechanism for creating a new PowerPoint Conversion service application in Central Administration.

Note that it is not necessary to attempt to start the PowerPoint Conversion service prior to the creation of the actual PowerPoint Conversion service application and proxy, due to MinRole service controls. When the PowerPoint Conversion service application has been configured, the corresponding service is activated automatically on SharePoint servers that host the Application role (as this application runs a batch process, similar to Word Automation Services).

CREATING A POWERPOINT CONVERSION SERVICE APPLICATION

Creating a service application and proxy for the PowerPoint Conversion service is a very basic SharePoint service application install requiring that the following steps be carried out via a PowerShell script:

1. Create the service application by using the New-SPPowerPointConversionServiceApplication cmdlet.

2. Assign the service application to a specified Service Application Pool.

3. Create a matching service application proxy by using the New-SPPowerPointConversionServiceApplicationProxy cmdlet and assign the proxy to a group (usually default).

After the service application has been configured, a local folder named PowerPoint Conversion should be created on each Application role server, and the WSS_WPG group should be given NTFS modify rights. The folder should be created in the C:\ProgramData\ Microsoft\SharePoint\ path.

CONFIGURATING THE POWERPOINT CONVERSION SERVICE APPLICATION

Unlike other service applications, the PowerPoint Conversion service application does not provide the ability to manage or set properties from Central Administration. In fact, a custom application needs to be created to use this service.

Configuring hybrid OneDrive for Business with Profile Redirection and Extensible App Launcher

Hybrid OneDrive for Business and the Extensible App Launcher are both part of the hybrid functionality present in SharePoint 2016.

- **OneDrive for Business** OneDrive for Business provides services that had previously been considered part of the on-premises OneDrive for Business configuration (also known as My Sites).

- **Extensible Hybrid App Launcher** The Extensible Hybrid App Launcher is a visual component in the interface that allows Apps (Add-ins) to be pinned to your session in Office 365; as these modifications are made, they are pushed down to the on-premises SharePoint 2016 environment.

Configuring OneDrive for Business with Profile Redirection

When configuring a SharePoint farm for a hybrid deployment, there are two options available from Office 365 in Central Administration:

- OneDrive and Sites
- OneDrive only

Regardless of the option chosen, the user will receive access to a OneDrive that replaces the on-premises version. The only configuration option available is the assignment of users to either an on-premises or cloud OneDrive via the use of Audiences.

Configuring the Extensible Hybrid App Launcher

The Extensible Hybrid App Launcher requires that OneDrive and Sites be configured on the Office 365 page in Central Administration. Once the App Launcher has been enabled, an administrator can log in to Azure Active Directory (either from the Azure Management Portal or from the Office 365 Admin Center) to configure new Apps on the launcher.

Two options exist for adding applications to the App Launcher:

- **Add An Application My Organization Is Developing** Uses the Add Application Wizard to capture fields including the App Name, Type, URI, and Sign-on URL.

- **Add An Application From The Gallery** Allows the user to search from and select an App in the Application Gallery.

In the case of applications added from the Gallery, each has a configuration menu that includes the ability to do the following:

- Enable single sign-on with Windows Azure Active Directory, including a selection from the following choices:
  - Windows Azure AD Single Sign-On
  - Password Single Sign-On
  - Existing Single Sign-On
- Enable automatic user provisioning to the App
- Assign users to the App

> **NEED MORE REVIEW?** For more information about how the App Launcher can be customized, review the MSDN article entitled "Have your app appear in the Office 365 app launcher" at *https://msdn.microsoft.com/office/office365/howto/connect-your-app-to -o365-app-launcher.*

Plan and install SharePoint Insights and SharePoint Server Telemetry features

SharePoint Insights allows SharePoint administrators to manage their on-premises infrastructure from Office 365 in a hybrid configuration. By using this service, Office 365 reports compile and relay information found in on-premises diagnostic and usage logs.

The Insights service taps local telemetry data to produce a dashboard showing SharePoint administrators which SharePoint features are being used and the actions users are taking, along with numerous advanced analytics about SharePoint use.

The Microsoft SharePoint Insights service will be configured in a similar fashion to hybrid OneDrive and Sites, from the Office 365 menu of Central Administration. The SharePoint Insights Hybrid scenario will be used to create the telemetry relationship between the on-premises SharePoint environment and Office 365. Should you attempt instead to start the Microsoft SharePoint Insights service from Central Administration, Services in Farm, you will be greeted with the following message:

Authentication for Hybrid scenarios is not yet set. Please start the service after SharePoint Insights Hybrid scenario is enabled on your SharePoint farm.

> **NEED MORE REVIEW?** At the time of publication for this Exam Ref, detailed instructions for configuring Microsoft SharePoint Insights in a SharePoint 2016 environment had not yet been released. Once this functionality is made available, the supporting documentation will be found in the TechNet article entitled "Microsoft SharePoint Insights" at *https:// technet.microsoft.com/library/86e0fc90-0ef8-4c22-9d3b-7af42bf882f1.*

Skill: Create and configure a Business Connectivity Services (BCS) and Secure Store application

Business Connectivity Services (BCS) is a powerful feature that allows both SharePoint and non-SharePoint data and information to be represented within the same interface. Successfully presenting this data requires that the SharePoint administrator be familiar with both BCS itself as well as the Secure Store, which is required for storing credentials to these external systems.

> **This section covers how to:**
> - Import and configure BCS models
> - Configure BCS model security
> - Configure BCS for search
> - Generate a Secure Store master key
> - Manage Secure Store Target Application permissions
> - Create Secure Store Target Applications
> - Configure hybrid BCS

Import and configure BCS models

Designing a data connection for use with BCS requires the use of a model. This model is an XML file that contains sets of descriptions of one or more external content types, the related external systems, and other environment-specific information, such as authentication properties.

> **IMPORTANT**   BCS used to be called Business Data Catalog (BDC) in previous versions of SharePoint. Throughout this section, this functionality is referred to by its name in Central Administration for clarity. One of the places where this naming standard appears is in the naming of models; the XML model imported into BCS is still referred to as a BDC model.

Four main data sources are available for use within BCS:

- Windows Communication Foundation
- SQL Server
- SQL Azure
- OData sources (including SQL OData sources)

Importing a BCS model

Once a BCS model has been made for the data source, it must be imported for use within SharePoint. Selecting the Business Data Connectivity service application allows for the management of the BDC service (Figure 4-10).

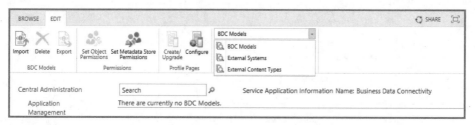

FIGURE 4-10 Managing the BDC service application

Selecting the Import icon on the ribbon begins the import process, with the following options:

- **BDC Model** Browse to and upload a BDC model XML file.
- **File Type** Choose the file type (model or resource).
  - **Model** A BDC model definition file contains the base XML metadata for a system.
  - **Resource** A resource definition file enables you to import or export only the localized names, properties, permissions, or any combination of the three.
- **Advanced Settings** Advanced Settings allows you to do the following:
  - **Choose Which Resources To Import** It is possible to select more than one of the following: Localized names (selected by default), Properties (selected by default), and Permissions (not selected).
  - **Custom Environment Settings** If you imported a resource file type, it can include custom settings.

EXAM TIP

A BDC model can be imported using a combination of both the Get-SPBusinessDataCat-alogMetadataObject and Import-SPBusinessDataCatalogModel cmdlets, as shown in the TechNet article "Import-SPBusinessDataCatalogModel" at *https://technet.microsoft.com /library/ff607757.aspx*. For the exam, be familiar with these cmdlets and also note that neither uses the phrase Business Connectivity Services or BCS.

Configuring an External Content Type Profile Page Host

Once the BCS model has been uploaded, Profile Pages can then be configured by selecting the Configure icon on the ribbon. The configuration process allows you simply to specify an External Content Type Profile Page Host, as shown in Figure 4-11.

FIGURE 4-11 Configuring an External Content Type

Profile Pages are used to display information for an entity (External Content Type). New Profile Pages are added by selecting the External Content Type and then selecting Create/Upgrade Profile Page (Figure 4-12).

FIGURE 4-12 Creating a new Profile Page

> **NEED MORE REVIEW?**   Creating and configuring BDC and BCS connections can be a very complex task. For a better understanding, review the TechNet article "Plan a Business Connectivity Services solution in SharePoint 2013" at *https://technet.microsoft.com/library /jj219580.aspx*.

Configure BCS model security

BCS often connects to other line-of-business systems, which can contain sensitive data. As with any other system, security requires that we plan for the authentication to the data source as well as the authorization (permissions) for accessing the data source.

Authentication

BCS supports three different authentication methods:

- **Credentials-based authentication**   User name and password credentials are passed directly from BCS to the external system.
- **Claims-based authentication**   The external system will accept credentials from a third-party authentication service (a security token provider). These credentials are comprised of assertions about the requestor (a claim).

- **Custom authentication**   If neither credentials- nor claims-based authentication is supported by the external system, then a custom solution will be required to translate credentials from BCS to a format understood by the external system.

Authorization

Once authentication has been performed, the next discussion is which roles will be assigned access to the solution. The security of this data should be assigned to three roles in a SharePoint farm:

- **Administrative roles**   Administrators are responsible for permissions management, creating and managing the BDC service application, importing BDC models, and managing permissions. If Add-ins are also used, then administrators will also publish the Add-in and create and manage connection objects.

- **Developer or Designer roles**   These roles create the external content types, BDC models, and the Add-ins for SharePoint by using BCS.

- **User roles**   Multiple groupings of users may be assigned to consume and possibly manipulate external data in the BCS solution.

Permissioning in BCS needs to be managed for four distinct components of the BCS solution:

- **External system**   The external system administrator will assign and manage permissions for the solution; if users are required to use their SharePoint credentials, the Secure Store service might need to be set up in SharePoint.

- **BCS central infrastructure**   This has to do with the security of the service application contained within Central Administration on the SharePoint farm; permissions to this service application can be delegated (as can happen on a number of other service applications in SharePoint).

- **Development environment**   As a development environment will likely be required for BCS design efforts, this environment can have fewer users but permissions can be a bit more relaxed, so as not to impede development efforts.

- **User environment**   User permissions differ based on the mechanisms used for accessing BCS data. For instance, it is a different matter (in terms of scope and execution) to configure external lists and columns, than to assign permissions via Office and SharePoint Add-ins.

> **NEED MORE REVIEW?**   BCS security extends from the SharePoint user, through administration, and into the destination system. Ensuring that these data connections are secure is a fundamental requirement for implementing successful BCS solutions. For a better understanding of the detailed tasks required for securing a BCS solution, review the TechNet article "Overview of Business Connectivity Services security tasks in SharePoint 2013" at *https://technet.microsoft.com/library/jj683116.aspx.*

Generate a Secure Store master key

The Secure Store service in SharePoint 2016 is a claims-aware service that stores authorization credentials in an encrypted database. These credentials can be used by other service applications in the farm, particularly to access external data sources.

Creating the Secure Store service application

As service applications go, setting up the Secure Store service application is quite easy. After selecting Manage Service Applications from within Central Administration, all that must be provided is a handful of information:

- **Service Application Name**   A name for the new service application.
- **Database**   The server and database names, along with the authentication mechanism used (Windows or SQL).
- **Failover Server**   Only used if you implement SQL mirroring.
- **Application Pool**   Create a new application pool (or reuse an existing one).
- **Enable Audit**   Choose whether or not to enable an Audit log for the Secure Store service (and how many days it spans), which will then be stored in the Secure Store database.

Several guidelines exist for the secure configuration of the Secure Store service application. These guidelines are designed to help secure this database, as it stores potentially sensitive credentials.

- Run the Secure Store service in a separate application pool from all other service applications.
- Run the Secure Store service in a separate application server not used for any other service.
- Deploy the Secure Store database to a different instance of SQL Server than is used for the SharePoint 2016 installation.

Creating a new key

Aside from creating the Secure Store service application (created from Central Administration, Service Applications), the only other task that remains is to create a new encryption key for use with the Secure Store database.

On the initial installation of the Secure Store service application, the service will not allow you to create new Target Applications until this key has been generated (Figure 4-13).

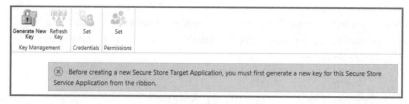

FIGURE 4-13 Warning message about generating a new key

Three guidelines exist for the creation and management of the encryption key:

- Back up the Secure Store database:
  - Before generating a new encryption key
  - After it's initially created
  - Each time credentials are re-encrypted
- Back up the encryption key (located in the Secure Store service application):
  - After initially setting up Secure Store
  - Each time it is regenerated
- Do not store the encryption key backup media in the same location as the backup media used for the Secure Store database.

Clicking the Generate New Key icon starts the process of generating and applying the encryption key. This process requires that you create a case-sensitive pass phrase for use with the encryption key, and which is used when adding new Secure Store service servers as well as restoring a backed-up Secure Store database (Figure 4-14).

FIGURE 4-14 Creating a new pass phrase while generating a new encryption key

Once the key has been generated, make sure to record the pass phrase, as both it and the encryption key are required to successfully restore the Secure Store database.

IMPORTANT At this point, you should perform a full backup of both the Secure Store service application (under Shared Services in Central Administration, Backup and Restore) as well as the Secure Store database.

Create Secure Store Target Applications

Creating a new Secure Store Target Application is a three-step process. On the ribbon, clicking the New icon begins this process.

First Configuration page

On the first configuration page, shown in Figure 4-15, you have the opportunity to provide the following values:

- **Target Application ID (name)** A unique, unchangeable identifier for your Target Application.
- **Display Name** A friendly (display) name for the Target Application.
- **Contact E-mail** The e-mail for the primary contact for this Target Application.
- **Target Application Type** Choose from an Individual Ticket, Individual Restricted, Individual (Default), Group Ticket, Group Restricted, or Group.
- **Target Application Page URL** Choose whether to use Default Page, a Custom Page (specify), or None.

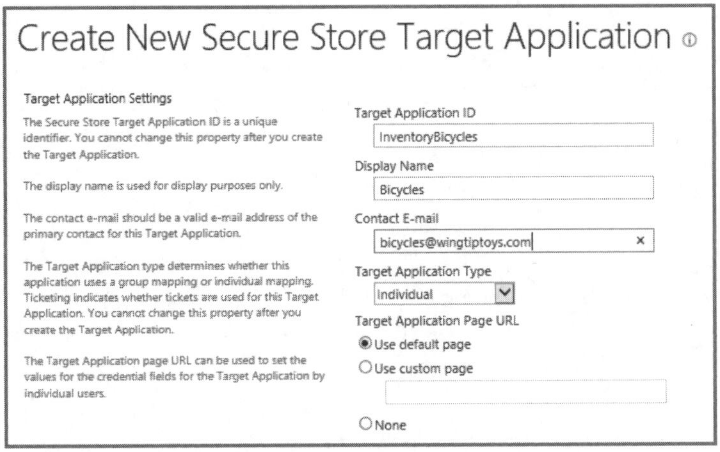

FIGURE 4-15 Creating a new Secure Store Target Application (Page 1)

NEED MORE REVIEW? **Target Application types have to do with the type of account used to map user credentials. More information on these items can be found in the MSDN article "How to: Use Secure Store Service to Connect to an External System" at *https://msdn.microsoft.com/library/office/ee554863(v=office.14).aspx.***

Second configuration page

On the second configuration page, you have the opportunity to provide both two field names and two matching field types (Figure 4-16). Field Name simply describes what the field is to be called, and is not a field for entering a user name or a password. The Masked check box can be selected to hide either the user name, password, or both when setting credentials, as you will see shortly.

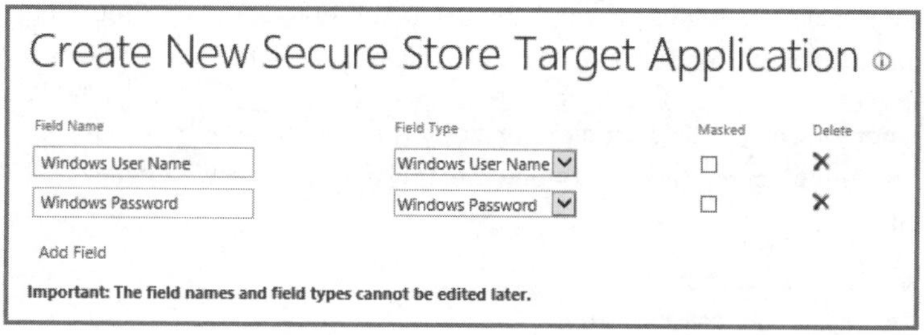

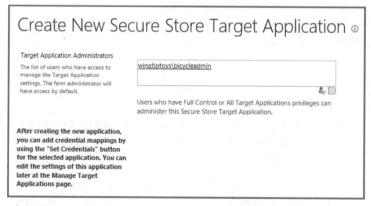

FIGURE 4-16   Creating a new Secure Store Target Application (Page 2)

Third configuration page

On the third and final configuration page, the Target Application Administrators can be selected. These users are then given privileges to manage the Target Application settings (Figure 4-17).

> **IMPORTANT**   Farm administrators automatically have access to the Target Application.

Create New Secure Store Target Application ⓘ

Target Application Administrators

The list of users who have access to manage the Target Application settings. The farm administrator will have access by default.

wingtiptoys\bicycleadmin

Users who have Full Control or All Target Applications privileges can administer this Secure Store Target Application.

After creating the new application, you can add credential mappings by using the "Set Credentials" button for the selected application. You can edit the settings of this application later at the Manage Target Applications page.

FIGURE 4-17   Creating a new Secure Store Target Application (Page 3)

> **NEED MORE REVIEW?**   The settings on this page depend greatly on which Target Application type was previously selected. For a clearer understanding of the effect this choice has on the Secure Store Target Application, review the TechNet article "Plan the Secure Store Service in SharePoint Server 2016" at *https://technet.microsoft.com/library /ee806889(v=office.16).aspx*.

Manage Secure Store Target Application permissions

Permissions for the Secure Store Target Application have to do with two actions: setting credentials and setting permissions.

Setting credentials

Once the Target Application has been created, user credentials need to be initially set. Selecting Target Application, Set Credentials provides the opportunity to specify a Credential Owner as well as individual or group user names and passwords (Figure 4-18).

> **IMPORTANT** This credential entry provides no opportunity for user lookups or validation; be careful of the values you enter here, as it would be easy enough to accidentally include a typographical error.

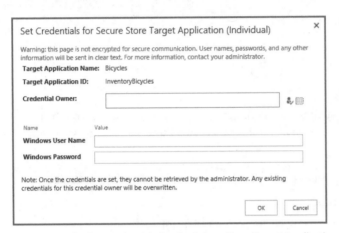

FIGURE 4-18 Setting credentials for the Secure Store Target Application

Setting permissions

After the Target Application is created, user permissions can be applied after the fact. Selecting the Target Application ID and then choosing to Set Permissions will give the ability to specify one or more permission sets (Target Application Administrators shown in Figure 4-19), depending on the Target Application type previously chosen.

FIGURE 4-19 Setting permissions

Configure BCS for search

To surface a BDC External Content Type in Search, the External Content Type needs to be configured as a Content Source in the Search service application.

Within the Search service application, selecting New Content Source begins this process, requiring the following fields (shown in Figure 4-20):

- **Name**   The name of the Search content source.
- **Type of content to be crawled**   Selections include SharePoint Sites, Web Sites, File Shares, Exchange Public Folders, Line Of Business Data (selected), and Custom Repository.
- **Select The Business Connectivity Service Application**   Allows for the selection of a BCS service application (assuming there is more than one).
- **Crawl**   Either Crawl All External Data Sources or Crawl Selected External Data Source, in this case Wingtiptoys.

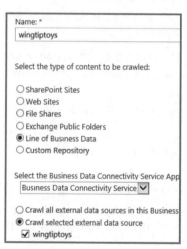

FIGURE 4-20 Configuring a BCS content source

Configure hybrid BCS

BCS is available both on-premises and in SharePoint online. By using the Microsoft BCS hybrid deployment scenario, you can publish on-premises data to an external list or add-in on SharePoint Online.

Prerequisites

Prior to its use, an environment must be configured for use with the BCS hybrid scenario. This configuration has several prerequisites:

- There must be an S2S trust with Azure Access Control Service for inbound hybrid connections.
- Ensure that all on-premises user accounts accessing the BCS hybrid solution are federated accounts.
- Create a service account in the on-premises domain intended to access the OData service endpoint.
- Create a global security group in the on-premises domain.
- Add the federated accounts from the on-premises domain to the global security group.

Configuration steps for hybrid BCS

Configuring the on-premises environment to use the hybrid BCS scenario requires several steps, intended to establish the relationship between the two environments:

- Create and configure a Secure Store Target Application, which links the global security group to the service account, both of which were created in the prerequisites section.
- Create and configure the OData service endpoint; this will also include the assignment of permissions to the data source represented by this endpoint.
- Prepare the SharePoint Online site and App Catalog, identifying the site through which the data will be offered, and configuring the App Catalog (if an Add-in for SharePoint will be used).
- Set permissions on the BDC Metadata Store in SharePoint Online (for use with manual imports of External Content Type method).
- Validate external access to the on-premises SharePoint environment using the URL published through your reverse proxy.
- Create and configure the External Content Type by using Visual Studio.
- From BCS in SharePoint Online, configure a connection settings object, which contains additional information used to establish the connection to the external system and OData source.

> **NEED MORE REVIEW?**   Establishing the relationship between environments is error-prone, often requiring a lot of troubleshooting. Fortunately, this process is documented in Chapter 3 ("BCS hybrid") of the ebook *Configuring Microsoft SharePoint Hybrid Capabilities*, available for free download at *https://blogs.msdn.microsoft.com /microsoft_press/2016/07/06/free-ebook-configuring-microsoft-sharepoint-hybrid -capabilities/.*

Skill: Manage SharePoint solutions and applications

From an extensibility standpoint, SharePoint has several options, depending on whether development efforts are specific to an on-premises deployment or meant for working in a hybrid situation. This skill begins with solutions (both sandboxed and full trust), then moves into the Add-in (previously referred to as App) model functionality.

This section covers how to:

- Manage sandbox solution quotas
- Configure sandbox solution management
- Deploy farm solutions
- Upgrade farm solutions
- Deploy Apps
- Upgrade Apps

Manage sandbox solution quotas

Sandbox solutions are code that runs in a very restricted execution environment. Maintaining these solutions in this space limits the amount of resources they consume from the SharePoint farm as a whole, perhaps preventing a poorly written solution from potentially taking down the entire SharePoint farm.

> **IMPORTANT** Sandbox solutions were deprecated in SharePoint 2013, but this functionality is provided with backward compatibility in mind. No new development should be using a sandbox solution.

Sandbox solutions are monitored by SharePoint for resource usage on a per-site-collection basis, and assigned points (via quota) that can be used on a daily basis. If this limit is reached, all sandboxed solutions within the site collection are disabled for the rest of the day, then reset by the Solution Daily Resource Usage Update timer job.

Creating a new quota template

A quota template provides a reusable mechanism for quickly assigning storage and resource limits to a series of site collections. Quota templates are assigned in Application Management, Site Collections, Specify Quota Templates, and require that the following fields be completed:

- **Template Name** Choose to either edit an existing quota template or create a new one.
- **Storage Limit Values** Limit site storage and set a warning threshold for an email notification in the site collection.
- **Sandboxed Solutions With Code Limits** Limit the maximum resource usage per day (default is 100 points), also setting a warning threshold for an email notification in the site collection.

Altering a site collection quota

It might be the case that a particular site collection needs a temporary change in resources or perhaps will be receiving a custom site collection quota, assigned without the use of a quota template. These quotas are assigned in Application Management, Site Collections, Site Collection Quotas and Locks, and require the following fields be completed:

- **Site Collection**   The site collection selected is the one for which the quota is being changed or unlocked.

- **Site Lock Information**   This indicates the existing website collection owner as well as the current lock status for the site (which can be altered): Not Locked, Adding Content Prevented, Read Only, or No Access.

- **Site Quota Information**   Allows for the selection of a predefined quota or the assignment of limits for both storage and resource quotas.

> **NEED MORE REVIEW?**   The creation, assignment, and alteration of quotas is described in the TechNet article "Create, edit, and delete quota templates in SharePoint 2013" at *https://technet.microsoft.com/library/cc263223(v=office.15).aspx.*

Configure sandbox solution management

Sandbox solution management can be found in Farm Management, under Manage User Solutions. This page allows the administrator to accomplish one of two distinct tasks:

- **Solution Restrictions**   Within this section, an administrator can do the following:
  - Name a solution that should be blocked and prevent it from running.
  - Optionally, display a message to the user, describing why this particular solution is disallowed in the farm.

- **Load Balancing**   This section has to do with performance and the load on a particular server.
  - Choosing to run all sandboxed code on the same machine as a request might perform better for smaller deployments, but not be able to handle a larger number of simultaneous requests.
  - Choose instead to use solution affinity to balance requests across multiple servers running the Microsoft SharePoint Foundation Sandboxed Code service.

> **NEED MORE REVIEW?**   A bit of confusion exists around sandboxed solutions, and specifically their use. Many SharePoint administrators think that they are deprecated, but this is untrue; not all sandbox solutions are deprecated, only those that use custom code.
>
> The Microsoft SharePoint Foundation Sandboxed Code Service is available in SharePoint 2016, although it's not provisioned or activated by default. For a better understanding of sandboxed solutions, review the TechNet article "Sandboxed solutions overview" at *https://technet.microsoft.com/library/ee721992(v=office.14).aspx.*

Deploy farm solutions

Farm solutions are a type of on-premises code deployment wherein dynamic-link libraries (DLLs) can be added to the global assembly cache. This type of deployment means that the solutions are "trusted," and therefore not subject to the same limitations placed on User (sandbox) solutions.

Although full trust solutions cannot be used in SharePoint Online, they are still a viable mechanism for deploying new functionality within an on-premises or cloud-hosted SharePoint farm, such as that found in Microsoft Azure. Before a solution package can be deployed in a SharePoint farm, it has to be submitted to the Solution Store in the configuration database by way of the Add-SPSolution cmdlet.

Adding and installing solutions

The process of deploying a farm solution is fairly straightforward:

1. **Add the farm solution** Before the solution can be deployed, it has to be added to the farm by using the Add-SPSolution cmdlet (there is no provision for adding a farm solution via Central Administration).

2. **Deploy the farm solution** Once the solution has been added, it can be deployed:
   - Via PowerShell by using the Install-SPSolution cmdlet
   - Via Farm Management, Manage Farm Solutions in Central Administration

Backward compatibility

As you are busily creating a new SharePoint 2016 environment, you might actually be ahead of the development curve. The full trust solutions you've maintained until now might be built for SharePoint 2013 (or even SharePoint 2010).

Fortunately, SharePoint has mechanisms in place that allow you to continue using older solutions, in the form of the -CompatibilityLevel switch, used with the Install-SPSolution cmdlet. On a SharePoint 2016 farm server, three folders exist at C:\Program Files\Common Files\ Microsoft shared\Web Server Extensions (Figure 4-21), representing three different modes:

- **14 folder** Installing a solution into the 14 folder indicates SharePoint 2010 compatibility mode.

- **15 folder** Installing a solution into the 15 folder indicates SharePoint 2013 compatibility mode.

- **16 folder** Installing a solution into the 16 folder indicates SharePoint 2016 compatibility mode.

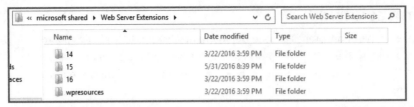

FIGURE 4-21 The Web Server Extensions folder, with the 14, 15, and 16 folders

> **IMPORTANT** There is no provision for specifying the compatibility level of a solution when deploying it from Central Administration. That said, obtain updated solutions for your farm whenever they become available, as older versions might not work as desired.

Upgrade farm solutions

After you've completed your SharePoint 2016 deployment and upgrade, your development teams or vendors might produce newer versions of the solutions present in your farm. When this occurs, you will need to work with these groups to better understand the changes made to the solution, as the act of upgrading a solution has two distinct flavors:

- **Updating a SharePoint solution** When the version of a SharePoint solution has been updated, the existing solution can be upgraded in place, if and only if the files and features are exactly the same as in the previous version. This replacement is done by using the Update-SPSolution cmdlet.

- **Replacing a SharePoint farm solution** More often than not, an updated solution means that new components, functionality, and (perhaps) bug fixes are also rolled in for good measure. This type of an update requires that the existing solution be retracted (Uninstall-SPSolution) and redeployed (Install-SPSolution).

Deploy Apps

Site Owners in a SharePoint farm have the ability to provide Add-ins in their sites from one of three locations:

- From a list of Add-ins that were already available for a site
- From the privately available App (Add-in) Catalog
- From the commercial Office Store

In particular, this section isn't about commercially available Add-ins from the SharePoint Store; it concentrates instead on in-house development and deployment of Add-ins. SharePoint Add-ins that are developed in house often provide a level of customization over and above what can be purchased in the store, but they must be maintained just like the older, full trust solutions. These Add-ins can be added to the organization's private Add-in Catalog.

> **IMPORTANT** When developing a new Add-in from the Microsoft Developer Tools for Visual Studio, the Add-in can be directly deployed to a test SharePoint site. This mechanism should not be used in a production SharePoint farm.

Installing an Add-in via the Add-in Catalog

Importing and installing an Add-in is as simple as uploading a document. Open the Add-in Catalog site for the particular web application, and then select the Apps for SharePoint library.

Within the library, the new Add-in can be uploaded. At this point, the Item Details box will appear, prompting for the Name, Title, Short Description, Icon URL, and other settings.

EXAM TIP

If your Add-in is not available in users' sites, ensure that you have selected the Enabled check box. Additionally, if you'd like to have the Add-in shown in the Featured Content view, simply select the Featured check box.

Importing and installing an Add-in via PowerShell

Prior to the installation of an Add-in, the installer must be a member of certain roles and groups:

- Securityadmin fixed role on the SQL server instance
- Db_owner fixed database role on all databases that are to be updated
- Administrators group on the local server where PowerShell cmdlets are to be run
- Site Owners group on the site collection to which you want to install the Add-in

> **IMPORTANT** Adding an individual by using the Add-SPShellAdmin cmdlet grants the ability to use SharePoint PowerShell cmdlets.

The process of deploying an App or Add-in in a farm via PowerShell is similar to deploying a solution:

1. **Import the Add-in package** Before the Add-in can be installed, it has to be added to the farm by using the Import-SPAppPackage cmdlet (there is no provision for adding an Add-in via Central Administration).

2. **Deploy the Add-in** Once the Add-in has been added, it can be deployed; in the case of Add-ins, there is no provision for installing them via Central Administration. Install the Add-in via PowerShell by using the Install-SPApp cmdlet.

EXAM TIP

It is not uncommon to see tasks that regularly occur in Central Administration represented instead by PowerShell commands in the exam.

Upgrade Apps

After an Add-in has been installed, development might begin on a newer version of the Add-in. At some point, you might wish to place this new Add-in within the Add-in Catalog. When this occurs, you will need to decide which of the following two mechanisms you will use:

- **Updating a SharePoint Add-in** When the version of a SharePoint solution has been updated, the existing solution can be upgraded in place if (and only if) the files and features are exactly the same as in the previous version. This replacement is done by using the Update-SPAppInstance cmdlet.

- **Migrating from an older Add-in to a newer Add-in** Depending on the need, you might decide to develop a new Add-in that replaces, rather than upgrades, the original Add-in. If this is the case, you will need to use the same friendly name and file name of the package, but have a different product ID in the manifest. This will allow the Add-in to effectively replace the original in the catalog.

> **IMPORTANT** The process of updating SharePoint Add-ins obviously is a lot more involved than we've covered here, with nuances such as update schedules, migrated data, modified functionality, and so on. For a clearer understanding of the process, review the MSDN article "SharePoint Add-ins update process" at *https://msdn.microsoft.com/library /fp179904.aspx.*

Summary

- The upgrade path to SharePoint Server 2016 uses the database attach method.
- The Test-SPContentDatabase indicates (but does not correct) issues with content databases.
- All content databases to be migrated must be first upgraded to a minimum level of 15.0.4481.1005, or Service Pack 1 and the March 2013 PU to be upgraded to SharePoint 2016. If the SharePoint 2013 farm was initially created with the combination SharePoint 2013 and Service Pack 1 media, then the farm is already at this version level.
- A correctly upgraded configuration database does not necessarily indicate that all the surrounding content databases are successfully upgraded.
- All SharePoint 2010 site collections in the SharePoint 2013 farm must be upgraded to 2013 site collections prior to the SharePoint 2016 upgrade process.
- Web Applications need to be upgraded from classic- to claims-aware authentication, as classic mode is no longer supported in SharePoint 2016.
- Consider making some content read-only and migrating content to expand migration scheduling opportunities.

- The installation sequence for a new SharePoint 2016 farm should begin at the data tier and work out, in accordance with MinRole guidance.

- Content can be migrated from SharePoint on-premises to SharePoint Online by using a Microsoft FastTrack partner, the SharePoint Online Migration API, or Windows PowerShell cmdlets. If you have a significant body of content (more than 10 TB), consider shipping the disk media to Microsoft for upload to your tenancy.

- Although you can create the App Management service application from Central Administration, you'll still have to create the Subscription Settings service application from PowerShell. You might as well build both at the same time from PowerShell.

- Building new service applications in a MinRole-compliant SharePoint 2016 farm does not require you to start the individual services (as you would have in 2013); the farm will start these for you.

- The App Catalog should live in its own DNS space, not in a subdomain or subsites or managed path because that introduces security issues. The FQDN is used with the app hash to create a unique URL.

- Office Online Server is an on-premises server, despite the name; it replaces the Office Web Apps Server in a SharePoint 2016 farm.

- SharePoint Insights and SharePoint Telemetry provide the ability to view on-premises server events and performance and user metrics from Office 365.

- BCS models are XML-based, and can represent four distinct data sources: Windows Communication Foundation, SQL Server, SQL Azure, and OData sources (including SQL OData sources).

- BCS supports three different authentication methods: Credentials-based authentication, Claims-based authentication, and Custom authentication.

- Hybrid BCS has four prerequisites: that all user accounts are federated, that there is a service account for the OData service endpoint, that there is a global security group in the on-premises domain, and that the federated accounts be added to the global security group.

- Apps (Add-ins) are available for deployment from three locations: a list of previously available Add-ins, from the Add-in Catalog, or from the Office Store.

- As is the case with solutions, Add-ins can be added from PowerShell.

- Add-ins can be either updated or migrated, depending on their complexity.

Thought experiment

In this thought experiment, demonstrate your skills and knowledge of the topics covered in this chapter. You can find the answer to this thought experiment in the next section.

You are designing a migration plan for moving from SharePoint Server 2013 to a hybrid SharePoint 2016 and SharePoint Online environment. The adoption of the previous environment was quite successful, and code-based customizations to the farm were fairly common. This environment has been in use since 2010, having been upgraded in 2013.

1. How would you approach the initial assessment of the SharePoint 2013 environment, particularly from a code standpoint?

2. What changes will be required from a productivity services standpoint to move the farm into the new hybrid configuration?

3. Management states that they cannot sustain an extended outage. How would you go about completing an upgrade?

Thought experiment answer

This section contains the solution to the thought experiment.

1. It's likely that you will have a combination of code and solutions in this farm. Document both the user solutions (sandboxed) and farm solutions as they exist today (including compatibility version), also capturing the Apps (now Add-ins) that were previously deployed. Work with the development team to determine which solutions and apps are no longer in use, then provide a window of time required to update earlier versions of solutions (if possible). Document the solutions that cannot (or will not) be updated, so they can be installed in a previous compatibility mode.

2. On the whole, most of the productivity services will successfully make the transition between SharePoint 2013 and SharePoint 2016. Create a new Office Online Server, and then work with your user base to determine which Excel Calculation Services components should be replaced by the Office Online Services farm. Remove any other Excel Calculation Services components, as the service is unavailable in SharePoint 2016. Capture the settings of the other Office-based services, such as Visio, Word Automation, and others, for migration to the new environment.

3. Work with management to understand which components of the environment can be down for extended periods (if available). Consider planning a parallel upgrade for certain components of the farm, and then work with the user stakeholders to schedule a freeze, during which they can still access content from the SharePoint 2013 environment, but not write or make changes (this includes workflows). Test the migration for each series of content databases, working with the SQL team to temporarily optimize components in the data layer to handle the upgrade of more than one content database at a time.

## CHAPTER 5

Manage search capabilities

Search in SharePoint 2016 maintains its position as a key feature of a SharePoint deployment. The configuration of this feature varies in complexity and scale, and can be deployed on a single server, multiple servers, or even a separate search-centric farm.

Skills in this chapter:

- Skill: Create and configure enterprise search
- Skill: Create and configure a managed metadata service application
- Skill: Manage search
- Skill: Manage taxonomy
- Skill: Plan and configure a search workload

Skill: Create and configure enterprise search

At first glance, the setup and administration of enterprise search in SharePoint Server 2016 might seem quite familiar to those administrators upgrading from SharePoint Server 2013. PowerShell cmdlets used to configure the topology are the same (except those used for hybrid configuration), and there is no change from a database or component standpoint.

In this chapter, the changes present in the search feature of SharePoint 2016 will be discussed, and you will have a chance to become acquainted (or perhaps, reacquainted) with SharePoint Search from both a configuration and administrative standpoint.

> **This section covers how to:**
> - Plan and configure a Search topology
> - Plan and configure content sources
> - Plan and configure crawl schedules
> - Plan and configure crawl rules
> - Plan and configure crawl performance
> - Plan and configure security trimming
> - Choose and configure hybrid search

Plan and configure a Search topology

When planning a Search topology, one of the first items to be considered should be which topology was initially chosen for the SharePoint 2016 farm.

- **Traditional topology** A series of servers, generally distributed in three tiers: Web, App, and Data.

- **Streamlined topology** A concept introduced with SharePoint 2013, this is specialized configuration for SharePoint servers, intended to optimize system resources and maximize performance to the end user.

Understanding which of these two selections has been chosen for your SharePoint 2016 farm directly influences the topology actions that will be taken during the configuration process.

Search application components

The Search application components in SharePoint 2016 are identical to those found in SharePoint 2013. As was the case in SharePoint Server 2013, there are a total of six components present in a SharePoint Server 2016 Search application, the topology of which is created and administered via PowerShell:

- **Crawl component** This component performs crawls of the content sources you specify, retrieving both metadata and crawled properties. This information is then propagated to the content processing component.

- **Content processing component** This component transforms the crawled items before sending them on to the index component. Crawled properties are mapped to managed properties by this component; other information is also provided to the analytics processing component.

- **Analytics processing component** This component has two major functions: analysis and reporting. It improves search relevance by analyzing the crawled items and how users interact with search results; it also creates search reports and recommendations.

- **Index component** This component has two major functions. This component receives items from the content processing component before writing them to the search index; it also handles both incoming and outgoing queries from the query processing component, retrieving information and returning result sets, respectively, to and from the search index.

- **Query processing component** This component analyzes queries before passing them to the index component for result set retrieval.

- **Search administration component** This component does not have an active role in handling incoming or outgoing search requests; it only runs system processes pertaining to Search and adds and initializes new search component instances.

Search application databases

From a database standpoint, SharePoint 2013 and SharePoint 2016 Search are also identical, requiring a total of four database types:

- **Administration database**   This database stores all the Search service application settings; for example, the topology, rules, and mappings between crawled and managed properties.
- **Crawl database**   This database stores tracking information and crawled items details, as well as crawl metrics (such as the last crawl time and ID).
- **Link database**   This database stores information about search clicks as well as information extracted by the content processing component; both types of information are analyzed by the analytics processing component.
- **Analytics reporting database**   Reports are generated from the contents of this database, which include analysis statistics as well as the results of usage analysis.

Search topology requirements gathering

SharePoint 2016 Search is capable of processing hundreds of millions of items within the context of a single SharePoint farm. It goes without saying that careful design of the initial topology is essential.

EXAM TIP

From a software boundaries and limits standpoint, the only real difference in search performance from SharePoint 2013 to SharePoint 2016 has to do with capacity. The maximum number of indexed items per partition has increased from 10 million in SharePoint 2013 to 20 million in SharePoint 2016. Both SharePoint versions allow 25 index partitions, thus the resulting maximum number of items available in search has also changed from 250 million in SharePoint 2013 to 500 million in SharePoint 2016. See *https://technet.microsoft.com /library/cc262787(v=office.16).aspx* for details.

Decision points for designing your SharePoint Search topology should include the following:

- Whether or not your SharePoint 2016 farm topology is to be MinRole compliant
- Resiliency requirements for your farm
- Overall volume of content to be searched
- Client load on the farm, in terms of queries and page views per second

MINROLE AND RESILIENCY

When discussing the business need for search resiliency within the farm, remember that a MinRole-compliant farm has no provision for allowing any Search component on the Application server, Distributed cache, or Front-end servers. Attempts to activate the Search service instance on one of these servers will result in MinRole noncompliance, as shown in Figure 5-1.

FIGURE 5-1 MinRole noncompliance due to the Search service

If the farm design will require search resiliency in a MinRole scenario, there are two available choices:

- **Add additional servers in the Search role**   Having more than two servers hosting the Search role in a MinRole-compliant SharePoint farm meets the requirements for resiliency.
- **Provide search features via a dedicated Search farm**   In enterprise scenarios, the decision is often made to create a farm responsible solely for search requests. In such a configuration, all the servers in that farm host the Search role.

EXAM TIP

From a MinRole standpoint, only the Front-end web, Application, and Distributed cache roles are required within a SharePoint farm. A Search role server is required only if the farm in question will be hosting Search.

SEARCH CORPUS AND CLIENT LOAD

In a larger environment, you might choose to add servers to host the Search role, or instead build a dedicated Search farm. In either case, the way you design your Search topology might also depend on usage requirements for the farm. For instance, a farm that only faces the Internet might require that performance be focused on the query processing and index components as the content corpus (body of content) does not change drastically. An enterprise intranet site might have just the opposite requirement due to the turnover in content, requiring that performance be focused on the crawl and content processing components.

The sheer size of the content corpus (body of content) could be an issue: If you are in a larger environment with thousands of people generating information to be included in the search, you might need to consider the addition of a dedicated Search farm and alter the topology to make these servers focus the processing and delivery of search information.

Finally, client load (particularly on Internet-facing sites) could be an issue; if your SharePoint site hosts a large amount of content, you must deliver an outstanding search experience to provide your customers with the information they need. To do so, you might decide to break the index into multiple partitions and add servers that are specifically focused on providing query functionality.

Viewing the Search application topology

You can view the Search topology of a SharePoint Server 2016 Search application from Central Administration. This topology map shows not only the members of the farm that host Search, but also the search components that they host within the farm and which database servers and databases are used by Search.

Selecting the Search service application from within Central Administration and then choosing Manage allows you to review the Search topology (Figure 5-2).

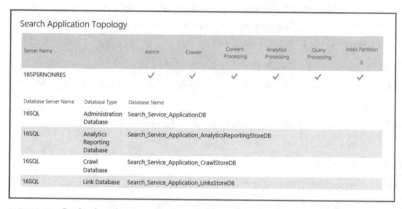

FIGURE 5-2 Reviewing the Search application topology

The color and icon beneath each component indicates its status on each server in the farm:

- **Green check**   A green check mark indicates that the search component is running correctly.

- **Yellow triangle**   A yellow triangle indicates that the search component cannot perform all operations correctly.

- **Red cross**   A red cross indicates that the search component is not running or that there are errors that prevent the component from running correctly.

EXAM TIP

If you need more detail on the status of Search in your farm, you should query the Search service application using the Get-SPEnterpriseSearchStatus cmdlet in Windows PowerShell.

Changing the Search topology

As was the case in SharePoint 2013, it is possible to review (but not alter) the Search topology of a SharePoint 2016 farm from within Central Administration. Changes in topology require the use of Windows PowerShell cmdlets for the Search service application.

If you have a single server hosting the Search role within your MinRole farm and choose to use the Farm Configuration Wizard (not the SharePoint 2016 Products Configuration Wizard), each search component will be deployed to only that server within the farm. This configuration is fine for an initial deployment, but does not address long-term growth or tuning needs.

> **IMPORTANT** Unfortunately, initial deployments of more than one MinRole Search server in a farm provide no configuration advantage, if using the Farm Configuration Wizard to generate the Search topology. In such a case, the wizard will simply deploy all Search roles to a single Search server (probably not what you had in mind from a resiliency standpoint). If you need to expand the Search topology to more than a single server in the farm, you'll have to use PowerShell and the search cmdlets.

At some point, you might encounter a requirement to change the Search topology in a SharePoint farm. Reasons for this change could include performance and scaling, or simply adding resiliency to the search layer of a MinRole farm.

There are two options for changing the Search topology of a farm:

- If you have a new farm or one that has an empty index, you can directly change the topology in Windows PowerShell.
- If you have a farm with an existing index that you want to keep, you must do the following:
    - Clone the active Search topology.
    - Make changes to the cloned topology.
    - Make the clone the active Search topology for the farm.

EXAM TIP

Know the differences between changing an active Search topology (a topology with an index requires cloning) and a no-content Search topology (no cloning required).

CHANGING THE SEARCH TOPOLOGY (EMPTY INDEX)

With a fresh installation, you have the opportunity to alter the topology without too much effort. To verify that your farm has an empty index, scroll up on the Search Administration page to the System Status section. Within this section, locate the Searchable Items section and verify that there are 0 searchable items (see Figure 5-3).

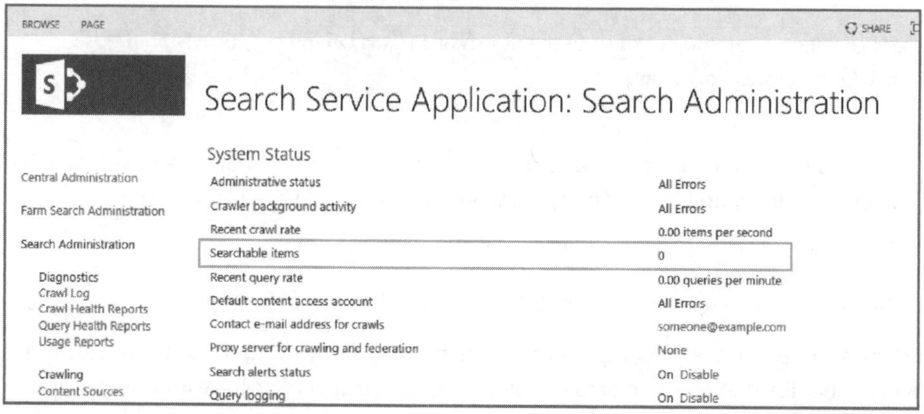

FIGURE 5-3 No searchable items found

> **NEED MORE REVIEW?** Although you technically can choose to empty your index and then run these configuration steps, doing so will render Search unusable for your users until you have completed a full crawl of your content sources. To reset the index, simply click the Index Reset link on the Search Application page. For a better understanding of the items affected by an index reset (including the permanent loss of analytics information), review the TechNet article "Reset the search index in SharePoint Server 2013" at *https://technet.microsoft.com/library/jj219652.aspx*.

If you have a farm with an empty index, you can use the following steps to alter the topology of your farm.

1. Assign the host name of each server to a variable using the Get-SPEnterpriseSearchServiceInstance cmdlet (the example server name shown is wtsearch01):

```
$hostA = Get-SPEnterpriseSearchServiceInstance -Identity "wtsearch01"
```

> **IMPORTANT** Note that this is not the fully qualified domain name (FQDN) of the server, but simply its NetBIOS (short) name.

2. If you are configuring your farm using a traditional topology (not MinRole-compliant), then you will need to start the search instance on each Search host server using the Start-SPEnterpriseSearchServiceInstance cmdlet. If not, skip to step 4:

```
Start-SPEnterpriseSearchServiceInstance -Identity $hostA
```

3. Verify the status of Search on each host using the Get-SPEnterpriseSearchServiceInstance cmdlet:

```
Get-SPEnterpriseSearchServiceInstance -Identity $hostA
```

> **IMPORTANT** You must wait until the Status line reads Online (not Provisioning) for each host before proceeding.

4. Create a new Search topology and set a reference using the Get-SPEnterpriseSearchSer viceApplication and New-SPEnterpriseSearchTopology cmdlets, respectively:

```
$ssa = Get-SPEnterpriseSearchServiceApplication

$newTopology = New-SPEnterpriseSearchTopology -SearchApplication $ssa
```

Add the appropriate search components to the new topology using the appropriate cmdlets (you will be distributing them across multiple hosts, replacing $hostA with the appropriate server variable, as shown in Table 5-1).

TABLE 5-1 Creating new components in the search topology

New Component Type	Windows PowerShell cmdlet
Admin component	New-SPEnterpriseSearchAdminComponent -SearchTopology $newTopology -SearchServiceInstance $hostA
Crawl component	New-SPEnterpriseSearchCrawlComponent -SearchTopology $newTopology -SearchServiceInstance $hostA
Content processing component	New-SPEnterpriseSearchContentProcessingComponent -SearchTopology $newTopology -SearchServiceInstance $hostA
Analytics processing component	New-SPEnterpriseSearchAnalyticsProcessingComponent -SearchTopology $newTopology -SearchServiceInstance $hostA
Query processing component	New-SPEnterpriseSearchQueryProcessingComponent -SearchTopology $newTopology -SearchServiceInstance $hostA
Index component	New-SPEnterpriseSearchIndexComponent -SearchTopology $newTopology -SearchServiceInstance $hostA -IndexPartition 0

EXAM TIP

In a MinRole-compliant farm, the Search servers already have an activated Search service, thus there is no need to start the service or inspect it to ensure that it started. SharePoint 2016 will allow you to activate the Search service on a non-Search role server, but will indicate noncompliance in the Servers in Farm page of Central Administration.

Plan and configure content sources

A content source specifies settings that define what types of content to crawl, what start addresses are used, what priority the crawl has, and on what schedule the content is crawled.

SharePoint 2016 enables content sources to be generated for any of eight possible content source types (see Table 5-2).

TABLE 5-2 Content source types

Content Source Type	For This Content
SharePoint Sites	SharePoint content from SharePoint 2013, 2010, and 2007-based systems, including SharePoint Foundation and Search server farms.
Web Sites	Intranet- or Internet-based, non-SharePoint sites.
File Shares	Information stored on file shares.
Exchange Public Folders	Exchange Server content on 2013, 2010, and 2007 versions.
Lotus Notes	Lotus Notes content (you must install and configure a connector before the Lotus Notes source type appears in the interface).
Documentum	EMC Documentum content (you must install and configure a connector before the Documentum source type appears in the interface).
Line-of-Business Data	Uses Business Connectivity Services (BCS) to crawl other line-of-business applications.
Custom Repository	Requires the development and installation of a custom connector to crawl external application data.

EXAM TIP

Know which content sources are available for use in a default setting: SharePoint Sites, Web Sites, File Shares, Exchange Public Folders, and (conditionally) Line-of-Business Data. The Line-of-Business Data content source type requires that at least one Business Data Connectivity service application has been created.

Each content source type displayed in the Search service application uses an indexing connector when crawling content. The BCS Connector Framework handles connections to the Lotus Notes and Exchange Public Folder content source types; a standard series of protocol handlers handles connections to SharePoint Sites, Web Sites, and File Shares.

NEED MORE REVIEW? The mechanism for creating custom connectors hasn't changed since SharePoint 2010. For more information about creating a custom connector for use with SharePoint Server, see the MSDN article "Creating a Custom Indexing Connector" at *https://msdn.microsoft.com/library/office/ff625806(v=office.16).aspx.*

Plan and configure crawl schedules

Content sources are most often configured to be crawled by SharePoint Search on a frequent basis. The frequency with which they are crawled is set by the crawl schedule (see Figure 5-4).

Crawl Schedules	
Select the crawl schedules for this content source.	⦿ Enable Continuous Crawls
	○ Enable Incremental Crawls
Continuous Crawl is a special type of crawl that eliminates the need to create incremental crawl schedules and will seamlessly work with the content source to provide maximum freshness. Please Note: Once enabled, you will not be able to pause or stop continuous crawl. You will only have the option of disabling continuous crawl.	Incremental Crawl
	Every 4 hour(s) from 12:00 AM for 24 hour(s) every day, starting 6/19/2016 ▼
	Edit schedule
	Full Crawl
	At 12:00 AM every day, starting 6/19/2016 ▼
	Edit schedule

FIGURE 5-4 Content source crawl schedules

There are three types of crawls available in SharePoint Server 2016: full, incremental, and continuous.

Full crawl

In a full crawl, all the content within a particular content source is crawled and then processed into the index. Depending on the volume of content to be crawled, this crawl could take hours or days, so full crawls are almost always scheduled for nonbusiness hours or weekends.

A full crawl can be scheduled to run monthly, weekly, or daily at a given time of day. It is also possible (although not recommended) to run the full crawl multiple times within a given day. You can also stagger the schedule using the Run Every/On option to crawl every X number of days (Daily setting), by choosing the days of the week in which to run the crawl, or by selecting a particular day to run the crawl each month (Monthly setting).

There are several reasons for running a full crawl on a regular basis, including the following:

- Creating or re-creating the search index
- Correcting issues or corruption within the search index
- Detecting security changes made on a file share
- Capturing changes made by crawl rules (additions, deletions, modifications)
- Capturing new metadata mappings in Search
- Capturing new server name mappings in Search
- Credential changes for the crawl account
- Software changes (hot fixes, cumulative updates, service packs) applied to the farm

EXAM TIP

If you ever need to reset the search index for your SharePoint farm, you have to do a full crawl of all content sources that should be included within the newly created index.

Incremental crawl

In an incremental crawl, changes made to the content within a particular content source are crawled and then processed into the index. An incremental crawl cannot be run alongside a full crawl; if a full crawl is taking an excessive amount of time to run, SharePoint waits to perform the next crawl until the first one completes.

An incremental crawl can be scheduled to run monthly, weekly, or daily at a given time of the day. Most often, an incremental crawl is scheduled a few times per day on every day of the week (again depending on the volume of content being crawled). The scheduling options for incremental crawls are identical to those of full crawls.

> **IMPORTANT** As is the case with full crawls, no two incremental crawls can occur simultaneously. If a crawl is already running (whether full or incremental) and you schedule another to start before the first crawl completes, the new crawl is delayed.

Continuous crawl

First introduced in SharePoint 2013, continuous crawls provide a mechanism for quickly and regularly updating content in a SharePoint farm. In a continuous crawl scenario, the index is constantly updated with new content (on a timed basis) as the content is added to a SharePoint site.

EXAM TIP

Continuous crawls are available for use only with content sources that are SharePoint sites.

Continuous crawls are unique among the crawl types, in that more than one can be running at a time. While a crawl of a content source is running (but in an incomplete state), the next scheduled crawl can begin on the same content source (thus the name *continuous*). By default, continuous crawls kick off every 15 minutes; there is no mechanism for scheduling these crawls in Central Administration.

PowerShell cmdlets exist that can be used to either shorten or lengthen the crawl interval. In the following example, the Local SharePoint Sites content source is set to crawl continuously, and then the crawl interval is reset to 1 minute:

```
$searchapp = Get-SPEnterpriseSearchServiceApplication "Search Service Application"
$contentsource = Get-SPEnterpriseSearchCrawlContentSource -SearchApplication $searchapp
-Identity "Local SharePoint Sites" $contentsource | Set-SPEnterpriseSearchCrawlContentSo
urce -EnableContinuousCrawls $true $searchapp.SetProperty("ContinuousCrawlInterval", 1)
```

> **IMPORTANT** From a performance and scaling standpoint, continuous crawls can be demanding. Shortening the crawl interval allows more crawls to run at one time. Consider your service-level agreements with your business stakeholders prior to altering this value. Also, if you are in a MinRole farm and find that the Search role server is becoming overcommitted, consider adding another server in this role and then add it to the Search topology.

Plan and configure crawl rules

Crawl rules are used in conjunction with both content sources and search, but are applied to all content sources within the Search service application. These rules have three functions:

- Exclude content from being crawled.
- Crawl only a portion of content from a site that is otherwise excluded from crawls.
- Specify authentication credentials.

Crawl rules are added on the Add Crawl Rule page within the Search service application (Figure 5-5).

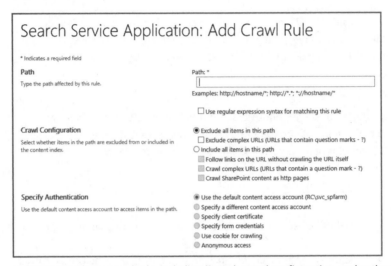

FIGURE 5-5 Adding a crawl rule, including its path, crawl configuration, and authentication

Each new crawl rule requires that three values be chosen: Path, Crawl Configuration, and Specify Authentication.

Path

This field captures the path that should be evaluated in this rule. The path should end with a final slash (front for a URL and back for a file share) and an asterisk (*), indicating a wildcard match.

The Use Regular Expression Syntax For Matching This Rule check box can be used to craft a regular expression that would omit potentially sensitive items such as credit card or Social Security numbers across an assortment of SharePoint sites.

Crawl configuration

While a crawl rule is being created, the author must choose whether it is intended to include or exclude content, using one of two possible selections:

- **Exclude All Items In This Path**   If you choose to exclude a path, you can optionally choose to only exclude complex URLs.
- **Include All Items In This Path**   If you choose to include a path, you can optionally select the following check boxes:
  - Crawl Complex URLs (URLs that contain a question mark - ?)
  - Crawl SharePoint Content As HTTP Pages

Specify authentication

The authentication component of crawl rules is easily the most complex. There are six main options, each of which has a different configuration:

- **Use The Default Content Access Account**   Choosing to use the default content access account requires no extra settings, and content will be crawled using the search crawl account specified in Central Administration.
- **Specify A Different Content Access Account**   If you choose to specify a different content access account, you will be prompted for the account name and password. You can optionally choose to not allow basic authentication, which will prevent your password from being transmitted without encryption during the crawl.
- **Specify Client Certificate**   If you choose to specify a certificate, a drop-down list will appear with a list of available certificates.
- **Specify Form Credentials**   If you choose to specify form credentials (Forms-based authentication on the site being crawled), you will need to specify the logon address and enter credentials (user name and password).
- **Use Cookie For Crawling**   If you choose to use a cookie for crawling content, you can either obtain a cookie from a URL or specify one from your system.
- **Anonymous Access**   If you choose to access the site anonymously, no extra settings are required. This rule crawls the content without attempting to authenticate.

Rule evaluation order

Rules are evaluated on a per-URL basis; the first rule that a URL matches is the one that is evaluated—all others are ignored. This configuration simply means that care must be taken to order the rules optimally for the intended purpose.

Plan and configure crawl performance

At first glance, it would seem that optimizing crawls would have to do with enhancing the performance of Search within the SharePoint farm; although this is true, optimizing Search has just as much to do with the destination servers being crawled. Adjusting the timing, duration, and intensity of the crawl being performed allows for the optimal retrieval of content from any external source.

There are three configuration options for optimizing performance of the crawl component within SharePoint Server 2016:

- Determining how much crawl interaction the destination content sources can handle
- Deciding how best to prepare and tune the servers that host the crawl component
- Understanding how to monitor the crawl component

Content source performance and crawl impact rules

Crawl performance can be a sensitive subject, especially if the source being crawled itself is not within your control. Factors such as the location, domain membership, and the hardware and software resources available to the content source can affect the performance of a crawl.

Some of these sources might be located across a wide area network (WAN) segment; aggressively crawling these sources could cause diminished performance across the WAN segment, affecting the business.

Performance levels for content sources not located on the SharePoint farm can be negatively affected by a well-provisioned crawl component. If the SharePoint farm is crawling a content source so aggressively that it winds up diminishing performance on the content source, there is a very good chance that the crawl account will be temporarily (or perhaps permanently) disabled from accessing the content source.

Consider coordinating crawls with the administrator(s) of the "crawled" system for potential configuration changes like these:

- **Time crawled** What time of the day is considered "nonbusiness" but also does not interfere with regular processes such as backup jobs?
- **Crawl duration** How long will the crawl take?
- **Items that are crawled** Perhaps it is only important to crawl certain folders or sites, thus reducing the overall load on the content source and improving crawl metrics.

Adding a crawler impact rule

Included in Search Administration is a link called Crawler Impact Rule, which enables you to govern how many resources are requested from a site at any one time. Crawler impact rule fields include the following:

- **Site** The name of the site (not including the protocol).
- **Request Frequency** Indicates how the crawler will request documents from the site. From here you can choose to do either of the following:
    - Request up to the specified number of documents at a time and do not wait between requests (also specifying the number of simultaneous requests).
    - Request one document at a time and wait the specified time between requests (also specifying a time to wait in seconds).

Monitoring crawl health reports

Crawl health reports are a series of graphical metrics that can be used to track the performance of the SharePoint Server 2016 crawl component at a granular level. These metrics are broken into seven report groupings, shown in Table 5-3.

TABLE 5-3 Crawl health reports

Report	Description
Crawl Rate	**Graphs** Crawl Rate Per Type and Crawl Rate Per Content Source **Metrics** Crawled rate, Total items, Modified items, Not modified items, Security items, Deleted items, Retries, and Errors
Crawl Latency	**Graphs** Crawl Load (filtered by component) and Crawl Latency (filtered by content source and component)
Crawl Freshness	**Graphs** Freshness trending, a summary of freshness for each content source, showing its aggregate freshness and number of documents crawled
CPU and Memory Load	**Graphs** Total % CPU Usage and Total % Memory Usage, filterable by machine and time interval
Content Processing Activity	**Metrics** Focusing on content sources, machines, content processing components, and content processing activity
Crawl Queue	**Metrics** Shows the number of items in these two crawl queues: Links to Process (number of uncrawled URLs queued for crawling) and Transactions Queued (number of uncrawled URLs queued to be processed in the crawl pipeline)
Continuous Crawl	**Graphs** Shows a graph of time in milliseconds versus discovery time in minutes for Time in Links Table, Time in Queue Table, Crawler Time, Protocol Handler Time, Repository Time, Content Pipeline Time, and SQL Time

Plan and configure security trimming

When viewed from a high level, Search in SharePoint 2016 follows a very basic process:

1. A content source is crawled (including the permissions applied) and then processed into an index.

2. A user issues a search query, which returns a result set.

3. The result set is security trimmed before being returned to the user.

If a user is granted permission to access an item, the item then appears in the result set. This does not mean that the information wasn't there all along (the index certainly contained the data), but that it was simply "held back" from view at query time.

Content access accounts

SharePoint uses the notion of content access accounts when crawling content sources. These accounts are granted permission to access the appropriate content, which is then crawled, processed for content, and stored in the index.

Content access accounts should be ordinary Active Directory accounts; in fact, these accounts should specifically have no special privileges at all.

- They should not be the same account as that used for SharePoint setup or farm administration.

- They should not be the same account as those that run any of the application pools or services.

- They should not have local administrative access granted to any of the SharePoint or SQL member servers in the farm.

The reason we should care about the status of these accounts is their effect on security trimming and the Publishing model. One of the most important components of SharePoint 2016, Publishing can be used for the life cycle of items contained within a SharePoint site:

1. An item is initially created and saved in draft mode.

2. After the document is deemed to be ready for publication by its creator, it is submitted.

3. If approvals are enabled, the item can be approved and then scheduled for publication.

4. After the item is approved, it can be published immediately or scheduled for publication at a later date.

> **NOTE** Items that are in draft mode, are not approved, or are not in a published state are unavailable in Search results.

Default content access account

Content is accessed via two types of content access accounts: default and specific. The default access account is used to access the content present in the SharePoint farm, whereas specific access accounts can be used to access content in a particular content source.

The default content access account is used to access most of the content in the SharePoint installation. If you want, this account can also be assigned Read permissions to other content sources; items crawled within these sources are also security trimmed as queries are issued by users. This account is shown (and can be assigned) in the System Status section of the Search Administration page.

Changing the default content access account is a very basic process:

1. Click the content access account name (in this case, RC\sp_svcfarm).

2. Type a new user name and password (you have to type the password twice).

3. Click OK.

After this account is designated as being the default content access account, it is assigned Read permissions on all published content in a SharePoint farm on each web application in the farm.

Specific content access accounts

There could be several reasons a specific access account should be required for a content source. Content sources range from file shares, to web sites, and everything in between.

If these sources are not under your control, you can be issued credentials to access these sources for crawling. The content source denotes what type of content is to be crawled, but does not assign specific access account permissions.

EXAM TIP

Specific content access accounts are assigned as part of crawl rules within the Specify Authentication section.

Choose and configure hybrid search

SharePoint 2013 and SharePoint 2016 both have the ability to configure cloud hybrid search between on-premises and Office 365 installations. In such a configuration, on-premises content is crawled and parsed on premises, then processed and indexed in Office 365. From a user standpoint, search results from both on premises and Office 365 are then presented in a single result set.

From a technical standpoint, cloud hybrid search removes technical obstacles present in the older federated search model, as neither a reverse proxy configuration nor a public Secure Sockets Layer (SSL) certificate is required for configuring cloud hybrid search. Cloud hybrid search also introduces a side benefit, namely the idea that the search index is no longer maintained on premises, but is instead stored in Office 365. Parsed content transferred from on premises to the cloud index is encrypted while in transit between the environments.

The configuration of a cloud Search service application involves a series of configuration actions. If you've already configured a hybrid relationship with your SharePoint farm, for OneDrive or Sites, you might have already completed some of these actions.

Preparing for cloud hybrid search

Before deploying cloud hybrid search, consideration should be given to preconfiguring the on-premises SharePoint environment, creating the necessary account information, downloading the necessary PowerShell scripts, and creating and reviewing a search architecture plan.

REVIEWING THE ON-PREMISES SHAREPOINT SEARCH ENVIRONMENT

When an on-premises search is reconfigured as a hybrid Search service application, there is a fundamental change in both the Search server components and database server search databases.

- **Search servers**   Normally, Search servers can host one of six possible search components: crawl, admin, query processing, index, analytics, and content processing. When the farm is configured for cloud hybrid search, the index, analytics, and content processing components still remain on the Search server but are inactive.

- **Database servers**   Servers hosting the search databases usually have four databases in use: Search admin, Crawl, Link, and Analytics. In a cloud hybrid search configuration, the Link and Analytics databases are rendered inactive, although they must still exist on the database server.

CREATING THE NECESSARY ACCOUNTS

The accounts required for configuring cloud hybrid search are those used for all SharePoint hybrid configuration and testing. Specifically required are a search account for cloud hybrid search in SharePoint Server 2016, and a managed account for default content access in SharePoint Server.

- **Global Administrator (Office 365 and Azure AD)**   Use an Office 365 work account that has been assigned to the Global Administrator role for Office 365 configuration tasks such as configuring SharePoint Online features, running Azure AD and SharePoint Online Windows PowerShell commands, and testing SharePoint Online.

- **Active Directory Domain Administrator (On-premises Active Directory)**   Use an Active Directory account in the Domain Admins group to configure and test Active Directory, Active Directory Federation Services (AD FS), Domain Name System (DNS), and certificates, and to do other tasks that require elevation.

- **SharePoint Farm Administrator (On-premises Active Directory)**   Use an Active Directory account in the Farm Administrators SharePoint group for SharePoint Server configuration tasks.

- **Federated Users (On-premises Active Directory)**   Use Active Directory accounts that have been synchronized with Office 365 to test access to specific resources in both SharePoint Server and SharePoint Online.

> **NEED MORE REVIEW?**   Accounts used with a hybrid configuration are detailed in the TechNet article "Accounts needed for hybrid configuration and testing" at *https://technet .microsoft.com/library/dn607319(v=office.16).aspx.*

DOWNLOADING THE NECESSARY POWERSHELL SCRIPTS

Microsoft makes the configuration of cloud hybrid search a bit easier by providing the CreateCloudSSA.ps1 and Onboard-CloudHybridSearch.ps1 PowerShell scripts, which should be downloaded in advance of deploying cloud hybrid search.

EXAM TIP

Although an in-depth understanding of these scripts is probably not required, it would be a good idea to be able to name the correct PowerShell scripts used when configuring cloud hybrid search. These scripts can be downloaded from the Microsoft Download Center at *https://www.microsoft.com/download/details.aspx?id=51490*.

CREATING AND REVIEWING A SEARCH ARCHITECTURE PLAN

Search architecture planning can be a fairly complex subject, as a search implementation might simply encompass a single server, might involve multiple servers, and might involve an entirely separate Search farm; cloud hybrid search can be added to any of these configurations.

NEED MORE REVIEW?　To gain an understanding of the depth and breadth of Search architecture planning, visit the Office article entitled "Plan cloud hybrid search for Share-Point" at *https://support.office.com/article/33926857-302c-424f-ba78 -03286cf5ac30#Plan_search_architecture*.

Configuring cloud hybrid search

Now that the preliminary items have been reviewed and completed, the configuration work can begin. Configuration steps for cloud hybrid search might include some that have already been configured (if you've previously configured hybrid OneDrive for Business or Hybrid Sites). Steps for this configuration (including some optional ones) are shown here.

1.　**Configure Office 365 for SharePoint hybrid**　Configure your Office 365 tenant for a hybrid environment, including registering your domain, configuring User Principal Name (UPN) suffixes, and synchronizing your user accounts.

2.　**Create a cloud Search service application in SharePoint on premises**　Use the CreateCloudSSA.ps1 PowerShell script to create the cloud Search service application on the search farm that's running SharePoint Server 2016.

3.　**(Optional) Alter the default Search architecture in SharePoint 2016 for cloud hybrid search**　If you planned a Search architecture that's different from the default one, set up the planned Search architecture.

4.　**Connect your cloud Search service application to your Office 365 tenant**　Use the Onboard-CloudHybridSearch.ps1 PowerShell script to onboard your cloud Search service application and Office 365 tenant to cloud hybrid search. The script sets up the cloud Search service application to interact with the Office 365 tenant and also sets up server-to-server authentication.

5.　**Create a test content source to crawl for cloud hybrid search**　Add a small file share first for testing the crawl, as you can add more on-premises content later.

6.　**(Optional) Set up a separate Search Center to validate hybrid search results in Office 365**　This recommended configuration allows you to validate and tune a new search experience in a separate Search Center, while keeping the original search experience entirely unchanged.

7. **Start a full crawl of on-premises content for cloud hybrid search**   When the crawl completes, your on-premises content shows up in the search results in your validation Search Center in Office 365 and in Office Delve.

8. **Verify that cloud hybrid search works**   Go to your Search Center in SharePoint Online in Office 365 and enter this query: **IsExternalContent:true**. The results you get should show content from the on-premises content source that you've crawled.

9. **Tune cloud hybrid search**   Set up and tune the search experiences you've planned for your users.

10. **Remove the validation Search Center and expose all users to hybrid search results**   Set your Search Center and any site search in Office 365 to use the default result source and set up the default result source with the search experiences that you've tuned. Your on-premises content shows up in the search results in your Search Center in Office 365, site search in Office 365, and in Office Delve.

> *NEED MORE REVIEW?*   These steps are covered in great detail within the TechNet roadmap entitled "Configure cloud hybrid search - roadmap" at *https://technet.microsoft.com /library/dn720906(v=office.16).aspx* and the free Microsoft Press eBook entitled *Configuring Microsoft SharePoint Hybrid Capabilities*, which can be downloaded at *https://blogs. msdn.microsoft.com/microsoft_press/2016/07/06/free-ebook-configuring-microsoft -sharepoint-hybrid-capabilities/.* Having a solid understanding of this roadmap, along with those for hybrid OneDrive and Hybrid Sites, is essential for administering hybrid configurations in SharePoint 2016.

Skill: Create and configure a managed metadata service (MMS) application

The managed metadata service (MMS) within a SharePoint farm provides a way to define taxonomical structures that can be carried out through the entire farm. These structures include term sets, which can be used for assigning metadata to lists and documents and controlling navigation, and content type hubs, which can be used to centralize and standardize the deployment of specific content types within your enterprise.

> **This section covers how to:**
> - Configure proxy settings for managed service applications
> - Configure content type hub settings
> - Configure sharing term sets

- Plan and configure content type propagation schedules
- Configure custom properties
- Configure term store permissions
- Configure MMS imports

Configure proxy settings for managed service applications

Most service applications present in a SharePoint 2016 farm are attached to a corresponding proxy. Using this proxy, a relationship can be established between a service application and a web application; this relationship is most often referred to as a service connection.

Consider a larger enterprise installation that wishes to prevent the availability of a particular service application (for example, Access Services) to a specific web application.

From a functional point of view, this effort requires three steps:

1. Create a new proxy group.
2. Associate all service application proxies to this group, *except* Access Services and Access Services 2010.
3. Associate the web application to the newly created proxy group.

Creating a new proxy group

A proxy group is a mechanism that defines the relationship between a web application and multiple service application proxies. These proxies enable the web applications associated with the proxy group to consume services (MMS, User Profile service application [UPA], and so on) from the associated service applications.

EXAM TIP

There is no mechanism in Central Administration for creating a proxy group. Proxy groups are created using PowerShell via the New-SPServiceApplicationProxyGroup cmdlet.

To create a service application proxy group, you would then issue the following PowerShell commands, first creating and then verifying the existence of a new proxy group, as shown in Figure 5-6.

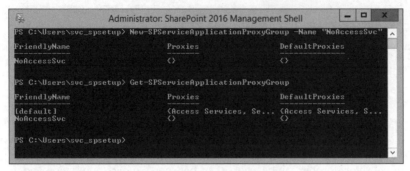

FIGURE 5-6 Creating a new service application proxy group

Associating proxies to a proxy group

Associating a service application proxy with a proxy group in Windows PowerShell requires only a few lines of code. Although it might seem like a lot of typing, it would be very easy to build several of these associations into a Windows PowerShell script.

EXAM TIP

A service application proxy can be associated with multiple proxy groups using Windows PowerShell. Also, a proxy group is not required to host each and every available service application available within the farm.

Two PowerShell cmdlets are required to associate a proxy with a proxy group. First, the service application proxy is assigned to a variable representing the proxy group member using the Get-SPServiceApplicationProxy cmdlet, and then the variable is assigned to the proxy group via the use of the Add-SPServiceApplicationProxyGroupMember cmdlet, as shown in Figure 5-7.

FIGURE 5-7 Assigning a proxy to a proxy group

IMPORTANT Removing a proxy from a proxy group is done using the same steps as when adding a proxy, except that Add-SPServiceApplicationProxyGroupMember is replaced by Remove-SPServiceApplicationProxyGroupMember. Removing a service application proxy from a proxy group *immediately* removes that service's functionality from all associated web applications.

Assigning proxy groups to web applications

Once the proxy and proxy group have been created and assigned, assigning the proxy group to a web application can be done from within Central Administration by selecting a web application and then selecting Service Connections. Doing so grants the web application the functionality provided by the associated service applications, as shown in Figure 5-8.

FIGURE 5-8 Configuring service application associations

Configure content type hub settings

A content type hub is a site collection that has been specified to provide content types, contained in a centralized or authoritative location, to other site collections. Content types must be configured for publication on an individual basis.

> **EXAM TIP**
>
> When a content type is published from the hub to a site collection, the published copy of the content type is considered to be "sealed," meaning that it cannot be modified. All modifications to this content type must occur within the context of the content type hub.

Publishing a newly created content type

The publication of content types stored in the hub is fully configurable from within the content type hub.

1. On the Content Type Hub page, select Site Settings (gear icon).
2. In the Web Designer Galleries section, select Site Content Types.
3. Select the link for your content type.
4. Select Manage Publishing For This Content Type.
5. The Content Type Publishing page opens (see Figure 5-9).

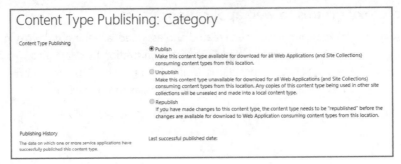

FIGURE 5-9 Content type publishing

6. Choose from the following:

   ■ *Unpublish* makes the content type unavailable; it also "unseals" each local copy of the content type.

   ■ *Republish* publishes the newly updated changes to your content type.

7. Click OK to close this dialog box.

> **IMPORTANT** Proceed with caution when you choose to unpublish a content type altogether. The act of unsealing the content type causes the content type in each site collection to become its own freestanding entity. All changes made from that point on will be made within each distinct site collection.

Configure sharing term sets

A particular web application should have a default MMS application (known as the primary) that enables users to enter and use keywords; this connection also provides the content hub that is used for the web application.

Editing the Managed Metadata Service Connection

The sharing of term sets is configured from the Edit Managed Metadata Service Connection page, found within the Manage menu of the Managed Metadata Service Connection (see Figure 5-10).

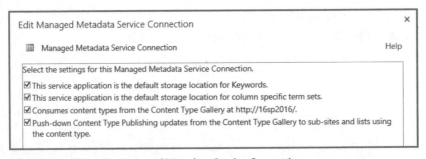

FIGURE 5-10 Editing the Managed Metadata Service Connection

The first two check boxes are the focus here; they determine the configuration of the MMS from a keyword or term set standpoint:

- Selecting the first check box (default keyword storage location) enables users to store new keywords into this term store.

- Selecting the second check box (default term set location) enables site admins to create new term sets.

Web applications are often associated with more than one MMS application; they can be used to create separate content type hubs. If you elect to have multiple MMS connections provided to a web application, leave these first two check boxes cleared on all but the primary connection.

EXAM TIP

Do not make more than one connection the default keyword storage location for any one web app. Also, do not make more than one connection the default term set location for any one web application.

Plan and configure content type propagation schedules

There are two types of timer jobs that control the flow and function of the content type hub:

- **Content Type Hub**   This is a singular job that controls the content type log maintenance and manages unpublished content types.

- **Content Type Subscriber**   If there are several web applications that are connected or proxied to the MMS, each is assigned a Content Type Subscriber job. This job retrieves content type packages from the hub and applies them to a local content type gallery.

Configuring the propagation schedule

The propagation of content types is controlled on a per-web application basis by the Content Type Subscriber timer job. To configure the propagation of a content type, follow these steps:

1. Open Central Administration and then select Monitoring.

2. On the Monitoring page, in the Timer Jobs section, select Review Job Definitions.

3. On the Job Definitions page, scroll down and select the Content Type Subscriber job for the intended web application.

4. Alter the Recurring Schedule settings for your job (see Figure 5-11).

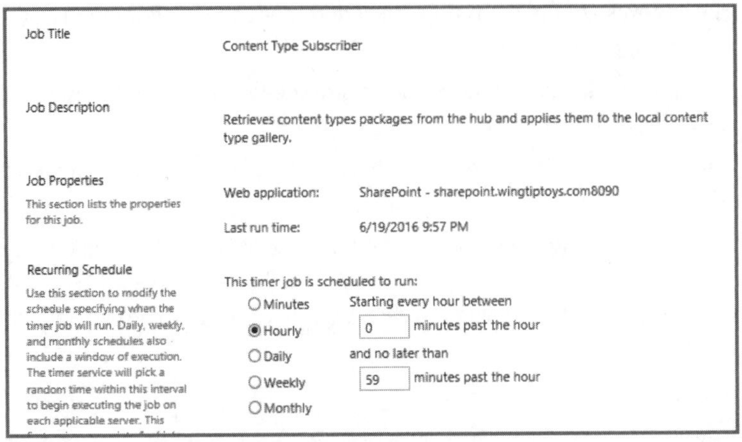

Job Title	Content Type Subscriber
Job Description	Retrieves content types packages from the hub and applies them to the local content type gallery.

Job Properties

This section lists the properties for this job.

Web application: SharePoint - sharepoint.wingtiptoys.com8090

Last run time: 6/19/2016 9:57 PM

Recurring Schedule

Use this section to modify the schedule specifying when the timer job will run. Daily, weekly, and monthly schedules also include a window of execution. The timer service will pick a random time within this interval to begin executing the job on each applicable server. This

This timer job is scheduled to run:

○ Minutes
● Hourly
○ Daily
○ Weekly
○ Monthly

Starting every hour between
[0] minutes past the hour
and no later than
[59] minutes past the hour

FIGURE 5-11 Altering the Recurring Schedule settings for the Content Type Subscriber timer job

> **IMPORTANT** The randomness of the time window for timer jobs is by design and enables each SharePoint server in the farm to process the job within a certain window of time. This randomness is beneficial in that the farm can better balance the load caused by its timer jobs.

5. At the bottom of this page, you can choose one of the following options:

   - Run Now starts the propagation cycle immediately.
   - Disable disables the job (not recommended).
   - OK accepts the changes you made to the propagation schedule.
   - Cancel discards all the changes made to the propagation schedule.

Configure custom properties

Custom properties can be added to an individual term or to a term set from within the Term Store Management Tool. These properties are useful for defining more advanced term attributes, which can then be used to develop custom code solutions for displaying and sorting terms and term sets within a SharePoint 2016 installation. These properties can also be used in conjunction with the Term Property Web Part.

There are two distinct property types: shared and local. Local properties are available only for a particular term in a term set, whereas shared properties are useful on all reused or pinned instances of the term anywhere within the term store.

Adding a new custom property

To add a new custom property to a term or term store, follow these steps:

1. Open the Term Store Management Tool for your MMS application.

2. Expand a Term Set Group.

3. Select a Term or Term Set.

4. Select the Custom Properties tab.

5. Add a new Shared Property Name and Value.

6. If you are adding a custom property for a term, you can instead choose to use a Local Property Name and Value.

7. Select Add to complete the addition and then click Save.

Configure term store permissions

Term store permissions operate in a hierarchical fashion and are assigned at the group level within a term store. These permission sets are mapped to one of three metadata roles:

- **Term Store Administrators** Members of this role can create new term set groups and assign users to the Group Manager or Term Store Manager roles.

- **Group Managers** Members of this role have contributor access and also can add users to the Contributor role.

- **Contributors** Members of this role have full permissions to edit terms and term set hierarchies within their term group.

EXAM TIP

Term store permissions for both Group Managers and Contributors are assigned at the term set group level. It is not possible to assign these permissions at the term set or individual term level.

Adding users to the Term Store Administrators role

The addition of new Term Store Administrators is done at the Managed Metadata site level within the Term Store Management Tool.

1. Select Manage Service Applications, then the link of your intended MMS application.

2. The General tab will appear for your MMS application. Add the new user in the Term Store Administrators text box (see Figure 5-12).

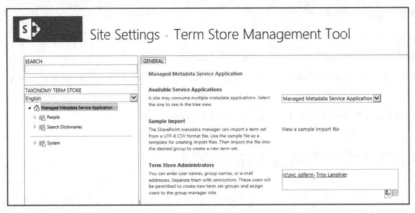

FIGURE 5-12 Adding a new Term Store Administrator

Adding users to Group Manager or Contributor roles

The addition of new Group Managers or Contributors is done at the term set group level within the Term Store Management Tool.

1. Select Manage Service Applications, and then the link of your intended MMS application.

2. Choose the link for the term set group to which you want to assign people.

3. On the General Tab, you can now add Group Managers and Contributors (see Figure 5-13).

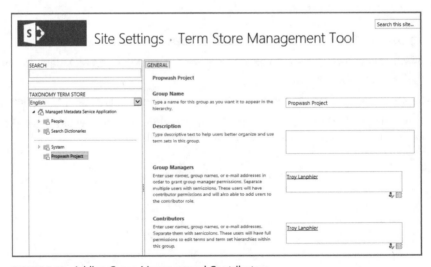

FIGURE 5-13 Adding Group Managers and Contributors

Configure MMS imports

Fortunately, it's not required to manually enter each and every term in a term set. Instead, a sample import file (.csv) can be downloaded and altered to meet your needs:

1. From Site Settings, Site Administration, choose Term Store Management.

2. Select the MMS application you intend to alter.

3. On the General tab, choose View A Sample Import File to download the ImportTermSet.csv file, and alter it to suit (Figure 5-14).

FIGURE 5-14 Importing a term set

4. Once you've completed your alterations to the import file, select the Import Term Set drop-down next to the group that will receive the uploaded terms.

5. Select the import file and then click OK to complete the upload.

Skill: Manage search

Although Search was a critical component of SharePoint 2013, it assumes an even larger role in SharePoint 2016 due to hybridization with the cloud. Search affects the content that can appear in navigation, filtering, search queries, and many other locations. Search is also capable of reaching across system boundaries, surfacing content present in other line-of-business systems.

> **This section covers how to:**
> - Manage result sources
> - Manage query rules
> - Manage display templates
> - Manage Search Engine Optimization (SEO) settings
> - Manage result types
> - Manage a search schema
> - Manage federated search, including integration with Delve and Office Graph

Manage result sources

Result sources in SharePoint have two core functions:

- They are used to scope search results to a certain type of content or subset of search results.

- They are also used to federate queries with the local SharePoint index, a remote SharePoint index, OpenSearch, or a Microsoft Exchange Server index.

If you created search scopes in prior versions of SharePoint, result sources will likely seem familiar. Search scopes have, in fact, been deprecated since SharePoint 2013, and have been replaced outright by result sources. If you upgraded from SharePoint 2010, you might find search scopes still exist and can be used in queries, but they will no longer be editable.

In SharePoint Server 2016, site collection administrators, site owners, and site designers can also create and configure result sources for use at the site collection and site levels. Search service administration privileges are required for creating farm-scoped result sources.

> **NEED MORE REVIEW?** Specific steps are required to build a result source at the Search service application, site collection, and site levels. These steps can be found in the TechNet article "Configure result sources for search in SharePoint Server 2013" at *https://technet.microsoft.com/library/%20jj683115(v=office.16).aspx.*

Creating a new result source in SharePoint 2016

Creating a new result source is done using the New Result Source link within the Result Sources section of the pertinent search application (Figure 5-15).

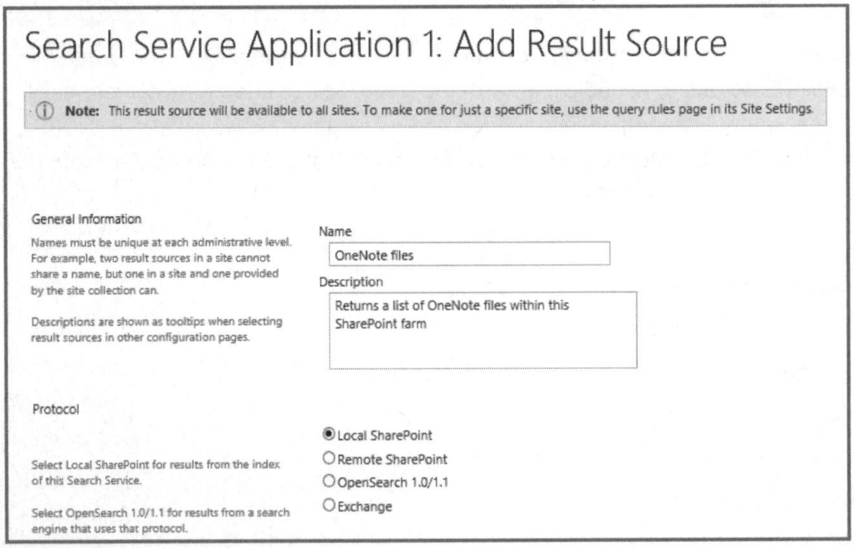

FIGURE 5-15 Adding a result source

The creation of a new result source involves five major groupings of tasks: providing general information, specifying a protocol, selecting a search result type, developing a query transform, and specifying credential information.

- **Providing general information**   Entering a Name and Description for the result source.

- **Specifying a protocol**   Allows the selection of the search protocol to be used.

  - Local SharePoint provides results from the index of this Search service.

  - Remote SharePoint provides results from the index of a Search service located in another farm.

  - OpenSearch 1.0/1.1 provides results from a search engine using this protocol.

  - Exchange provides results from an Exchange source.

- **Selecting a search result type**   Depending on the protocol chosen, different options are presented.

  - For local SharePoint, either SharePoint or People search results can be searched.

  - For remote SharePoint, the Remote Service URL must be entered for the remote farm, then SharePoint or People search results can be searched.

  - No options are presented for OpenSearch 1.0/1.1.

  - Exchange sources request that you specify the Source URL (or optionally, use AutoDiscover).

- **Developing a query transform**   By using the query builder, transforms can be entered to focus on a particular type of content. For instance, a search for OneNote files might use a transform such as "{searchTerms} fileextension=one".

- **Specifying credential information**   Each protocol type requires a different set of credentials for authentication.

  - Local SharePoint can select either Default Authentication (using their default SharePoint authentication credentials) or Basic Authentication (the same user name and password are provided regardless of user).

  - Remote SharePoint can select either Default Authentication or Single Sign-On ID credentials.

  - OpenSearch can either select Anonymous (no authentication required) or choose from Basic, Digest, NTLM/App Pool Identity, NTLM/user name and password, Form Authentication, or Cookie Authentication.

EXAM TIP

As a reminder, a total of four protocol types are available for use in result sources: Local SharePoint (this farm), Remote SharePoint (a different farm), OpenSearch 1.0/1.1 (used to crawl OpenSearch-compatible sources), and Exchange (used to crawl Exchange information).

Predefined result sources in SharePoint 2016

There are a total of 16 built-in result sources provided by SharePoint 2016 (see Table 5-4). Each of these result sources uses the Local SharePoint protocol and a query transform to retrieve the appropriate content.

TABLE 5-4 Predefined result sources in SharePoint 2016

Name	Type	Description
Conversations	SharePoint search results	Results from conversation results and community sites
Documents	SharePoint search results	Office and PDF documents
Items matching a content type	SharePoint search results	Results with a given content type
Items matching a tag	SharePoint search results	Results with a given tag
Items related to current user	SharePoint search results	Results related to the user
Items with same keyword as this item	SharePoint search results	Results sharing a keyword with a given item
Local people results	People search results	People results from the profile database
Local reports and data results	SharePoint search results	Excel, Office Data Connection (ODC), Report Definition Language (RDL), and reports library results
Local SharePoint results (default selection)	SharePoint search results	All local index results except people
Local video results	SharePoint search results	Video results from the local index
Pages	SharePoint search results	SharePoint web page results
Pictures	SharePoint search results	Picture and image result items
Popular	SharePoint search results	Documents and list items sorted by view count
Recently changed items	SharePoint search results	Documents and list items sorted by modified date
Recommended items	SharePoint search results	Items that are recommended for a specific item
Wiki	SharePoint search results	SharePoint Wiki pages

Manage query rules

Query rules are used to promote certain search results, show blocks of additional results, or influence the ranking of search results. This functionality is made available not only to the Search application administrator but also to the site collection and site administrators within a SharePoint farm.

Query rules can be defined at one of three possible levels:

- **Search service application** Applies to all site collections in the web applications that consume the Search service application
- **Site collection** Applies to all sites within a particular site collection
- **Site** Applies to a particular site

Creating a new query rule

A query rule is composed of three possible components: the query conditions that cause the rule to fire, the actions that occur when the rule is fired, and (optionally) the ability to provide a time window for when the rule is available to fire.

> **NEED MORE REVIEW?** Specific steps are required to build a query rule at the Search service application, site collection, and site levels. These steps can be found in the TechNet article "Manage query rules in SharePoint Server 2013" at *http://technet.microsoft.com /library/jj871676(v=office.16).aspx.*

Creating a new query rule at the Search application level requires only a few steps. In this example, you will build a new query rule that acts much like a best bet would have in prior versions of SharePoint. This rule will fire when the user queries for the following words: 401K, Hiring, Interviewing, Retirement, or Termination.

To create this example query rule at the Search application level, follow these steps.

1. Select Manage Service Applications, then the link of your intended Search service application.

2. In the Queries And Results section of the Search Administration page, select Query Rules.

3. On the Manage Query Rules page, choose the For What Context Do You Want To Configure Rules drop-down list and select Local SharePoint Results (System). Next, select the New Query Rule link (see Figure 5-16).

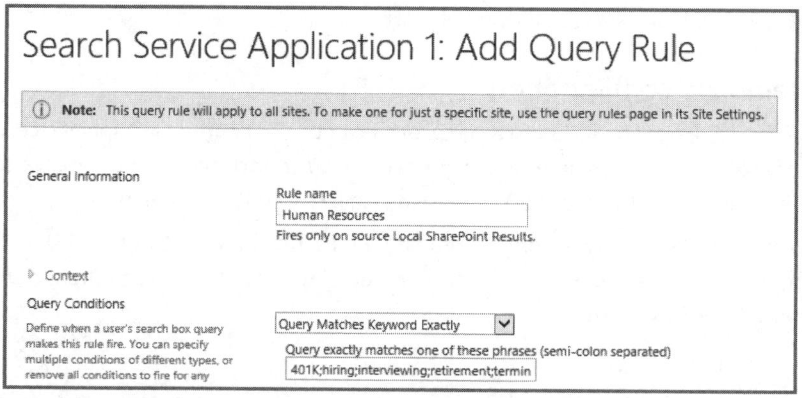

FIGURE 5-16 New query rule

1. In the General Information Rule Name text box, type **Human Resources**.

2. In the Query Conditions section, choose the Query Matches Keyword Exactly drop-down value. In the text box beneath the drop-down list, enter the following string of terms in the field: **401K;hiring;interviewing;retirement;termination.**

EXAM TIP

Be familiar with each of the query conditions and the potential effect each one can have on the query rules.

3. In the Actions section, click the Add Promoted Result link, then enter the following values for Title and URL:

   ■ Title: **Human Resources**

   ■ URL: **http://hr.wingtiptoys.com**

   You can optionally choose to render the URL as a banner instead of a plain hyperlink.

   Users who search for a term present in the Query Conditions (Retirement) now see the promoted site (Human Resources—hr.wingtiptoys.com).

Manage display templates

Search results in SharePoint 2016 are presented by a series of search-specific Web Parts. These Web Parts, in turn, rely on a series of display templates to control the formatting and presentation of search results.

IMPORTANT Display templates are available only for search-driven Web Parts.

There are two major groupings of display templates:

■ **Control templates** These control the organization and layout of search results as well as the overall look of the Web Part.

■ **Item templates** These provide the display characteristics of individual items displayed in search results within the Web Part.

Display template configuration

As new search Web Parts are added to a page, each can be configured with specific control and item templates. These templates are changeable; new control and item templates can also be defined and stored within the Master Page Gallery to suit your needs.

Editing a search Web Part (the Content Search Web Part is shown in Figure 5-17) enables you to configure its properties. Within the Display Templates section, you see the Control and Item selection drop-down boxes.

FIGURE 5-17 Web Part properties (Content Search Web Part)

Creating new display templates

The first step of building a new display template is finding its location within the SharePoint file system and mapping a location from your client system.

EXAM TIP

Be familiar with the four different display templates folders and which affect the result type functionality.

Display templates are housed within the Master Page Gallery of a given SharePoint site. Probably the easiest way to document this location is to use Design Manager to tell you the location.

1. On the Settings menu (click the gear icon) in your site collection, select Design Manager.
2. After the Design Manager page appears, select item 3, Upload Design Files. The URL shown (for example, *http://intranet.wingtiptoys.com/_catalogs/masterpage/*) is the location of the Master Page Gallery. Copy this URL to your clipboard.

EXAM TIP

If you look at your Settings menu, but do not see the Design Manager link, there is a good chance that you do not have the Publishing features activated in this site collection. These features are a requirement for much of the ease-of-design functionality in SharePoint Server 2016.

1. Map a network drive from your client machine using the URL you previously captured.
2. In the newly mapped drive, open the Display Templates folder (Figure 5-18). Note that the Content Web Parts, Filters, Search, and System folders each maintain both control and item templates (not shown).

Name	Date modified	Type	Size
Content Web Parts	12/12/2012 5:23 PM	File folder	
Filters	12/12/2012 5:23 PM	File folder	
Language Files	12/12/2012 5:23 PM	File folder	
Search	12/12/2012 5:23 PM	File folder	
Server Style Sheets	12/12/2012 5:23 PM	File folder	
System	12/12/2012 5:23 PM	File folder	

FIGURE 5-18 The contents of the Display Templates folder

3. Open the Content Web Parts folder to display a series of control and item templates. Among them are the Control_List and the Item_Picture3Lines templates, which correspond to the List and Picture On Left, 3 Lines On Right item templates you saw in the Search Web Part.

> **NEED MORE REVIEW?** Creating display templates can be a fairly involved process. For more details on how to create a new display template, see the article "SharePoint 2013 Design Manager display templates" at *http://msdn.microsoft.com/library/jj945138.aspx*.

Manage Search Engine Optimization settings

Previous versions of SharePoint (prior to SharePoint 2013) did not provide any sort of built-in mechanism for controlling Search Engine Optimization (SEO). SharePoint Server 2016 now includes native, easy-to-configure SEO support for publishing sites that can be administered by site collection administrators and site owners.

There are three distinct levels of SEO configuration within SharePoint 2016: publishing pages, site collection, and XML site mapping.

Configuring SEO properties for publishing pages

Each publishing page on a SharePoint site can be configured with a series of SEO properties:

- **Name** A name for the page that could appear in the URL.
- **Title** A phrase that can be used in search for keyword-based queries.
- **Browser Title** A friendly title for the page that can appear in the title bar of web browsers viewing the page (must be between 5 and 25 characters).
- **Meta Description** A description for the page that would appear on a search results page.
- **Keywords** Individual words that describe the intent of the page. These words will be used during keyword searches, influencing the ranking of the page in Search. This field allows between 25 and 1,024 characters.
- **Exclude From Internet Search Engines** This option enables you to include or exclude this page from the sitemap (if used) and search engines.

Most of these properties are stored as columns within the Pages library, although some are mapped a bit differently (for instance, Exclude From Internet Search Engines becomes Hide From Internet Search Engines in the page's properties).

Additionally, you can use the last property, Exclude From Internet Search Engines, to both hide the page from an XML-generated sitemap and hide it from search engines.

To configure SEO properties for a publishing page, follow these steps.

1. Check the page out.

2. On the ribbon, select the Page tab and then select the Edit Properties drop-down list. Select the Edit SEO Properties menu item.

3. Change the values for the SEO Property fields and click OK to commit your changes. Note that changes made in this menu appear instantly on the site (such as changing the title of the page from Home to Intranet Home).

4. Check your page back in and publish it for the change to take effect.

EXAM TIP

SEO properties are only available for Publishing pages (those contained within the /Pages library). The SEO properties icon in the ribbon is unavailable for any other page type (a standard team site page, for instance).

Configuring SEO settings for site collections

In addition to the SEO properties on Publishing pages, SharePoint 2016 enables you to configure the following settings on a per-site-collection basis:

- **Verify Ownership Of This Site With Search Engines** You can go to a search engine's webmaster tools page and request the appropriate <meta> tag that is specific to your URL.

- **Consolidate Link Popularity With Canonical URLs** Allows you to specify filter link parameters that can help search engines combine the appropriate URLs on your site from a search metric point of view.

To configure SEO properties for a site collection, follow these steps.

1. Navigate to the root site of your site collection.

2. On the Settings menu (gear icon), select Site Settings.

3. In the Site Collection Administration section, select Search Engine Optimization Settings.

4. On the Search Engine Optimization Settings page, select the appropriate values for the two optimization settings sections and then click OK.

Be familiar with the structure of a meta tag and the way it can be added for your Internet-facing SharePoint site.

Configuring SEO for the XML sitemap

If you have a site that enables anonymous access, you can also enable the Search Engine Sitemap site collection feature. This feature improves SEO of your site by automatically generating a sitemap on a regular basis that contains all the valid URLs in your website.

Enabling this feature adds two additional fields to the SEO Properties page, Sitemap Priority and Sitemap Change Frequency (Figure 5-19).

- **Sitemap Priority**   This value indicates the weighting (between 0.0 and 1.0) of the importance of one page over another within your site collection; the higher the number, the more important your page.

- **Sitemap Change Frequency**   This selection enables you to tell the search engine how regularly you expect the page to change to help improve search engine efficiency.

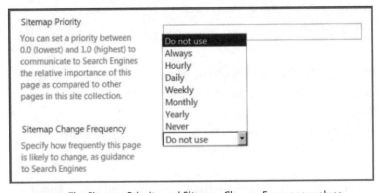

FIGURE 5-19 The Sitemap Priority and Sitemap Change Frequency values

Manage result types

Result types evaluate a query based on a set of rules and then apply the appropriate display template. The display templates in use here are located in a different folder from the ones we used earlier in this section (located within the Content Web Parts folder).

When a query is made via Search (for instance, a series of Microsoft Word documents), the result set that is returned is evaluated for the way the returned information should be presented. The Result Type defines the fields for evaluating the result set in terms of conditions and actions.

- **Conditions** For the Microsoft Word result set, two conditions are evaluated:
  - Which result source should the item match? (All sources)
  - What types of content should match? (Microsoft Word)
- **Actions** One action is applied, consisting of two parts:
  - What should these results look like? (Word item)
  - What is the appropriate display template URL? (for example, *~sitecollection/ _catalogs/masterpage/Display Templates/Search/Item_Word.js*)

Display templates associated with result types

The display templates that are associated with result types are located in the Search folder within the Master Page Gallery (see Figure 5-20).

Name	Date modified	Type	Size
Item_WebPage	2/9/2016 5:01 AM	HTML Document	3 KB
Item_WebPage	2/9/2016 5:01 AM	JavaScript File	4 KB
Item_WebPage_HoverPanel	2/9/2016 5:01 AM	HTML Document	5 KB
Item_WebPage_HoverPanel	2/9/2016 5:01 AM	JavaScript File	7 KB
Item_Word	2/9/2016 5:01 AM	HTML Document	3 KB
Item_Word	2/9/2016 5:01 AM	JavaScript File	5 KB
Item_Word_HoverPanel	2/9/2016 5:01 AM	HTML Document	8 KB
Item_Word_HoverPanel	2/9/2016 5:01 AM	JavaScript File	10 KB

FIGURE 5-20 Display Template HTML and JavaScript

Manage a search schema

As a document is crawled, metadata is extracted as crawled properties. This metadata can include structured content (such as columnar metadata; for example, title, author) or unstructured content (such as keywords extracted from the body of the document).

For a user to be able to search on a piece of metadata, this crawled property must be mapped to a managed property. After this task is complete, queries can be performed against this metadata (such as looking up an item's order number, stored in a list column).

To view the properties that have been crawled, select Search Schema from within the Queries And Results section of your Search service application. The resulting page shows a series of three links: Managed Properties, Crawled Properties, and Categories.

Managed Properties

The first page displayed is Managed Properties (Figure 5-21). On this page, you can selectively filter which managed property is shown and also see what managed properties are mapped to which crawled properties.

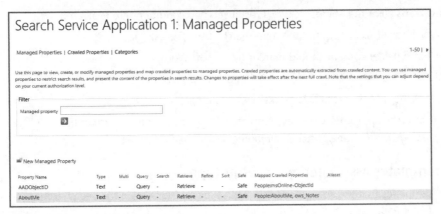

FIGURE 5-21 Managed Properties page

Crawled Properties

Selecting the Crawled Properties link inverts the view. Selecting a category (such as People) then enables you to see which crawled properties are mapped to a particular managed property (see Figure 5-22).

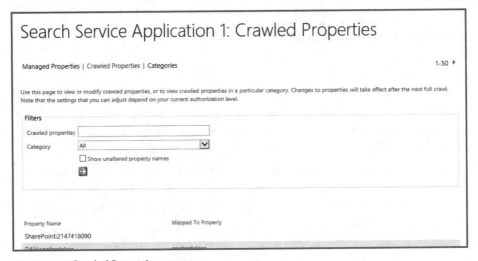

FIGURE 5-22 Crawled Properties page

Categories

The Categories selection enables you to see a summary of all available categories and the properties each possesses (see Figure 5-23).

Search Service Application 1: Categories

Managed Properties | Crawled Properties | Categories

Use this page to view or modify categories, or view crawled properties in a particular category. Note that the settings that you can adjust depend on your current authorization level.

Category Name	Number of Properties
Basic	0
Business Data	0
Document Parser	0

FIGURE 5-23 Categories page

EXAM TIP

Be familiar with the configuration and process of converting a crawled property to a managed property. This process is detailed in the TechNet article "Manage the search schema in SharePoint Server 2013" at *https://technet.microsoft.com/library/jj219667.aspx*.

Manage federated search, including integration with Delve and Office Graph

Delve is powered by Office Graph in Office 365, and shows users the most relevant content based on who they work with and what they are working on. This relevance is a direct result of the search capabilities present in Office 365. From a permissions standpoint, Delve respects the permission structure put in place, just as Search does.

Granting access to Delve

Access to Delve is granted within the SharePoint Online menu of the Office 365 Admin Center, and is located within the Office Graph section. Granular control of access to this feature is not available, leaving the administrator with two possible choices:

- Allow access to the Office Graph (default).
- Don't allow access to the Office Graph.

Removing access to Delve

Preventing user access to Delve primarily affects the user experience when visiting an individual user's page:

- A person's page in OneDrive for Business will only show user profile information.
- Users can search for other people in the organization, but have no ability to search for documents or boards in a Delve-like fashion.

Skill: Manage taxonomy

Term sets contained within MMS work together with SharePoint 2016 Search to provide functionality such as navigation and product catalogs. After the correct information has been located in Search, term sets continue to provide benefits, enabling you to both refine search results and filter content within a list.

> **This section covers how to:**
>
> - Manage site collection term set access
> - Manage term set navigation
> - Manage topic catalog pages
> - Configure custom properties
> - Configure search refinement
> - Configure list refinement

Manage site collection term set access

In SharePoint 2016, it's possible to have one site collection refer to another's term set. Of course, you could also generate the term set within the MMS application, but perhaps this level of availability (having the term set available across the entire farm) is not required.

 EXAM TIP

Although the designated site collections do indeed have Read access to the original term set, they cannot change its contents.

You might have a team that generates and maintains its own term set in one site collection, and then wants to provide that term set to several other site collections. This cross-site collection term set access is Read-only, meaning that the sites allowed access are not themselves allowed to configure any new term sets or terms; however, the consuming site collections can bind and pin term sets from this group into their own term sets.

Configuring term set access in SharePoint 2016 can be done in a few steps.

1. Select Term Store Management.

2. Select the term set group for your site collection.

3. On the General tab for your term set group, scroll down to the Site Collection Access section.

4. Within the Site Collection Access section, enter the names of each site collection that should have access to this term set group (one per line, shown in Figure 5-24).

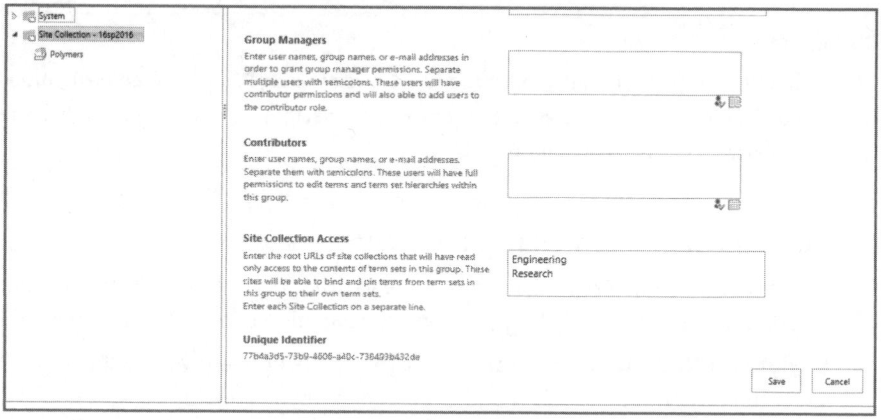

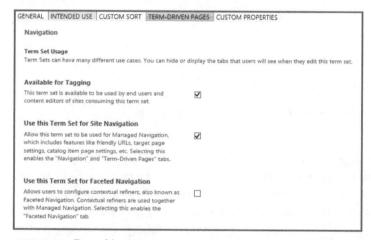

FIGURE 5-24 Adding site collection access to a term set

Manage term set navigation

Configuring a site collection to use managed navigation requires the use of a new term set to house the navigational structure. This term set can then be configured to be used for site navigation, faceted navigation, or both (see Figure 5-25).

| GENERAL | INTENDED USE | CUSTOM SORT | TERM-DRIVEN PAGES | CUSTOM PROPERTIES |

Navigation

Term Set Usage
Term Sets can have many different use cases. You can hide or display the tabs that users will see when they edit this term set.

Available for Tagging
This term set is available to be used by end users and content editors of sites consuming this term set. ☑

Use this Term Set for Site Navigation
Allow this term set to be used for Managed Navigation, which includes features like friendly URLs, target page settings, catalog item page settings, etc. Selecting this enables the "Navigation" and "Term-Driven Pages" tabs. ☑

Use this Term Set for Faceted Navigation
Allows users to configure contextual refiners, also known as Faceted Navigation. Contextual refiners are used together with Managed Navigation. Selecting this enables the "Faceted Navigation" tab. ☐

FIGURE 5-25 Term-driven pages

Choosing to have a term set be used for site navigation activates the Navigation and Term-Driven Pages tabs on individual navigation terms. After a term set is configured to be used as site navigation, its individual terms can function as navigation nodes.

EXAM TIP

Understand the differences between these two types of navigation. Faceted navigation has to do with refining content based on the context; site navigation enables you to use a term set for global and current navigation.

Term store management (Navigation tab)

On the Navigation tab, the Navigation Node Appearance section enables you to configure how the node will appear in the global and current navigation of the site (see Figure 5-26):

- **Navigation Node Title** You can choose to use the title as given by the term set or select the Customize check box and enter a more appealing name.

- **Navigation Hover Text** Editing this text enables more helpful information to be displayed when the user moves a mouse over the link.

- **Visibility In Menus** This setting enables you to determine whether the link will be available to global navigation, current navigation, or both.

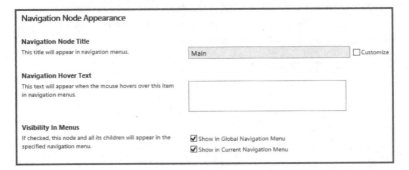

FIGURE 5-26 Navigation Node Appearance

Also located on the Navigation tab is the Navigation Node Type and the Associated Folder. The Navigation Node Type enables you to specify whether the node is simply a link or header, or whether the node sends users to a term-driven page. The Associated Folder allows you to specify a folder of pages that will be associated with this node (see Figure 5-27).

- If you choose the Simple Link Or Header option, you can either choose to enter the URL of a link or simply a header that can have links beneath it.

- If you choose the Term-Driven Page With Friendly URL option, this node will be a friendly URL to a term-driven page (configured on the Term-Driven Pages tab).

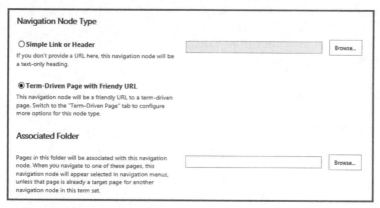

FIGURE 5-27 Navigation Node Type and Associated Folder

Term Store Management (Term-Driven Pages tab)

On the Term-Driven Pages tab (for a selected term), you can specify four different groups of settings (Figure 5-28):

- **Configure Friendly URL For This Term**   Defaults to a friendly URL that matches the name of the individual term. Selecting the optional Customize check box allows you to change the friendly URL from its default.

- **Target Page Settings**   Enables you to choose both the target page for a term as well as specifying another target page for children of the term.

- **Category Image**   Allows you to specify a display image meant to represent this term in the Term Property Web Part.

- **Catalog Item Page Settings**   If you are using the term as a catalog category (covered in the next section), this setting enables you to choose both the Catalog Item Page for the category and another Catalog Item Page for children of the category.

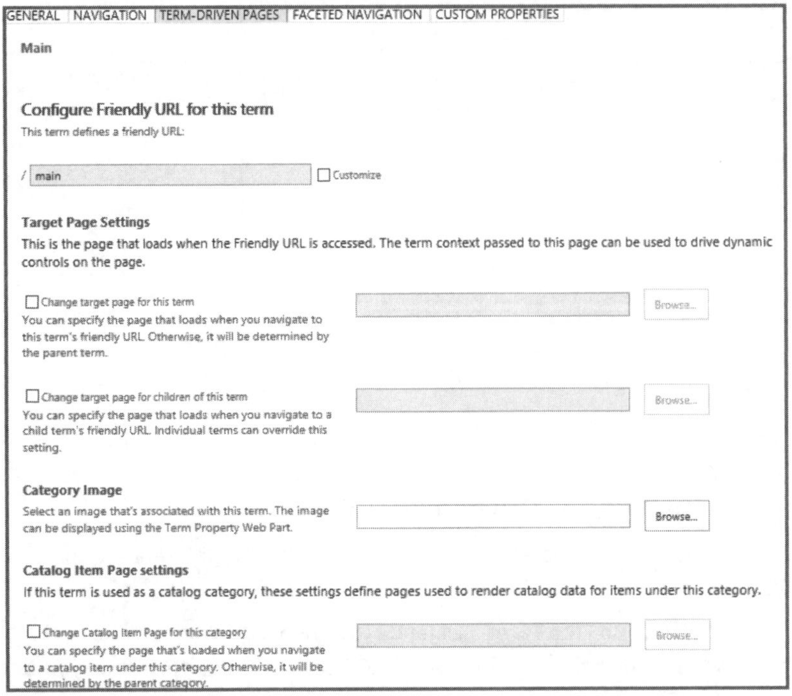

FIGURE 5-28 Specifying the settings within Term-Driven Pages

> **IMPORTANT** If the page you are viewing has neither a Friendly URL field nor a Category Image selection field on the Term-Driven Pages tab, you have selected a term set, not an individual term.

Manage topic catalog pages

Topic catalog pages are used to render items within the products list on a product catalog site. These pages are used to show structured content in a consistent fashion across a SharePoint site.

Most often, these pages are used within the confines of a site collection that has been enabled with the cross-site collection publishing feature. There are two distinct page types available:

- **Category pages** Used specifically to display a series of catalog items.
- **Item pages** (also called catalog item pages in some documentation) Used to display an item in detail.

> **IMPORTANT** If you previously deployed the Product Catalog Site template, available in SharePoint 2013, it is no longer available in SharePoint 2016. This is not much of an issue however, because the Cross-Site Collection Publishing feature is still available and quite useful within a SharePoint farm.

EXAM TIP

Be familiar with the process of creating a product catalog, assigning terms in the term set, and then allowing another Publishing site to consume the result. Most important, remember to crawl the content source after enabling a list or library as a catalog.

Assigning master pages to the category and item pages

Because category and item pages are standard publishing fare within SharePoint 2016, it only stands to reason that they follow the same structure that all other Publishing pages do. When a Publishing site is initially configured to connect to a product catalog, the opportunity arises to specify a master page for both category and item pages.

To specify the catalog pages' master page as part of the connect-to-catalog process (Figure 5-29), follow these steps.

1. Navigate to the root site of your Publishing site collection, and in Site Settings, Site Administration, choose Manage Catalog Connections.

2. On the Manage Catalog Connections page, select Connect To A Catalog.

3. On the Connect To Catalog page, click Connect for your product catalog.

4. In Catalog Source Settings, scroll to the bottom of the page.

5. The last section of the page enables you to choose from the two out-of-the-box (OOB) master page types (or use an existing one if you have it created; see Figure 5-29). Category and item pages can also be configured within this section.

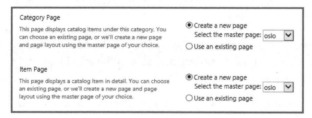

FIGURE 5-29 Specifying a master page for category and item pages

IMPORTANT When you initially make the connection between the product catalog site and the Publishing site that consumes its navigational hierarchy, you have the chance to choose the master page for both category and item pages. Selecting Catalog Source Settings after the fact does not give you the opportunity to make the choice again.

Options on the Term-Driven Pages tab

As discussed in the term set navigation section, there are options available on the Term-Driven Pages tab that enable you to specify catalog page settings; these choices are just that, optional. Catalog pages work just fine without making changes at this level.

The number of options available has to do with whether you are changing this setting at the term set or term level:

- If you are making this change at the term set level, your only option is to specify a custom page for the catalog item.

- If you are making this change at the term level, you have two options: change the catalog item page for a category, and also change the catalog item for children of the category.

Configure custom properties

Within a term set, you can define properties that aren't a necessary part of the term, term set, or group. Sometimes these properties are useful as part of a custom development effort; at other times, they might just be there to identify information that surrounds a term or term set.

EXAM TIP

Custom properties are almost never used outside of custom development efforts.

These custom properties have two distinct scopes, shared and local, that define at which levels a custom property can be applied.

- **Shared properties**   Properties that can be used on all reuses of pinned instances of the term anywhere in the term store.

- **Local properties**   Properties that can be used only for a term contained within the term set being configured.

> **IMPORTANT**   Custom property configuration can differ based on the item. At the term set level, shared properties are the only configuration available; at the individual term level, both shared and local properties can be configured.

Configuration of a custom property is done within the Term Store Management Tool. To build a new custom property, follow these steps.

1. In the Site Administration section of your site collection, select Term Store Management.

2. Expand your term set until you get to the desired location for your custom property, then select the term or term set and click the Custom Properties tab (see Figure 5-30).

3. Click the Add link for either Shared Properties or Local Properties and then enter values for the property name and a matching value.

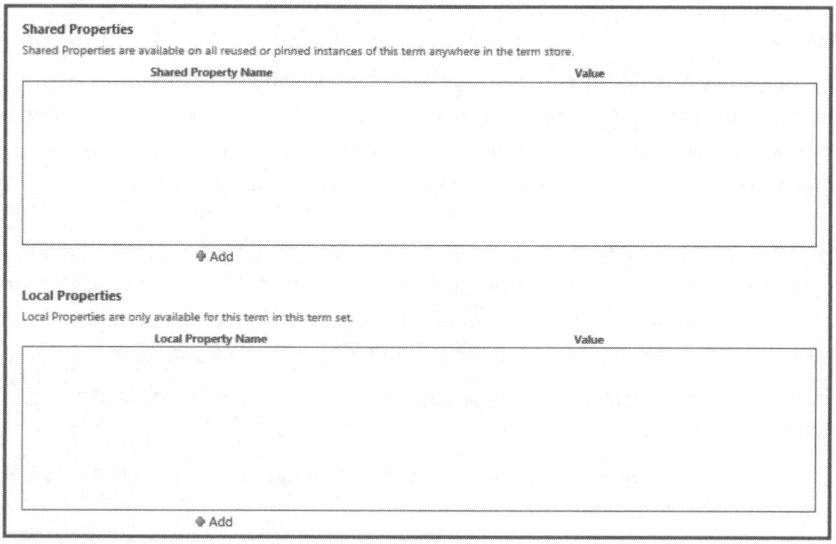

Shared Properties

Shared Properties are available on all reused or pinned instances of this term anywhere in the term store.

Shared Property Name	Value

⊕ Add

Local Properties

Local Properties are only available for this term in this term set.

Local Property Name	Value

⊕ Add

FIGURE 5-30 Shared and local custom properties

Configure search refinement

When you issue a search query in SharePoint 2016, you not only get the returned results of your query but also a series of categories that you can use to narrow your search (shown on the left side of Figure 5-31) that are known as *search refiners*.

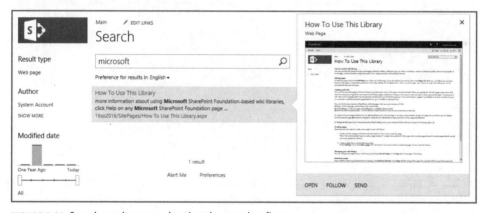

FIGURE 5-31 Search results page, showing the search refiners

Search refiners are represented within the Refiner Web Part, which is exposed by editing the search results page from within the Enterprise Search Center site.

Be familiar with which different refiners are available OOB and what each one can provide from a functionality standpoint (such as the modified date slider control). Within the Refiners section, you can select to either use the refinement configuration as defined in the managed navigation term set or you can define refiners within the Web Part.

Easily the more reusable of the two refinement options, using managed navigation for refinement enables you to set up refiners at the term or term set level. If you need more granular controls over refiners, you can configure each and every term; however, most refiners are applied at the term set level and then inherited by the individual terms.

1. In the Site Administration section of your site collection, select Term Store Management.

2. Expand your term set until you get to the desired location for your refiner to be applied and then select the term or term set.

3. Select the Faceted Navigation tab, shown in Figure 5-32. In this instance, the term selected already has custom refiners, but you can add refiners as well.

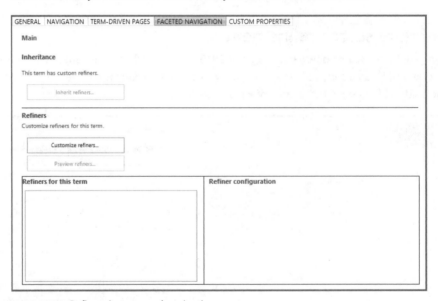

FIGURE 5-32 Refiners in managed navigation

4. Clicking Customize Refiners causes refiner tags to be added to the Selected Refiners section, shown in Figure 5-33. Near the bottom of the screen, you can also see the sample values for the selected refiner. If you scroll down, you will see a Preview Refiners button; clicking this button enables you to see a preview of the Refinement Web Part output using this refiner.

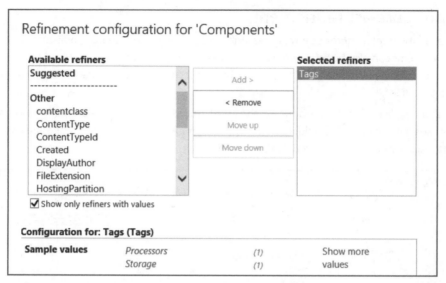

FIGURE 5-33 New refiner for "Components"

5. Completed refiners for a term appear on the Faceted Navigation tab. Returning to the site where the Refinement Web Part was configured and selecting the Use The Refinement Configuration Defined In The Managed Navigation Term Set option completes the action (Figure 5-34).

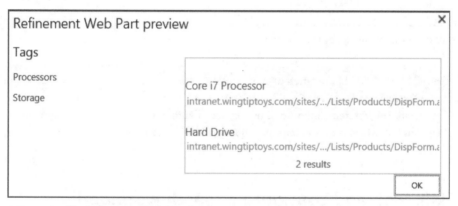

FIGURE 5-34 The Refinement Web Part preview

EXAM TIP

Be familiar with the steps required to configure a refiner both in the term set as well as a Web Part.

Configure list refinement

The ability to refine items doesn't necessarily end with enterprise search; individual list and library items can also be refined because they are also part of the items indexed by Search. This functionality is similar to views, in that particular items can be filtered and selected from the overall list.

Enabling list refinement is done via the list's Settings page, from the Metadata Navigation Settings link (Figure 5-35). Adding a Key Filter component enables you to refine the contents of the library based on Selected Key Filter Fields.

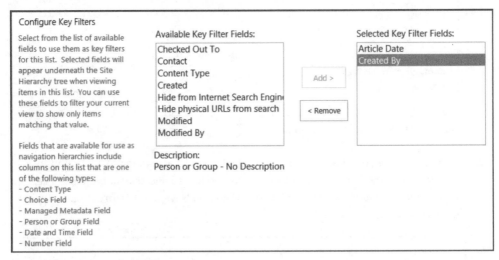

FIGURE 5-35 Configuring Key Filters settings

> **IMPORTANT** Within the metadata navigation settings for a list, you can configure one of three things: the list's navigation hierarchy, key filters for the list, and automatic column indexing. The last item, Indexing, is usually set to Automatically Manage Column Indices On This List, which results in improved query performance for the filtering and hierarchy used in a list.

Skill: Plan and configure a search workload

Setting up and configuring enterprise search is simply the beginning of a continuous process for improving search relevance. As users become more aware of Search from both an Internet and intranet standpoint, their expectations for Search become more and more detailed.

Configuring a search workload consists of the steps necessary to initially gauge the desired relevancy within a SharePoint 2016 farm as well as the balancing act between overall performance and keeping Search up to date. Taking the long view of optimization, search analytics reports can be used to track trends in customer Search usage, providing feedback on the optimization changes that have already taken place.

> **This section covers how to:**
> - Plan and configure search result relevancy
> - Plan and configure index freshness
> - Plan and configure result sources
> - Plan and configure the end-user experience
> - Plan and configure a search schema
> - Analyze search analytics reports

Plan and configure search result relevancy

Search relevancy (also known as relevance ranking) is a result of ranking models present within the SharePoint 2016 platform. These models fall into one of three categories:

- **General purpose**   Compute the relevance rank for most types of search results.
- **People search**   People search ranking models compute the relevance rank for search results that are related to people. They calculate, among other things, how relevant search results are based on social distance and expertise.
- **Special purpose**   Special purpose ranking models compute the relevance rank for search results related to various specific ranking scenarios. For example, there is a ranking model to calculate the ranking score for recommendations, and there are ranking models to calculate relevance ranks for cross-site Publishing sites that have an associated product catalog.

> *NEED MORE REVIEW?*   SharePoint 2013 had a total of 16 ranking models, all of which have been carried over to SharePoint 2016, which has a total of 19, including three new models: the 2016 Highlights ranking model, the Graph Only model, and the Second Level Colleagues ranking model. For more information about ranking models, review the TechNet article "Overview of search result ranking in SharePoint Server 2013" at *https://technet.microsoft.com/library/dn169065.aspx*, and the MSDN article "Customizing ranking models to improve relevance in SharePoint 2013" at *https://msdn.microsoft.com/library /c166ecdd-7f93-4bbb-b543-2687992dd2bc.aspx*.

Rank evaluation

Rank evaluation is a two-stage process, combining the calculations from each to achieve an overall score for a search result. These models use five pieces of information, shown in Table 5-5.

TABLE 5-5 Ranking model information

Search Index Item Info	Description
Content	These are the words contained in the items. For items that are text based, such as documents, this is typically most of the text. For other types of items, such as videos, there is little or no content.
Metadata	The metadata associated with items such as title, author, URL, and creation date. Metadata is automatically extracted from most types of items.
Web graph data	This is information such as authority (from authoritative pages settings) and anchor text (from the hyperlinks associated with the item, and items linking to the item).
File type	Some file types can be considered more important for ranking than others. For example, Word and PowerPoint results are typically more important than Excel results.
Interaction	Information about the number of times a search result is clicked, and which queries led to a result being clicked.

Influencing search result rank

There are three major ways to influence the ranking of search results in SharePoint 2016:

- **Query rules**   Define which actions to take when a query matches a condition.
    - Use promoted results.
    - Add a results block for promoted results.
    - Change the query itself.
- **Search schema**   Configure the context of a managed property.
    - Change the context of a managed property in Advanced Searchable Settings.
- **Create custom ranking model**   As you have already seen, there are several ranking models already in use; before attempting to create a new one, use query rules with an existing one to try and meet your goals.

Plan and configure index freshness

Index freshness is directly influenced by the type and frequency of search crawls configured for a SharePoint 2016 farm. These search crawls require resources and can affect resource allocation within a SharePoint farm, so there must be a balance struck between index freshness and overall farm performance.

There are three major factors in a SharePoint farm that can negatively affect index freshness:

- **Crawl frequency**   Search indexes that are not updated frequently ultimately cannot be fresh. Although full and incremental crawls work together to index content, the minimum window of freshness can be no smaller than the incremental crawl time. Moving instead to a continuous crawl mechanism by default causes the index freshness to be a minimum of 15 minutes, although this interval can be altered in PowerShell.

- **Crawler impact rules for external servers** Similarly, the rate and frequency with which external servers are crawled has a direct bearing on index freshness for those content sources. Where possible, configure the crawler impact rules to give the absolute best possible crawl performance without causing undue load to the external system.

- **Permissions assignment** Assigning users individual permissions on a site can negatively influence crawl performance. Where possible, combine these users into SharePoint groups and assign the permissions to the groups. For the absolute best crawl performance (and thus, index freshness), assign permissions via Active Directory group where reasonable and possible.

Plan and configure result sources

Result sources in SharePoint are used to gather content using three distinct items:

- **Search provider or source URL** Search results are retrieved from a location, such as the search index of the local SharePoint Search service.

- **Protocol used for search results** The search crawler can use many distinct protocols (shown earlier in this chapter: Local SharePoint, Remote SharePoint, OpenSearch, or Exchange) to parse content into an index.

- **Query transform** This is used to narrow results to a specified subset of content.

Search experiences in the Enterprise Search Center each line up to a respective result source. Four result sources are configured in an OOB SharePoint 2016 implementation:

- **Local SharePoint Results** Provides the Everything Search experience, retrieving any and every type of matching content in the SharePoint farm.

- **Local People Results** Narrows the items queried to information concerning people in the organization.

- **Conversations** Narrows the items queried to simply conversations in microblogs, newsfeed posts, and community sites.

- **Videos** Local videos in the SharePoint farm.

> **NEED MORE REVIEW?** There are more than a dozen preconfigured result sources that you can take advantage of, turning any or all into search experiences for your users. These result sources are listed in the TechNet article "Understanding result sources for search in SharePoint Server 2013" at *https://technet.microsoft.com/library/dn186229.aspx*.

EXAM TIP

Understanding how to present result sources in the user interface is a fundamental skill, and could turn up on the certification exam.

Plan and configure the end-user experience

The end-user search experience in SharePoint 2016 combines some of the features already covered to streamline the end-user experience when interacting with Search.

Search interfaces

Users performing a search query do so from one of three possible locations:

- **List level**   Within a list or document library, the option is given to Find A File, thus limiting a search query to the contents of the current list or library (Figure 5-36).

FIGURE 5-36 Find A File

- **Site level**   Site-level searches are performed from the standard Search box, near the upper right corner of a site. Search This Site is the default search experience in this box, although selecting the drop-down list allows the user to select from the Everything, People, Conversations, or This Site search experiences (Figure 5-37).

FIGURE 5-37 Search This Site

- **Search Center**   An Enterprise Search Center expands on the abilities of Search, providing search experiences in combination with refiner information to further tune search results (Figure 5-38).

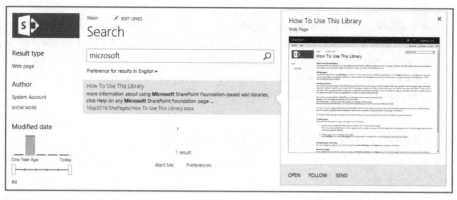

FIGURE 5-38 Enterprise Search Center

Shaping the user search experience

The user search experience is a combination of these three Search interfaces with some of the technologies we've already covered.

- **Query rules** Used to promote specific search results, show blocks of additional results, or influence the ranking of search results.
- **Result types** Use a combination of keywords and synonyms, managed properties, search experiences, and result sources to narrow the search result.
- **Display templates** Used in search-specific Web Parts, these templates are based on a combination of HTML and JavaScript to control the appearance and formatting of the search results.

Plan and configure a search schema

Earlier in this chapter, we discussed the process of converting crawled properties into managed properties. This process formalizes the capture of metadata into something that can then be used to optimize search queries.

1. The Search service application must be created, and content sources must have an initial, full crawl run on them.

2. The results of a crawl are crawled properties; certain crawled properties can then be selected and then mapped to managed properties, which can be used to narrow search results.

3. Changing certain items within the search schema requires a reindex of the content, including crawled to managed property mapping, token normalization, complete matching, company name extraction, custom entity extraction, and enabling the queryable, retrievable, refinable, and sortable property settings.

Analyze search analytics reports

SharePoint 2016 uses the same analytics architecture found in SharePoint 2013, consisting of three main parts:

- **Analytics processing component**   This component runs the different analytics jobs used to extract information as it's being crawled.
- **Analytics Reporting database**   This database stores statistical information from the different analyses.
- **Link database**   This database stores extracted information from the analytics processing component along with information about clicks in search results.

EXAM TIP

Although it's unlikely that you'll be expected to answer questions about the minutia of the search analytics architecture, you should be able to recap the three different parts that comprise it.

Summary

- SharePoint 2016 Search is comprised of six components: crawl, content processing, analytics processing, index, query processing, and search administration.
- SharePoint 2016 Search requires four application databases: Administration, Crawl, Link, and Analytics Reporting.
- SharePoint 2016 allows 25 index partitions, each with 20 million indexed items per partition for a total of 500 million items.
- In a MinRole-compliant farm, all search components exist on servers hosting the Search role.
- Changing a Search topology with an active index requires that you clone the existing topology, alter the clone, and then activate the cloned topology as the active topology.

- Search content sources can include SharePoint sites, websites, file shares, Exchange public folders, Lotus Notes (connector install required), Documentum (connector install required), LOB data (using BCS), and custom repositories (requires custom development).

- The three search crawl types are full, incremental, and continuous (which defaults to running at 15-minute intervals).

- Crawler impact rules can be used to minimize the effect of a SharePoint crawl on external systems.

- Search results are security trimmed by default.

- A SharePoint 2016 hybrid search environment requires the same six components and four databases, though the index, analytics, and content processing components and Link and Analytics databases are all rendered inactive.

- The managed metadata service provides a mechanism for defining taxonomical structures throughout your SharePoint 2016 farm.

- Several service application proxies can be assigned to a single proxy group. Each service application proxy can also be assigned to multiple proxy groups.

- The content type hub relies on two timer jobs to function correctly: the Content Type Hub job and the Content Type Subscriber job.

- Terms in a term set can be entered manually or added to an import file that can configure multiple terms at one time.

- Result sources can use one of four possible protocols: Local SharePoint, Remote SharePoint, OpenSearch, and Exchange.

- Display templates control the formatting and presentation of search results.

- Crawled properties can be mapped to managed properties for use within Search.

- Topic catalog pages include category pages and item pages.

- User search experience is shaped by query rules, result types, and display templates.

Thought experiment

In this thought experiment, demonstrate your skills and knowledge of the topics covered in this chapter. You can find the answer to this thought experiment in the next section.

You are designing a hybrid search configuration between SharePoint 2016 and Office 365. As Office 365 interacts with multiple technologies, you have been asked several questions, intended to help shape how SharePoint will interact in the Office 365 space.

1. What sort of PowerShell scripts must be run to connect your SharePoint 2016 cloud Search service application to the Office 365 tenant?

2. What components might you use that tie the on-premises environment of SharePoint to SharePoint Online?

3. As your organization has previously implemented SharePoint, management would like to know what benefits hybrid search offers.

Thought experiment answer

This section contains the solution to the thought experiment.

1. Two PowerShell scripts are required for this configuration, CreateCloudSSA.ps1 (used to create the cloud Search service application) and Onboard-CloudHybridSearch.ps1 (used to onboard your cloud Search service application).

2. Your organization could use OneDrive for Business, Hybrid Sites, and cloud hybrid search to unify the on-premises and cloud deployments of SharePoint.

3. Hybrid search offers the opportunity to provide a fully secure search index in Office 365. This index will be used for both on-premises and cloud search results, unifying the search experience for users. Search also provides the benefit of Delve and Office Graph, allowing users to find people both on their team and in others that work on similar projects within the organization.

## CHAPTER 6

Plan and configure cloud services

SharePoint Server 2016 is unique among all the other versions of SharePoint, simply because it is firmly rooted in the cloud. Development for what would become the on-premises version of SharePoint Server 2016 has been taking place over the last few years in Office 365, which itself is constantly progressing.

As Office 365 moves ahead, functionality found in the cloud can be expected to start appearing in on-premises environments in the form of software updates. As you work through this chapter, you will note that only a small amount of back-ported (providing older functionality not found in the cloud) content exists in SharePoint 2016.

Skills in this chapter:

- Skill: Plan and configure a BI infrastructure
- Skill: Create and configure work management
- Skill: Plan and configure cloud and hybrid federated search

Skill: Plan and configure a BI infrastructure

SharePoint Server 2016 improves on the business intelligence (BI) components found in SharePoint 2013, while taking advantage of new external BI functionality surfaced by SQL Server 2016 Database Services and Analysis Services. Functionality that was once limited to on-premises use in previous versions can now be made available to both internal and external users, and (with few exceptions) the supporting BI components are moving quickly toward the use of HTML5 standards of presentation.

> **This section covers how to:**
> - Plan and configure PerformancePoint
> - Plan and configure Reporting Services
> - Plan and configure Power Pivot
> - Plan and configure Excel Services (Office Online only)

- Plan and configure Power View
- Plan and configure BI security

Plan and configure PerformancePoint

PerformancePoint Services was folded into the SharePoint Server product line starting with the 2010 version of the product, and is used to create dashboards, scorecards, and key performance indicators (KPIs). This information can then be used by an organization to make informed business decisions around the reported metrics and trends.

> **IMPORTANT** PerformancePoint Services is a back-ported product, meaning that this older feature was added into the newer SharePoint Server 2016 product.

Introducing the Business Intelligence Center

As you work through this chapter, most of the technologies shown refer to some use of the Business Intelligence Center. This SharePoint site template provides a convenient way to unify the BI components of SharePoint into a single location for review and interaction (Figure 6-1).

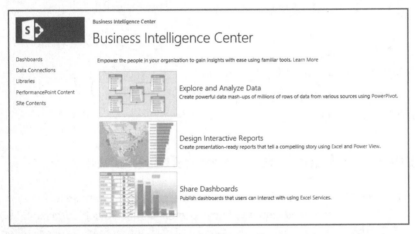

FIGURE 6-1 The SharePoint 2016 Business Intelligence Center

Reports and scorecards

Generating a report or scorecard for use with PerformancePoint Services is done via the use of the Dashboard Designer tool set. Probably the easiest way to start this tool is to open the PerformancePoint Content section of your Business Intelligence Center and then click New Item. Creating a new item requires the use of the Dashboard Designer tool, shown in Figure 6-2.

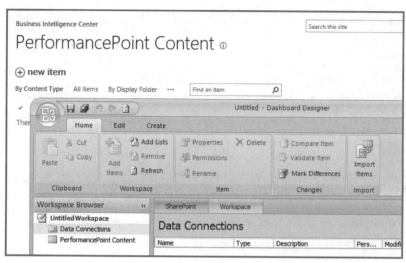

FIGURE 6-2 The PerformancePoint Content library and Dashboard Designer tool

PerformancePoint Services report templates

Although it's quite possible to generate custom reports within PerformancePoint by using Dashboard Designer, seven different templates are shipped out-of-the-box (OOB), as seen in Table 6-1.

TABLE 6-1 PerformancePoint report templates

Template	Description
Analytic Chart	An analytic chart is an interactive line, bar, or pie chart that you create and configure by using Dashboard Designer. Analytic charts use data that is stored in SQL Server Analysis Services.
Analytic Grid	An analytic grid is an interactive table that you create and configure by using Dashboard Designer. Analytic grids use data that is stored in SQL Server Analysis.
KPI Details	A KPI Details report is a report that serves as a companion to a scorecard to provide additional information about scorecard KPI values and properties. A KPI Details report does not contain or display information by itself. The KPI Details report derives all its information directly from the scorecard to which it is connected. Dashboard users click a value in a scorecard, and the KPI Details report updates to display additional information about that particular scorecard value without cluttering up the scorecard.
Reporting Services	A Reporting Services report is a view that was published to SQL Server Reporting Services Report Server. In Dashboard Designer, you do not actually create a Reporting Services report. Instead, you create a PerformancePoint Web Part to display an existing Reporting Services report.
Strategy Map	A strategy map is a report that serves as a companion to a scorecard to show relationships between objectives, goals, and KPIs at a glance. Strategy maps are based on the Balanced Scorecard framework. A strategy map uses a scorecard as its data source and a Visio diagram as its display structure.

Template	Description
Web Page	A Web Page report is a fully functional internal or external website that you can display alongside other reports in your dashboard. In Dashboard Designer, you do not actually create a Web Page report. Instead, you create a PerformancePoint Web Part to display an existing website.
Decomposition Tree	A decomposition tree is an interactive view that dashboard users open from a scorecard or a report that uses SQL Server Analysis Services data. However, as a dashboard author, you do not create the Decomposition Tree by using PerformancePoint Dashboard Designer. Instead, the Decomposition Tree is opened by users from a report in a dashboard that has been deployed to SharePoint Server 2016.

> **NEED MORE REVIEW?** For a clearer understanding of how to use the Decomposition Tree in PerformancePoint Dashboard Designer, review the TechNet article entitled "Overview of the PerformancePoint Decomposition Tree" at *https://technet.microsoft.com/library /gg576962(v=office.16).aspx.*

PerformancePoint Services scorecard templates

Scorecards are a specialized type of report intended to provide high-level progress summary information. Using the Scorecard Wizard within Dashboard Designer allows the author a choice of four possible template types, shown in Table 6-2.

TABLE 6-2 PerformancePoint scorecard templates

Template	Description
Analysis Services	The Analysis Services scorecard template enables you to create a scorecard that uses an Analysis Services data source for at least one KPI in the scorecard.
Blank Scorecard	The Blank Scorecard template enables you to create an empty scorecard that has no KPIs or other information. You would typically create a blank scorecard when you and other dashboard authors have already created KPIs.
Fixed Values Scorecard	The Fixed Values Scorecard template enables you to create a scorecard that does not use a separate data source. When you use this template, you specify the values for the scorecard while you use the wizard.
Tabular templates for Excel Workbooks, SharePoint Lists, and SQL Server Tables	The three tabular templates (Excel Workbook, SharePoint List, and SQL Server Table) enable you to create a scorecard that uses a tabular data source for at least one KPI in the scorecard. Similar to the Analysis Services scorecard template, when you use a tabular data scorecard template, you can create KPIs that are based on measures in the data source, or you can select existing KPIs that you or other dashboard authors have created.

> **NEED MORE REVIEW?** Although this depth of information is not likely to be on the SharePoint 2016 certification test, detailed information concerning the types of reports and scorecards for PerformancePoint Services is available in the TechNet article entitled "Overview of PerformancePoint reports and scorecards" at *https://technet.microsoft.com /library/gg410942(v=office.16).aspx.*

Configuring PerformancePoint Services

Installing and configuring PerformancePoint Services requires only a few steps:

1. Install ADOMD.NET from the SQL Server 2012 Feature Pack.

2. Configure the PerformancePoint Services application pool account and service application.

3. Configure service application associations.

The installation of ADOMD.NET from the SQL Server 2012 Feature Pack provides access to some of the built-in reports present in the Power Pivot management dashboard, particularly those that use ADOMD.NET to access internal data for query processing and farm server health.

> **IMPORTANT** The SQL Server 2012 Feature Pack can be downloaded from *https://www .microsoft.com/download/details.aspx?id=29065*. Remember that PerformancePoint is a back-ported application, and thus makes use of this older component.

Creating the service application pool account and service application for PerformancePoint Services is no different than those we configured earlier in this book, and can be accomplished from either Service Applications in Central Administration or via PowerShell.

Before PerformancePoint Services can be used in SharePoint 2016, its service application must be associated with one or more proxy groups. This service application is intentionally not associated with any proxy groups for web applications, specifically because security considerations might need to be required prior to deployment.

Configuring the service application associations is quite straightforward; from Service Application Associations in Central Administration, a proxy group must be selected and then the PerformancePoint Services check box can be enabled (shown in Figure 6-3).

> **IMPORTANT** The PerformancePoint Service Application can also be provisioned by using the New-SPPerformancePointServiceApplication cmdlet.

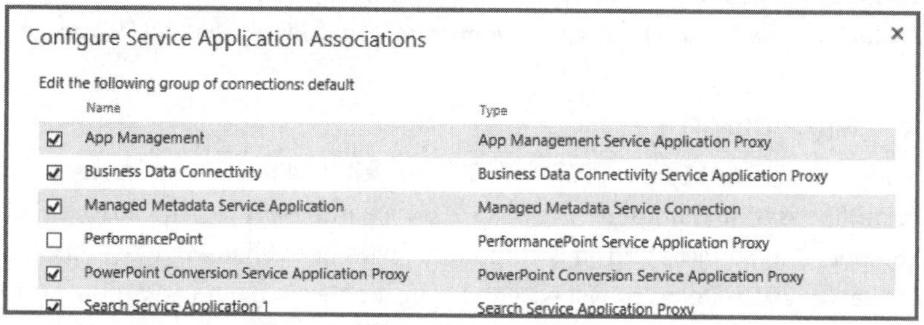

FIGURE 6-3 Configure service application associations

The final step in the core activation process is to activate the PerformancePoint Services feature for use within a site collection, as shown in Figure 6-4.

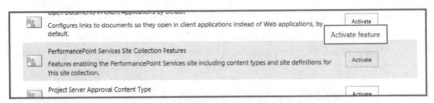

FIGURE 6-4 Activating the PerformancePoint Services site collection features

NEED MORE REVIEW? A detailed view of the configuration process for PerformancePoint Services on SharePoint Server 2016 is shown in the TechNet article "Configure PerformancePoint Services (SharePoint Server 2016)" at *https://technet.microsoft.com /library/ee748644(v=office.16).aspx*.

Plan and configure Reporting Services

An SQL Server Reporting Services (SSRS) environment, integrated with the SharePoint Server 2016 farm, enables report creation and viewing within the context of a document library, also providing the subscription delivery of reports via email, Power View, data alerting, and report management.

NEED MORE REVIEW? SQL Services allows users to create any number of report types, from basic tabular reports to data-driven and drill-through reports. A series of tutorials for using Report Builder can be found in the MSDN article entitled "Reporting Services Tutorials (SSRS)," which can be found at *https://msdn.microsoft.com/library/bb522859.aspx*.

Preparing your environment

If you are currently using SharePoint Server 2013 with SQL Server 2014 Reporting Services, the guidance for upgrading is to first upgrade the SSRS 2014 environment to SSRS 2016, as the SQL Server 2016 Reporting Services add-in is compatible with both SharePoint Server 2013 and SharePoint Server 2016. Doing so will ease the transition from a data and reporting standpoint when moving forward with a SharePoint Server 2016 migration.

NEED MORE REVIEW? For a complete breakdown of which SharePoint and Reporting Services components versions are compatible, review the MSDN article entitled "Supported Combinations of SharePoint and Reporting Services Server and Add-in (SQL Server 2016)" at *https://msdn.microsoft.com/library/gg492257.aspx*.

Configuring SharePoint Server 2016 integration with SSRS 2016

The process for integrating these two systems together is functionally identical to the previous configuration used with SharePoint 2013. In this configuration, the SQL Reporting environment is set up and configured in SharePoint Integrated mode, and then an add-in is installed in the SharePoint 2016 farm.

- **Report server**   The report server handles the data and report processing and rendering as well as subscription and data alert processing. The SharePoint mode report server is designed and installed as a SharePoint Shared Service.

- **SSRS SharePoint add-in**   The Reporting Services add-in (rssharepoint.msi) installs the user interface (UI) pages and features on a SharePoint 2016 server. The UI features include Power View, administration pages in SharePoint Central Administration, feature pages used within SharePoint document libraries, and Reporting Services Data Alerting pages.

> **IMPORTANT**   SharePoint Server 2016 is only compatible with SQL Server 2016 Reporting Services servers; components from either SQL 2012 or SQL 2014 will not work. SharePoint 2016 support, including Power View integration, requires the Reporting Services report server and the Reporting Services add-in version of SQL Server 2016 or later.

The actual deployment of SSRS 2016 in a SharePoint farm is largely unchanged from configuring SSRS 2014 in a SharePoint 2013 farm, with a few notable differences.

- **SQL Server 2016 and SharePoint 2016**   Regardless of the BI component chosen, SQL Server 2016 is required to enable BI support in SharePoint 2016.

- **SSRS and MinRole compliance**   A server configured for SSRS use must be assigned the Custom role from a MinRole compliance standpoint. The installation of SSRS on any other MinRole server will indeed be successful, but will abruptly be stopped by MinRole during the next SharePoint maintenance window.

EXAM TIP

The SSRS service application only supports the Custom role.

> **IMPORTANT**   The installation and configuration of SSRS integration in a SharePoint 2016 farm is thoroughly examined in the MSDN article and document entitled "Deploying SQL Server 2016 Power Pivot and Power View in SharePoint 2016" at *https://msdn.microsoft .com/library/mt614795.aspx*.

Plan and configure Power Pivot

Power Pivot is a built-in component within the Excel 2016 client. This tool allows the user to import data from several data sources into a workbook, then create relationships between heterogeneous data, create calculated columns and measures using formulas, build Pivot

Tables and Pivot Charts, then analyze data to make business decisions without requiring assistance from an IT standpoint.

> **IMPORTANT** If you open Excel 2016 on your desktop, you will not immediately see the Power Pivot add-in. However, this add-in is included in the client and can be activated from within the Options menu.

Power Pivot in SharePoint extends this client functionality, working with the Excel Online functionality present in the Office Online Server. This arrangement allows the Power Pivot workbook to exist within a web browser, and only requires an SQL 2016 Analysis Services server, configured in Power Pivot mode. This server must be registered with the Office Online Server connected to the SharePoint 2016 farm. The functional arrangement of these servers is shown in Figure 6-5.

FIGURE 6-5 SharePoint, Office Online, and Analysis Server arrangement

Installing Analysis Services in Power Pivot mode (SQL Server and Office Online Server)

SharePoint administrators are often required to understand (at a high level) configuration steps essential to activating certain functionality in a SharePoint 2016 farm. In the case of Analysis Services, we have to understand the steps required in SQL Analysis Services to make this integration a success.

Assuming SQL Server has been installed and an Analysis Services instance is available, there are four required steps for configuring Power Pivot mode.

- **Install Power Pivot for SharePoint** This series of steps is usually carried out by an SQL database administrator (DBA), and involves the installation of SQL Server Analysis Services on a server. During the installation, the DBA will select Power Pivot Mode, as shown in Figure 6-6.

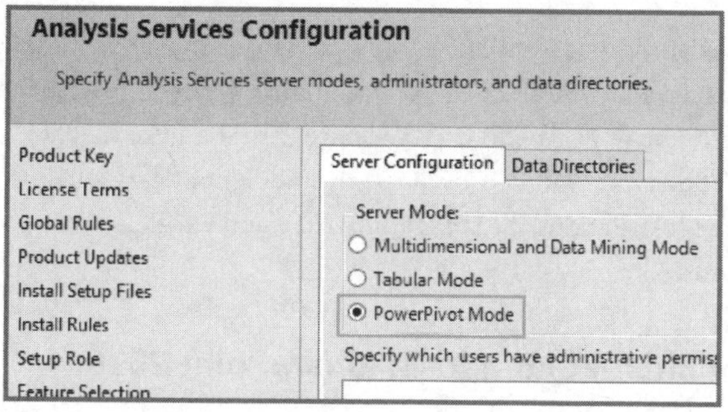

FIGURE 6-6 Selecting Power Pivot Mode

IMPORTANT As Analysis Services is being set up, the option is given to also designate accounts requiring administrative access to the Analysis Services server instance. The following accounts should be granted this level of access: the Office Online Server machine account, the SharePoint farm account, and the service accounts for Power View and PerformancePoint Services.

- **Configure Windows Firewall to allow Analysis Services access** If there are no firewalls present between the Analysis Server and the Office Online Server, this step can be skipped. This series of steps to be performed depends greatly on how the Analysis Services implementation is intended to be configured.

NEED MORE REVIEW? The process for configuring this access is thoroughly detailed in the MSDN article "Configure the Windows Firewall to Allow Analysis Services Access" at *https://msdn.microsoft.com/library/ms174937.aspx*.

- **Configure Basic Analysis Services SharePoint integration** This series of steps requires participation from both the SQL DBA and the Office Online Server administrator.

  - The SQL DBA must grant the Office Online Server machine account administrative access to the Analysis Server instance (you can skip this step if previously completed).

  - The Office Online Server administrator must register the Analysis Server with Office Online Server. This process is accomplished via PowerShell cmdlets, and involves importing the OfficeWebApps module, then accomplishing the registration itself:

```
Import-Module OfficeWebApps
New-OfficeWebAppsExcelBIServer -ServerId <servername\instancename>
```

- **Verify the integration** This series of steps is accomplished as a user, and involves the creation and upload of a workbook to verify the Analysis Services integration with Office Online Server.

Install the Power Pivot for SharePoint add-in (SharePoint 2016)

Power Pivot for SharePoint 2016 is a collection of application server components and back-end services that provide Power Pivot data access in a SharePoint Server 2016 farm. These components allow for the use of workbooks as a data source, scheduled data refresh, and the Power Pivot Management Dashboard.

The Power Pivot for SharePoint add-in is an installer package used to install the application server components, and is downloaded separately.

Installing Power Pivot for SharePoint causes four components to be deployed to the SharePoint server.

- **Power Pivot for SharePoint** Includes PowerShell scripts, SharePoint solution packages, and the Power Pivot for SharePoint 2016 configuration tool to deploy Power Pivot in a SharePoint 2016 farm. It is recommended that at least two servers in the farm should have the configuration tool installed.

- **Microsoft OLE DB Provider for Analysis Services (MSOLAP)** Used by Microsoft Excel to connect to Microsoft SQL Server.

- **ADOMD.NET data provider** A Microsoft .NET Framework provider designed to communicate with Microsoft SQL Server Analysis Services.

- **SQL Server Analysis Management Objects** A library of objects that enables an application to manage a running instance of Microsoft SQL Server Analysis Services.

EXAM TIP

Power Pivot for SharePoint 2016 is a Microsoft Windows Installer package (spPowerpivot16.msi) that deploys Analysis Services client libraries and copies Power Pivot for SharePoint 2016 installation files to the computer. This add-in should be installed on all servers in the SharePoint 2016 farm for consistency. This is useful because PerformancePoint Services and Power View can also use this functionality in their respective configurations. As an example, PerformancePoint can connect to Analysis Services data sources (including Power Pivot workbooks), but this functionality requires that Power Pivot for SharePoint be installed on every farm server running the PerformancePoint service.

Configure Power Pivot and deploy solutions (SharePoint Server 2016)

This process is a SharePoint-specific effort, and should be carried out by logging on as the SharePoint farm account. During this process, two major tasks are completed.

- The SharePoint solution files for Power Pivot are installed.
- The Power Pivot service application is created and configured.

IMPORTANT Prior to running the Power Pivot for SharePoint 2016 Configuration utility, you should either log on as the account that installed SharePoint, or configure the setup account as the primary administrator of the SharePoint Central Administration site.

These two tasks are completed by running the Power Pivot for SharePoint Configuration utility. Although this utility is run on a SharePoint 2016 server, it uses the Configuration Tools section of the Microsoft SQL Server 2016 installation media, and requires the use of the SharePoint farm passphrase.

IMPORTANT The installation process for this tool calls for the prior installation of the Power Pivot for SharePoint add-in. If you attempt to install the Power Pivot for SharePoint Configuration utility and cannot seem to find this link in the interface, you've neglected to install the add-in first.

To verify that this installation has successfully completed, you will look in four distinct locations.

- **Services** In Central Administration, Manage Services On Server, verify that the SQL Server Power Pivot System Service is started.
- **Farm Feature** In Central Administration, Manage Farm Features, verify that the Power Pivot Integration Feature is Active.
- **Site Collection** The Power Pivot configuration tool creates a new site collection. In the settings of that site collection, click Site Collection Features, and then verify that the Power Pivot Feature Integration for Site Collections is Active.
- **Power Pivot Service Application** In Central Administration, Application Management, click Manage Service Application, and verify that the Power Pivot service application status is Started.

IMPORTANT The SQL 2014 Power Pivot and Power View add-ins for SharePoint cannot be used in SharePoint 2016. To deploy these add-ins, you will need to upgrade to SQL Server 2016.

FOR MORE INFORMATION The configuration of Power Pivot can be quite detailed in scope. For a more complete understanding of this process, review the MSDN article entitled "Configure Power Pivot and Deploy Solutions (SharePoint 2016)" at *https://msdn.microsoft.com/library/mt595855.aspx*.

Plan and configure Excel Services (Office Online only)

Excel Online loads Excel workbooks and renders them for display and interaction via a user's web browser. If the workbook contains a data model, Excel Online streams the model to SQL Server 2016 Analysis Services and then queries the data to update the workbook data, although this is an on-demand update.

Although you will continue to find references to Excel Services in some SharePoint 2016 documentation, it is important to note the differences between Excel Services functionality in SharePoint 2013 and Excel Online functionality in SharePoint 2016.

Excel Services proper has been deprecated, as Excel Online (a component of the Office Online Server) replaces its function within a SharePoint 2016 farm. This change results in the removal of some familiar Excel Services functionality:

- Trusted data providers
- Trusted file locations
- Trusted data connection libraries
- Unattended service account
- Excel Services PowerShell cmdlets
- Opening of Excel workbooks from SharePoint Central Administration

IMPORTANT The switch to Excel Online requires a couple of functional behavior changes. SharePoint managed accounts are no longer able to open Excel workbooks in Excel Online, requiring that any test be carried out with a standard user account. Also, Excel workbooks can no longer be accessed from directly within Central Administration.

Excel Online in Office Online Server provides the following Excel functionality:

- Viewing and editing Excel workbooks in a browser (with or without the Data Model)
- Excel Web Access Web Part for SharePoint
- Office data connection (ODC) file support (no longer requires Data Connection Libraries)
- Programmability features such as JavaScript OM, User Defined Function Assemblies, SOAP and REST protocol support

Configuring Excel Online for BI

Three steps are included in the configuration of Excel Online for BI:

- **Analysis Services availability** The SQL Server 2016 Analysis Services server instance in Power Pivot mode must be accessible over the network, from the perspective of Office Online Server.

- **Service instance registration** The SQL Server 2016 Analysis Services server instance needs to be registered in the Excel Online configuration.

- **Permissions assignment for Excel Online** The Excel Online service account must be added to the list of Analysis Services server administrators. You might have previously accomplished this when setting up Analysis Services for use with Power Pivot.

Aside from these three steps, there is one more registration that's implied. Usually this has already been configured, but Excel Online has to be registered so that users can open workbooks in the browser, and Claims to Windows Token Service (c2WTS) has to be enabled such that Excel Online can resolve SharePoint identities into Windows identities.

> **NEED MORE REVIEW?** The configuration of Excel Online is a part of a larger BI configuration process, and is covered in great detail (including the necessary scripts) within the MSDN article and document called "Deploying SQL Server 2016 Power Pivot and Power View in SharePoint 2016" at *https://msdn.microsoft.com/library/mt614795.aspx*.

Plan and configure Power View

Although we've mentioned Power View several times in this chapter, we have not yet defined it. Power View is a browser-based Silverlight application supporting interactive data exploration, visualization, and presentation. This functionality is heavily dependent on SSRS, which is used to render the Power View reports.

> **IMPORTANT** Power View reports embedded in Excel Online workbooks cannot be displayed unless the workbooks reside in a SharePoint farm with SharePoint-integrated Reporting Services installed. Excel Online relies on Reporting Services to render the Power View reports.

EXAM TIP

Power View still relies on Silverlight for the display of some items.

Power View is installed and configured alongside SQL Server 2016 Reporting Services. The SQL 2014 Power Pivot and Power View add-ins for SharePoint cannot be used in SharePoint 2016. To deploy these add-ins, you will need to upgrade to SQL Server 2016.

Plan and configure BI security

As you've already seen in this section, implementing BI in SharePoint 2016 can be a challenge because there are multiple technologies to configure (for example, PerformancePoint, Power Pivot, Excel Services, and others) across a series of servers, including SQL Server 2016 Analysis Services, SQL Server Reporting Services, Office Online Server, and SharePoint Server 2016.

While implementing an environment this complex, we are also charged with finding effective ways to secure it. As is the case with any infrastructure effort, the resulting design must not only be secure, but also able to perform at a desired level, so as to be useful to the business.

Authentication mechanisms for BI

Each of the services in the BI stack behaves similarly from an authentication point of view, although how the authentication is implemented varies from service to service, as listed in Table 6-3.

TABLE 6-3 BI services, data sources, and authentication methods

Shared Service	Data Source	Authentication Method
Excel Online	SharePoint lists	SharePoint user identity
	Excel workbooks	SharePoint user identity
	SQL Server	Windows user identity (integrated security), Secure Store Service, unattended service account, or SQL authentication
	Analysis Services	Windows authentication (integrated security), Secure Store Service, or unattended service account
	Third-party OLE DB, ODBC, ADO.NET	User name and password in the connection string
PerformancePoint Services	SharePoint lists	SharePoint user identity
	Excel workbooks	SharePoint user identity
	SQL Server	Windows user identity (integrated security), Secure Store Service, unattended service account, or SQL authentication
	Analysis Services	Windows authentication (integrated security), Secure Store Service, or unattended service account

Shared Service	Data Source	Authentication Method
Power View	Workbook data models	SharePoint user identity
	Analysis Services	Windows authentication (integrated security) or credentials stored in a Reporting Services data source (RSDS) file
Reporting Services in SharePoint-integrated mode	SharePoint lists	SharePoint user identity
	SQL Server	Windows user identity (integrated security) or credentials stored in an RSDS file
	Microsoft Azure SQL Database	Credentials stored in an RSDS file
	Analysis Services	Windows user identity (integrated security) or credentials stored in an RSDS file
	XML Web Services or documents	Windows user identity (integrated security) or no credentials
	Oracle, SAP NetWeaver BI, Hyperion Essbase, or other third-party OLE DB, ODBC, ADO.NET	Credentials stored in an RSDS file

> **NEED MORE REVIEW?**   These authentication mechanisms are discussed in detail within the "Microsoft BI Authentication and Identity Delegation" Word document located at *https://msdn.microsoft.com/library/dn186184.aspx.*

Kerberos constrained delegation and BI

Kerberos is a network authentication protocol that has been available for use within a Microsoft environment since the Windows 2000 Server product was introduced. In a standard SharePoint Server 2016 configuration, Kerberos can be used to improve performance and further secure connectivity between a client and their SharePoint 2016 server farm.

When BI components are introduced to a SharePoint 2016 farm, Kerberos becomes a vital component in the overall BI stack. The reason for this is simple: BI components most often connect to external data sources such as external databases, Analysis Services data cubes, and SSRS reports; NTLM authentication cannot delegate client credentials, thus it cannot authenticate the user to the back-end system.

> **NEED MORE REVIEW?**   An understanding of what double-hop authentication is (and more important, why NTLM can't do it) can be found in the MSDN blog article "Double-hop authentication: Why NTLM fails and Kerberos works" at *https://blogs.msdn.microsoft .com/besidethepoint/2010/05/08/double-hop-authentication-why-ntlm-fails-and -kerberos-works/.*

For example, in SharePoint Server 2016, Excel Services is no longer part of the SharePoint farm (Excel Online is part of Office Online Server); as a result, authentication mechanisms for connecting to this external system must be capable of delegating client credentials in this two-hop scenario.

NEED MORE REVIEW?   Analysis Services and its use of Kerberos constrained delegation is detailed in the MSDN article entitled "Configure Analysis Services and Kerberos Constrained Delegation (KCD)" at *https://msdn.microsoft.com/library/mt126226.aspx*.

Is Kerberos the only mechanism for providing this access? Absolutely not. In fact, there are drawbacks to using Kerberos:

- **Active Directory integration**   Kerberos is closely tied to Active Directory.
- **Internet readiness**   Kerberos is not something that can be used over the Internet.

Secure Application Markup Language claims authentication and BI

As it happens, SharePoint 2016 requires that users authenticate via claims. Because the SQL 2016 BI stack has been updated, it is also claims aware, meaning that you can use it together with c2WTS in your SharePoint farm.

IMPORTANT   If you are still using a Kerberos infrastructure, do not worry; Kerberos is also fully supported in SharePoint 2016.

The service account for c2WTS requires three different rights on each application server running this service:

- Act as part of the operating system
- Impersonate a client after authentication
- Log on as a service

Once these permissions have been granted, the c2WTS service account needs constrained delegation with protocol transitioning and permissions to delegate to the BI services it will work with (for example, Analysis Services).

NEED MORE REVIEW?   A very good example of this configuration is the MSDN article entitled "Claims to Windows Token Services (c2WTS) and Reporting Services" at *https://msdn .microsoft.com/library/hh231678.aspx*.

Skill: Create and configure work management

SharePoint Server 2013 was a good start toward uniting systems in the enterprise, with the ability to connect disparate systems such as Exchange and Skype. This solidarity meant that users were able to move fairly seamlessly between environments, especially for the purposes of eDiscovery.

SharePoint Server 2016 improves on this trust functionality, bringing systems such as Exchange and Skype to the forefront of the data loss prevention and eDiscovery curve. Sensitive information policies that exist in Exchange are identical in SharePoint ensuring that, no matter which system hosts sensitive content, privacy and other governance policies are carried out in a uniform fashion.

SharePoint Server 2016 also brings Project Server 2016 users into the fold, literally combining the two distinct systems into a single server vertical capable of providing both functionality sets.

This section covers how to:
- Configure a connection to Exchange
- Activate and configure a connection to Microsoft Project Server 2016
- Manage trusts
- Plan Exchange configuration for eDiscovery

Configure a connection to Exchange

Chapter 2, "Authentication and security," discusses how to go about establishing server-to-server trusts between SharePoint 2016 and other on-premises servers; one of the servers discussed was Exchange Server 2016.

Establishing a trust between these environments allows eDiscovery to take place in a SharePoint 2016 environment, allowing the user to query, hold, and export content from Exchange as required. Setting up the trust is fairly straightforward, and requires three distinct steps:

- Configure the SharePoint 2016 farm to trust the Exchange 2016 farm by using a JavaScript Object Notation (JSON) endpoint located on the Exchange 2016 farm.
- Configure permissions on the SharePoint 2016 farm for the server-to-server trust.
- Configure the Exchange 2016 farm to trust the SharePoint 2016 farm by using the ConfigureEnterprisePartnerApplication.ps1 PowerShell script.

> ***NEED MORE REVIEW?*** For a walk-through of this configuration, visit the TechNet site "Configure server-to-server authentication between SharePoint 2013 and Exchange Server 2013" at *https://technet.microsoft.com/library/jj655399.aspx.*

Activate and configure a connection to Microsoft Project Server 2016

Project Server 2016 is now included in the SharePoint Server 2016 Microsoft Installer (MSI) file; thus, no additional media downloads are required for installation. The activation of the Microsoft Project Server components will require a specific Product ID (PID) key and supporting licensing from Microsoft.

For Project Server to be used in a SharePoint Server 2016 farm, it must be enabled by using PowerShell:

```
Enable-ProjectServerLicense -Key <LicenseKey>
```

Once Project Server is active, you will then need to configure the Project Server service application and create a Project Web App site.

Deployment option details

There are two ways to deploy a Project Web Application:

- Create a Project Web App site within a given site collection, giving you the ability to add Project Server functionality to sites in that site collection.
- Create the Project Web App site as the top level of a site collection to centralize the deployment of project sites.

> **NEED MORE REVIEW?** Detailed information about the installation and configuration of Project Server 2016 is available on TechNet. The configuration of the Project Server service application (Step 2 of the core requirements just shown) is discussed in the TechNet article entitled "Install and configure Project Server 2016" at *https://technet.microsoft.com /library/ee662109(v=office.16).aspx*. The creation of the Project Web App site is discussed in the TechNet article entitled "Deploy Project Web App" at *https://technet.microsoft.com /library/jj200303(v=office.16).aspx*.

 Quick check

- Your corporate Project Management Office is looking to start using the Project Server functionality present in SharePoint Server 2016. What needs to happen to spin the technology, and what might be the optimal Project Web Application deployment?

Quick check answer

- The Project Management Office will need to secure Project Server licensing. Once this is done, you will need to activate the license by using PowerShell. The Project Web Application might be best deployed in its own web application, with project sites deployed beneath it.

Manage trusts

Server-to-server (S2S) trusts in SharePoint 2016 can be established with on-premises servers, Office 365, or Infrastructure as a Service (IaaS) farms in Azure. Regardless of the option chosen, these trusts are all administered via PowerShell cmdlets; there is no option in Central Administration for inspecting existence or health of trust relationships currently established with the SharePoint 2016 farm.

Two different types of trusts are required to be used with SharePoint Server 2016:

- **Farms with web applications** The configuration of S2S on a receiving farm (having web applications) requires that the JSON endpoint of the sending farm be specified by using the New-SPTrustedSecurityTokenIssuer cmdlet with the -MetadataEndpoint switch.

- **Farms without web applications** The configuration of S2S on a receiving farm (having no web applications) requires that the SharePoint Security Token Service certificate be exported and then incorporated on the trusting farm by using the New-SPTrustedSecurityTokenIssuer cmdlet along with the -Name, -Certificate, and -RegisteredIssuerName switches.

EXAM TIP

When reviewing the index of Windows PowerShell cmdlets for SharePoint Server 2016 at *https://technet.microsoft.com/library/ff678226(v=office.16).aspx*, you might notice that there are four cmdlets that all look a great deal alike: Set-SPTrustedIdentityTokenIssuer, Set-SPTrustedRootAuthority, Set-SPTrustedSecurityTokenIssuer, and Set-SPTrustedService-TokenIssuer.

Only the last two of these four cmdlets are used to set up and administer trusts from within PowerShell. Set-SPTrustedIdentityTokenIssuer is used to set the identity providers for a web application (not for S2S). Set-SPTrustedRootAuthority is used to create a new trusted root authority (also not for S2S). Set-SPTrustedSecurityTokenIssuer is used to set the trusted token issuer as part of setting up S2S. Set-SPTrustedServiceTokenIssuer is used to update the trust with the SharePoint farm (S2S).

NEED MORE REVIEW? For more information about the process of maintaining trusts between farms, see the TechNet Article "Configure server-to-server authentication between SharePoint 2013 farms" at *https://technet.microsoft.com/library/jj655400.aspx*.

Plan Exchange configuration for eDiscovery

Configuring the trust with Exchange Server 2016 is not the only step required to enable eDiscovery from SharePoint Server 2016 to Exchange Server 2016. For users to be able to use Exchange Server 2016 In-Place eDiscovery, you need to add these users to the Discovery Management role group from within Exchange.

Members of the Discovery Management role group have Full Access mailbox permissions to the default discovery mailbox, also known as the Discovery Search Mailbox. Members of this role group have the ability to access sensitive message content, as they can use In-Place eDiscovery to:

- Search all mailboxes in the organization (no restrictions).
- Preview the search results (and other mailbox items).

- Copy these results to a discovery mailbox.
- Export the search results to a .pst file.

> **IMPORTANT** Given the unfettered access to mailboxes presented by the Discovery Management role group, it would be wise to heavily limit the membership of this group to legal, compliance, or human resources personnel.

The Discovery Management role group can only have security principals added, including user mailboxes, mail users, security groups, and other role groups.

Adding a user to the Discovery Management role group

Users can be added to the Discovery Management role group in one of two ways:

- **Exchange Admin Center (EAC)** Within the Permissions section of the EAC, select Admin Roles, Discovery Management, and then add new members.
- **Exchange Management Shell** Use the Add-RoleGroupMember cmdlet on the Discovery Management role group to add individual users or groups.

> **NEED MORE REVIEW?** Assigning eDiscovery permissions is a fairly straightforward process, requiring only a handful of steps. An understanding of this process and other eDiscovery processes can be gained by reviewing the TechNet article entitled "In-Place eDiscovery in Exchange 2016" at *https://technet.microsoft.com/library/dd298021(v =exchg.160).aspx*.

Skill: Plan and configure cloud and hybrid federated search

Although Chapter 5 covered Search in great detail, this section discusses some of the nuances present in the configuration of cloud hybrid search and its older relation, hybrid federated search (also known as classic hybrid search). Cloud hybrid search can work on its own, or if desired, in concert with hybrid federated search; this allows a best-of-breed configuration experience, capable of meeting any hybrid search need from the enterprise.

> **This section covers how to:**
>
> - Plan and configure on-premises and Office 365 search and encrypted metadata when content is transferred to the search index in Office 365
> - Configure user-specific queries and inbound and outbound or bidirectional hybrid topologies

Plan and configure on-premises and Office 365 search and encrypted metadata when content is transferred to the search index in Office 365

Search is a pervasive topic throughout this book; it stands to reason that it will be the same on the certification test. With this in mind, this section drills a bit deeper into the Cloud Search service application as well as its ability to transfer metadata from an on-premises SharePoint 2016 farm to the cloud.

It is often the case that people believe that their content is transferred to the cloud, immediately prompting a discussion of encryption and safety concerns. Fortunately, this configuration is not what happens in a SharePoint cloud hybrid search configuration; in fact, the only content that is transferred to the cloud (and this transfer is, in fact, encrypted) is the metadata itself, retrieved by crawling on-premises content sources.

Cloud versus on-premises search components

When a Cloud Search service application is created, all six search components are required: crawl, admin, query processing, index, analytics, and content processing. Although they are required (and continue to be so after cloud hybrid search is configured), the index, analytics, and content processing components are inactive on an on-premises Search role server.

In an on-premises, MinRole-compliant SharePoint 2016 farm, Search is its own role within the farm. Servers in the other standard tiers (Front-end, Application, and Distributed cache) are unable to host any of the search components, as doing so would violate MinRole requirements within the farm. This leaves the administrator with two MinRole-compliant choices: Either scale the Search role out (two or more servers would achieve resiliency requirements), or perhaps (if the environment is big enough) designate a Search-specific farm to provide search functionality to one or more SharePoint 2016 farms.

For cloud hybrid search, the only scaling that is required comes in the form of the crawl component. For most search architectures, having two crawl components in the farm should produce a reliable crawl rate.

Avoid throttling issues

Office 365 is, by its nature, a multitenant environment. This shared arrangement means that multiple tenants often share the same networking, memory, processing, and storage I/O resources. To keep one environment from consuming all available resources at any given time, Microsoft implements application *throttling*; this good neighbor policy ensures that no individual user (or group of users) in an Office 365 tenant can affect others by using unreasonable amounts of networking bandwidth or resources.

> **NEED MORE REVIEW?** Cloud hybrid search planning is a central component for implementing a successful SharePoint 2016 and Office 365 hybrid environment. For more information about this planning effort, review the Office.com article entitled "Plan cloud hybrid

search for SharePoint" at *https://support.office.com/article/Plan-cloud-hybrid-search-for
-SharePoint-33926857-302c-424f-ba78-03286cf5ac30?ui=en-US&rs=en-US&ad=US#BKMK
_Unused_search_components.*

Configure user-specific queries and inbound and outbound or bidirectional hybrid topologies

In SharePoint 2013, three distinct hybrid search topologies exist, and can be selected for federated search with Office 365:

- **One-way outbound topology** In this configuration, the on-premises SharePoint Server farm has a connection to SharePoint Online, and allows the on-premises users to view both local and remote search results. Users from SharePoint Online only see results from the SharePoint Online Search portal.

- **One-way inbound topology** In this configuration, SharePoint online connects to the SharePoint farm through a reverse proxy device, and allows Office 365 users to view results from both the online and on-premises environments. Users from the SharePoint on-premises environment only see the local results from that environment.

- **Two-way, bidirectional topology** In this configuration, the search query results for both on-premises and SharePoint Online environments are presented in both environments.

EXAM TIP

Cloud hybrid search environments no longer require the use of a reverse proxy device, streamlining installation and maintenance of the hybrid search environment.

Federated search has been largely replaced by cloud hybrid search (which is the default in SharePoint 2016 and the August PU for SharePoint Server 2013 and uses a Cloud Search service application). In this arrangement, search crawls of both on-premises and online content wind up in an Office 365 search index. For every 1 TB of pooled storage in the tenant, you are allowed to index 1 million items of on-premises content to the Office 365 search index (with a default limit of 20 million items).

Cloud hybrid search topologies and user-specific queries

When using cloud hybrid search, the default topology is to allow two-way searches; after all, the index is stored online (rather than maintaining two distinct indexes), and users in both environments (on-premises and online) can easily review search results from the index.

In special cases, a combination of cloud hybrid search and federated search can be used to prevent metadata from sensitive, on-premises content from appearing in the Office 365 index, allowing for different query results, based on the user's location. In such an arrangement, the content sources for the Cloud Search service application cover all on-premises content except the sensitive content, whose metadata is retained in an on-premises index.

> **NEED MORE REVIEW?** Detailed information about the configuration and administration of cloud hybrid search can be found in the Office.com article entitled "Plan cloud hybrid search for SharePoint" at *https://support.office.com/article/Plan-cloud-hybrid-search-for -SharePoint-33926857-302c-424f-ba78-03286cf5ac30.*

Summary

- The BI stack in SharePoint Server 2016 includes PerformancePoint, SQL Server Reporting Services, Power Pivot, Excel Online, and Power View.

- PerformancePoint Services is a back-ported product that has been folded into SharePoint Server 2016.

- PerformancePoint Services provides a series of reporting and scorecard templates, although other templates can be created by an administrator.

- SQL Server 2016 Reporting Services is a BI component that runs in SharePoint-integrated mode.

- An SSRS server must be assigned the Custom role in a SharePoint Server 2016 MinRole configuration.

- Power Pivot is a built-in component within the Excel 2016 client that is capable of working in concert with SQL Server Analysis Services (configured in Power Pivot mode) to import data from several sources into a workbook and then create relationships between this data.

- Office Online Server is required for use with Power Pivot to provide Excel Online functionality.

- The Microsoft SQL Server 2016 Power Pivot for Microsoft SharePoint 2014 add-in is downloaded separately and provides the necessary Power Pivot application server components.

- Three steps are required for the configuration of Excel Online for BI: Analysis Services availability, service instance registration, and permission assignment for Excel Online.

- Power View is a browser-based Silverlight application that supports interactive data exploration, visualization, and presentation.

- Power View reports in Excel Online workbooks cannot be displayed unless the workbooks reside in a SharePoint farm with SharePoint-integrated SQL Reporting Services installed.

- The SQL Server 2014 Power Pivot and Power View add-ins for SharePoint cannot be used in SharePoint 2016.

- SharePoint Server 2016 uses a series of trusts to integrate functionality provided by Exchange Server 2016 (and others).

- Two different types of trusts are required for use in SharePoint 2016: trusts for farms with web applications and trusts for farms with no web applications.

  A Cloud Search service application still requires that all six search components be installed: crawl, admin, query processing, index, analytics, and content processing. These last three, index, analytics, and content processing, are all inactive in a Cloud Search service application.

Thought experiment

In this thought experiment, demonstrate your skills and knowledge of the topics covered in this chapter. You can find the answer to this thought experiment in the next section.

You are designing a BI infrastructure for your enterprise using SharePoint Server 2016 and SQL Server 2016. Management would like to ensure that the environment will be supported going forward:

1. Which components might you opt to omit in your BI solution to ensure forward compatibility?

2. What are the differences between using Kerberos and Secure Application Markup Language claims in your environment?

3. What supporting SharePoint components might you need to ensure that your environment is complete?

Thought experiment answer

This section contains the solution to the thought experiment.

1. PerformancePoint, although useful, is a back-ported solution; this could mean that further development efforts might not take place. Power View is a component that is heavily dependent on SSRS, but uses Silverlight for the display of some of its data. If possible, you might even choose to forgo the use of Kerberos, replacing it with Secure Application Markup Language claims.

2. In an on-premises environment, both are quite effective means of overcoming the double-hop issue between SharePoint 2016 and other back-end BI functions and data sources. Kerberos is not useful in a cloud environment, as a user must be able to contact an Active Directory domain controller for its use.

3. As the BI stack in SharePoint 2016 has become claims-aware, a key design component might be c2WTS, which can be used to provide constrained delegation with protocol transitioning and permissions to the BI stack in your farm.

## CHAPTER 7

Monitor and optimize a SharePoint environment

Up to this point, we've been talking about what steps are required to design a viable SharePoint 2016 environment. Designing the topology, planning security, installing, and configuring the environment lead to the eventual completion of the implementation phase, but this isn't the end; in fact, it's just the beginning.

Moving forward, the environment will need to be evaluated prior to its release to production, to ensure that services are running as desired and that the scaling of the farm is as required to meet service level agreement (SLA) and capacity expectations. Once the farm has been released, it will continue to require careful maintenance, planning, and management to ensure service to a growing user base.

In this chapter, we focus on three major tasks: monitoring, tuning and optimization, and troubleshooting. Monitoring is concerned with the use of tools and metrics to minimize system failures or loss of performance. Tuning and optimization expand on these concepts, providing insight into how to optimize the performance of not only SharePoint, but SQL and Internet Information Services (IIS) as well. Troubleshooting is perhaps the most complex of these tasks and is concerned with establishing performance baselines as well as using both client and server tools to troubleshoot issues as they occur.

Skills in this chapter:

- Skill: Monitor a SharePoint environment
- Skill: Tune and optimize a SharePoint environment
- Skill: Troubleshoot a SharePoint environment

Skill: Monitor a SharePoint environment

The first few steps after implementation are often the most critical. The organization sets about getting to use this new environment, causing a sudden uptick in user adoption. As users begin to evaluate the farm, the extra resource load on the farm places stress on it and could expose any design inconsistencies not discovered during performance testing. Previously defined SLAs with the business might also be in effect, beginning to restrict the times that the system can be down for maintenance.

Ensuring reliability and performance levels during this period is a key requirement for user adoption of the new platform. Effective administration and monitoring of the SharePoint environment can capture events, addressing any misconfigurations or design shortfalls before they affect user adoption rates.

This section covers how to:
- Define monitoring requirements
- Configure performance counter capture
- Configure page performance monitoring
- Configure usage and health providers
- Monitor and forecast storage needs
- Monitor SharePoint hybrid cloud deployments

Define monitoring requirements

Monitoring is the art of using instrumentation to analyze and predict the behaviors of a given system. Knowing what instrumentation items are available for use and the expected values for each enables the administrator of a system to be able to adjust for performance idiosyncrasies of a system without experiencing any downtime.

Each new revision of SharePoint has introduced greater potential for monitoring at a more granular level than in previous versions. SharePoint 2016 continues this pattern by providing insight into the operations of major subsystems such as Microsoft SQL, ASP.NET, IIS, and other services.

Service guarantee metrics

In the planning stages of your farm design, you should develop SLAs that define the service guarantee of functionality provided by the farm to your user base. This guarantee defines not only the times that a system can be up or down entirely, but also the availability and enforceability of scheduled outage windows.

Within the SLA for your environment, you will define terms such as downtime, scheduled downtime, and uptime percentage. These metrics merely describe at a high level what the goals of monitoring are.

IMPORTANT Reviewing a production SLA will give you a good idea of what to incorporate into your own organizational SLAs. The Microsoft Office 365 SLA is a good example of what's included in this documentation; a version of this SLA that applies to most regions and is written in English can be found on the Microsoft Volume Licensing site at *http://www.microsoftvolumelicensing.com/Downloader.aspx?DocumentId=10758*.

As an example, Microsoft produces an SLA for each of the component features within the Office 365 platform. For instance, within the Microsoft Office 365 SLA agreement for SharePoint Online, you will find definitions for the following:

- **Downtime**   Each of the services in Office 365 has its own definition of downtime. The definition for SharePoint Online is "any period of time when users are unable to access SharePoint sites for which they have appropriate permissions."

- **Scheduled Downtime**   This is defined as "periods of Downtime related to network, hardware, or Service maintenance or upgrades." The SLA goes on to define the advance notification period as "five (5) days prior to the commencement of such Downtime."

- **Monthly Uptime Percentage**   Although this is defined for each service in Office 365, each of the definitions follows roughly the same formula. For SharePoint Online, downtime is measured in user-minutes, and for each month is the sum of the length (in minutes) of each incident that occurs during that month, multiplied by the number of users affected by that incident, as shown in Figure 7-1.

$$\frac{User\ Minutes - Downtime}{User\ Minutes} \times 100$$

FIGURE 7-1 Monthly uptime percentage formula

Immediately after these definitions, the SLA goes on to define what service credit is offered in the event of monthly uptime percentage falling below 99.9 percent ("three nines"), 99 percent ("two nines"), and 95 percent ("one nine").

Monitoring levels

Now that you know what your monthly uptime percentage is (for example, three nines would give you a maximum of approximately 24*60*.001, or 1.44 minutes per day of downtime) and what constitutes downtime, you can begin to monitor the SharePoint farm (or farms) to prevent these incidents.

A single SharePoint farm has three major levels at which it can be monitored (from largest to smallest):

- **Server level**   At this level, you will be monitoring each tier of the servers that constitute a farm, including Front-end, Application, Distributed cache, Search, Custom role, and SQL database servers.

- **Service application level**   At this level, you will be monitoring all the services provided within the farm, such as Managed Metadata, User Profile, Search, and others.

- **Site and site collection level**   At this level, you monitor all the sites and site collections contained within the farm.

> **IMPORTANT**   It's important to remember that outages do not necessarily require the failure of an entire farm; an improperly deployed feature or a misconfigured service application can result in downtime for a considerable segment of the user base without rendering the entire farm inoperable.

Monitoring tools

There are four on-premises tools that can be used to monitor SharePoint 2016 farms: Central Administration, Windows PowerShell, system- and SharePoint-specific logs, and System Center 2012 R2 Operations Manager.

CENTRAL ADMINISTRATION

Central Administration allows for the configuration and monitoring of the SharePoint logs as well as configuration of usage and health providers. Additionally, Health Analyzer runs a series of rules on a regular basis that check on the status of metrics such as these:

- Free disk space on both SharePoint and SQL servers
- Service issues such as problems with State service, InfoPath Forms Services, and Visio Graphics Service
- SQL-specific issues, such as overly large content databases, databases in need of upgrade, and the read and write status for a given database

> **NEED MORE REVIEW?** A complete listing of all SharePoint Health Analyzer rules can be found on TechNet at *https://technet.microsoft.com/library/ff686816(v=office.16).aspx*.

WINDOWS POWERSHELL

Windows PowerShell focuses on the diagnostic capabilities found in the Unified Logging Service (ULS) logs. The ULS logs can be quite detailed in scope, meaning that quite literally hundreds and thousands of entries can be found on a given server. When you choose to use the Get-SPLogEvent cmdlet, you can view trace events by level, area, category, event ID, process, or message text.

EXAM TIP

Using the -MinimumLevel switch with Get-SPLogEvent enables you to look for events that are equal to or more severe than the level you specify. There are only two valid values: Error or Warning.

Additionally, you can pipe its output to the Out-GridView cmdlet to produce tabular log output in a graphical format (as shown in Figure 7-2), which can be easily refined or exported to an Excel spreadsheet for further analysis.

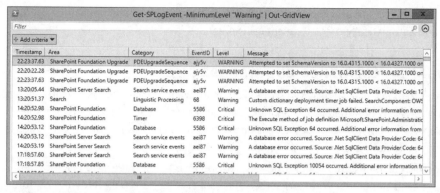

FIGURE 7-2 Using the Out-GridView cmdlet

NEED MORE REVIEW?   For a more detailed discussion of the use of Windows PowerShell for viewing SharePoint diagnostic logs, see the TechNet article "View diagnostic logs in SharePoint 2013" at *https://technet.microsoft.com/library/ff463595.aspx*.

SYSTEM AND SHAREPOINT LOGS

Logs for monitoring and diagnosing SharePoint come from two distinct sources. At the operating system level, you find the standard event logs, in which events that concern SharePoint and its supporting technologies (SQL, IIS, and so on) are recorded (primarily in the Application and System logs). As previously mentioned, SharePoint also records information in its own series of trace logs, otherwise known as the ULS logs.

SYSTEM CENTER 2012 R2 OPERATIONS MANAGER

If you have a larger SharePoint farm (or multiple farms), you might find that the monitoring of each individual system becomes too time consuming, and that even the use of the usage and health providers is not enough to provide a complete picture of the systems required to support SharePoint.

For this purpose, Microsoft produces a product known as System Center 2012 Operations Manager R2. Using this tool set with the System Center Management Pack for SharePoint 2016 not only allows for the effective monitoring of multiple SharePoint farms and their component systems, but also for the alerting and preventative actions required to assist in the maintenance of service level guarantees.

NEED MORE REVIEW?   System Center 2016 will be released soon (as of this writing, it is at Technical Preview 5). Until then, the current version is System Center 2012 R2, and the management pack used by this version for SharePoint 2016 can be found on the Microsoft Download Center at *https://www.microsoft.com/download/details.aspx?id=52043*.

The System Center Monitoring Pack monitors Microsoft SharePoint Server 2016 by collecting SharePoint component-specific performance counters in one central location and raising alerts for operator intervention as necessary. This tool allows you to proactively manage

SharePoint servers and identify issues before they become critical by detecting issues, sending alerts, and automatically correlating critical events.

Configure performance counter capture

As your SharePoint installation grows in scope, you might want to evaluate the performance of particular servers within the farm. Examining the performance level of each server in the farm from an operating system perspective is one way to predict areas in which more system resources or configuration changes are required.

One tool that can be used for this purpose is Performance Monitor (PerfMon), a tool that is natively installed along with Windows Server. This tool enables you to monitor and capture metrics about your individual servers using a series of performance counters.

As SharePoint, SQL, and other applications are added to a server, additional performance counters for those applications are made available to PerfMon. These new counters describe performance and health metrics that are specific to each application (or its major components).

Starting a performance monitoring capture

To start a new performance capture, begin by opening the PerfMon App. In Windows Server 2012 R2, you can do this by going to your Start screen and selecting the tile for PerfMon (see Figure 7-3).

FIGURE 7-3 Performance Monitor (tile)

IMPORTANT If you are having difficulty locating PerfMon, there is another way to start it. Simply start a search and then type **PerfMon** into your Search box and select its icon.

Selecting the Performance Monitor menu item causes the capture graph to appear, as shown in Figure 7-4.

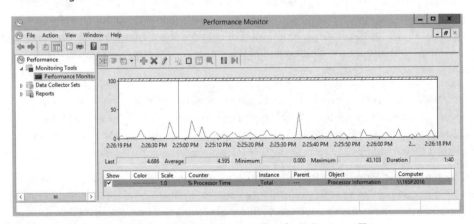

FIGURE 7-4 Performance Monitor (default view), capturing the % Processor Time

Not too impressive, is it? As PerfMon is intended to be customized, there isn't much to see when it first appears. By default, all PerfMon captures is the % Processor Time performance counter over roughly a 100-second interval.

Adding SharePoint counters to Performance Monitor

All sorts of SharePoint-specific counters can be added to a PerfMon capture. Counters are included for SharePoint, but other represented subsystems counters include the following:

- Access Services (2010 and 2013 versions)
- InfoPath Forms Services 16
- Office Online
- PerformancePoint Services
- Project Server
- Search (including Graph, Gatherer, and so on)
- Visio Services

Adding a counter to an existing performance capture is fairly straightforward, requiring only that you select the plus (+) icon in the toolbar and then choose a counter (for example, Current Page Requests, All Instances, as shown in Figure 7-5).

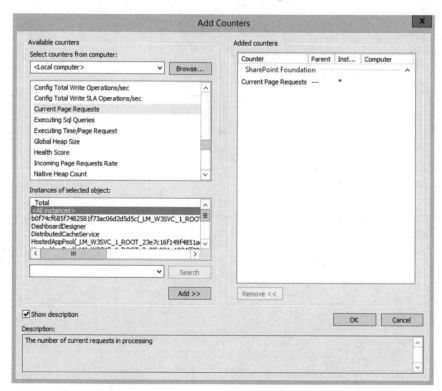

FIGURE 7-5 Adding a counter

> **IMPORTANT** One of the most valuable pieces of information in the Add Counters dialog box is the often overlooked Show Description check box. Selecting this box shows a description of what the counter actually does within the system.

Building and reporting performance using a data collection set

In the previous example, we added counters one by one. Performing such an ad hoc capture has limited usefulness, and generally means two things:

- Starting another new PerfMon session would require that the counters be added back in.
- Although a point-in-time view is useful, there is no meaningful way to capture and replay the counters as they appear.

The next logical step would then be to build a data collector set to monitor the performance counters, and then use the Reports feature of PerfMon to replay the captured metrics. Creating a data collector set isn't terribly difficult, and becomes a useful tool in capturing baseline server and farm behavior for later comparison.

Within Performance Monitor, select Data Collector Sets, right-click User Defined, and then select New, Data Collector Set, as shown in Figure 7-6.

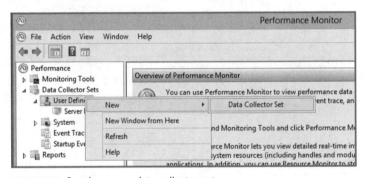

FIGURE 7-6 Creating a new data collector set

Enter a name for your new data collector set, select Create Manually (Advanced), and then click Next (see Figure 7-7).

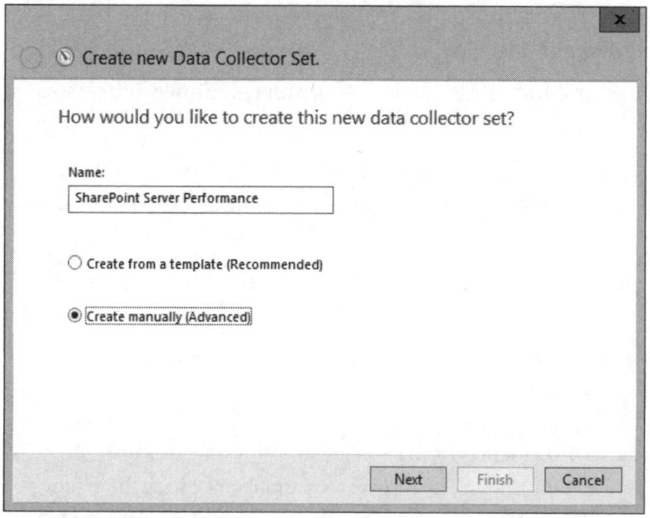

FIGURE 7-7 Creating a data collector set (not using a template)

> **IMPORTANT** There are no OOB data collector sets for SharePoint 2016.

Selecting Create Data Logs Using Only Performance Counters prompts you to choose which counters you'd like to log by clicking Add, which results in the options listed in Figure 7-8.

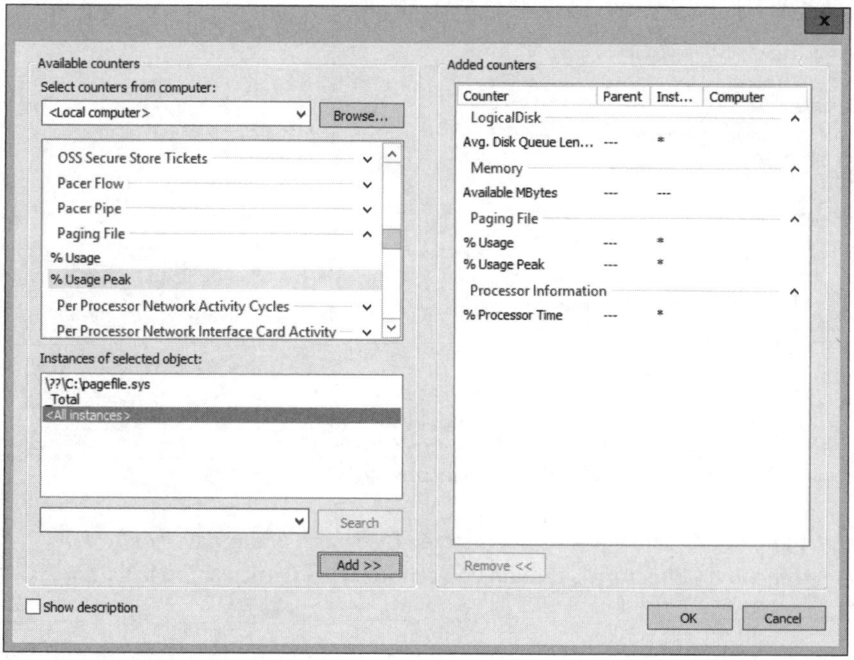

FIGURE 7-8 Selected counters

The five counters shown in Figure 7-8 are those that are often used to check the basic health of the server on which SharePoint is installed:

- **% Processor Time** (Processor Information section, All Instances) Shows processor usage over time.

- **Avg. Disk Queue Length** (Logical Disk section, All Instances) Shows the average number of both read and write requests that were queued for the selected disks during the sample interval.

- **Available MBytes** (Memory section) Shows how much physical memory is available for allocation.

- **% Usage and % Usage Peak** (Paging File section, all instances) Shows the current and peak values for paging file used.

> **NEED MORE REVIEW?** The counters listed previously are those commonly used to troubleshoot core performance levels on a SharePoint server. Optimal values for the major performance counters can be found in the TechNet article "Monitoring and maintaining SharePoint Server 2013" at *https://technet.microsoft.com/library/ff758658.aspx*.

In the Create New Data Collector Set page, the selected counters are displayed, along with a sampling interval. You might wish to change this interval (time between counter samples in seconds). Click Next to continue (see Figure 7-9).

FIGURE 7-9 Logged performance counters in the new data collector set

The data captured in this data collector set is stored by default in the *%systemdrive%\ Perflog\Admin\<set name>* directory, although you can specify a particular log location (Figure 7-10).

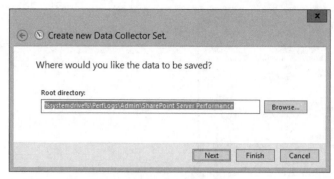

FIGURE 7-10 The default root directory

The final step in creating the new data collector set is to choose which account it runs under and then choose from a series of actions:

- **Open Properties For This Data Collector Set** Enables you to specify additional selections for your log, such as its duration.
- **Start This Data Collector Set Now** Saves and immediately starts the data collector set capture.
- **Save And Close** Saves and then closes this configuration process (selected in Figure 7-11).

FIGURE 7-11 Completing the data collector set

Now that the data collector set has been created, it can be used repeatedly. To start the capture, simply right-click the data collector set and select Start (see Figure 7-12).

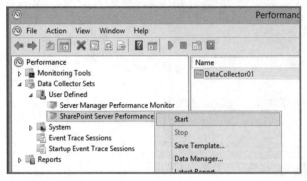

FIGURE 7-12 Starting a performance counter capture from a user-defined data collector set

Looking in the Reports section, under User Defined, you can see that the SharePoint Server Performance capture is running (Figure 7-13).

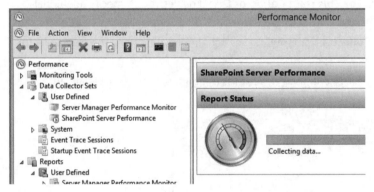

FIGURE 7-13 SharePoint Server Performance capture, collecting data

After about five minutes, you should have a fairly good capture, but you could extend this duration if you want. After you capture enough data, select Stop, then select a report to display the metrics for a given time period along with some maximum, minimum, and average values (see Figure 7-14).

Now that you have created a data collector set, you have the option of saving this as a template. Simply selecting the user-defined data collector set and right-clicking it gives you the option to save this set as a template for later use (Figure 7-15).

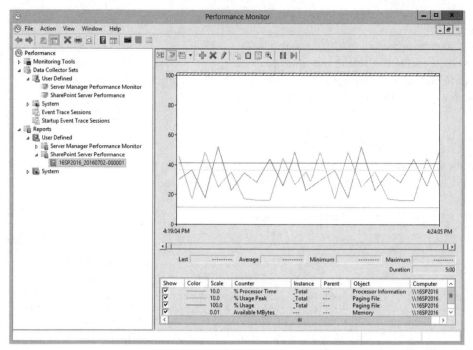

FIGURE 7-14 Metrics captured by the SharePoint Server Performance report (data collector set)

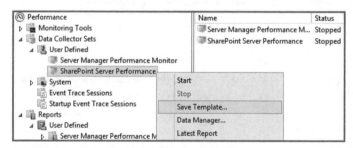

FIGURE 7-15 Saving the data collector set as a template

Configure page performance monitoring

Page performance is dependent on a number of variables: whether the user has caching enabled on the desktop, whether the IIS web servers are caching artifacts such as graphics and text content, how SharePoint is caching information, and how quickly SQL Server can provide content to the SharePoint farm.

SharePoint can make use of three distinct caching mechanisms: ASP.NET output cache, Binary Large Object (BLOB) cache, and the object cache. Each of these caching mechanisms has a representative set of counters in Performance Monitor.

EXAM TIP

Although these caching mechanisms all enhance performance in a SharePoint farm, know which are enabled by default and which you must enable manually. Each of these cache types can result in a shortage of resources in the SharePoint farm; know which resource types might be affected by each of the three cache types.

ASP.NET output cache counters

Output cache setting effectiveness can be monitored by viewing the values for the following ASP.NET Apps counter group in Performance Monitor (shown in Table 7-1).

TABLE 7-1 Output cache counters and optimal values

Counter name	Optimal Value	Notes
Cache API Trims	0	Increases the amount of memory that is allocated to the ASP.NET output cache.
Cache API Hit Ratio	1 for read-only sites <1 for read-write sites	Low hit ratios have mostly to do with content that has not been cached, frequently edited pages, or customized cache profiles that prevent effective caching.

IMPORTANT In PerfMon, the name of this counter is specifically listed as ASP.NET Apps, but is appended by the version number (for example, this might read ASP.NET Apps v.4.0.30319).

BLOB cache counters

BLOB cache setting effectiveness can be monitored by viewing the values for the SharePoint Publishing Cache counter group in Performance Monitor shown in Table 7-2.

TABLE 7-2 BLOB cache counters and optimal values

Counter name	Optimal Value	Notes
Total number of cache compactions	0	A consistently high number indicates that the cache size is too small.
BLOB cache % full	< 80%	Values between 80 percent and 100 percent indicate that the cache size is too small.
Publishing cache flushes/second	0	When the cache is flushed, performance is negatively affected. Site owners might be performing actions on the sites that are causing the cache to be flushed. To improve performance during peak-use hours, make sure that site owners perform these actions only during off-peak hours.
Publishing cache hit ratio	1 for read-only sites <1 for read-write sites	Any time that unpublished or draft items are being interacted with, the read-write ratio is less than 1.

Object cache counters

Object cache setting effectiveness can be monitored by viewing the values for the SharePoint Publishing cache counter group in Performance Monitor shown in Table 7-3.

TABLE 7-3 Output cache counters and optimal values

Counter name	Optimal Value	Notes
Total number of cache compactions	0	If this number is high, the cache size is too small for the data being requested. To improve performance, increase the size of the cache.
Publishing cache flushes/second	0	Site owners might be performing actions on the sites that are causing the cache to be flushed. To improve performance during peak-use hours, make sure that site owners perform these actions only during off-peak hours.
Publishing cache hit ratio	1 for read-only sites <1 for read-write sites	If the hit ratio starts to fall, either the cache has been flushed or a significant amount of content has been added to the site.

Configure usage and health providers

Monitoring is an integral part of any IT administrator's job; although this person is occasionally called on to perform reactionary maintenance (to fix things that go wrong during production hours), the lion's share of duties should be focused on preventive administration. Monitoring logs and other metrics provided by the systems they support is a key component of long-term IT success.

SharePoint presents a special challenge from an administrative standpoint because it is dependent on a lot of other technologies such as SQL, IIS, ASP, the operating system, and SharePoint.

At any given time, a SharePoint administrator might need to know metrics such as these:

- How well is IIS serving pages?
- Are SharePoint farm member servers functioning correctly, from an operating system standpoint?
- How are the data tier servers functioning with respect to the load placed on them by the SharePoint farm?

Add the monitoring of several SharePoint servers into the mix, and there are a lot of logs to be checked, especially for a smaller IT team. IIS, SharePoint, and SQL logs can be individually monitored, but each individual logging system paints only a partial picture of the health and well-being of a SharePoint farm.

Event selection

When you are configuring the usage and health data collection for the farm, you will be given the opportunity to choose from a series of events to capture. Several of these events are enabled by default, although you can choose to deselect them before enabling the usage and health data provider to enhance performance.

Table 7-4 shows a listing of events that can be logged along with their initial logging state.

TABLE 7-4 Potential logging events

Events to log	Enabled by default?
Analytics Usage	Yes
App Monitoring	Yes
App Statistics	Yes
Bandwidth Monitoring	No
Content Export Usage	Yes
Content Import Usage	Yes
Database Wait Statistics	Yes
Definition of usage fields for microblog telemetry	Yes
Definition of usage fields for service calls	Yes
Definition of usage fields for SPDistributedCache calls	Yes
Definition of usage fields for workflow telemetry	Yes
Feature Use	Yes
File IO	Yes
Page Requests	Yes
REST and Client API Action Usage	Yes
REST and Client API Request Usage	Yes
RUM Global Provider Description	Yes
Sandbox Request Resource Measures	Yes
Sandbox Requests	Yes
Sandbox Requests (new)	Yes
Sandbox Site Resource Measure	Yes
Sandbox Solution Resource Measure	Yes
Simple Log Event Usage Data_RUMUsage	Yes
Simple Log Event Usage Data_SPUnifiedAuditEntry	No
Simple Log Event Usage Data_UserEngagement	Yes
SQL Exceptions Usage	No

Events to log	Enabled by default?
SQL IO Usage	No
SQL Latency Usage	No
Task Use	Yes
Tenant Logging	No
Timer Jobs	Yes
Tracks Response Times/Processing Time Metrics for Access Services ADS and WFE Subsystems	No
User Profile ActiveDirectory Import Usage	Yes
User Profile to SharePoint Synchronization Usage	Yes
Web Part Use	Yes

Configuring usage and health data collection

A newly created SharePoint installation creates the usage and health data collection services, but does not activate or configure them by default. These services can affect performance; as a result, they should not be activated until after the farm is fully configured, but prior to user acceptance testing.

To display the usage and health data collection configuration, on the Monitoring page in Central Administration, in the Reporting section, select Configure Usage And Health Data Collection.

EXAM TIP

Be familiar with the steps required to both enable and configure usage and health providers—specifically how to schedule the log collection and select the events being captured.

There are six major components to the configuration of usage and health data collection:

- **Usage Data Collection**   Choose to either enable or disable data collection (selected to be enabled by default).

- **Event Selection**   The selection of which events are to be captured within the logging database, as shown in the last section.

- **Usage Data Collection Settings**   Specifies the log file location on all SharePoint farm servers (defaults to *%ProgramFiles%\Common Files\Microsoft Shared\Web Server Extensions\16\LOGS*).

- **Health Data Collection**   Choose whether or not to enable health data collection settings and edit the health logging schedule (if necessary).

- **Log Collection Schedule**   Choose whether you want to edit the log collection schedule via the Usage Data Imports and Usage Data Processing timer jobs.

- **Logging Database Server** Displays the current database server and name for the logging database along with the authentication method used to connect to SQL (Windows authentication or SQL authentication).

> ***IMPORTANT*** The database server and name are intentionally unavailable; these values can be reconfigured via Windows PowerShell cmdlets.

After you have made your selections on this page, click OK to activate the usage and health data collection functionality.

> ***NEED MORE REVIEW?*** Obviously, special care should be taken to ensure that the logging database does not fill all its available space. The benefit of having operating system, SharePoint, and SQL counters captured in the logging database is to gather a complete picture of your farm and all its member servers (including database servers) for analysis as required. For more information on this functionality, see the TechNet article "Monitoring and maintaining SharePoint Server 2013" at *https://technet.microsoft.com/library /ff758658.aspx*.

Logging database functionality

As the SharePoint farm is being created, the WSS_UsageApplication (default name) database is created for use in logging performance metrics. Individual metrics, captured by each member server of the SharePoint farm, can be combined on a regular basis and stored in a series of partitioned tables within the logging database. This database also provides a series of predefined SQL views that can be used to produce output using Microsoft Excel.

> ***NEED MORE REVIEW?*** This logging database is unlike any other in SharePoint 2016 because it is the only one created for the express purpose of querying via SQL Server Management Studio (SSMS). For more details about the views and stored procedures present within the logging database, see the article "View data in the logging database in SharePoint 2013" at *https://technet.microsoft.com/library/jj715694.aspx*.

After the usage and health data collection has been configured in Central Administration, logged events are stored in a series of tables (partitioned by day), as shown in Figure 7-16. Each table has a total of 32 partitions, one for each possible day of a given month (Partitions 1 through 31) and another specifically intended to contain the current day's logs (Partition0).

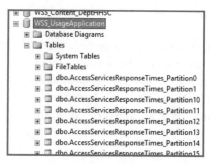

FIGURE 7-16 WSS_UsageApplication database tables

There are three timer jobs responsible for the collection and aggregation of logging data in a SharePoint 2016 farm:

- **Microsoft SharePoint Foundation Usage Data Import**   This job runs every five minutes by default and imports usage log files into the logging database.

- **Microsoft SharePoint Foundation Usage Data Maintenance**   This job runs hourly and performs maintenance in the logging database itself.

- **Microsoft SharePoint Foundation Usage Data Processing**   This job runs once daily and expires usage data older than 30 days.

The usage data import timer job is fairly self-explanatory: All it does is extract logging data from every member of the farm and load this information into the logging database tables (by category) for further analysis. This information is temporarily stored in the _Partition0 table so logging information can be regularly added throughout the day. At day's end, the usage data processing job accumulates and analyzes the current day's log information, removing it from _Partition0 and storing it in one of the 31 different daily partitions.

As an example, if today were July 10 and you selected the top 1,000 rows from the dbo. AccessServicesMonitoring_Partition10 table, you would likely be seeing logs from June 10; today's logs would still be stored in the _Partition0 table until the date rolls over to July 11. At that point, the logs for July 10 would be moved by the usage data processing timer job to the _Partition10 table, and the _Partition0 table would be reset.

Monitor and forecast storage needs

Predicting the storage requirements of SharePoint installation requires a combined effort from both farm and site collection administrators. Either of these can monitor storage and also record the data growth rate for predicting future database size requirements.

Although the farm administrator can often "drill down" to the same administrative level as the site collection administrator, his or her unfamiliarity with the data or its retention requirements makes the administration of storage at this level quite a bit more difficult. Likewise, the site collection administrator often has no insight into the available storage outside of a particular site collection.

EXAM TIP

Capable monitoring of individual content databases is important, but understanding and addressing growth trends is even more important. Be extremely familiar with the process of moving site collections from one content database to another using PowerShell cmdlets, how to create a new content database attached to the same web application, and how to restrict the addition of new site collections to a content database that is already quite large.

Monitoring content databases

Central Administration does not provide a way for farm administrators to review the size of content databases. Windows PowerShell, on the other hand, provides a couple of different cmdlets for reviewing SharePoint databases.

- **Get-SPDatabase**   This is the more generic of the two commands, and it will retrieve information about all databases within a SharePoint farm: configuration, content, and service application.

- **Get-SPContentDatabase**   This focuses specifically on databases that possess SharePoint content.

EXAM TIP

Be familiar with these two very similar sounding cmdlets and the differences in their output.

A single web application might have multiple content databases; using the Get-SPContentDatabase cmdlet along with the -webapplication switch displays all the content databases associated with a particular web application (*http://departments.wingtiptoys.com*, shown in Figure 7-17).

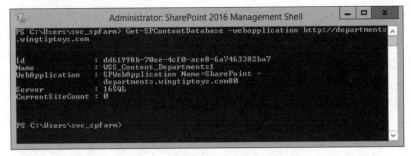

FIGURE 7-17 Retrieving content databases with the -webapplication switch

It's also possible to obtain the size of any individual database by assigning a variable to the Get-SPContentDatabase cmdlet along with the name of the individual content database and then querying the disksizerequired property to get the size in bytes:

```
$CDb = Get-SPContentDatabase -id <databasename>
```

```
$CDb.disksizerequired
```

This number can be divided by 1 GB to get the size in gigabytes:

```
$CDb.disksizerequired/1GB
```

IMPORTANT   There are certainly more sophisticated ways of retrieving the size of each content database, even grouping them by their associated web applications and URLs. This example was meant to be a very basic walkthrough.

Monitoring individual site collections via Windows PowerShell

Retrieving the size of a single site collection in Windows PowerShell is much less complicated than retrieving the size of an entire content database. The Get-SPSite Windows PowerShell cmdlet can be used along with a site collection's URL to retrieve its information. The size of the site collection is returned by using the usage property, as shown here:

```
$site = get-spsite -identity http://departments.wingtiptoys.com
```

```
$site.usage
```

Monitoring site collection content

Site collection administrators can monitor the consumption of storage within their respective site collection by using the new Storage Metrics page. This page is located in the Site Collection Administration section of Site Settings, and shows a graphic representation of all content within the current site collection (see Figure 7-18).

Product Catalog

Site Settings · Storage Metrics ⓘ

🗐 Site Collection

Type	Name	Total Size↓	% of Parent	
🗔	_catalogs	3.3 MB	77.56 %	▆
🗔	Style Library	333.5 KB	7.69 %	▪
🗔	Lists	59.8 KB	1.38 %	▪
🗔	Images	48.7 KB	1.12 %	▪
🗔	Site Collection Images	48.2 KB	1.11 %	▪

FIGURE 7-18 Storage metrics for a site collection

This report is far from being one dimensional; from here, a site collection administration can drill down into the content of an individual site collection, retrieving its storage metrics.

Monitor SharePoint hybrid cloud deployments

SharePoint hybrid is the sum of two different systems and the component functionality that binds them together. Items that might be hybridized between the two environments currently include Cloud Hybrid Search, OneDrive for Business, Hybrid Team Sites, Business Connectivity Services (BCS),, and Hybrid profiles.

Up to this point, monitoring of these two systems has been done individually:

- On-premises SharePoint installations can be monitored by using either out-of-the-box toolsets (ULS logs, event logs, and so on) or more advanced components, such as Systems Center Operations Manager 2012 or later.

- SharePoint Online installations have had little in the way of monitoring from a systems standpoint.

Microsoft Insights and Telemetry services will allow the SharePoint administrator to effectively monitor both on-premise and online versions of SharePoint, providing both systems-based and user analysis in one interface.

> **IMPORTANT**   At the time of publication for this Exam Ref, Microsoft SharePoint Insights has not yet been rolled out for use in a SharePoint 2016 hybrid environment. Once this functionality is made available, the supporting documentation will be found in the TechNet article entitled "Microsoft SharePoint Insights" at *https://technet.microsoft.com /library/86e0fc90-0ef8-4c22-9d3b-7af42bf882f1*.

Skill: Tune and optimize a SharePoint environment

Creating an effective SharePoint environment isn't a one-size-fits-all task. A careful examination of how the farm is intended to be used often exposes perceived weaknesses in the original design requirements. Add to that any requirements changes placed on the system by the user base, and you have a situation that is ripe with tuning potential.

The tuning and optimization portion of your project is the chance for you to tweak the underlying configuration of the farm, enabling you to both enhance performance metrics and avoid any limitations placed on the system by its original design.

> **This section covers how to:**
> - Plan and configure SQL optimization
> - Implement database maintenance rules
> - Plan for capacity software boundaries

- Estimate storage requirements
- Plan and configure caching and a caching strategy
- Tune network performance
- Plan and configure Zero Downtime Patching

Plan and configure SQL optimization

SharePoint administrators occasionally assume the role of itinerant SQL administrators for one of two reasons:

- Because the performance of the data tier directly affects the performance of an entire SharePoint farm, and SharePoint has very specific SQL requirements.

- If the organization has an SQL database administrator, there is an off chance that they might have never before been required to support the data tier of a SharePoint environment.

Knowing the behaviors, maintenance requirements, and performance characteristics of your content, configuration, and service application databases enables you to more clearly relate your desired strategy for long-term performance and growth goals to the SQL team.

Choosing a storage type

The type of storage configuration chosen for the SQL data tier will have a direct bearing on the performance of the completed SharePoint farm. In a server-based environment, storage is most often attached either directly to the server using direct attached storage (DAS) or attached via a storage area network (SAN). In either type of storage implementation, the way in which these disks are organized and grouped together can have a direct bearing on performance.

> **NEED MORE REVIEW?** Network attached storage (NAS) is supported only for Remote Blob Storage (RBS) in SharePoint 2016, and then only if the time to first byte in a response is less than 40 ms for more than 95 percent of the time. For more information about supported limits in SharePoint 2016, review the TechNet article entitled "Software boundaries and limits for SharePoint Server 2016" at *https://technet.microsoft.com/library/6a13cd9f-4b44-40d6-85aa-c70a8e5c34fe(v=office.16)*.

Within a SharePoint farm, the design of the farm and which service applications or functions are to be implemented determine what type of storage arrangement should be chosen. There are several configuration items that should be considered:

- Is the service application or function more sensitive to read or write speeds? Is there a balance to be had between the two?

  - On an Internet site on which people consume a lot of data, but that does not change often, you might want to focus on read speeds for your storage.

- For a series of collaboration sites in which the data itself is changing on a regular basis, you might choose to balance read and write speeds.
- For a service application such as Search or for the TempDB of an SQL instance, you might want to focus on write speeds for your storage.
- Is the storage mechanism chosen appropriate for the content being stored?
    - A RAID-5 storage array containing five 600-GB drives could store 2.4 TB of data (600 GB would be lost to maintain data parity). This array would be capable of withstanding a single drive failure and would have excellent read characteristics but less than optimal write performance characteristics.
    - A RAID-10 array using the same drives would require a total of eight 600-GB drives to provide the same amount of storage (2.4 TB for the data; 2.4 TB mirrored). This array would theoretically be able to withstand the failure of up to four drives (but only one per mirror set), but would offer superior read and write performance characteristics.

> **IMPORTANT**   RAID configurations are discussed in the next section.

RAID configuration levels

Redundant array of independent disks (RAID) is a technology that uses either hardware or software to group and organize hard drives into one or more volumes. The RAID level chosen can meet one of two possible objectives:

- **Redundancy**   Allows for the grouping of drives to be able to withstand the failure of one or more individual drives within the group.
- **Performance**   Altering the arrangement and configuration of drives within the group results in performance gains.

> **IMPORTANT**   Although you can choose to use software RAID in a production SharePoint farm, it is not recommended because the operating system of the server that hosts the storage is itself responsible for maintaining the RAID configuration. This maintenance consumes both memory and processor resources on the host system.

There are four RAID levels commonly used within the storage subsystems of a SharePoint farm (particularly within the data tier): 0, 1, 5, and 10:

- **RAID Level 0 (striping)**   This array type distributes the reads and writes across multiple physical drives (or spindles).
    - **Performance**   This arrangement offers the absolute best performance for both reads and writes in your storage subsystem.
    - **Redundancy**   This arrangement has absolutely no tolerance for any individual drive failures; if a single drive fails, the entire array is destroyed.
- **RAID Level 1 (mirroring)**   This array type uses an identical pair of disks or drive sets to ensure redundancy.

- **Performance**   This arrangement offers the same read performance as RAID Level 0 (assuming the same number of physical disks or spindles), but write speed is reduced as the number of input/output (I/O) write operations per disk is doubled.

- **Redundancy**   This arrangement can withstand the failure of a single drive or an entire drive set.

- **RAID Level 5 (block level striping with distributed parity)**   This array type distributes reads and writes across all drives, but also writes parity in a distributed fashion across all drives.

    - **Performance**   This arrangement offers the same read performance as RAID Level 0, but it incurs a fairly steep write penalty as the parity operation increases write overhead.

    - **Redundancy**   This arrangement can withstand the failure of a single drive within the drive set.

- **RAID Level 10 (striped mirror)**   This array type (known as a nested or hybrid RAID) combines RAID Levels 0 and 1 together, providing a high-performance and high-resiliency drive arrangement.

Performance prioritization

Within an SQL data tier, there are four distinct groupings of databases and files you should consider from a performance perspective. The assignment of these groupings to different storage types can have a dramatic effect on performance.

Although you could theoretically put all your databases on RAID-10 disk sets, doing so could be wasteful from a cost standpoint, providing limited benefit in some cases. Conversely, assigning write-heavy databases to a RAID-5 disk set would result in a heavy performance penalty.

From a performance standpoint, then, the four groupings of storage to consider are (in terms of priority from highest to lowest) as follows:

- TempDB files and transaction logs

    - If possible, assign these to RAID-10 storage.

    - Allocate dedicated disks for TempDB.

    - Number of TempDB files should be equal to the number of processor cores (hyper-threaded processors should be counted as one core).

    - All TempDB files should be the same size.

    - An average write operation should require no more than 20 ms.

- Database transaction log files

    - These should be on a separate volume from the data files.

    - If possible, assign them to RAID-10 storage.

    - These are write-intensive.

- Search databases

  - If possible, assign these to RAID-10 storage.

  - These are write-intensive.

- Database data files

  - These can be assigned to RAID-5 storage with the understanding that writes might be slower (for better performance, consider using RAID-10 storage).

  - These are read-intensive, especially useful for Internet-facing sites.

Pregrowing content databases and logs

Pregrowth is the act of preemptively growing a content database (or its associated log file) to a designated initial size. This size can be an estimate of how big you might expect the database or log to grow because the database administrator (DBA) can also shrink the files somewhat if not all of the space is eventually used.

Pregrowing a database has two benefits:

- **A reduction in overall I/O**   A database that has not been pregrown or grows in very small increments has to be expanded every time data is added, resulting in additional I/O load on the disk array and server.

- **A reduction in data disk fragmentation**   Small or frequent incremental data growth can result in defragmentation, reducing performance.

> **IMPORTANT**   The SQL model database (part of the system databases) can be used to control the initial size of newly created content databases. If you choose to do so, just remember that any new service application, configuration, or other databases will all echo the model database's initial size. Often, SharePoint administrators will configure the entire farm first (Central Administration/Configuration/Service Applications) and then alter the model database prior to creating content databases.

Pregrowing the database is done from within SQL Server Management Studio, as there is no way to configure initial database size from within Central Administration. Altering the initial size of a database is done by simply opening the properties of the content database and choosing a new initial size number, as shown in Figure 7-19.

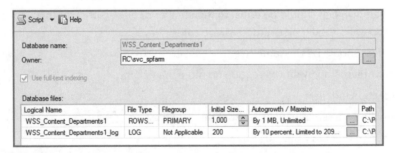

FIGURE 7-19 Altering the Initial Size setting of a database (pregrowth)

Configuring content database autogrowth

Autogrowth is the amount at which a database or its log grows after it reaches its current size limit. When a SharePoint content database is created from within Central Administration, its default autogrowth rate is set to 1 MB.

Such a configuration is far from ideal; if you had a database that was at its current size limit and you added a 10 MB file, the database file would have to be grown a total of 10 times before it would have enough room to store the file. Imagine how much I/O this could generate multiplied over 1,000 files!

> **IMPORTANT** The SQL model database (part of the system databases) cannot be used to control the autogrowth rate of newly created content databases. Get in the habit of altering the initial size and autogrowth metrics for a content database after its initial creation.

Configuring the autogrowth number for a database is done from within SQL Server Management Studio, as there is no way to configure this growth from within Central Administration. Altering the autogrowth of a database is done by simply opening the properties of the content database and choosing a growth number (in MB) or growth percentage, as shown in Figure 7-20.

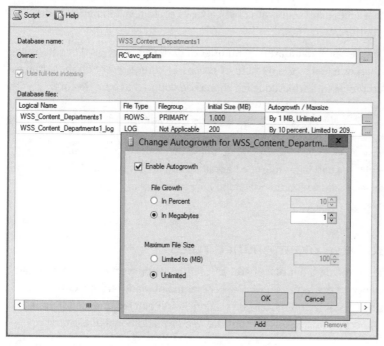

FIGURE 7-20 Altering the autogrowth values for a database

> **IMPORTANT**   It is never a good idea to limit the maximum file size of a SharePoint content database or its associated transaction log. Doing so can have unintended results and appear as an error to your users if the database attempts to exceed a hard limit.

> **EXAM TIP**
>
> Choosing to either adjust autogrowth rates or pre-grow a database might trigger the SharePoint Health Analyzer rule called Database, which has large amounts of unused space. This message can be safely ignored because you intend to eventually fill the available space with data.

Advanced content database performance

As content databases grow, their overall size can cause performance degradation. Depending on the content present in the database, separating the database into multiple smaller content databases might be impractical.

One of the potential solutions to this issue is to split a larger content database file into multiple smaller files that are still part of the same database. If you decide to go with this approach, spreading these files across separate physical disks could result in performance improvements, due to better I/O metrics.

As is the case with the TempDB database, the number of data files for any split content database should be less than or equal to the number of processor cores present on the database server. If hyperthreaded processors are used, each should be counted as a single core.

> **IMPORTANT**   Choosing to split content databases across multiple database files has a side effect where SharePoint administration is concerned: SharePoint Central Administration cannot be used to back up and restore a content database that is comprised of multiple files. After they are split, the databases must be backed up and restored from SQL Server because SharePoint specifically does not understand how to restore multiple files to the same content database.

Implement database maintenance rules

Errors or inconsistencies in the data tier of a SharePoint farm environment can have dramatic effects on the performance of the farm as a whole. Regular maintenance from a database standpoint results in a more stable and better performing SharePoint experience for your users, often resulting in performance gains without the need for additional equipment or reconfiguration.

Health Analyzer rules

In previous versions of SharePoint, it was often necessary for either the SharePoint administrator or SQL DBA to perform this behind-the-scenes maintenance from within SQL Server Management Studio. Fortunately, the newer versions of SharePoint have new Health Analyzer rules that address both defragmentation and statistics maintenance, removing these administrative tasks as regular maintenance items.

A Health Analyzer rules definition can be found in Central Administration in the Monitoring, Health, Review Rule Definitions menu. Within the Performance section, there are three rules that are all enabled and set to automatically repair any related issues on a daily basis (see Table 7-5).

TABLE 7-5 Health rules for database indexing and statistics

Health Rule	Schedule	Enabled	Repair Automatically
Databases used by SharePoint have fragmented indices	Daily	Yes	Yes
Databases used by SharePoint have outdated index statistics	Daily	Yes	Yes
Search: One or more crawl databases may have fragmented indices	Daily	Yes	Yes

Plan for capacity software boundaries

Boundaries are absolute limits within SharePoint that were created by design and cannot be exceeded. Although these boundaries are few in number when compared with the sheer quantity of options and settings available, they shape the design of a SharePoint infrastructure.

This boundary structure is present in many of the logical components of a SharePoint farm. Although not present in each level, boundaries exist at the following levels:

- Web applications
- Content databases
- Site collections
- Lists and libraries
- Search
- Business Connectivity Services
- Workflows
- PerformancePoint Service
- Word Automation Service
- Office Online Service
- Project Server
- SharePoint Add-ins
- Distributed Cache Service
- Miscellaneous limits

EXAM TIP

Although there are dozens of supported limits and boundaries in SharePoint, there are a few that every administrator should know by heart. Items such as maximum file size, zones in a farm, and crawl document size limits are all good metrics to be familiar with.

Estimate storage requirements

Because SharePoint is heavily dependent on SQL for its storage needs, the proper allocation of storage resources is a critical design element for the SharePoint farm. This design can be broken down into two major components, storage and I/O operations per second (IOPS).

Storage variables

Storage is simply the amount of available space configured for a particular database. If the database happens to be a content database, the overall size of the database can vary dramatically based on two features: recycle bins and auditing.

Recycle bins are enabled by default at both the site (web) and site collection (site) levels. A document that is deleted from a site occupies space in the associated content database until it is deleted from both the first- and second-stage recycle bins. If you foresee the need to delete many documents in the interest of reclaiming space, the documents must be deleted from both recycle bins.

Auditing can place a lesser storage demand on a content database. If you expect to use auditing in a particular content database, try to restrict the levels at which it is enabled rather than enabling auditing on entire site collections.

EXAM TIP

Recycle bins are some of the most straightforward and most misunderstood components in SharePoint. Knowing and understanding how a document moves from one stage recycle bin to another is key to understanding how documents that are "hidden" might be consuming space.

I/O operations per second

IOPS is the measure of how many input and output operations per second are available from your I/O subsystem (storage). The storage configuration influences both the read and write speeds available for use.

Stress testing a storage subsystem enables you to know the limits of your storage and also gives you an opportunity to tune it to your requirements. There are three main tools used for this purpose (see Table 7-6), each of which is free of charge.

TABLE 7-6 I/O subsystem testing tools

Tool	Provided By	Purpose	Download Location
SQLIO	Microsoft	Performance capacity (single I/O type at a time)	*https://www.microsoft.com/download/details .aspx?id=20163*
IOMeter	Open source	Performance capacity (combination of I/O types at one time)	*http://sourceforge.net/projects/iometer/*
SQLIOSim	Microsoft	Simulates SQL I/O patterns	*http://support.microsoft.com/kb/231619*

Estimating configuration storage and IOPS requirements

The SharePoint configuration database and Central Administration content database have fairly meager storage requirements. Both databases use a negligible amount of space; you can safely plan for less than 1 GB each for the configuration database and Central Administration content database storage. Although the configuration database itself will not grow to a great degree, the supporting transaction log can grow to be quite large and should be backed up (for truncation purposes) on a regular basis.

Estimating service application storage and IOPS requirements

Service applications vary wildly in terms of storage and IOPS requirements. The largest consumer of service application resources is Search, consuming the lion's share of available storage and IOPS resources. At the other end of the scale are the State, Word Automation, and PerformancePoint Service applications, each of which requires minimal IOPS and approximately 1 GB of allocated storage.

> **NEED MORE REVIEW?** Detailed information concerning performance and scaling metrics is given in the TechNet article "Storage and SQL Server capacity planning and configuration (SharePoint Server 2016)" at *https://technet.microsoft.com/library/cc298801(v=office.16) .aspx*.

Plan and configure caching and a caching strategy

Caching within SharePoint 2016 is an effective mechanism for increasing the performance of page and content delivery to the requesting user. As stated earlier in this chapter, SharePoint uses a combination of three distinct technologies to deliver this enhanced performance: ASP. NET output cache, BLOB cache, and object cache.

> **IMPORTANT** Some of the following configurations involve altering the Web.config of a web application. When this file is saved after having been changed, it automatically recycles its associated web application, potentially disrupting service to your users. It is advisable to make these configuration changes after hours.

Planning and configuring the ASP.NET output cache

The output cache present in SharePoint 2016 stores several different versions of a rendered page; these versions are permissions dependent, based on the permissions level of the person who is attempting to view the page. Settings for this cache can be configured at the site collection and site levels, and also configured for page layouts. Additionally, the Web.config file for a web application can be altered with the output cache profile settings; these settings will then override any settings made at the site collection level (or below).

> **IMPORTANT** SharePoint implements the ASP.NET output cache, but refers to it simply as the page output cache in most site settings menus; from this point forward, we'll use this reference.

CACHE PROFILES

Prior to enabling the page output cache, you can review the site collection cache profiles that will be used in the output cache in the site settings of your site collection. In Site Settings, select the Site Collection Administration section; under Site Collection, select Cache Profiles.

Four profiles exist by default:

- **Disabled**   Caching is not enabled.
- **Public Internet (Purely Anonymous)**   Optimized for sites that serve the same content to all users with no authentication check.
- **Extranet (Published Site)**   Optimized for a public extranet in which no authoring takes place and no Web Parts are changed by the users.
- **Intranet (Collaboration Site)**   Optimized for collaboration sites in which authoring, customization, and other write-intensive operations take place.

You can also create a new cache profile if none of these suits your needs.

EXAM TIP

The use of the page output cache requires that the Publishing Infrastructure feature be active for the site collection and that the Publishing feature be active for the particular site. After the Publishing feature is enabled, so, too, is the output cache (using default settings).

ENABLING THE PAGE OUTPUT CACHE (WEB APPLICATION LEVEL)

Enabling the page output cache at the web application level overrides all other page output cache settings at the site collection, site, or page layout levels.

To enable the page output cache, follow these steps:

1. Open Internet Information Services (IIS) Manager and select the Website that you want to configure.

2. Select Web.config and then open with the editor of your choice.

3. Search for the OutputCache Profiles XML entry:

```
<OutputCacheProfiles useCacheProfileOverrides="false" varyByHeader=""
varyByParam="*" varyByCustom="" varyByRights="true" cacheForEditRights="false" />
```

4. Change the useCacheProfileOverrides attribute from false to true, then save and close the Web.config file.

> **IMPORTANT** Saving this change will result in an outage while the site is restarted in IIS.

EXAM TIP

Although setting the page output cache at the web application level is highly effective, changes made at this level have to be made on the Web.config files of each front-end server and should be included in your farm documentation. Unless there is a compelling reason not to, it is recommended to instead enable configuration of the page output cache at the site collection level, which requires no system outage for additional changes.

ENABLING THE PAGE OUTPUT CACHE (SITE COLLECTION LEVEL)

Enabling the page output cache within a publishing site collection is done within the Site Collection Administration menu.

1. In Site Settings, select the Site Collection Administration section and then select Site Collection Output Cache.

2. In the Output Cache section, choose to enable or disable the output cache.

3. In the Default Page Output Cache Profile section, you have the opportunity to choose from the cache profiles mentioned earlier:

   A. For the Anonymous Cache Profile: Choose from Disabled, Public Internet, Extranet, or Intranet.

   B. For the Authenticated Cache Profile: Choose from Disabled, Extranet, or Intranet.

4. Page Output Cache Policy enables you to delegate control of the cache policy:

   A. Whether publishing subsite owners can choose a different page output cache profile.

   B. Whether page layouts can use a different page output cache profile.

5. Debug Cache Information (optional) enables you to enable debug cache information on pages for troubleshooting cache contents.

ENABLING THE PAGE OUTPUT CACHE (SITE LEVEL)

If previously delegated by the site collection administrator, page output cache settings can be configured at the subsite level from the Site Administration menu.

1. In Site Settings, select the Site Administration section and then select Site Output Cache.

2. On the Publishing Site Output Cache page, you can choose the Page Output Cache Profile:

    A. Anonymous Cache Profile can either inherit the parent site's profile or select a profile (Disabled, Public Internet, Extranet, or Intranet).

    B. Authenticated Cache Profile can either inherit the parent site's profile or select a profile (Disabled, Extranet, or Intranet).

3. Optionally, you can select the check box to apply these settings to all subsites.

ENABLING THE PAGE OUTPUT CACHE BY PAGE LAYOUT

If previously delegated by the site collection administrator, page output cache settings can be configured on a per-page layout basis from the Master Pages And Page Layouts menu.

1. In Site Settings, in the Web Designer Galleries section, select the Master Pages And Page Layouts section.

2. On the Master Page Gallery page, choose a page layout and then select its drop-down menu.

3. After selecting the Edit Properties value, you are presented with the Properties page. Scroll down to the bottom and you can select either or both authenticated or anonymous cache profiles.

4. On the ribbon, in the Commit section, click the Save icon to close the settings.

Planning and configuring the BLOB cache

The BLOB cache is used to prestage branding (*.gif, .jpg, .css, .js*), image, sound, video, and other files that are stored in SQL as BLOBs. This is a disk-based caching technique that stores these items on the web tier servers within your farm.

The purpose of storing these items on the web tier is to directly benefit from not having to retrieve these larger files from the content databases stored on the SQL data tier. This caching mechanism is enabled or disabled on each web tier server on a per-web application basis by modifying Web.config and adding the following XML:

```
<BlobCache location="{drive letter}:\BlobCache\16" path="\.(gif|jpg|jpeg|jpe|jfif|bmp|d
ib|tif|tiff|themedbmp|themedcss|themedgif|themedjpg|themedpng|ico|png|wdp|hdp|css|js|as
f|avi|flv|m4v|mov|mp3|mp4|mpeg|mpg|rm|rmvb|wma|wmv|ogg|ogv|oga|webm|xap)$" maxSize="10"
enabled="false" />
```

There are a few settings in this piece of XML that are of interest.

- Although both the location and file folder details can be changed, the change should be uniform on all web tier servers.

- The path item does not indicate the path on the file system, but instead the types of files (BLOB) that can be stored on the file system.

- The maxSize entry indicates the size in gigabytes (GB) for the BLOB cache; any changes to this value should be made uniformly on all web tier servers.

- The maxSize value should never be less than 10 GB, but can (and should) be grown to roughly 20 percent bigger than the expected BLOB content.

- Changing the enabled value from false to true activates the BLOB cache.

Planning and configuring the object cache

The object cache in SharePoint 2016 is used to store objects in the memory of the front-end SharePoint farm servers, thus reducing the amount of traffic between these servers and the SQL data tier. These objects—which include lists and libraries, site settings, and page layouts—are used by the Publishing feature when it renders webpages on the site.

> **IMPORTANT** The use of the object cache requires that the Publishing feature be active on your site. After the Publishing feature is enabled, so, too, is the object cache (using default settings).

ACTIVATING THE OBJECT CACHE

The object cache relies on a series of settings, which can be found at Site Settings, Site Collection Administration, Site Collection Object Cache:

1. In Site Settings, select the Site Collection Administration section and then select Site Collection Object Cache.

2. In the Object Cache Size section, specify the maximum cache size in MB (default is 100 MB). Remember that this cache space comes directly out of RAM of each server in your web tier.

3. In the Object Cache Reset section, you will normally leave these values cleared. From here, you can not only flush the object cache of the current server (by selecting Object Cache Flush) but also that of the farm (by selecting Force All Servers In The Farm To Flush Their Object Cache).

4. In the Cross List Query Cache Changes section, you can configure the behavior of cross list queries, such as Content Query Web Parts. You have the choice of either precaching the results of such a query for a specified period of time (the default is 60 seconds) or forcing the server to check for changes every time a query is performed (which is more accurate from a results standpoint, but results in slower performance).

5. In the Cross List Query Results Multiplier section, you can choose a multiplier value ranging from 1 to 10 (3 is the default). This number should be increased if your site has unique security applied to many lists or libraries, but it can also be reduced if your site does not have as many unique permissions. A smaller multiplier uses less memory per query.

> **IMPORTANT** The object cache size can also be controlled at the web application level by altering the Web.config <ObjectCache maxSize="100" /> line.

Tune network performance

Although there are significant networking improvements present in both the Windows Server 2002 and 2016 platforms, some minor alterations to your SharePoint 2016 network environment can result in significant performance gains.

Domain controllers and authentication

A SharePoint Server 2016 farm can potentially place a significant authentication load on domain controllers (DCs) within your network. As general guidance, Microsoft recommends that you deploy a new DC per every three web tier servers present in your SharePoint farm.

> **IMPORTANT** It should be noted that the DC for this task should not be a read-only DC.

Separating client and intrafarm network traffic

A SharePoint Server 2016 environment can start on only a single server and grow into an environment consisting of several servers in a MinRole environment. Depending on the arrangement chosen, a SharePoint environment could potentially have client and intraserver traffic traversing the same interfaces, potentially disrupting or slowing services for SharePoint users.

Consider installing two network adapters on each front-end server:

- One connected to a client subnet/virtual local area network (VLAN) that serves client requests.
- The other connected to an intraserver subnet/VLAN that enables interserver connectivity.

EXAM TIP

Network administration is not a core requirement for being a SharePoint administrator; however, knowing how concepts such as subnets and VLANs can work to separate client and server communications might be key to understanding a very simple way to improve SharePoint connectivity and performance.

Plan and configure Zero Downtime Patching

In Chapter 1 we discussed how an environment could be made resilient using at least two servers for each role (three for the distributed cache service), as shown in Figure 7-21. Designing a farm with resiliency in mind not only improves farm availability, but also provides the opportunity to maintain the farm without the need to provide an outage window.

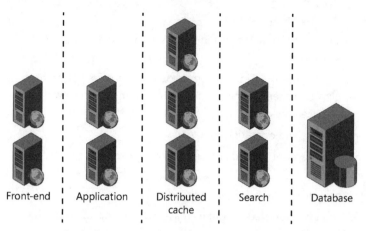

FIGURE 7-21 Designing an environment for resiliency using a five tier server farm.

In SharePoint 2013, it was possible to approximate a zero downtime schedule for software updates to SharePoint 2013. SharePoint update binaries could be applied to a server that had been temporarily removed from rotation; when added back in, that server would continue to run in backward compatibility mode. This process could be completed on each SharePoint server in the farm, resulting in no downtime.

Once the binaries had been installed to the SharePoint farm, the next step was to update the farm as a whole. At this point, using the SharePoint Configuration Wizard would not be the preferred option, as it would upgrade content databases sequentially; instead, using multiple instances of the Upgrade-SPContentDatabase cmdlet with the -UseSnapshot option would allow you to upgrade the databases in parallel (shortening the overall upgrade window) and allowing read-only access to the snapshot.

During this process, the SharePoint farm is available from a read-only standpoint during the upgrade, but cannot be used in a read-write capacity until the process is complete; thus, it doesn't technically meet the definition of Zero Downtime.

> **NEED MORE REVIEW?** The -UseSnapshot option will not be used in SharePoint 2016 Zero Downtime operations, as it places the content databases in a read-only state. For more information, review the TechNet blog article by Stefan Goßner called "SharePoint Server 2016 Zero-Downtime Patching demystified" at *https://blogs.technet.microsoft.com /stefan_gossner/2016/04/29/sharepoint-2016-zero-downtime-patching-demystified/*.

Preparing for a Zero Downtime update

Given the resiliency requirements for this process, it is recommended that an inspection of the current farm status is in order before proceeding. The following upgrade conditions should be met:

- All front-end servers should be in a functioning load balancer rotation.
  - During the upgrade process, the SharePoint farm administrator will need to work closely with the administrator of any external load balancer appliance.

- All farm servers should be operating properly.
  - Perform checks such as reviewing any errors in Event Viewer and determining if enough disk space is available.
  - For the Search role servers, use the Get-SPEnterpriseSearchStatus cmdlet or the Manage Service Applications menu within Central Administration to review the status of the Search service application.
- All databases should be active and operating properly.
  - Make sure that databases are set to read and write in SharePoint and that they are online.
  - Check the Health Analyzer for any database orphans.
  - Notify the SQL DBA that your upgrade might increase I/O demands on both the SQL and storage (SAN) subsystems.

> **IMPORTANT** Never proceed with any upgrade (whether it's build-to-build or version-to-version) on a farm that is in an inconsistent state.

Using the in-place upgrade method (with backward compatibility)

In a Zero Downtime cycle, the Web, App, and Distributed cache tier servers are individually removed from rotation, patched, and then returned to service. Search is also included in this cycle, but it is the one component that does have a minimal downtime window (while the Search service application is suspended).

The Zero Downtime cycle is broken into two major phases:

- **Update phase** During this phase, the contents of the SharePoint update are installed to each server in the farm, in a sequence that starts with the Front-end servers and continues through Application, Search, and Distributed cache servers.
- **Upgrade phase** During this phase, member servers in the farm are upgraded, starting with the Application server hosting Central Administration and continuing through the Front-end, Search, and other Application servers.

> **IMPORTANT** Neither the Configuration Wizard nor the Upgrade-SPContentDatabase cmdlet should be run in the Update phase.

> **NEED MORE REVIEW?** The process for updating an entire SharePoint 2016 farm using Zero Downtime Patching can be complex, depending on the roles you've enabled. For an in-depth understanding of exactly what needs to occur during this process, review the TechNet article entitled "Install a software update for SharePoint Server 2016" at *https://technet.microsoft.com/library/ff806338(v=office.16).aspx*.

Skill: Troubleshoot a SharePoint environment

Now that users and departments are being migrated to the SharePoint environment, the focus of the SharePoint administrative team changes to the monitoring and troubleshooting of the new environment. Monitoring thus far has been a reactionary tactic, as production SLAs might not yet be in place; as a result, the current user load (and any remaining configuration items) have the potential to create issues that will require attention.

Administering the new farm from a proactive versus reactive standpoint is critical at this juncture. Establishing a baseline for how the farm will perform provides the SharePoint administrative team with the ability to quickly identify any performance or configuration anomalies before they become issues observed by the user base as a whole.

This section covers how to:
- Establish baseline performance
- Perform client-side tracing
- Perform server-side tracing
- Analyze usage data
- Enable a developer dashboard
- Analyze diagnostic logs
- Troubleshoot SharePoint hybrid cloud issues

Establish baseline performance

Immediately after your staging environment (or production, if you don't have the resources for staging) has been finalized, you have an opportunity to define the baseline performance of your SharePoint environment.

At this point, we are not talking about performance testing (what the system is capable of when it is working at maximum capacity), but rather what the nominal or expected operation of the system looks like from a logging standpoint. The optimal goal is to have a statistical sampling of what the environment looks like as it adjusts to varying levels of user demand on a regular interval. For instance, odds are that a system is much busier at 9:00 on Monday morning than it is at 9:00 on Saturday night (assuming a standard work week).

Baselining your SharePoint environment

A core SharePoint 2106 MinRole-compliant farm includes Front-end, Application, and Distributed cache servers. Moving beyond the core configuration, farm services can be provided by servers that perform Search, Workflow Manager, Office Online, and Custom roles within the farm.

Performing a baseline capture of the chosen architecture prior to releasing it to production status allows the administrator to glean some understanding of how each of the service configurations performs in the completed farm, both from a duration and initial capacity standpoint.

> **IMPORTANT** The baseline monitoring changes here are not intended to be left running for an extended period of time, as they can be resource intensive from a processor, memory, and storage standpoint. Use these items to establish a baseline for the farm, then return the configured values to their normal settings in the early production stages of the SharePoint 2016 farm.

Configuring monitoring

Monitoring a SharePoint 2016 farm can use a combination of settings from the Monitoring section within Central Administration:

- **Diagnostic Logging** Diagnostic Logging can be used to select the categories and severity of events that will be recorded to the Event log and Trace log. At this point, Event log flooding protection should be disabled, after first ensuring that enough disk space is available where the Event log is stored.

- **Timer Job Scheduling** The Timer Jobs, Job Definitions menu can be used to ensure that the Microsoft SharePoint Foundation Usage Data Import is scheduled to run every five minutes.

- **Diagnostic Providers** While still in the Job Definitions menu, all following Diagnostic Data Providers should be enabled (except for SQL Blocking Queries, which is already enabled by default). The schedule for the Performance Counters—Database Servers and Performance Counters—should be already set to run every minute.

- **Usage Data Collection** On the Configure Usage And Health Data Collection page, you can choose to enable usage data collection (this should be enabled for monitoring purposes), and in the Events To Log section, the following items should be selected: Content Import Usage, Content Export Usage, Page Requests, Feature Use, Search Query Use, Site Inventory Usage, Timer Jobs, and Rating Usage.

> **NEED MORE REVIEW?** In addition to the SharePoint items that can be recorded in the usage database, performance counters can be added from both an operating system and SQL standpoint using the Add-SPDiagnosticsPerformanceCounter cmdlet. For a clearer understanding of how monitoring is configured for SharePoint, review the TechNet article "Monitoring and maintaining SharePoint Server 2013" at *https://technet.microsoft.com /library/ff758658.aspx*.

Perform client-side tracing

Trace logs, which contain information such as stack traces and informational messages, are available on both Windows clients and Windows servers. The example shown here configures the only SharePoint functionality currently available for a client-side trace: BCS.

IMPORTANT Client-side tracing using PerfMon is only available in Windows Vista, Windows 7, Windows 8, and Windows 8.1 clients. Windows 10 does not have this functionality, which has largely been replaced by the Developer Dashboard.

Enabling a new client-side trace

Trace logging is not enabled by default, but it can be activated from within PerfMon by generating a new data collector set on a Windows client machine. Trace logging can have an effect on performance, so it is recommended that this functionality not be enabled unless required for troubleshooting efforts.

To perform client-side tracing, follow these steps:

1. Run *Perfmon.exe*.

2. In the left pane, expand the Data Collector Sets section and then right-click User Defined.

3. From the New menu, select Data Collector Set.

4. When the Create New Data Collector Set dialog box opens, enter a name for the set and select Create Manually (Advanced). Click Next.

5. On the What Type Of Data Do You Want To Include? page, leave the Create Data Logs option selected and select the Event Trace Data check box. Click Next.

6. On the Which Event Trace Providers Would You Like To Enable? page, select Add.

7. In the Event Trace Provider dialog box, scroll down and select the Microsoft-Office-Business Connectivity Services event trace provider and then click OK.

8. Returning to the Which Event Trace Providers Would You Like To Enable? page, verify that your new provider is shown and then click Next.

9. On the Where Would You Like The Data To Be Saved? page, you can choose a new location or leave the default. Make a note of this location and then click Finish.

Running the new client trace

Now that the trace has been configured, it is available to run as desired from within PerfMon, as follows:

1. Run *Perfmon.exe*.

2. In the left pane, expand Data Collector Sets and then expand User Defined, selecting your recently configured trace.

3. Right-click your data collector set and click Start.

4. Perform the BCS activities for which you want to capture trace data.

5. After you complete your activities, stop the trace by right-clicking the data collector set and selecting Stop.

Reviewing the client trace results

The results of the client trace can be reviewed from within Event Viewer. Follow these steps:

1. Run *Eventvwr.exe*.

2. On the Action menu, select Open Saved Log.

3. In the Open Saved Log dialog box, navigate to the location in which you specified the data should be saved when you created the data collector set.

4. Within this folder, you see one or more folders. The name of each of these subfolders begins with the machine name and then the year, month, and date in which the trace was performed. Expand this folder.

5. Within this folder is an *.etl* file. Open this file in Event Viewer.

6. Correlation (activity) IDs are generated on both the server and the client when items are created, updated, or deleted in external data. The Correlation ID column might not appear by default.

7. To display the Correlation ID column, on the View menu, select Add/Remove Columns.

Perform server-side tracing

Server-side tracing is captured within the trace log on the SharePoint Server. Used in conjunction with client-side tracing, it is possible to watch a particular activity from both the server's and the client's point of view.

Continuing with the previous example, the logging of BCS is already enabled on the SharePoint farm. To verify its logging trace level, do the following:

1. Open Central Administration and select Monitoring.

2. In the Reporting section, select Configure Diagnostic Logging.

3. Expand the Business Connectivity Services entry and ensure that Business Data is set to at least the Medium trace level.

4. Analyze the ULS log entries, looking for information about two categories:

   - BDC_Shared_Services
   - SS_Shared_Service

Analyze usage data

Using the built-in views provided in the logging database, you can review the different metrics that are captured in the SharePoint usage and health collection intervals. This information not only can be viewed in SSMS, but can also be exported as a comma-separated value (*.csv*) file to Microsoft Excel for further analysis.

EXAM TIP

SharePoint farm administrators are becoming more and more versatile. One of the key tool sets we are learning to master is the simple SQL Server Management Services tool. Understand how to connect to a server, run a simple query, and view the result.

To begin viewing logging data in SSMS, do the following:

1. Open SSMS and connect to the SQL instance providing data services to your SharePoint farm (see Figure 7-22).

FIGURE 7-22 Connecting to SQL Server

2. Select the logging database (WSSUsageApplication, by default) and then select the plus (+) sign to show all its components. Expand Views and then select a view from which you'd want to collect information (dbo.FileUsage is shown in Figure 7-23).

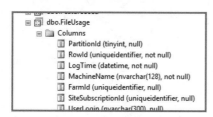

FIGURE 7-23 The dbo.FileUsage view

3. Right-click the view and choose Select Top 1000 Rows. The SQL Query appears in the top pane, and the lower pane shows the query results (see Figure 7-24).

FIGURE 7-24 Query results for the selection

These results can now be exported to a *.csv* file for viewing and analysis in Microsoft Excel by choosing Save Results As in the Results window at the bottom of the console. Opening and importing the *.csv* file in Excel enables you to display and interact with the data (see Figure 7-25).

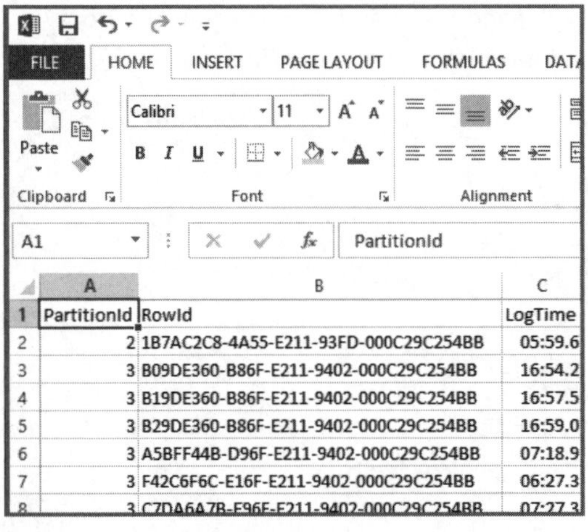

FIGURE 7-25 The results shown in an Excel file

Enable a developer dashboard

The Developer Dashboard is a tool that can be used to analyze the performance of your SharePoint pages. When enabled, this tool can be used by anyone with the Add and Customize Pages permission level (or greater).

The Developer Dashboard now appears in its own browser window, making it easier to interact with and navigate to the desired SharePoint page while still providing a dedicated view into the performance of that page.

Developer Dashboard settings

In SharePoint 2016, three properties still exist in Windows PowerShell (Off, On, and On Demand), but there are effectively only two settings: Off and On. When you specify On, you are really specifying On Demand because you must select the Developer Dashboard icon in the ribbon to cause it to appear. If you choose On Demand, you receive the same result.

EXAM TIP

The Developer Dashboard is an indispensable tool for a SharePoint troubleshooter, especially because it can retrieve correlation IDs and their meaning from the back-end server. Understand how to enable this tool via Windows PowerShell and also how to activate, deactivate, and use this tool at a basic level.

Enabling Developer Dashboard using Windows PowerShell

To enable Developer Dashboard, you have to set a variable for the Developer Dashboard Settings object and then change its Properties:

```
$devdash=[Microsoft.SharePoint.Administration.SPWebService]::ContentService.
DeveloperDashboardSettings

$devdash.DisplayLevel = "On"

$devdash.Update()
```

To reverse the change, all you have to do is set the DisplayLevel property to a value of "Off" and then do another Update().

Activating Developer Dashboard from a SharePoint page

Once the Developer Dashboard is enabled, a new icon appears on the header to the right of Share, Follow, and Focus on Content links, as shown in Figure 7-26.

FIGURE 7-26 The Developer Dashboard icon

When this icon is selected, the Developer Dashboard appears in a new browser window. Selecting any of the HTTP GET Requests displays the overall metrics required for the particular page to be rendered, as shown in Figure 7-27.

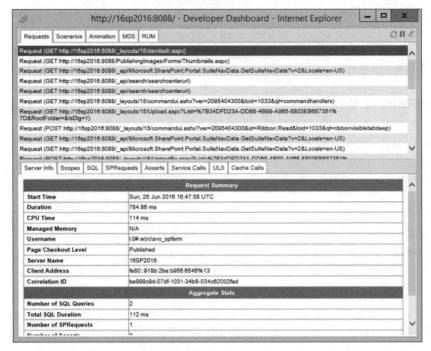

FIGURE 7-27 Developer Dashboard, displaying the request and summary information

Analyze diagnostic logs

Each server in a SharePoint farm maintains a series of diagnostics logs known as ULS logs, which are contained by default in *%ProgramFiles%\Common Files\Microsoft Shared\Web Server Extensions\16\Logs* and are saved in 30-minute increments (default).

> **IMPORTANT** ULS log files are in standard *.txt* format. ULS log files are named in the format *servername-yyyymmdd-hhhh* where the hour indicated (in 24-hour format) indicates the beginning time of the log.

These logs are not available to be viewed through Central Administration, but can be viewed by using the following:

- A text editor such as Notepad
- Windows PowerShell
- Developer Dashboard
- A third-party tool

ULS logging levels

There are six possible logging levels available to be reported within the trace log: none, unexpected, monitorable, high, medium, and verbose. Table 7-7 provides insight into what each level of logging entails.

TABLE 7-7 ULS logging levels

Level	Definition
None	No trace logs are written to the file system.
Unexpected	This level is used to log messages about events that cause solutions to stop processing. When set to log at this level, the log includes only events at this level.
Monitorable	This level is used to log messages about any unrecoverable events that limit the solution's functionality but do not stop the application. When set to log at this level, the log also includes critical errors (unexpected level).
High	This level is used to log any events that are unexpected but do not stall the processing of a solution. When set to log at this level, the log will include warnings, errors (monitorable level), and critical errors (unexpected level).
Medium	When set to this level, the trace log includes everything except verbose messages. This level is used to log all high-level information about operations that were performed. At this level, there is enough detail logged to construct the data flow and sequence of operations. This level of logging can be used by administrators or support professionals to troubleshoot issues.
Verbose	When set to log at this level, the log includes messages at all other levels. Almost all actions that are performed are logged when you use this level. Verbose tracing produces many log messages. This level is typically used only for debugging in a development environment.

Troubleshoot SharePoint hybrid cloud issues

The process required for understanding issues within a hybrid implementation is nearly identical to that required for an entirely on-premises solution. Diagnostic logging is configured using a series of counters that are used to capture metrics for both on-premises and Office 365 implementations of SharePoint.

A series of categories, shown in Table 7-8, can be monitored to gather a better understanding of issues within the SharePoint farm.

TABLE 7-8 Monitoring Categories

Category	Requirement
Secure Store Service	Select this top-level category and all subcategories.
SharePoint Foundation	Select this top-level category and all subcategories.
Services Infrastructure	Select this top-level category and all subcategories.
SharePoint Portal Server	Select the Claims Authentication, User Profiles, and Soap Server Exception subcategories.

Category	Requirement
SharePoint Server	Select the Distributed Cache, Logging Correlation Data, and Shared Services subcategories.
SharePoint Server Search	Select this top-level category and all subcategories (only if configuring a hybrid search solution).
Business Connectivity Services	Select this top-level category and all subcategories (only if configuring a hybrid BCS solution).

Troubleshooting toolsets

Aside from the soon-to-be-released SharePoint Insights hybrid service (more on this in a bit), there are a series of tools that can be used to troubleshoot SharePoint installations, but these still primarily focus on onsite deployments, and can generally only provide basic monitoring (up or down) of the relationship between on-premises and online deployments of SharePoint. These tools are shown in Table 7-9.

Resource	Scope	Notes
Remote Connectivity Analyzer	Single Sign On	Remote Connectivity Analyzer is a free connectivity test platform for Office 365. It tests the availability of the required Office 365 SSO service endpoint for expected behavior by acting upon those services from the Internet.
SharePoint Server ULS logs	SharePoint Server	ULS logs are the single most important source of SharePoint Server troubleshooting information.
ULS Viewer	SharePoint Server	ULS Viewer allows users to open SharePoint Server ULS log files and display their contents in a user-friendly format, with advanced functions such as filtering, sorting, highlighting, and reading real-time logging data.
Log Parser 2.2	SharePoint Server and other on-premises logs	Log Parser is a powerful, versatile tool that provides universal query access to text-based data such as log files, XML files, CSV files, and key data sources on the Windows operating system such as the Event Log, the Registry, the file system, and Active Directory.
Fiddler	Web traffic debugging	Fiddler is a web debugging proxy that logs all HTTP and HTTPS traffic between your computer and the Internet. Fiddler allows you to inspect traffic, set breakpoints, and "fiddle" with incoming or outgoing data.
Microsoft Network Monitor 3.4	Network protocol analysis	Network Monitor 3.4 is a protocol analyzer. It allows you to capture network traffic and view and analyze it and is extensible with a range of experts and parsers for the analysis of specific kinds of traffic.

NEED MORE REVIEW? For a more in-depth understanding of how to troubleshoot hybrid SharePoint environments, review the TechNet article "Troubleshooting hybrid environments" at *https://technet.microsoft.com/library/dn518363.aspx*.

IMPORTANT Help is on the way! The Microsoft Insights and Telemetry components are not present in the product (as of the publication date of this book), but the Microsoft Insights service is already in place, awaiting activation via cumulative update. Once this tool is in place, monitoring of both environments should become a much easier process. When this functionality is made available, the supporting documentation will be found in the TechNet article entitled "Microsoft SharePoint Insights" at *https://technet.microsoft.com/library/86e0fc90-0ef8-4c22-9d3b-7af42bf882f1*.

Summary

- SLAs provide an understanding of performance between IT and the business, consisting of definitions for downtime, scheduled downtime, and monthly uptime percentages.

- SharePoint Server 2016 farms can be monitored at the server, service application, site collection, and site levels.

- Performance Monitor (PerfMon) captures component information about the member servers of the SharePoint farm, including information about the application itself as well as operating system metrics.

- Data collection sets are used to gather groupings of metrics together for use in performance monitoring.

- Data collection sets can be saved as templates for regular use.

- Page performance monitoring includes counters for the ASP.NET output cache, the BLOB cache, and the page object cache.

- Usage and Health Data Collection allows the SharePoint administrator an effective mechanism for gathering counters and other logging information from all farm member servers into a centralized database.

- Three timer jobs are responsible for the collection and aggregation of logging data in a SharePoint 2016 farm: the Microsoft SharePoint Foundation Usage Data Import, Usage Data Maintenance, and Usage Data Processing jobs.

- The Get-SPDatabase cmdlet is used to retrieve information about all databases within a SharePoint farm (configuration, content, and service application), whereas the Get-SPContentDatabase cmdlet is focused specifically on SharePoint content databases.

- SharePoint-supported storage includes DAS and SAN. NAS is also supported, but only for RBS and only if the time to first byte in a response is less than 40 ms for more than 95 percent of the time.

- Performance prioritization (from highest to lowest) from an SQL standpoint would include TempDB files and transaction logs, database transaction logs, Search databases, then database data files.

- Content databases should never be configured to have a maximum size in SSMS.
- Health Analyzer rules handle routine database maintenance such as correcting fragmented indices and outdated index statistics.
- SQLIO, IOMeter, and SQLIOSim are tools that can be used to accurately gauge the performance potential of a disk subsystem.
- The page output cache can be enabled at the web application, site collection, site, or page layout levels.
- The BLOB cache stores large content on the local drive of a Front-end server.
- The object cache stores content in the memory of the Front-end server, reducing the amount of memory available to the rest of the system.
- Zero Downtime Patching requires resiliency at all server roles within a MinRole farm.
- Monitoring in SharePoint for the purposes of baselines can include metrics from diagnostic logging, the rescheduling of timer jobs, the addition of new diagnostic providers, and usage and health data collection.
- Server-side tracing is done within the ULS logs.
- The Developer Dashboard must be enabled for use within the farm using PowerShell.

Thought experiment

In this thought experiment, demonstrate your skills and knowledge of the topics covered in this chapter. You can find the answer to this thought experiment in the next section.

You are in the process of completing your SharePoint farm implementation, and want to release it in a limited fashion to an early group of users.

1. Are you providing a prerelease SLA to these users? What SLA considerations might you document?

2. What steps might you take to ensure that monitoring can be data mined for further analysis?

3. From a troubleshooting standpoint, what tools do you have at the ready to evaluate a server (or servers) that are causing issues?

Thought experiment answer

1. An SLA (even a preliminary one) is never a bad idea, as it sets the stage for an understanding between IT, the SharePoint administration team, and the business users that are participating in the early adopter program. Perhaps a minimal SLA of one nine (95 percent) would be an appropriate starting place for the farm.

2. Setting up the requirements for the Usage and Health Data Collection would provide a mechanism for capturing baseline information as well as any performance eccentricities with respect to the SharePoint 2016 environment.

3. Although the Usage and Health Data Collection functionality is useful, it captures a lot of data that must be parsed to be useful. From a troubleshooting standpoint, a combination of data collector sets in PerfMon and logging events in the ULS logs will allow the administration team to time-box any issues, retrieving only the logging information required to ad hoc troubleshoot a particular event.

Index

A

G

H

K

L

M

O

P

T

V

W

X

Y

Z

About the author

TROY LANPHIER, MCTS, MCITP, MCP, MCSE, and Managing Consultant for Catapult Systems, is a senior-level IT professional with extensive infrastructure, architecture, and design experience. As a long-standing member of the computer geek community, he has been hooked on computers since 1980, when his father brought home a brand new TRS-80 microcomputer (and the all-important TRS-80 computer cassette recorder for storing bits of BASIC language code).

Troy has been involved in enterprise server infrastructure design since the mid-1990s, when Banyan VINES, DEC Alpha, Novell Netware, SGI Indy, and Windows NT 3.1 servers roamed the IT world. Since the early 2000s, he has been training, working on, or writing about Windows server technologies, including the Microsoft SharePoint family of technologies (since the 2003 beta).

When he's not working on (or writing about) SharePoint, Troy enjoys spending time restoring vintage cars and motorcycles, playing video games with his daughters Samantha and Katherine, browsing antiques with his wife Marlene, and collecting Hot Wheels and Star Wars memorabilia.

Hear about it first.

Get the latest news from Microsoft Press sent to your inbox.

- New and upcoming books

- Special offers

- Free eBooks

- How-to articles

Sign up today at MicrosoftPressStore.com/Newsletters

Microsoft

Free ebooks

From technical overviews to drilldowns on special topics, get *free* ebooks from Microsoft Press at:

www.microsoftvirtualacademy.com/ebooks

Download your free ebooks in PDF, EPUB, and/or Mobi for Kindle formats.

Look for other great resources at Microsoft Virtual Academy, where you can learn new skills and help advance your career with free Microsoft training delivered by experts.

Microsoft Press

Now that you've read the book...

Tell us what you think!

Was it useful?
Did it teach you what you wanted to learn?
Was there room for improvement?

Let us know at http://aka.ms/tellpress

Your feedback goes directly to the staff at Microsoft Press,
and we read every one of your responses. Thanks in advance!

 Microsoft